Amsterdam
Rotterdam & The Hague

Derek Blyth

Prentice Hall Travel

New York • London • Toronto • Sydney • Tokyo • Singapore

W9-BON-209

THE AMERICAN EXPRESS ® TRAVEL GUIDES

Published in the United States by
Prentice Hall General Reference
A division of Simon & Schuster, Inc.
15 Columbus Circle
New York, NY 10023

PRENTICE HALL and colophon are
registered trademarks of Simon &
Schuster, Inc.

First published in the United
Kingdom by Mitchell Beazley
International Ltd, Michelin House
81 Fulham Road, London SW3 6RB

Edited, designed and produced by
Castle House Press, Llantrisant,
Mid Glamorgan CF7 8EU, Wales

First published 1988 as *The American
Express Pocket Guide to Amsterdam.*
This new and expanded edition
published 1992.

© American Express Publishing
Corporation Inc. 1992
All rights reserved including the right
of reproduction in whole or in part in
any form
Library of Congress Catalog
Card Number 92-060350
ISBN 0-13-028713-X

The author wishes to thank in
particular Mary Maclure, who
provided essential moral support and
suggested innumerable
improvements both to this edition
and to its predecessor. He also wishes
to thank the following for their help,
advice, accommodation and the
occasional loan of a bicycle: A.L.
Bakker of the Dutch Tourist Office in
Brussels, Helen Bannatyne, Alan
Blyth, Abi Daruvalla, Jules Farber,
Mark Fuller, Jane Hedley-Prôle, Doug
Hutchinson, Yvette Rosenberg and
Menno Spiering. The editor and
publisher wish to thank the
Netherlands Board of Tourism in
London for their assistance during the
preparation of this edition. Warm
thanks are due also to Neil Hanson,
David Haslam, Hilary Bird and Tim
Charity.

FOR THE SERIES:
General Editor:
  David Townsend Jones
Map Editor: David Haslam
Indexer: Hilary Bird
Cover design:
  Roger Walton Studio

FOR THIS EDITION:
Edited on desktop by:
  Sharon Charity
Art editor:
  Eileen Townsend Jones
Illustrators:
  Sylvia Hughes-Williams,
  Karen Cochrane
Gazetteer: Anne Evans
Cover photo:
  Hayson/Colorific

FOR MITCHELL BEAZLEY:
Art Director: Tim Foster
Managing Editor: Alison Starling
Production: Sarah Schuman

PRODUCTION CREDITS:
Maps by Lovell Johns, Oxford,
  England
Tram & metro maps by
  TCS, Aldershot, England
Typeset in Garamond and
  News Gothic
Desktop layout in Ventura Publisher
Linotronic output by
  Tradespools Limited, Frome,
  England

Contents

The Randstad

Amsterdam

Rotterdam

The Hague

How to use this book

Few rules and pointers are needed to understand how this travel guide works. Your enjoyment and efficiency in reading and using it will be enhanced if you note the following remarks.

HOW TO FIND WHAT YOU WANT

- For the general organization of the book, see CONTENTS on the pages preceding this one.
- Wherever appropriate, chapters and sections are arranged alphabetically, with headings appearing in **CAPITALS.**
- Often these headings are followed by location and practical information printed in *italics*.
- As you turn the pages, you will find subject headers, similar to those used in telephone directories, printed in CAPITALS in the top corner of each page.
- If you still cannot find what you need, check in the comprehensive and exhaustively cross-referenced INDEX at the back of the book.
- Following the index, a LIST OF STREET NAMES provides map references for all roads and streets mentioned in the book that are located within the areas covered by the main city maps.

CROSS-REFERENCES

These are printed in SMALL CAPITALS, referring you to other sections or alphabetical entries in the book. Care has been taken to ensure that such cross-references are self-explanatory. Often, page references are also given, although their excessive use would be intrusive and ugly.

FLOORS

We use the European convention in this book: "ground floor" means the floor at ground level (called by Americans the "first floor").

KEY TO AREA MAP SYMBOLS

■	Place of Interest	═O═	Superhighway / Motorway (with access point)
	Built-up Area		
	Wood or Park	═ ═	Superhighway / Motorway (under construction)
† †	Cemetery		
✈	Airport	═══	4-Lane Highway / Dual Carriageway
✦	Airfield		
♜	Castle	▬▬	Other Main Road
⌐⌐⌐⌐	Canal	▬	Secondary Road
◉	Metro Station	▭▬▭	Railway

KEY TO SYMBOLS

☎	Telephone	AE	American Express
Tx	Telex	◉	Diners Club
Fx	Facsimile (fax)	◎	MasterCard/Eurocard
★	Recommended sight	VISA	Visa
♣	Good value (in its class)	⅋	Facilities for disabled
i	Tourist information		people
⬅	Parking	◄€	Outstanding views
⊡	Free entrance	▣	Secure garage
⊠	Entrance fee payable	◠	Quiet hotel
⛪	Building of architectural	⬍	Elevator
	interest	☐	TV in each room
⌨	Photography forbidden	☎	Telephone in each
∤	Guided tour		room
▣	Cafeteria	≋	Swimming pool
✳	Special interest for children	↯	Gym/fitness facilities
◇	Hotel	⛼	Conference facilities
▣	Simple hotel	☗	Bar
▥	Luxury hotel	≒	Restaurant
☐	Cheap	☗	Simple restaurant
☑	Inexpensive	☗	Luxury restaurant
☑	Moderately priced	☗	Open-air dining
☑	Expensive	☗	Good for wines
☑	Very expensive	☗	Casino/gambling

PRICE CATEGORIES

These are denoted by the symbols ☐ (cheap), ☑ (inexpensive), ☑ (moderately priced), ☑ (expensive) and ☑ (very expensive). For **hotels** and **restaurants** they correspond approximately to the following actual local prices, which give a guideline **at the time of printing**. Naturally, prices rise, but hotels and restaurants tend to remain in the same price category.

(Guilders: Fl.)		Corresponding to approximate prices for **hotels** *double room with bath; single slightly cheaper*	for **restaurants** *meal for one with service, taxes and house wine*
☑	very expensive	over Fl.500	over Fl.95
☑	expensive	Fl.300-500	Fl.80-95
☑	moderately priced	Fl.200-300	Fl.65-80
☑	inexpensive	Fl.100-200	Fl.50-65
☐	cheap	under Fl.100	under Fl.50

About the author

Born in Scotland, **Derek Blyth** is a European writer, journalist and translator. During more than a decade spent exploring the art and culture of Northern Europe, he has published several travel books including *Flemish Cities Explored, American Express Berlin* (1992) and this book's predecessor, *The American Express Pocket Guide to Amsterdam* (1988), and he is co-writing with Rory Watson the forthcoming *American Express Brussels*. He is currently based in Brussels, where he writes for the *Bulletin* magazine, but he still frequently returns to his former home-town of Amsterdam to drink a beer at De Engelbewaarder or take his daughters cycling down the banks of the Amstel.

A message from the series editor

In designing *American Express Amsterdam, Rotterdam & The Hague* we aimed to make this brand-new edition simple and instinctive to use, like all its sister volumes in our new, larger paperback format.

The hallmarks of the relaunched series are clear, classic typography, confidence in fine travel writing for its own sake, and faith in our readers' innate intelligence to find their way around the books without heavy-handed signposting by editors.

Readers with anything less than 20:20 vision will doubtless also enjoy the larger, clearer type, and can now dispense with the mythical magnifying glasses we never issued free with the old pocket guide series.

Author **Derek Blyth** and editor **Sharon Charity** have worked enormously hard to ensure that this edition is as accurate and up to date as possible at the moment it goes to press. But time and change are forever the enemies, and in between editions we appreciate it when you, our readers, keep us informed of changes that you discover.

As ever, I am indebted to all readers who wrote during the preparation of this book. Please remember that your feedback is extremely important to our efforts to tailor the series to the very distinctive tastes and requirements of our sophisticated international readership.

Send your comments to me at Mitchell Beazley International Ltd, Michelin House, 81 Fulham Road, London SW3 6RB; or, in the US, c/o American Express Travel Guides, Prentice Hall Travel, 15 Columbus Circle, New York, NY 10023.

David Townsend Jones

Amsterdam
Rotterdam & The Hague

Randstad — an evolving metropolis

Amsterdam, Rotterdam and The Hague are the three largest cities in an evolving conurbation at the heart of northern Europe, known as the Randstad. Occupying the low-lying western region of the Netherlands, the crescent-shaped metropolis incorporates, in addition to the three cities that are the subject of this book, the historic Dutch towns of Dordrecht, Delft, Leiden, Haarlem and Utrecht. A tour of this region offers the traveler an enormous variety of sights and sensations within a relatively compact area.

The appeal of the Randstad lies in the diversity of its cities and landscapes. If you want contrasts, you can flit in one day from a gallery of Van Goghs to a breezy dike on the Rhine. The range of options in this tiny region is staggering: you can hunt for rare books in Rembrandt's Amsterdam, cycle out to a windmill, listen to a Baroque concert in Franz Hals' Haarlem, take a boat trip on the busiest waterway in Europe, watch rare birds on a windswept shore, drink a Belgian beer in a 17th century tavern, feast on an authentic Indonesian banquet, shop for tulips on a canalside market, or simply watch the world go by from a window table in an aged brown café.

RANDSTAD TOWNS AND CITIES

You can almost think of the Randstad as one city, and a relatively small one at that, with a total population of just 2.5 million. Excellent rail connections mean that you can easily stay overnight in one Randstad city and travel to another for business or sightseeing. The tree-lined canals of Delft are just 15 minutes by train from the steely glass skyscrapers of central Rotterdam. And you can flit from Amsterdam's cosmopolitan crush to the jaunty port of Hoorn in only 30 minutes.

The individual cities that make up the Randstad may be close, but they retain entirely different characters due to a long Dutch tradition of municipal independence. Amsterdam, capital of the Netherlands, is radical and tolerant, while The Hague, the seat of government, has a quiet dignity. Rotterdam, boasting the world's busiest port, is dazzling and futuristic, whereas Schiedam and Dordrecht are decaying old harbors. Utrecht, Leiden and Delft are lively university towns, and Haarlem is more retiring.

Most visitors opt to stay in Amsterdam, but the other Randstad cities have points in their favor. The Hague offers the brisk charms of the nearby North Sea beaches, and Rotterdam provides the stimulation of a busy seaport. Delft is a good base for those wanting to stay in a small, but lively town, while Utrecht has the youthful energy of Amsterdam without the anarchy.

EXPLORING THE RANDSTAD

The postwar growth of the Randstad has been carefully checked to preserve large rural regions within easy reach of the cities. The metropolitan crescent encloses an area known as *het groene hart* (the green heart), with misty polders and old wooden windmills. The windswept

11

beaches along the west coast provide another escape route from the pressures of urban living.

Zandvoort is where Amsterdammers like to bask in the sun, while Scheveningen on sunny days is mobbed by off-duty Hagenaars. Quieter beaches such as Egmond aan Zee are found north of IJmuiden, and the dunes inland are wonderfully wild places for rambles or cycle trips. Brightly-patterned bulb fields flourish on the landward side of the dunes, creating a spectacular artificial landscape reminiscent of a modern abstract painting.

Farther north, you can explore the wooden houses of Waterland and the Zaanse Schans, or wander in the once decaying, but now primly restored ports on the shores of the IJsselmeer, such as Enkhuizen, Edam and Marken.

The Randstad offers plenty of opportunities to pursue a specialized interest: you might plan a trip around a particular theme such as Dutch paintings, contemporary architecture, or gardens of the Randstad. You might be inspired to plan a tour of maritime Holland taking in Dordrecht, Rotterdam's Waterstad, Amsterdam's maritime quarter, and the ports of Hoorn and Enkhuizen. Or you might spend a few days investigating Dutch markets.

The Randstad's very diversity can sometimes be dismaying. The typical Dutch mixture of earthiness and sophistication, sex and piety, business and art, can be too much, especially in Amsterdam, where many tourists gaze in disbelief at the cluster of seedy brothels surrounding the Gothic Oude Kerk. But there is a point to it all: the spirit of the Randstad stems from a deep commitment to tolerance and freedom. The secret of survival for the visitor is to single out the pursuits that appeal, and ignore all the rest.

Culture, history and background

Landmarks in the Netherlands' history

THE COUNTS OF HOLLAND

c. 1250: Count William II of Holland built a castle at The Hague. His son, Floris V, erected the Ridderzaal within the castle walls. **1275:** Count Floris V of Holland granted Amsterdam exemption from tolls — the first document to refer to Amsterdam. **Late 13thC:** Conflict between Counts of Holland and Bishops of Utrecht; Count Floris V of Holland was assassinated and his son died 2 years later; Holland then passed to John of Hainault, who defeated the Bishop of Utrecht and installed his brother Gwijde as Bishop. In 1300 Gwijde granted Amsterdam its first charter.

1317: Amsterdam annexed to Holland. **1345:** Count William IV of Holland died and the county passed to the son of his sister, Margaretha, wife of Ludwig of Bavaria. This led to feuds between "Hooks" and "Cods." **Mid-14thC:** Amsterdam became an important entrepôt for goods from N Germany, the Baltic and Flanders, especially beer and grain.

THE BURGUNDIANS

1428: Philip the Good, Duke of Burgundy, acquired Holland from his cousin Jacoba of Bavaria. Burgundy, now controlling much of the Low Countries, pursued a policy of centralization that eroded the privileges enjoyed by the cities; but the *Pax Burgundica* brought stability and prosperity to trading cities, especially Amsterdam, which vied with the Hanseatic League for Baltic trade.

1477: Death of Charles the Bold, son of Philip the Good. He was succeeded by his daughter, Mary of Burgundy, who restored the privileges to the cities in the *Groote Privilegie* to secure the loyalty of the Low Countries. She married Maximilian Hapsburg, later Holy Roman Emperor, who in 1489 granted Amsterdam the privilege of placing the imperial crown above its coat of arms. **1496:** Philip the Fair, son of Mary and Maximilian, wed Juana the Mad, heiress to Castile and Aragon. **1500:** Birth of Charles V, their son.

1515: Charles V assumed control of the Low Countries and of Spanish and German territories. **1535:** A group of Anabaptists (radical Protestants), following the example of Münster (1533), seized Amsterdam town hall, but were evicted the following day and executed. **1555:** Charles V abdicated in favor of his son, Philip II of Spain. Philip pursued an increasingly intolerant policy toward Protestantism and tried to assert the power of the crown over cities and nobles.

1566: The Iconoclasm *(Beeldenstorm)*, an outburst of popular unrest, during which numerous Catholic works of art were destroyed. **1568:** William of Orange led the Dutch Revolt against Spain; the Eighty Years' War began. **1576:** The Pacification of Ghent briefly united 17 provinces of the Low Countries, but stalled on religious grounds. **1578:** Amsterdam, previously loyal to the Catholic (Spanish) side, finally converted to the Protestant side in a peaceful revolution *(Alteratie)*.

1579: The Union of Utrecht was signed by the seven northern provinces of the Netherlands, guaranteeing mutual assistance yet leaving provinces with considerable independence. **1581:** The Northern provinces renounced Philip II as their sovereign. **1584:** Assassination of William of Orange at Delft. **1585:** Antwerp fell to the Spanish and Amsterdam seized the chance to attract trade; the influx of refugees from Antwerp also benefited Amsterdam economically.

THE REPUBLIC

1588: The defeat of the Spanish Armada eroded Spanish naval power. Beginning of Holland's Golden Age, a period of economic prosperity and scientific and artistic brilliance. **1594-97:** Willem Barents made several unsuccessful attempts to discover a northern route to China. **1594:** Nine Amsterdam merchants established the Compagnie van Verre to exploit the spice trade; Cornelis de Houtman discovered Java. **1599:** The Compagnie's second expedition to the East Indies yielded 400-percent profits. **1602:** Dutch East India Company established.

1603-11: Construction of Amsterdam's Zuiderkerk, the first Dutch Protestant church to be built. **1604:** Publication of *De Jure Praedae* by Hugo Grotius proclaimed freedom of the seas. **1609:** The plan of the three canals was drawn up for Amsterdam. **1609-21:** A 12-year truce with Spain was concluded; during this period a dispute flared up between two Protestant factions — the Remonstrants and Counter-Remonstrants — leading to the execution of Van Oldenbarnevelt and the imprisonment of Grotius.

1620: The Pilgrim Fathers departed from Delfshaven on the *Speedwell,* bound for the New World. **1621:** Dutch West India Company established. **1626:** Peter Minuit purchased Manhattan from Indians for beads and other fripperies worth about 60 guilders ($24) and built a fort at the s end of the island. This became the settlement of New Amsterdam, which in 1664 ejected the Dutch governor Pieter Stuyvesant in favor of the English; the settlement was then renamed New York.

1628: Descartes settled in Amsterdam. **1632:** A university, the Athenaeum Illustre, was established in Amsterdam. **1634-37:** Tulip fever led to spectacular price increases, which then collapsed causing many bankruptcies. **1642:** Rembrandt painted the *Night Watch;* his wife Saskia died in the same year.

1642-43: The Dutch navigator Abel Tasman, searching for a route to south America through the East Indies, discovered Tasmania and New Zealand. **1648:** The Treaty of Münster concluded the Eighty Years' War;

in the same year work began on a new Baroque town hall for Amsterdam. **1652:** A Dutch settlement was established at Cape Town. **1652-54:** The First Anglo-Dutch War broke out as a result of the English Navigation Act. **1665-67:** The Second Anglo-Dutch War began, in the course of which Admiral de Ruyter sailed up the Medway and set fire to the English fleet.

1672: The "Year of Disasters." Louis XIV invaded the Netherlands, and Johan and Cornelis de Witt were murdered by an angry mob in The Hague. **1672-74:** Hostilities broke out once more between the Dutch and the English in the Third Anglo-Dutch War. **1683-88:** John Locke, the English philosopher, lived in Holland. **1685:** The revocation of the Edict of Nantes by Louis XIV brought a flood of Huguenot refugees from France. **1688:** The Glorious Revolution: Stadholder William III of Holland and his wife Mary became King and Queen of Great Britain. **1697:** Czar Peter the Great visited the Netherlands to study shipbuilding.

18thC: Decline of Amsterdam's role as an entrepôt due to competition from France and England. **1747:** French invasion; civil unrest in the Netherlands. **1780-84:** The Fourth Anglo-Dutch War was caused by Dutch assistance given to American rebels. **1782:** Persuaded by John Adams, the Netherlands was the first European government to recognize the United States. **1795:** The Batavian Republic was established in the Netherlands by Dutch radicals, with the aid of French revolutionary troops.

THE KINGDOM OF THE NETHERLANDS

1806: The Kingdom of the Netherlands was established with Louis Napoleon as head of state. **1813:** Liberation of the Netherlands; creation of a Kingdom under William I; this briefly reunited the N and S Netherlands. **1830:** The Belgian Revolt; Belgium (formerly S Netherlands) became an independent state. **1848:** In the Year of Revolutions a new Dutch constitution drafted by Thorbecke was approved. **1876:** Construction of the North Sea Canal brought new prosperity to Amsterdam.

1901: The Housing Act led to a dramatic improvement in the design of public housing. **1907:** Completion of the Peace Palace in The Hague. **1928:** Olympic Games held in Amsterdam. **1932:** Completion of the Afsluitdijk, a dike enclosing the Zuider Zee, to create the IJsselmeer.

1940: Holland capitulated to the invading German army after the bombing of Rotterdam. **1941:** Amsterdam dock workers went on strike in protest at the deportation of Jews. **1942:** Japan occupied the Dutch East Indies. **1944-45:** Liberation of Holland. **1949:** Dutch East Indies achieved independence; the Republic of Indonesia was created. **1953:** Disastrous floods in Zeeland killed 1,800 people. **Mid-1960s:** Provo demonstrations in Amsterdam resulted in short-lived radical policies such as free municipal bicycles and public electric cars *(Witcars)*. **1970s:** Clashes in Amsterdam over metro construction, housing, squatting and new opera house. **1986-7:** Completion of town hall and opera house complex in Amsterdam. **1992:** Completion of new parliament building in The Hague.

15

Who's who

For a small country, Holland has produced a remarkable number of great scientists, scholars, navigators and merchants. The following selection deals mainly with people mentioned in this book. (Painters are listed separately under DUTCH PAINTING.)

Barents, Willem (1550-97)
Dutch navigator and cartographer who made three unsuccessful attempts to discover a northeast passage to China, and finally died after a winter on Novaya Zemlya. The expedition's camp and journal were found in the late 19thC.

Bicker, Andries (1586-1652)
Powerful Amsterdam merchant who, with his three brothers Cornelis, Jacob and Jan, monopolized city government in the 17thC. Andries served ten times as burgomaster; his brother Jan built and gave his name to Bickerseiland in Amsterdam.

Blaeu, Willem Jansz. (1571-1638)
Founder of an Amsterdam printing firm that specialized in maps and globes. His son Jan published the 11-volume *Atlas Major* in 1663.

Bredero, Gerbrant (1585-1618)
Satirical playwright and poet, author of *De Spaanse Brabander*.

Coornhert, Dirck Volckertsz. (1522-90)
Humanist, reformer, and proponent of tolerant penal policies at a time of Spanish atrocities.

Elsevier, Louis (1540-1617)
Refugee from the Spanish Netherlands, founder of a publishing house in Leiden that later moved to Amsterdam.

Erasmus, Desiderius (1466-1536)
Europe's foremost 16thC humanist, born in Rotterdam and later professor at Leuven University. He was a friend of Thomas More and opponent of the absolutism of Luther's doctrines.

Frank, Anne (1929-44)
German-born Jewish girl who, with her family, hid from occupying Nazi troops in a house on Amsterdam's Prinsengracht. The family was eventually betrayed, and Anne died in Bergen-Belsen concentration camp.

Frederik Hendrik (1584-1647)
The youngest son of William of Orange and his fourth wife Louise de Coligny. He was an able soldier, following in the footsteps of his half-brother Maurits (1567-1625), and a tolerant politician.

Grotius, Hugo (1583-1645)
Jurist, politician, poet and historian, born in Delft. He was imprisoned in 1618 for his support of the Remonstrant cause, but escaped to France with the help of his wife. His greatest work, *De Jure Belli ac Pacis,* is a cornerstone of international law.

Mata Hari (1876-1917)
The stage name of a Dutch dancer who was executed in Paris as a German spy during World War I.

Heyn, Piet *(1578-1629)*
Flamboyant Dutch sea captain who in 1626 captured the Spanish silver fleet, valued at some 12 million guilders, in the Cuban port of Matanzas. He was made an admiral, and died in a sea battle near Dunkirk.

Multatuli *(1820-87)*
The pseudonym of Amsterdam-born writer Eduard Douwes Dekker. He served in the Dutch colonial service in Java, and criticized its abuses in his most famous work, *Max Havelaar* (1860).

Louis Napoleon *(1778-1846)*
Brother of Napoleon I of France. He was King of the Netherlands from 1806-10, and converted the town hall of Amsterdam into one of his palaces.

Oldenbarnevelt, Johan van *(1547-1619)*
Politician and lawyer who in 1609 concluded a truce with Spain. His support for tolerance at a time of religious strife brought him into conflict with the Stadholder, Prince Maurits, and resulted in his arrest and execution as a traitor.

Robinson, John *(c. 1576-1625)*
English religious leader, who fled to Amsterdam in 1608, and in 1609 settled in Leiden, where he established a church. Here the Pilgrim Fathers (as they later became known) worshiped before departing in 1620 for the New World.

Ruyter, Michiel Adriansz. de *(1607-76)*
Born in Vlissingen, he ran off to sea as a cabin boy and eventually rose to the rank of admiral. His most daring exploit was to sail up the Medway in 1667 and set fire to the English fleet. He died of wounds at Syracuse while fighting the French.

Six, Jan *(1618-1700)*
Son of a Huguenot merchant. He was a friend of Rembrandt (who painted his portrait in 1654) and wrote poetry and plays. He served as burgomaster and married a daughter of Dr Nicolaes Tulp.

Spinoza, Baruch *(1632-77)*
Jewish philosopher who was born in Amsterdam of Sephardic parents. In 1656 he was expelled from the Jewish community for his Cartesian beliefs and was forced to earn a living polishing spectacle lenses. His greatest work, *Ethica*, used mathematical deduction to justify ethical beliefs.

Stuyvesant, Pieter *(1592-1672)*
Dutch governor of Nieuw Amsterdam (later New York). An unpopular leader, in 1664 he was forced to hand the colony over to the English.

Swammerdam, Jan *(1637-80)*
Naturalist and collector, born in Amsterdam. He laid the foundations of entomology and was the first to observe red blood corpuscles.

Tasman, Abel *(1603-c. 1659)*
Dutch navigator who discovered Tasmania (originally named Van Diemen's Land) and New Zealand on a voyage (1642-43) in search of a route from the Dutch East Indies to South America.

Thorbecke, Johan *(1798-1872)*
Liberal politician, architect of the 1848 Constitution.

Trip, Louis and Trip, Hendrick *(1605-84 and 1607-66)*
Dutch industrialists, famed for the manufacture of armaments and the development of iron and copper mines in Sweden.

Tromp, Maarten *(1597-1653)*
Admiral, born in Briel. He won several victories against the Spanish in the Eighty Years' War, fought in the First Anglo-Dutch War and died in a battle against the English off the Dutch coast.

Tulp, Nicolaes *(1593-1674)*
Physician and professor of anatomy, painted by Rembrandt in 1632. He was active in the city government and served four terms as burgomaster. One of his daughters married Jan Six.

Vondel, Joost van den *(1587-1679)*
Dutch poet and playwright of the Golden Age. He was born in Cologne of Anabaptist parents, but converted to Catholicism late in life. He worked in business and later in a pawn shop, using his literature to comment on political issues.

William of Orange *(1533-84)*
Also known as William the Silent. Brought up as a Catholic at the court of Charles V in Brussels, he converted to protestantism in 1570 and in 1572 led the Dutch Revolt against Philip II of Spain. He was assassinated in Delft.

Witt, Johan de *(1625-72)*
Leading politician of the 17thC, who guided the United Provinces through the First and Second Anglo-Dutch Wars. He became a scapegoat in the Year of Disasters (1672), and he and his brother Cornelis (1623-72) were lynched by an angry mob in The Hague.

Randstad architecture

AMSTERDAM

As befits a trading city, Amsterdam's principal buildings are merchants' homes, warehouses, shops, weigh houses, banks, exchanges and insurance offices. Small-scale architecture has always flourished in Amsterdam and most styles are to be found here, trimmed to fit the narrow facades on the canals. What is delightful about Amsterdam is the profuse detail, from the sculpted gable tops to the witty facade stones illustrating the trade or name of the house owner. Interior design in shops, cafés and restaurants is equally diverse, from the creaking, wooden ambience of traditional Dutch interiors to minimalist modern styles.

GOTHIC: The street pattern of the Middle Ages — and something of the social pattern as well — is preserved in the narrow lanes around Amsterdam's two pre-Reformation parish churches, the **Oude Kerk** (pictured on page 106) and **Nieuwe Kerk** (old and new churches). After Amsterdam's conversion to Protestantism in 1578, the numerous convents and monasteries of the old city were used for secular purposes — as orphanage, university, hospital or barracks — leaving only the lovely **Begijnhof** on Spui and the two chapels s of Oude Hoogstraat as reminders of the city's Catholic origins. Stringent town-planning regulations in the 17thC also led to the virtual extinction of the picturesque wooden Gothic houses, which were a notorious fire hazard in the crowded, industrious city. Here and there, however, the odd glimpse of a jettied wall indicates a resilient medieval framework to which a more modern facade has been attached.

DUTCH RENAISSANCE: Dutch Renaissance architecture was a late and rather eccentric development of Italian and French Renaissance styles. The early Dutch Renaissance emerged during the reign of the Emperor Charles V, when Dutch architects were able to travel to Italy, while Italian architects were often employed by Dutch patrons. The Revolt of the Netherlands severed these links with Italy, however, and architects of the late Dutch Renaissance had to rely largely on books of engravings. The most influential of these source books was published by Hans Vredeman de Vries in Antwerp in 1577, illustrating a style that had much in common with the explosive **Mannerism** of Michelangelo. The best examples of this neurotic style in Amsterdam are the ornate **gates** of the **Orphanage** (now the Amsterdams Historisch Museum) and the **Athenaeum Illustre** at Oude Zijds Voorburgwal 231.

Hendrick de Keyser (1565-1621) was city architect at just the moment Amsterdam's economy began to take off, and he was appointed to build three new Protestant churches, several spires, the first stock exchange and many private houses. One soon learns to spot a De Keyser building by its animated **step-gabled facade** of whitened sandstone set off against rosy red brick. Lieven de Key's **Stadhuis** in Leiden and **Vleeshal** in Haarlem are other striking examples of this style.

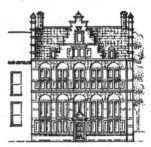

The **Groenland Pakhuizen** and **House on the Three Canals**, two elegant examples of 17thC architecture distinguished by their fine **step gables**.

DUTCH CLASSICISM: De Keyser's Mannerism was a touch too swashbuckling and jovial for the humorless temperament of the Dutch Calvinist rulers of the second quarter of the 17thC. They much preferred the sober and rational Classicism of **Jacob van Campen** (1595-1657). Constantijn Huygens, the powerful secretary to Prince Frederik Hendrik, put his weight behind Van Campen because he "admonished Gothic curly foolery with the stately Roman, and drove old Heresy away before older Truth." Van Campen's stately style can be seen in the house at

Keizersgracht 177 built in 1624 for the Coymans brothers, and the **Royal Palace** (formerly Town Hall; see KONINKLIJK PALEIS, pictured on page 97) in Amsterdam (1648-55). These simple, reserved buildings reflect the quiet dignity of the Dutch Golden Age as perfectly as do the paintings of Vermeer.

Philips Vingboons (1608-75) developed a less austere Classicism that retained a lingering fondness for the Gothic gable. Vingboons' distinctive contribution to the Amsterdam skyline was the **neck gable** — a simplified step gable with ornate claw pieces — as in his four stately houses built for the Cromhout family at **Herengracht 364-70**. His brother **Justus Vingboons'** 1660 Trippenhuis on Kloveniersburgwal shows an even more stately form of Dutch Classicism.

A 1638 **neck-gabled house** on Herengracht, built by Philips Vingboons

Daniel Stalpaert (1615-76) had a significant impact on Amsterdam as city architect during the mid-17thC. His first task was to complete the Town Hall after Jacob van Campen mysteriously dropped out of the project, and he then went on to design a number of massive public buildings such as the austere 1656 **Admiralty Arsenal** on Prins Hendrikkade, the 1661 **Prinsenhof** on Oude Zijds Voorburgwal, the **German Synagogue** on Waterlooplein and the **Amstelhof** on the River Amstel.

Even more sober were the residences built by **Adriaen Dortsman** in the 1660s and '70s on fashionable sites close to the Amstel. Dortsman's houses stand out sharply against the colorful pluralism of Amsterdam, with their grim, gray sandstone facades purged of all decoration — except for lithe sculptures of Grecian gods perched on the balustrades. Few Dortsman houses have survived intact, but there is a splendid pair at Keizersgracht 672-74, housing the **Museum Van Loon**.

FRENCH STYLES OF THE 18THC: After the decline of Classicism at the end of the Golden Age, Dutch architecture fell under the spell of French styles introduced by Protestant refugees who fled from France after Louis XIV's Revocation of the Edict of Nantes in 1685. **Daniel Marot**

A stately 18thC **canal house** with a Louis XIV-style cornice

(1661-1752) brought the grand **Baroque** style of **Louis XIV** to Holland, carefully compressing its features to fit the modest proportions of Dutch houses. This Dutch Louis XIV style is characterized by monumental double staircases, splendidly decorated centerpieces, grand entrances, and cornices laden with heavy, symmetrical decoration. A handsome example of this style is the **Museum Willet-Holthuysen** at **Herengracht 605**. The gorgeous frothy tops of Keizersgracht 244-46 and the haughty pair of neck gables at Keizersgracht 606-8 illustrate the tendency at this time for architects to be over-zealous in their work.

During the mid-18thC, the heavy Baroque symmetry of Louis XIV softened into the delicious **Rococo** style of **Louis XV**. The Herengracht and Keizersgracht élite had already spent their money on Louis XIV improvements, and so Louis XV details tend to appear on more modest dwellings on the less prestigious canals such as Singel, Prinsengracht and Kloveniersburgwal. The style is characterized by capricious **bell gables** and other touches of whimsy. **Prinsengracht 126** shows this style at its most flamboyant.

An elegant example of an 18thC **bell-gabled house**

After the sensual abandon of Rococo, a sober reaction set in — the **Louis XVI** style — which reached Amsterdam from France in the 1770s. During this cooling-off period, exactly 100 years after the gray sobriety of Dortsman and Stalpaert, necks, bells and crests were brutally chopped off to be replaced by flat cornices. This resulted in the permanent ruin of large tracts of Amsterdam's skyline, although the consequences were far more dire in Utrecht, Delft and The Hague.

The French occupation in the late 18th and early 19thC brought the **Empire** style to Holland. This was a continuation of the geometrical Louis XVI style, with various oddities such as cushion doors and palm motifs. The economy of Amsterdam was in poor shape at this time, however, and the Empire style had little impact beyond the decoration of fanlights with attractive geometrical designs.

ECLECTICISM: A somber tone persisted through to the **Greek Revival** architecture of the early 19thC, as seen in the austere **law courts** at Prinsengracht 436 and the solid 1840 **Willemspoort** at the w end of Haarlemmerstraat.

After the economic doldrums of the French occupation, Amsterdam's economy began to take off with the opening of the North Holland Canal in 1823 and the Amsterdam-Haarlem railway in 1839. The palaces on the Golden Bend of Herengracht ceased to be fashionable and new mansions were commissioned on the edge of the **Vondelpark** or overlooking the **Amstel**. Architects flirted with various historical styles, from musty **Old Dutch Renaissance** (favored by Protestants) to fussy **neo-Gothic** (admired by Catholics).

Architects of public buildings tended to adopt a diplomatic compromise between these two styles, although **P.J.H. Cuypers** (1827-1921) could not fail to conceal his strong Catholic prejudices in his neo-Gothic designs for the **Rijksmuseum** (1876-85, pictured on page 110), **Centraal Station** (1881-89) and numerous churches. On the other hand, A. N. Weissman's **Stedelijk Museum** is a solid piece of neo-Renaissance design. Eventually, the dispute was solved by the adoption of a haughty international **Classicism**, seen in A. L. van Gendt's dignified 1888 **Concertgebouw**, which could almost belong in Vienna.

Art Nouveau architecture failed to make much headway in Amsterdam. The finest Art Nouveau work in Amsterdam was produced by the

21

versatile **Gerrit van Arkel**, who skipped deftly from **neo-Renaissance** (Heiligeweg 35) and **neo-Gothic** (Plantage Middenlaan 36) to outrageous Art Nouveau in his 1905 office building overlooking Keizersgracht at Leliegracht.

MODERN ARCHITECTURE: The **Amsterdam Beurs** (stock exchange) on Damrak, completed in 1903 by **H.P. Berlage** (1856-1934),

Amsterdam Beurs

represents a decisive break with 19thC eclecticism and a firm assertion of a new architectural ethic based on rigorous proportions and an honest use of building materials.

Berlage was also responsible for drawing up the **Expansion Plan for Amsterdam Zuid** (1905-17), which brought an end to the ruthless urban growth of the 19thC and a return to the harmonious ideals of the 17thC. The Plan was drawn up under the 1901 Housing Act, which required municipal authorities to subsidize and control the construction of working-class housing. The first wave of new housing after the 1901 Act was designed by the **Amsterdam School**, a group of passionately idealistic socialist architects who developed a brilliantly inventive **organic** style and launched it with gusto in the 1911-16 design for the **Scheepvaarthuis**. This large office building on Prins Hendrikkade is encrusted with fabulous seafaring motifs. Dazzling blocks of surreal **workers' housing** were later designed by **Michel de Klerk** (1884-1923) at **Spaarndammerbuurt** in W Amsterdam and in the s at **Henriette Ronnerplein**. **P. L. Kramer** (1881-1961) displayed similarly restless energy in his matching blocks on **P. L. Takstraat**, and in many highly unusual bridge designs.

Despite its unbounded creative vitality, the Amsterdam School style lasted barely a decade. It lost much of its impetus with the early death of De Klerk in 1923, but there were deeper reasons for its demise, such as its high production costs and its concentration on surface decoration.

The **Dutch Modern Movement** architects roundly renounced the theatrical flights of the Amsterdam School. They were inspired by a rational, rather than romantic, socialism and sought to design spacious, light-filled buildings that were crisply functional. The **Ciné-**

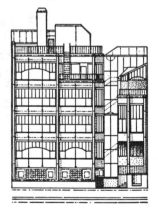

Aldo van Eyck's **Moederhuis**

tol at Tolstraat 154 (now a public library) is one of the best examples of Modern Movement architecture in Amsterdam, designed in 1926 by J.A. Brinkman and L. C. van der Vlugt. A much later building in this same tradition is the **Van Gogh Museum**, designed by Gerrit Rietveld (1888-1964).

The key figure in the development of postwar Amsterdam architecture is **Aldo van Eyck**, whose 1978 **Moederhuis**, pictured on the previous page, combines functionalism with an enchanting rainbow of colors. The city council's "compact city" policy in the 1980s led to the filling in of numerous gap sites in the Nieuwmarkt and the Jordaan with imaginative small-scale housing projects, while **Cees Dam** and **Wilhelm Holz-bauer's** controversial **Muziektheater** (concert hall), pictured on page 168, and **Stadhuis** (town hall) complex has brought the allure of international modern architecture to the old Jewish quarter. But the careful creativity that has been a hallmark of Amsterdam architecture through the centuries is perhaps best illustrated by Tony Alberts' **NMB Bank** headquarters in Amsterdam Zuid-Oost, with its eccentric angles precisely calculated to maximize energy efficiency.

NMB Bank headquarters, Amsterdam

ROTTERDAM

Central Rotterdam was destroyed in a German air raid in 1940, and entirely reconstructed in the 1950s in a bold modern style that enormously influenced international postwar architecture. Only a few isolated buildings still stand from before World War II, of which the oldest is the heavily-restored **Grote Kerk**, a majestic Gothic church blending Flemish and Dutch influences.

Virtually nothing remains of Rotterdam's Dutch Classical architecture except for the handsome **Schielandshuis**, tucked away amid modern offices. Built during the prosperous 1660s, it now houses Rotterdam's historical museum.

Nor are there many merchants' houses left in Rotterdam, apart from the row of modest 17thC and 18thC dwellings on the **Wijnhaven**, recently dismantled to allow the construction of a rail tunnel under the Nieuwe Maas, but scheduled to be rebuilt when the work is done. The

23

17thC scale of the Wijnhaven was broken in 1898 by **Het Witte Huis** (the white house), a 10-story Art Nouveau office building modeled on late-19thC American skyscrapers.

Rotterdam's transformation into a modern city began in the 1920s. Several key works of 20thC modern architecture were built here, including the **Van Nelle tobacco factory**, designed by **Brinkman** and **Van der Vlugt** in 1927-29, which pioneered a new architectural style based on functionalism and transparency.

Rotterdam's City Architect **J.J.P. Oud** was influenced by De Stijl paintings in his 1924 design for the **Café De Unie**. The geometrical red and blue facade was destroyed in 1940, but rebuilt in 1986. Oud's **Kiefhoek** public housing project, built in 1928-30 for low-income families, is still impressive for its careful attention to detail.

The 1940 bombardment offered Rotterdam architects an irresistible opportunity to apply their strict functionalist principles on a grand scale. The **Lijnbaan** shopping center, built by **Bakema and Van den Broek** in 1949-53, was the world's first pedestrianized shopping mall. The Lijnbaan's leafy streets, lined with low-rise buildings, inspired countless postwar shopping malls throughout the world, many of which were horribly unsuccessful imitations. It is still pleasant to stroll along the Lijnbaan, with its carefully-designed street furniture including benches, sidewalk display cases and newspaper kiosks.

There are recent signs that Rotterdam has finally begun to turn away from sober functionalism in favor of a more playful style. Quirky buildings now enliven the waterfront around the old harbor (**Oude Haven**). The most adventurous project to date is the complex of tilted cube houses known as **Het Blaakse Bos** (the Blaak forest), pictured on page 221. The nearby **Gemeentebibliotheek**, built in 1983 by Van den Broek & Bakema, is a Dutch version of the Pompidou Center in Paris, with bright yellow exposed pipes on the exterior and a vast terraced well filled with escalators in the belly of the building. Construction cranes are currently clustered around Centraal Station, where an enormous skyscraper is to be built.

THE HAGUE

The Hague has neither the Baroque harmony of Amsterdam, nor the stimulating modernity of Rotterdam, yet it boasts several buildings of architectural merit. The oldest edifice is the **Ridderzaal**, a 13thC hall fastidiously restored to its original state in the 19thC by P.J.H. Cuypers. The **Grote Kerk** on the Groenmarkt is an interesting blend of 14th, 15th and 16thC Gothic, with a magnificent painted wooden roof. The hexagonal **Nieuwe Kerk**, built on the Spui in 1649-56, was The Hague's first Protestant church.

Little survives of 17thC Dutch Renaissance architecture except for the **Stadhuis**, built in 1565. The elegant restraint of 17thC Dutch Classicism is represented by several buildings, including the beautiful **Mauritshuis**, built in 1633-44 by Jacob van Campen and Pieter Post, who collaborated again on the construction, in 1640, of the **Paleis Noordeinde**, for Stadholder Frederik Hendrik.

Glossary of architectural terms

Art Deco   Geometric style of the 1920s and 1930s, named after the Paris Arts Décoratifs Exhibition of 1925

Art Nouveau   Sinuous style of the early 20thC, deriving inspiration from natural forms

Basilica   Church with nave higher than the flanking aisles

Bell gable   An 18thC gable top in the shape of a bell

Capital   The carved top of a column

Cartouche   A decorative frame enclosing a window or panel

Caryatids   Female figures supporting an architectural element

Claw piece   Sculpture, often in the shape of a dolphin, filling the steps of a gable

Cornucopia   Sculpture depicting a horn overflowing with fruit, symbolizing abundance

Entablature   The horizontal structure supported by the columns in Classical architecture, comprising architrave, frieze and cornice

Facade stone   A decorative stone attached to the front of a house to indicate the address; the stones often refer to a trade or are puns on the owner's surname

Fanlight   Window above a door, admitting light to the hallway

Gable   Ornate upper part of a wall between the sloping roofs

Garland   Sculpture depicting hanging fruit or flowers

Hall church   Gothic church in which the nave and aisles are of equal height

Hofje   Almshouses grouped around a quiet courtyard

Mask   Renaissance decoration showing either a human or an animal face

Nave   The central section of a church, running W to E

Neck gable   A gable with an elevated centerpiece

Pediment   Triangular or rounded form above door or window

Pilaster   A flat column projecting slightly from a wall

Putto   Charming sculpture representing a small boy, cherub or cupid

Sash window   An 18thC window that slides up and down in its frame

Spout gable   A simple triangular gable often used on warehouses

Step gable   A Gothic gable ascending by a series of steps

Strapwork   Mannerist decoration curled at the edges like old parchment or leather

Tracery   Pattern of intersecting ribs in windows and walls of Gothic buildings

Transepts   Transverse arms of a cruciform church

The Hague gradually acquired an elegance that set it apart from the crowded mercantile cities of the Netherlands. The poet and diplomat **Constantijn Huygens** took a keen interest in town planning, designing a square (the **Plein**), an avenue (the **Korte Vijverberg**) and a road through the woods to Scheveningen (now the route of trams 7 and 8). The house he built himself in the suburb of **Voorburg** is still standing (see HUYGENS MUSEUM HOFWIJK, page 253).

Several elegant buildings in 18thC **Dutch Baroque** style grace the waterfront of the Lange Vijverberg and the tree-lined Lange Voorhout. The **Huis Schuylenburch** at Lange Vijverberg 8 was designed in 1715 by the Huguenot refugee Daniel Marot, who introduced the French

Baroque style of Louis XIV to the northern Dutch cities. The former **Koninklijke Bibliotheek** (royal library) at Lange Voorhout 34 is another Marot town house, designed in 1734 but with wings added by Pieter de Swart in 1761.

H.P. Berlage designed several important buildings in The Hague, including the geometrical **First Church of Christ Scientist** in 1925 (Andries Bickerweg), and the brick-clad concrete **Gemeentemuseum**, completed posthumously in 1935.

A cluster of new buildings next to Centraal Station represent an attempt to rebuild the city center on a grand scale. The complex includes the brash **Babylon** shopping center, the new **Koninklijke Bibliotheek** (royal library) designed by the **OD 205 group**, and the **Ministry of Foreign Affairs**. Another group of big buildings is gradually taking shape in the Spui quarter, including the new **Danstheater** and the **Stadhuis** (town hall). P. de Bruijn's new building for the **Tweede Kamer** (Lower House) on Hofweg represents a sensitive attempt to create a modern building that also harmonizes with the old Binnenhof architecture.

Dutch painting

To most people Dutch painting means the art of the **Golden Age**: the peaceful landscapes of Jacob van Ruisdael and Hobbema, the quiet domestic interiors of Vermeer and De Hoogh, the merry banqueting scenes of Frans Hals and the vibrant portraits by Rembrandt.

The Rijksmuseum in Amsterdam boasts the world's finest collection of Dutch art of the Golden Age, and there are also excellent collections at the Mauritshuis in The Hague and at the Museum Boymans-van Beuningen in Rotterdam. Other well-known Dutch artists are Van Gogh, to whom a museum is devoted in Amsterdam, and the abstract painter Piet Mondrian, whose work can be studied in The Hague's Gemeente-museum.

It is also interesting while in Holland to explore some of the less well-known areas of Dutch art, such as the exquisite Delft Masters of the 15thC, the Haarlem Mannerists of the 16thC and the Impressionists of the 19thC.

EARLY NETHERLANDISH PAINTING
Early Dutch painting has its roots in the realism of **Flemish Masters** such as **Jan van Eyck** and **Hans Memling**, who were active in the Southern Netherlands (present-day Belgium) during the 15thC. The most notable Dutch artist of this period was **Geertgen tot Sint Jans** (1460s-90s), whose fascination with rich jewelry and clothes is typically Flemish.

The most bizarre artist of the 15thC was **Hieronymus Bosch** (c. 1450-1516), whose paintings present a disturbing vision of burning cities, erotic fantasies and fabulous beasts, often verging on the surreal.

RENAISSANCE

Hints of the Renaissance can be detected in early 16thC paintings by **Jan Mostaert** (c. 1475-c. 1555) from Haarlem, whose works abound in delightful details, and **Jacob Cornelisz. van Oostsanen** (c. 1470-1533). But it was Van Oostsanen's pupil **Jan van Scorel** (1495-1562) who introduced the techniques of the Renaissance to the Northern Netherlands. As keeper of the Vatican art collection from 1522-23 under the Dutch Pope Adriaen IV, Van Scorel was able to study the works of Leonardo da Vinci and Raphael. Paintings such as his *Mary Magdalene* in the Rijksmuseum are unmistakably Italian in style, although lingering traces of Flemish realism can be detected in the group portraits he painted in Utrecht and Haarlem. His pupil **Maerten van Heemskerck** (1498-1574) displays a similar blend of Renaissance and Flemish styles in his portraits.

A more dynamic and fluid style was achieved by **Lucas van Leyden** (1494-1533) in works such as *The Last Judgment,* which hangs in the Lakenhal in his home town of Leiden, and the *Dance around the Golden Calf* in the Rijksmuseum. A strange, exotic **Mannerism** was developed in the nearby town of Haarlem by artists such as **Cornelis Cornelisz** (1562-1638).

THE GOLDEN AGE

For most of the 17thC, artists produced the type of painting that is thought of as typically Dutch. The Golden Age is characterized by its placid landscapes with grazing cattle, tranquil domestic scenes, dramatic sea battles, empty white churches, and portraits of civic guards sporting magnificent moustaches. During this period, the church ceased to be an important patron of the arts, and merchants, burgomasters and even shopkeepers became avid collectors of paintings. This led to a shift from religious themes to mundane subjects such as quacks, prostitutes, household tasks and local landscapes.

The mood of the Golden Age is faithfully reflected in group portraits by **Frans Hals** (c.1580-1666), which range from merry civic guards celebrating festive occasions to grim, tight-lipped governors of hospitals and old people's homes.

Holland's greatest artist is **Rembrandt van Rijn** (1606-69), who in 1632 moved from Leiden to Amsterdam. He painted a number of group portraits, such as *The Anatomy Lesson of Dr Tulp* (1632), *Night Watch* (1642) and *The Wardens of the Amsterdam Drapers' Guild* (1661). The mysterious golden light that suffuses these works is also present in his numerous portraits, historical scenes and biblical episodes. Rembrandt was also a skilled etcher, as can be seen in the remarkable collection of portraits and landscapes in the Rembrandthuis.

Numerous pupils studied under Rembrandt in his atelier on Jodenbreestraat, including Gerrit Dou, Ferdinand Bol, Nicholas Maes and the mysterious **Carel Fabritius** (1622-54). Fabritius may have influenced **Johannes Vermeer** (1632-75), whose meticulous paintings convey a serene, almost spiritual quality. Vermeer produced about 30 paintings in his lifetime, of which six remain in Holland. Perhaps the most extraordi-

27

nary is the *View of Delft* (c.1658) in the Mauritshuis, which the French writer Marcel Proust praised as "the most beautiful painting in the world." The Mauritshuis also owns the simple, enthralling *Head of a Girl* (c. 1660), while the Rijksmuseum boasts another fond view of Delft, and two tranquil portraits — *The Kitchen Maid* (c. 1658) and *Woman Reading a Letter* (c. 1662) — that demonstrate Vermeer's exceptional skill at capturing the elusive qualities of light.

Other Delft painters of the 17thC include **Pieter de Hoogh** (1629-c.1684), who painted domestic interiors rich in spatial complexity, and **Gerrit Houckgeest** (1600-61), painter of whitewashed church interiors. The purity of Protestant churches also preoccupied the supremely fastidious Haarlem artist **Pieter Saenredam** (1597-1665).

Landscape painting also flourished during the Golden Age, when artists acquired a taste for the low horizons, cloudy skies and watery meadows of Holland. **Salomon van Ruysdael** (c. 1600-70) was fond of depicting tranquil, windless days, while his nephew **Jacob van Ruisdael** (c. 1628-82) preferred stormy, changeable skies as a romantic backdrop to his scenes. **Hobbema** (1638-1709) was more drawn by peaceful vistas, while **Jan van Goyen** (1596-1656) portrayed the bleak, desolate scenery of the eastern provinces. Under the influence of the Italianizing landscape painters of Utrecht such as Jan Both, **Albert Cuyp** (1620-91) from Dordrecht produced idealized Dutch scenes in which the mellow golden light and the rolling landscape do not ring quite true. Much more realistic are the merry winter skating scenes painted by **Hendrick Avercamp** (1585-1634) of Kampen.

Still-life paintings came into vogue in the 17thC, reaching a peak of technical virtuosity in the works of **Pieter Claesz.** (c. 1597-1661) and **Willem Claesz. Heda** (1599-c. 1680). These somewhat academic paintings tended to conceal some hidden meaning such as transience (a tumbled glass, a history book, an extinguished pipe) or deception (a peeled lemon).

The paintings of **Jan Steen** (1625-79) are also packed with hidden messages, sometimes surprisingly erotic, such as the red stockings in *Woman at her Toilet* in the Rijksmuseum, which symbolized prostitution, and the oysters (a popular aphrodisiac) in *Girl Eating Oysters* in the Mauritshuis, which symbolized copulation. Other familiar symbols in these *genre* paintings (which were moralistic reminders of death or the folly of infidelity) include dead birds (symbolizing impotence), musical instruments (vanity) and needlework (domesticity).

EIGHTEENTH TO NINETEENTH CENTURY PAINTING

Dutch art of the 18thC was a pale reflection of French styles, and perhaps the most pleasing artists were **Jan de Beijer** and **Isaac Oudewater**, who confined themselves to the careful portrayal of charming urban scenes.

A fresh vitality entered Dutch art in the middle of the 19thC when the artists of the **Hague School** (Haagse School), inspired by French painters of the Barbizon School, turned their attention to the peculiarities of Dutch landscape and light. The leading figure of the Hague School was **Josef**

Israels (1824-1911), whose paintings display a sad, pensive quality, while his son **Isaac Israels** (1865-1934) painted cheerful Impressionistic views of the dunes at Scheveningen. Other artists of the Hague School include **Hendrik Weissenbruch** (1824-1903), painter of watery meadows and luminous skies; **Hendrik Willem Mesdag** (1831-1915), a prolific marine painter; and **Jacob Maris** (1837-99), who depicted rain-swept Dutch skies.

The Amsterdam artist **George Breitner** (1857-1923) used Impressionism to capture the bustle of Amsterdam in the heady days of the Industrial Revolution, while at other times his paintings showed the sad melancholy of the old port area, where he had a studio.

The languid style of the Hague School stands in sharp contrast to the feverish vitality of **Vincent van Gogh** (1853-90), born in the village of Nuenen near Eindhoven. Van Gogh's earliest works show the same dark tones and somber mood as the works of Josef Israels, but later, after moving to Paris and falling under the spell of Impressionism, his works became increasingly colorful and at times dazzling, particularly after his move to Arles in 1888. The Provençal landscape, which initially inspired the famous series of apple blossom paintings, quickly seems to have become oppressive, however, for two years later Van Gogh killed himself, shortly after completing the desolate *Crows over the Wheatfield*.

MODERN ART

Modern art in the Netherlands began with **Piet Mondrian** (1872-1944), a methodical artist whose life-style developed in perfect harmony with his art. In the early 20thC, Mondrian affected a thick bohemian beard, inhabited a cluttered atelier in Amsterdam and exhibited dreamy moonlit Symbolist paintings, but in 1912 he moved to Paris, shaved off his beard, and began to develop an increasingly abstract style. After helping to set up the **De Stijl** (The Style) movement in 1917, he slowly evolved his distinctive use of horizontal and vertical lines enclosing vivid blocks of primary color. Other influential De Stijl artists were **Theo van Doesburg** and **Bart van der Leck**.

Contemporary Dutch artists continue to experiment with a series of colors and abstractions, and the innocent optimism of the postwar years is reflected in the delightfully colorful and childlike works of Karel Appel, Constant, Corneille and Brands, who formed the Dutch branch of the international **Cobra** group. Works by Cobra artists and other modern Dutch artists can be seen at the Stedelijk Museum in Amsterdam and in many small commercial galleries (see page 176).

Basic information

Before you go

DOCUMENTS REQUIRED

For citizens of the EC, US, Canada, Australia and New Zealand, a valid **passport** is the only document required for visits not exceeding three months. For some other nationals a **visa** must be obtained in advance from a Dutch consulate in the country of departure. **Vaccination certificates** are not normally required. Foreign visitors not staying in a hotel, pension, campground or youth hostel must register with the local **Aliens Police** (*Vreemdelingenpolitie*) within eight days of arrival. Visitors arriving by **private boat** should report to the nearest customs office on entering and leaving the Netherlands.

If you are driving a vehicle in the Netherlands, you must have a valid national **driver's license**, the **vehicle registration certificate** and a **national identity plate**.

TRAVEL AND MEDICAL INSURANCE

It is advisable to take out an insurance policy covering loss of deposits paid to airlines, hotels, tour operators, etc., and emergency costs, such as special tickets home, as well as a medical insurance policy.

Free medical treatment is administered by **Ziekenfonds ANOZ** (*Postbus 9069, 3506 GB Utrecht* ☎ *(030) 618881*). Treatment is available in an emergency from a Ziekenfonds doctor, pharmacist or hospital to visitors from countries having reciprocal agreements with the Netherlands (*UK travelers should obtain form E111 from a DSS office before leaving*).

The **IAMAT** (International Association for Medical Assistance to Travelers) has a directory of English-speaking doctors who will call, for a fixed fee. There are member hospitals and clinics throughout the world, including IAMAT Centers in Amsterdam, Rotterdam and The Hague. Membership is free. For further information on worldwide traveling and a directory of doctors and hospitals, write to **IAMAT** headquarters in the US or in Europe (*417 Center St., Lewiston, NY 14092 USA or 37 Voirets, 1212 Grand-Lancy, Genève, Switzerland*).

MONEY

The unit of currency is the guilder (Fl.), divided into 100 cents (ct). There are coins for 5ct (known as *stuivers*), 10ct (*dubbeltjes*), 25ct (*kwartjes*), Fl.1 (*guldens*), Fl.2.5 (*rijksdaalders*) and Fl.5 (*vijf gulden*).

Brightly-colored banknotes, with embossed markings for the blind, are issued in denominations of Fl.5, Fl.10, Fl.25, Fl.50, Fl.100, Fl.250 and Fl.1,000. There are no restrictions on the amount of currency that may be imported or exported.

Travelers checks issued by all major companies are widely recognized. Make sure you read the instructions included with your travelers checks. It is important to note separately the serial numbers of your checks and the telephone number to call in case of loss. Specialist travelers check companies such as **American Express** provide extensive local refund facilities through their own offices or agents.

Currency may be changed and travelers checks and Eurocheques cashed at all banks and at the **Grenswisselkantoren (GWK** — bureaux de change) found in many rail stations and at frontier posts. Branches of the GWK have the advantage of being open longer hours than ordinary banks and they allow you to use major charge and credit cards to obtain cash. Post offices, some tourist offices, long-distance trains and major department stores will also handle foreign exchange. You may have to show your passport when cashing a check.

The major **charge and credit cards** such as American Express, Diners Club, Eurocard (MasterCard) and Visa are widely, although not universally, accepted in shops, hotels and restaurants. **Eurocheques**, written in guilders, are the most common method of payment for larger sums. American citizens who also bank in Europe can make use of the Eurocheque Encashment scheme whereby they can cash personal checks with a **Eurocheque Encashment Card**.

American Express also has a **MoneyGram** ® money transfer service that makes it possible to wire money worldwide in just minutes, from any American Express Travel Service Office. This service is available to all customers and is not limited to American Express Card members. See under USEFUL ADDRESSES in each city.

CUSTOMS

The completion of the European Single Market takes place at the end of 1992. Under the Single Market arrangements due from January 1, 1993, travelers between EC countries need only make a declaration to Customs for prohibited or restricted goods. Limits on duty- and tax-paid goods purchased within the EC will end after 1992, although there will be certain higher limits on tobacco goods and alcoholic drinks, designed to prevent unfair commercial exploitation of the new arrangements.

These new higher limits will be: **Tobacco** — 800 cigarettes *plus* 400 cigarillos *plus* 200 cigars *plus* 1kg tobacco; **Alcohol** — 10 liters of liquor (spirits) *or* 20 liters fortified wine *plus* 90 liters wine (not more than 60 percent sparkling) *plus* 110 liters beer.

Limits that apply within the EC until the end of 1992 only are widely publicized in duty-free shops and at ports, airports and international crossing-points. All allowances apply to travelers aged 17 and over.

The EC decision is that duty- and tax-free shopping will continue until July 1999 based on what is referred to as a "vendor control system." What this appears to mean is that no duty or tax will be charged within the appropriate stores, but prices charged for goods on sale will be up to the store management. Our best advice is: be on your guard.

Travelers from countries outside the EC will still have to declare any goods in excess of the Customs allowances. If you are in any doubt at all, inquire before you depart.

Prohibited or restricted goods include drugs, weapons, meat, fruit, plants, flowers and protected animals. Dogs and cats brought into the Netherlands from countries other than Belgium and Luxembourg must have a certificate of vaccination from the official veterinary service of the country of departure.

TOURIST INFORMATION
Useful information on all aspects of travel in the Netherlands can be obtained from the **Netherlands Board of Tourism** *(355 Lexington Ave., 21st Floor, New York, NY 10017* ☎ *(212) 370-7367* ℻*(212) 370-9507; 25-28 Buckingham Gate, London SW1E 6LD* ☎ *(071) 630-0451* ℻ *(071) 828-7941).* Other NBT offices are located in Brussels, Tokyo and Cologne.

GETTING THERE
By air: Amsterdam's Schiphol Airport *(* ☎ *(020) 6010966)* is a major international airport with direct flights from all over the world including many cities in the US. It is regularly voted the world's most popular airport. KLM and British Airways fly from London Heathrow, Transavia from London Gatwick and Air UK from other major British airports.

By ferry: The main car ferry link from Britain is operated from Harwich to Hoek van Holland by **Sealink Stena** *(London* ☎*(071) 834-2345),* taking 7 hours by day and 8 hours by night. There is also a comfortable service operated by **Olau Line** *(Sheerness* ☎*(0795) 666666)* between Sheerness and Vlissingen, taking 7 hours by day and 9 hours by night. This service is good for drivers, and for those taking bicycles across from Britain, but foot passengers have to rely on bus transfers at either port. **North Sea Ferries** *(Hull* ☎*(0482) 77177)* operate night crossings from Hull to Rotterdam, taking 14 hours. The ship docks at Europoort, some distance from Rotterdam, but a bus runs to Rotterdam Centraal Station. Another option is to take the Dover-Oostende car ferry, which takes $3\frac{3}{4}$ hours, or the **Jetfoil** *(no cars, reservation required* ☎*Dover (0304) 203203 ext. 3428),* which takes $1\frac{3}{4}$ hours.

By train: Trains from the UK run from London Liverpool Street to Harwich and from London Victoria to Dover and Sheerness *(bus connection to port).* Direct train services run between Hoek van Holland and all the major Randstad cities. The total journey time to Amsterdam from London is about 12 hours by boat on any route, and about 10 hours by Jetfoil.

By bus: There are many cheap bus services from London to Amsterdam, Rotterdam and The Hague, via Dover. One company to try is **Eurolines UK** *(* ☎*(071) 730-0202).*

The fastest way of getting to the Randstad cities by sea from the UK is via the jetfoil from Dover to Oostende ($1\frac{3}{4}$ hours), but this service is prone to cancellation due to stormy seas or technical problems. Undoubtedly, the cheapest way to get there is by bus. Inquire at a travel agent for further details.

CLIMATE

Holland has a breezy maritime climate with mild winters and cool summers. The driest months are, surprisingly, in the spring, while the warmest months tend to be July and August. Although the Dutch may apologize for the wet, unreliable weather, it does create exceptional cloud formations reminiscent of landscape paintings by Jacob van Ruisdael and the Hague School.

CLOTHES

Visitors to the Netherlands should be prepared for rain and wind, and bring comfortable shoes for walking; high-heeled and thin-soled shoes spell disaster on the uneven, bricked sidewalks of Holland. The Dutch are colorful, casual dressers, and Amsterdammers are particularly flamboyant and creative. Dress up by all means for the smarter hotels and for restaurants and concerts, but few places, apart from casinos, will insist on formality.

GENERAL DELIVERY (POSTE RESTANTE)

Letters to be collected should be marked **General Delivery** and addressed to **Hoofdpostkantoor PTT** in the relevant city (see under USEFUL ADDRESSES in each city). These can be collected at the main post office: take identification. **American Express** (write to: **Client Mail** at American Express; see under USEFUL ADDRESSES for the local offices in Amsterdam, Rotterdam and The Hague) and **Thomas Cook** offer the same service to their customers.

Getting around

FROM SCHIPHOL AIRPORT

There is a main **rail station** at Schiphol Airport, lying on the main line from Amsterdam to Leiden, The Hague and Rotterdam. The night train service links the main cities of Holland, namely Utrecht, Amsterdam, Leiden, The Hague and Rotterdam. *(For train information ☎ 06-899 1121 (Dutch services) or (020) 620-2266 (international services), Mon-Fri 8am-10pm, Sat and Sun 9am-10pm.)* **Taxis** are a convenient and not unduly expensive alternative to public transportation.

PUBLIC TRANSPORTATION

All Dutch cities have excellent integrated public transportation systems. City **buses** *(stadsbussen)* are usually **maroon**, while buses serving outlying districts or other towns *(streekbussen)* are **yellow**. Amsterdam,

33

Rotterdam and The Hague both have extensive **tram** networks, and Amsterdam and Rotterdam also have **metro** systems, maps of which are included at the back of this book. To help you find your way around, it is advisable to obtain a public transportation map when you visit any of these cities. Tram and metro maps of Amsterdam and Rotterdam can be found at the back of this book.

The same **tickets** are used on buses, trams and metro throughout the Netherlands. You can buy a ticket for a one-way journey *(eenritskaart)* from the driver, but it is much cheaper to buy in advance a multistrip ticket, known as a *strippenkaart,* sold in units of 15. Buy these at post offices, rail stations, public transportation offices, VVV tourist offices and in newsdealers (newsagents) and tobacconists displaying the *strippenkaart* symbol. Drivers also sell 6- and 10-strip tickets, but at a higher price.

The country is divided into **zones** and the *strippenkaart* has to be folded and stamped according to the number of zones traveled, plus a flat rate of one strip per journey. Therefore if you are traveling within a single zone (e.g., from Dam to Spui in Amsterdam), you should stamp the ticket on strip 2, and if you travel through two zones, the ticket should be stamped on strip 3. It is possible for one ticket to be used by more than one person — just stamp the required number of strips for each person. The machine for stamping tickets is usually located at the back of the tram.

If you need to begin a new card, simply stamp the last strip of the old card and then the remaining strips required on the new card. As well as stamping the zone in which you begin your journey, the machine records a time on the ticket. Your ticket will then be valid for connections on any tram, bus or metro for one hour after the time stamped if you are traveling through 1-3 zones, or for $1\frac{1}{2}$ hours if you are traveling through 4-6 zones.

The system works on the basis of trust on trams and on the metro, while on buses the driver will check your ticket as you enter. However, random checks are made by inspectors who can fine you on the spot if you do not have a valid ticket.

If you are baffled, you should state your destination to the driver, who will then stamp your ticket. (Or buy a *dagkaart* for unlimited travel in one city, valid for one or more days.)

A **route map** is usually displayed above the doors on trams, while the name of the stop is given on a signpost, together with the zone number, timetable and map of zones. Stops are requested by pressing a red button.

Trams and metros usually run until midnight, while **night buses** *(nachtbussen)* run throughout the night on certain routes.

BUSES

The Randstad has a dense network of local buses serving small towns and villages. The *strippenkaart* (multistrip ticket) is valid on all buses in the Netherlands. Most of the bus drivers speak English and will announce the stop if you are unsure where to get off. Timetables are usually displayed at bus stops.

TAXIS

Taxis can be ordered by telephone, in which case they arrive almost immediately, or picked up at the taxi stands located at rail stations, hotels and near major sights and museums. Taxis cannot be hailed in the street. The charge displayed on the meter will include a service charge, but a small tip is normally added.

GETTING AROUND BY CAR

Driving in the Netherlands tends to be monotonous and frustrating. The flat freeway landscape is dreary, and parking in cities is seldom easy. The Dutch government is currently striving to restrict car-use in an attempt to alleviate congestion and pollution, and ecologically concerned travelers should think seriously before they take their car to the Netherlands. Travel by train, bus or bicycle is relatively easy, and far less harmful to the fragile Dutch environment.

The **speed limit** in built-up areas is generally 50kph (31mph), in some designated areas 30kph (19mph), and in special residential districts known as *woonerven* (indicated by a blue sign showing a white house), cars are restricted to a crawl. Main roads outside the city have a limit of 100kph (62mph), and superhighways (motorways) 120kph (74mph).

Traffic coming from the right has priority unless otherwise indicated. Drivers should take particular care when turning right, as cars must yield to cyclists on their inside that are proceeding straight ahead. Trams have priority, and pedestrians on a pedestrian crossing must be given right of way. Seat belts are compulsory.

RENTING A CAR

Most major international **car rental firms** have branches in Amsterdam and at Schiphol Airport. Payment by charge or credit card is generally required. A current driver's license is required, and the minimum age is usually 18.

RAIL SERVICES

Travel by rail in the Netherlands is quick, efficient and reasonably priced. **NS (Netherlands Railways)** operates frequent services between all the main towns, as well as night trains between Utrecht, Amsterdam, Schiphol, Leiden, The Hague and Rotterdam. An *intercity* is a fast train linking main cities, while a *stoptrein* calls at intermediate stations as well. A full timetable *(spoorboekje)*, with explanatory notes in English, can be purchased at rail stations.

One-way tickets *(enkele reis)* and return tickets *(dagretours)* are valid in the Netherlands on the day of issue only. There are various **special tickets** such as day tickets *(dagkaarten,* for unlimited travel throughout the Netherlands for one day); 3-day and 7-day Rovers *(Holland Rail Pass)* entitling the holder to unlimited train travel for a specified length of time (for an extra charge, these can be used on other forms of public transportation); weekly tickets *(weeknetkaarten);* and group tickets *(meer man's kaart,* for unlimited travel on one day for 2-6 people traveling together). Children under 4 travel free, while those aged 4-9 pay a nominal fare.

The NS also offers a number of bargain trips *(dagtochten)* to popular sights, museums, exhibitions and parks, which include the round-trip rail fare, any bus or boat fares necessary, entrance charges and perhaps a refreshment. These make excursions easy and economical, while leaving you free to decide when to travel and how long to stay. A free brochure entitled *NS-Dagtoerisme,* which is available only in Dutch, lists special excursions, and further information can be obtained from NS (☎ *(020) 623-8383).*

Information on train services can be obtained from **Netherlands Board of Tourism** offices (see page 32), or from **Netherlands Railways** *(25-28 Buckingham Gate, London SW1E 6LD* ☎ *(071) 630-1735).* In the Netherlands, **NS Travel Information Offices** provide full information:

Amsterdam CS   ☎(020) 622-0451
Eindhoven   ☎(040) 461480
Den Haag CS (The Hague)   ☎(070) 347-1681
Haarlem   ☎(023) 340116
Leiden   ☎(071) 127722
Rotterdam CS   ☎(010) 411-7100
Schiphol   ☎(020) 601-0541
Utrecht CS   ☎(030) 332555

DOMESTIC AIRLINES
Domestic flights are operated by **KLM Cityhopper** (☎ *(020) 674-7747).*

GETTING AROUND BY BICYCLE
Holland is, of course, the land of the bicycle. There are 11 million bicycles in the country and 9,900km (6,200 miles) of cycle lanes. People of all ages use their bicycles in all weather to commute to work, to go shopping, to transport their children and exercise their dogs, quite apart from long-distance touring and racing.

Sturdy black one-speed bicycles with pedal-operated brakes can be rented at more than 100 rail stations in the Netherlands. Special attachable seats for small children are also available. Train travelers can obtain reductions on rentals at stations if they have a valid rail ticket to that destination — simply ask for a *fietsdagkaart* (bicycle day ticket) when you buy a ticket. There are hourly, daily and weekly rates, and you will be required to pay a deposit. A passport or other identification is also required.

Before you set off, it is advisable to check that the brakes, lights and bell are in working order. Be sure also to take a few minutes to get used to the bicycle — and in particular the brakes, which are operated by pedaling backward — before you set off into the traffic. When planning a route, it is better to take meandering roads along rivers and dikes than straight routes along canals or across polders, which quickly become monotonous.

Proceed cautiously until you are accustomed to the rules of the road. Riding in cycle lanes — designated by a blue sign with a white bicycle, or marked *fietspad* or *rijwielpad* — is compulsory. Routes particularly suitable for bicycles are indicated by signposts with a red bicycle. There are often separate traffic lights for bicycles, and you are permitted to cycle the wrong way down one-way streets if the no-entry sign declares *m.u.v. fietsen* (bicycles excepted). Finally, you should keep in mind that cars usually have priority when entering a road from the right.

If you leave your bicycle outside, you should use a strong lock to attach it to something solid and remove all detachable parts such as lamps and pump. Most rail stations provide manned bicycle sheds where, for a small charge, you can keep your bicycle locked up overnight or for longer periods.

You can take your bicycle with you by train, but you will have to pay rather a lot to do so. Rates for sending bicycles unaccompanied are considerably cheaper. Bicycles can also be taken on the Amsterdam metro — the fare is the same as for children.

The most useful maps for the cyclist are the ANWB 1:100,000 scale series. The Amsterdam region is covered by map 5 (See SHOPPING for map suppliers). An informative booklet, *Cycling in Holland,* can be obtained from the Netherlands Board of Tourism (see page 32 for addresses).

GETTING AROUND BY BOAT
Holland's dense web of rivers, canals and lakes makes it possible to reach almost anywhere by boat. The **IJsselmeer**, which can be reached from Amsterdam via the IJ, is ideally suited to dinghies, and its coastline is dotted with historic towns offering mooring facilities. The **Loosdrechtse plassen** (an area of lakes between Amsterdam and Utrecht) offer more sheltered sailing conditions. One of the most attractive routes for cruising is from Amsterdam to Utrecht via the Amstel, Holendrecht, Angstel and Vecht rivers. The NBT publishes an excellent guide to sailing in the Netherlands, *Holland Watersports Paradise,* available from Netherlands Board of Tourism offices.

GETTING AROUND ON FOOT
Dutch cities tend to be compact and traffic-free, which makes walking around them a pleasure. In the countryside, however, public footpaths are rare.

On-the-spot information

PUBLIC HOLIDAYS
New Year's Day, January 1; Easter Monday; Queen's Birthday, 30 April; Ascension Day (sixth Thursday after Easter); Whit Monday (second Monday after Ascension); December 25; December 26. All banks and most shops are closed on these days, although museums are sometimes open. Good Friday is also a bank holiday, but most shops open for at least part of the day. Some government offices close on Liberation Day (May 5).

TIME ZONES

The Netherlands is 6 hours ahead of Eastern Standard Time and from 7-9 hours ahead of the other time zones in the US. It is one hour ahead of Greenwich Mean Time (GMT) in winter and 2 hours ahead in summer.

BANKS AND CURRENCY EXCHANGE

Banks in the Netherlands are normally open Monday to Friday 9am-4pm and sometimes later on *koopavond* (late-night shopping) days. Branches of the **Grenswisselkantoor (GWK)**, located at major rail stations, airports and superhighway (motorway) frontier crossings, are open additionally in the evenings and on weekends. The GWK branches at **Amsterdam Centraal Station** (☎ *06-0566 — free, map 11 B6)* and **Schiphol airport** (☎ *06-0566 — free, map 1 C3)* stay open 24 hours. Check exchange rates and commission charges at other *Wisselkantoren,* as these are occasionally outrageous.

SHOPPING HOURS

Shop opening hours are strictly regulated in the Netherlands. Normally, shops are open Monday 1-6pm, from Tuesday to Friday 9am-6pm, and Saturday 9am-5pm. Shops in city centers may also remain open late one evening a week *(koopavond):* this is Thursday in Amsterdam, The Hague and Utrecht and Friday in Rotterdam and Delft.

POSTAL AND TELEPHONE SERVICES

Post offices *(postkantoren),* marked **PTT**, are normally open from Monday to Friday 8.30am-5.30pm. In large cities, the main post office is also open on Saturday morning.

Stamps can be obtained in post offices, from coin-operated machines and from many newsstands selling postcards. Letter boxes are red and marked PTT; the slot marked *streekpost* is for local mail only. Allow 7-10 days for letters between the Netherlands and the US; 4 days between the Netherlands and the UK. There is also an express mail service *(expresspost)* for urgent mail. Call for information on postal services (☎ *0017-free).* Telegrams can be sent from any post office or over the telephone (☎ *009).*

Public telephones are green and marked **PTT Telecom**. They are found in post offices, cafés, museums, large department stores and occasionally in the street. Dialing instructions are given in numerous languages (including Esperanto). Some telephones take only 25ct coins, while others take 25ct, Fl.1 and Fl.2.5 coins. Coins must be inserted before dialing. Certain telephones can only be operated with a card *(telefoon-kaart),* sold at post offices. Telephone numbers beginning with the digits **06-0** are free. The dialing code for Amsterdam and Schiphol is **020**, Rotterdam is **010**, and The Hague is **070**. The code is omitted when dialing within the city. The ringing signal is a long, low intermittent tone, the busy signal a higher and more rapid tone. A three-tone sound indicates the number is not available. Public telephones have an amplifying button.

Emergency information

EMERGENCY SERVICES
For **Police**, **Ambulance** or **Fire** ☎06-11.

AUTOMOBILE ACCIDENTS
- Do not admit liability or incriminate yourself.
- Ask any witness(es) to stay and give a statement.
- Contact the police.
- Exchange names, addresses, car details and insurance company details with any other drivers involved.

Give a statement to the police who will compile a report that insurance companies will accept as authoritative.

CAR BREAKDOWNS
- Put on flashing hazard warning lights and place a warning triangle 50m (55 yards) behind the car.
- Telephone police or ring the **ANWB Wegenwacht (road patrol)** *(☎06-0808—free, 24hr)*

LOST PASSPORT
Contact the local police and your consulate immediately.

LOST TRAVELERS CHECKS
Notify the local police immediately, then follow the instructions provided with your travelers checks, or contact the issuing company. Contact your consulate or American Express if you are stranded with no money.

LOST PROPERTY
Report all losses to the police immediately as insurance companies may not accept a claim without a police report.

EMERGENCY PHRASES
Help! *Help!*
There has been an accident. *Er is een ongeluk gebeurd.*
Where is the nearest telephone/hospital? *Waar is hier een telefoon/ziekenhuis?*
Call a doctor/ambulance. *Roep een dokter/ambulance!*
Call the police. *Roep de politie!*

International calls should be preceded by **09** and the country code (e.g., 1 for the US, 44 for the UK), then the number minus the initial 0 digit of the area code. Country codes are listed in the telephone directory, which contains instructions in English. To make a collect call to a UK number, insert a 25ct coin (which is returned at the end of the call), then ☎06-0229944. This connects you with a UK operator who will call the number you need.

Directory inquiries Holland ☎008; abroad ☎06-0418 (free)
Travel information ANWB ☎(070) 3313131
Telegrams ☎009 (free number)

MUSEUMS

The Netherlands spends lavishly on its 800 or so museums, and every sizeable town has at least one interesting collection. Most are closed on Sunday morning, all day Monday and on certain public holidays. If you plan to visit several museums, it is well worth investing in a *Museumjaarkaart* (one-year museum card), which gives free access to the 300 museums listed on the card (although for some special exhibitions an entrance fee may be charged). The *Museumjaarkaart,* valid from January 1 to December 31, is sold at VVV (tourist) offices and in major museums (passport photograph required).

PUBLIC REST ROOMS (WCs)

There are very few public WCs in Dutch cities. You will find clean facilities in rail stations, museums, art galleries, cafés and major department stores such as the Bijenkorf and Vroom en Dreesmann. Expect to pay about 25ct in rail stations and department stores.

ELECTRIC CURRENT

The electric current is 220V. As in most of mainland Europe, plugs have two round prongs.

LAWS AND REGULATIONS

The Dutch Criminal Code certainly does not read like a manifesto for license, yet many visitors are astonished, even shocked, by the permissive attitude adopted in Amsterdam and other large cities toward soft drugs, prostitution and pornography, which are to a large extent decriminalized. There are limits, however, and you should not assume that a practice is legal simply because it is widespread.

CUSTOMS AND ETIQUETTE

Holland is relaxed about etiquette and there are few unusual conventions. People usually say, "*Dag* (good morning/afternoon)," on entering or leaving a shop; in restaurants you will usually be exhorted to, "*Eet smakelijk* (enjoy your meal)," on being served; and at the end of the meal asked, "*Heeft het gesmaakt?* (did you enjoy your meal?)." Other cultural quirks include leaving front-room drapes undrawn at night and treating dogs with the reverence other countries bestow on sacred cows.

EATING IN HOLLAND

The Dutch tend to look for *gezelligheid* (conviviality) or good interior design in a restaurant, rather than gastronomic perfection. Dutch cuisine tends to rely on solid staples such as Gouda cheese, meat and vegetables. Specialties such as *erwtensoep* (thick pea soup) and *hutspot* (stew) may be sustaining on winter days, but are hardly the stuff of gourmets' dreams. Probably the most succulent food in Holland is yielded by the seas, estuaries and lakes, including *maatjes haring* (cured raw herring), *gerookte IJsselmeer paling* (smoked IJsselmeer eel) and *Zeeuwse mosselen* (Zeeland mussels).

There are also a few specialties based on exotic herbs and spices brought back by the Dutch East India Company's ships in the 17th century, such as the distinguished *Friese nagelkaas* (Frisian clove cheese).

Dutch pancakes *(pannekoeken)* are also worth sampling, particularly the mini-pancakes called *poffertjes* sold at gaudy fairground stands set up permanently on main squares such as the Dam and Westermarkt in Amsterdam, and the Neude in Utrecht.

Another legacy of Holland's Far Eastern trade is the large number of Indonesian, Chinese, Japanese and Thai restaurants, which offer exotic and spicy alternatives to traditional Dutch food. Holland is particularly famous for Indonesian restaurants, which lay on spectacular *rijsttafels* (rice tables). These consist of a huge spread of dishes — sometimes requiring additional tables to hold them all — that include a large bowl of white rice *(nasi)*, prawn crackers *(kroepoek)*, a cooked vegetable salad *(gado-gado)*, several types of spicy meats, peanuts, coconut, fruit and various hot sauces. The *rijsttafel*, generally accompanied by tea, beer or water, forms a complete meal, and it is neither customary nor wise to order starters or desserts.

The main types of Indonesian cuisine are Javanese (fairly mild), Balinese (hot) and Sumatran (almost unbearably hot). It is prudent to sample a small amount of each dish to avoid unpleasant shocks, and to extinguish hot tastes with rice, *kroepoek* or vegetables. Many of Holland's best Indonesian restaurants are found in The Hague, where a large number of ex-colonials settled after Indonesian independence, but Amsterdam also offers some interesting restaurants, such as the grand **Indonesia** and the convivial **Speciaal**. For those whose palates are not accustomed to such spicy dishes, Holland also boasts numerous Chinese and Japanese restaurants.

Since the early 18th century, Holland has looked toward France for much of its culinary inspiration. This is reflected today in the growing number of elegant (and often expensive) restaurants offering French-style *nouvelle cuisine*. At its best, this involves delightful and imaginative dishes presented with flair, although sometimes it seems to be merely an excuse to charge inflated prices for deflated portions. The acknowledged masters of *nouvelle cuisine* in Holland are the Fagels, a family of chefs who at the last count were running no fewer than ten restaurants in Holland, including John Fagel's **Tout Court** in Amsterdam.

Amsterdam's Utopian zeal has led to the establishment of numerous vegetarian restaurants in recent years. Unfortunately, they are less than alluring to those who wish to combine gastronomic joys with moral beliefs or dietary requirements, since there is often no alcohol available and kitchens tend to close early. Generally, gourmet vegetarians do better to choose an ordinary restaurant offering a vegetarian menu such as **Sancerre**, or simply order the vegetarian dish *(vegetarische schotel)* in a café such as **Het Molenpad**.

Probably the most horrifying experience a food-lover will ever encounter is a Dutch Sunday, when most restaurants (especially in the provinces) are closed, and often the only place to obtain food is a slot machine at the rail station. Fortunately, Amsterdam is not afflicted by this Protestant curse, although the choice in Rotterdam and The Hague is limited. It is wise not to venture into remote areas without first ascertaining that there is somewhere open from which to obtain food. The best bet is usually an Indonesian or Chinese restaurant, or, in the country, a pancake house. Otherwise, take your cue from the Dutch and never embark on a journey without a supply of cheese sandwiches.

TIPPING

In restaurants and cafés in the Netherlands, service charges and sales tax are almost invariably included in the price *(inclusief btw en bediening)* and you need not leave a tip unless you want to show your appreciation for the service. Taxi fares also include service and taxes, but drivers still expect an additional tip. Small tips are given to hairdressers, porters and cloakroom attendants, but not movie-theater ushers.

DISABLED VISITORS

The provisions for disabled people in Holland are generally good, although in cities such as Amsterdam there are numerous obstacles to mobility such as steep, narrow staircases in old buildings, and uneven, narrow sidewalks often blocked with cars. Netherlands Railways (NS) will provide information and assistance for disabled people on request *(☎ (030) 331253 Mon-Fri 8.30am-4pm)*. General information and advice can also be obtained from **Mobility International Nederland** *(Postbus 165, 6560 AD Groesbeek ☎ (08891) 71744)*. The **Netherlands Board of Tourism** publishes a useful booklet entitled *The Handicapped,* which lists hotels, restaurants and sights accessible to disabled people.

TELEVISION

Randstad cities receive about 14 television channels by cable, including three Dutch stations, three N German, two French, BBC 1 and 2, Belgian Flemish and Belgian French. Movies on Dutch stations and Belgian Flemish are broadcast in the original language; those on French and German channels are dubbed.

LOCAL AND FOREIGN PUBLICATIONS

KLM's magazine *Holland Herald* contains a short listings section and some restaurant tips. For those who have not picked up a copy on the plane, it is on sale in newsdealers.

Newsstands and English-language bookstores are listed in the SHOP-PING sections for each of the three cities.

BOOKS ON THE NETHERLANDS

Simon Schama's *The Embarrassment of Riches* is essential reading for anyone curious about the Dutch Golden Age. It is packed like a cabinet of curiosities with anecdotes about everyday life in the 17thC, including an intriguing chapter on children. Adam Hopkin's *Holland* offers a sober survey of Dutch history and politics, with much of interest on World War II.

The German occupation of the Netherlands still obsesses Dutch novelists and film-makers; Harry Mulich's *De Aanslag* (The Attack) is a recent attempt to come to terms with the war experience. But for millions of readers worldwide, the years of terror in occupied Amsterdam are most vividly described in *The Diary of Anne Frank*.

Randstad planning

Orientation

The Randstad dominates the provinces of Noord-Holland, Zuid-Holland and Utrecht in the densely-populated western region of the Netherlands.
- Rotterdam and Dordrecht lie on the southern edge of the Randstad at the estuary of the River Maas.
- The Hague, Leiden and Haarlem stand just behind the dunes on the western edge of the region.
- Amsterdam stands on the northern edge of the Randstad.
- Utrecht occupies the eastern extremity, close to a region of wild heaths and sandy hills.

When to go

Tourists increasingly visit the Randstad throughout the year and the only hint of an off-season is from November to March, when certain museums are closed, or open only for restricted hours. Amsterdam is mobbed by northern Europeans at Easter and other religious holidays. In summer, the Netherlands attracts the seasonal migration of backpackers and, a recent development, increasing numbers of Spanish and Italian tourists. In flight from their sweltering southern cities, they rush toward the rain showers and relative cool of Amsterdam.

The Randstad looks its best in the spring, when stalls selling daffodils and tulips bring a blaze of color to street corners, while the skies are filled with billowy clouds. Summer is good for cycling, although the weather is frequently unreliable, and Amsterdam becomes somewhat crowded. Watch out for posters announcing open-air concerts in city parks.

The Dutch tend to go on vacation in July, and many city theaters, small restaurants and boutiques close at that time. Early fall can be mild and pleasant, while raw, foggy days in November add a romantic edge to old ports such as Schiedam and Enkhuizen. A winter visit might be rewarded by the sight of animated skating scenes on the frozen canals and lakes of Holland.

Amsterdam, Rotterdam and The Hague make ideal weekend destinations from Britain, France or Germany. When booking, avoid Mondays if possible, as many shops and almost all museums are closed.

Calendar of events

FEBRUARY

‡ Early February: **International Film Festival**, Rotterdam. ‡ February 25: **commemoration of dock workers' strike**, 1941, at J. D. Meijerplein, Amsterdam.

MARCH

‡ End March/beginning April to late May: the **Keukenhof gardens and greenhouses**, with their dazzling display of daffodils and tulips, are open to the public. ‡ Late March to early April: **art and antiques fair** in the Nieuwe Kerk, Amsterdam.

APRIL

‡ Mid-April to mid-May: **World Press Photo exhibition** in the Nieuwe Kerk, on Dam in Amsterdam. ‡ Late April to mid-September: **cheese market** staged on Friday mornings in Alkmaar. ‡ April 30: **Queen's Birthday** (Koninginnedag). The Queen descends on rural Dutch communities, while chaos reigns in Amsterdam as the streets become jammed with thousands of makeshift stalls where enterprising locals sell redundant clothes, dog-eared books, Fifties furniture and ethnic food. Lively **street parties** are held in the **Jordaan** quarter, but the rest of the country stays home to watch the solemn ceremonies on television.

MAY

‡ Early May to mid-June: the public are admitted to the **Japanese Garden**, Clingendael, The Hague. ‡ Early May to late September: **antique market** held on Thursday and Sunday along Lange Voorhout, The Hague. ‡ May 4: **Remembrance Day** (Dodenherdenking). **Ceremonies to honor the dead of World War II** at the National Monument on the Dam in Amsterdam. ‡ May 5: **Liberation Day** (Bevrijdingsdag). ‡ Second weekend in May: **National Bicycle and Windmill Day**. Working windmills throughout the country unfurl their sails and turn in the breeze. The Dutch take to their bikes to visit rural windmills and watch demonstrations of traditional milling. This would be a good day on which to visit Schiedam, Kinderdijk or the Zaanse Schans. ‡ End May: **opening of the herring season** in ports such as Scheveningen and IJmuiden. Dutch gourmets crowd greedily around the fish stalls to sample the first delicious batch of *maatjes* (cured young herring).

JUNE

‡ June to August: **Royal Palace,** Amsterdam, open to the public. ‡ June 1-30: **Holland Festival**. International festival of music, dance and theater. ‡ **International Organ Festival**, Haarlem. ‡ Mid-June: **international art fair** (Kunst RAI) at the RAI exhibition center, Amsterdam. ‡ Late June to late August: **cheese and craft market** takes place on Thursday mornings in Gouda.

JULY

‡ July to August: **open-air concerts** in the Vondelpark, Amsterdam.
‡ July to September: vast **display of roses** in Westbroekpark, The Hague. ‡ July: **festival of alternative theater**, Amsterdam (Zomerfestijn). ‡ Mid-July: **North Sea Jazz Festival** at Congresgebouw, The Hague.

AUGUST

‡ End August on Friday: **open-air evening concert** takes place on barges moored on Prinsengracht, Amsterdam (outside the Pulitzer Hotel). ‡ Last weekend in August: **Uitmarkt** in Amsterdam. Promotion of forthcoming cultural attractions, with occasional drama and music performances. ‡ Late August to early September: **Festival of Ancient Music** (Festival van Oude Muziek) at Vredenburg, Utrecht.

SEPTEMBER

‡ Early September: **Openmonumentendag** (open monuments day); normally inaccessible historic buildings throughout the Netherlands open to the public free of charge for one day; a flag decorated with a key indicates each open monument. ‡ Third Tuesday in September: the Dutch monarch rides in procession through The Hague in a gilded carriage for the **State Opening of Parliament (Prinsjesdag)**. ‡ Mid-September: Old-fashioned street games and crowded cafés during the **Jordaan Festival** in Amsterdam. ‡ Last Saturday in September: flamboyant **floral parade** proceeds from Aalsmeer to Amsterdam.

OCTOBER

‡ October to November: **Antiques Fair** takes over the Prinsenhof, Delft. ‡ October 3: **parade** in Leiden to commemorate the relief of the siege in 1574.

NOVEMBER

‡ End November: **arrival of St Nicholas** celebrated.

DECEMBER

‡ December 5: Dutch families get together on **Sinterklaasavond** (St Nicholas' Eve), to read rhymes, exchange gifts and eat miniature marzipan pigs. ‡ Tuesday in mid-December: **Gouda by candlelight**. ‡ December 31: **New Year's Eve** celebrations. **Fireworks** on the Dam in Amsterdam.

Organizing your time

THREE-DAY REMBRANDT TOUR

Travelers can immerse themselves in Rembrandt by touring the places in the Randstad where the artist lived and worked, and the museums where many of his most important works hang.

First, buy a three-day Holland Rail Pass. Spend **day 1** in Leiden (15 minutes by train from Schiphol airport), where Rembrandt was born in 1606, the eighth child of a miller. Buy a *Museumkaart* at the tourist office, and visit the **Lakenhal** museum, where you can see works by Isaac van Swanenburgh, Rembrandt's first teacher, and Jan Lievens, with whom the young artist shared a studio. A solitary Rembrandt from 1626 shows his hesitant early style.

Move to Amsterdam for the evening. Those who want to sleep in the heart of Rembrandt's Amsterdam should reserve a room at the **Doelen Karena Hotel** (see WHERE TO STAY, page 132). A fragment of wall where *The Night Watch* once hung has been piously preserved in the fabric of the building (the receptionists are happy to show you the way). Two statues flanking the hotel clock on the Kloveniersburgwal facade are roughly modeled on the captain and lieutenant in Rembrandt's painting.

After breakfast on **day 2**, walk down Kloveniersburgwal to look at the **Trippenhuis**, where Rembrandt painted a portrait of Maria Trip, the somewhat pampered daughter of a wealthy arms dealer, on her 21st birthday in 1639 (now in the RIJKSMUSEUM). Continue to Nieuwmarkt, where you will see a looming brick building known as the **Waag**. Look for the doorway marked *Theatrum Anatomicum*, which once led to the anatomy theater where Rembrandt painted *The Anatomy Lesson of Dr Tulp* in 1632 (now in the MAURITSHUIS, in The Hague). Turn down St Antoniesbreestraat to visit the **Rembrandthuis**, where Rembrandt lived from 1639 until his bankruptcy in 1658. His wife Saskia died here in 1642, shortly after giving birth to his son Titus. She is buried in the OUDE KERK under a stone slab carved with the word "Saskia." After Saskia's death, Rembrandt frequently went on long walks down the River Amstel to sketch landscapes full of wistful tenderness.

Now walk down Zwanenburgwal and turn into Staalstraat to look at the **Saaihal** (Serge Hall). The five Syndics of the Drapers' Guild (and one servant) were painted here in 1661 by Rembrandt. Walk on to **Spui** — a good place for lunch — to pick up a tram to the **Rijksmuseum**, where you can look upon 19 Rembrandt paintings, including *The Night Watch* and the portrait of Maria Trip. Some of the greatest masterpieces in the collection were painted after Rembrandt's bankruptcy, when he lived in a modest house on Rozengracht (since disappeared). They include a *Self-Portrait as the Apostle Paul* (1661), the *Syndics of the Drapers' Guild*, and *The Jewish Bride* (1665). Finally, try to fit in a visit to the **Westerkerk**, where Rembrandt was buried in 1669. His second mistress Hendrickje Stoffels is buried here too, as is Titus and his wife Magdalena.

Go to **Rotterdam** on **day 3** to visit, first, the **Boymans-van Beuningen Museum**, which owns a tender portrait of *Titus at his Desk* (1655). Eat lunch in the museum restaurant, then take the train to Den Haag CS to look at the Rembrandts in the **Mauritshuis**, amassed by the former director Abraham Bredius. You will find *The Anatomy Lesson of Dr Tulp*, painted in Amsterdam one year before the Mauritshuis was begun, and two self-portraits. Compare the youthful confidence of the 1629 portrait in soldier's armor to the sad resignation of the 1669 painting, probably the artist's final self-portrait.

THREE-DAY DUTCH INTERIORS TOUR

A visit to the Randstad gives the traveler an opportunity to see a variety of Dutch interiors, from handsome 17thC rooms with tiled floors reminiscent of Vermeer paintings, to daring modern designs. The guiding principle in almost every Dutch interior is to obtain as much space and light as possible.

Before setting out on this tour, buy a three-day Holland Rail Pass. If you want to immerse yourself in a 17thC Dutch interior, stay at the **Pulitzer** or **Canal House** hotels in Amsterdam (see WHERE TO STAY, pages 134 and 131).

Begin **day 1** with a visit to the **Museum Amstelkring**, a handsome 17thC house where daylight is ingeniously manipulated to illuminate dark stairs and a deep kitchen. Go to the **Rijksmuseum** in the afternoon to wander through the period rooms illustrating Dutch Classicism (rms 252), Chinoiserie (rm 261), Baroque (rms 164-65 and 167-69), Rococo (rms 173-76), Louis XVI (rm 179), Empire (rm 33) and Art Nouveau (rm 34). The paintings of Vermeer and De Hoogh (rm 222) show Dutch interiors of the 17thC. Look up the current cinema listings for **Tuschinski 1** or **The Movies**, both movie theaters worth visiting for their exceptional **Art Deco** interiors.

Spend the morning of **day 2** in **Delft** at the **Stedelijk Museum Het Prinsenhof**, a former convent furnished in 16thC style with tiled floors and wooden cabinets. Move on to The Hague after lunch to wander around the intimate Classical rooms of the 17thC **Mauritshuis**. On **day 3**, travel to Utrecht to look at the six period rooms in the **Centraal Museum** in the morning, then visit the **Rietveld-Schröder Huis** (☎ *in advance to reserve*) to see an inspiring modern Dutch interior.

THREE-DAY DUTCH ART TOUR

Several of the world's greatest art galleries are located in the Randstad. The student of art can gain a deep knowledge of Dutch art in a brief visit, looking at masterpieces by Rembrandt, Vermeer, Van Gogh and Mondrian.

Start **Day 1** in Amsterdam, with a visit to the **Rijksmuseum** in the morning. See the 17thC Dutch paintings before tracking down the 19thC Dutch Impressionists. Marvel at the paintings of St Rémy and Arles in the **Van Gogh Museum** in the afternoon.

On **Day 2**, take the train to Den Haag CS and visit the **Mauritshuis**. In the afternoon, take tram 10 to the **Haags Gemeentemuseum** to look at 19thC Dutch Impressionists and the world's biggest Mondrian collection.

Spend **Day 3** in Haarlem, and visit the **Frans Hals Museum**.

TWO-DAY TOUR OF DUTCH GARDENS IN SPRING

Dutch landscape gardening alternates between the formal French style and casual English intimacy. The greatest gardens in the Netherlands are the Baroque acres laid out for William and Mary at **Het Loo** *(90km/ 56 miles E of Amsterdam)*. In general, however, the gardens of the Randstad, although small, are secret and seductive spots in which to escape the urban crush.

In the morning of **Day 1**, take the train to Leiden, looking out for bulbfields on the way, then catch the bus to **Keukenhof** (see EXCURSIONS, page 200) to visit the landscaped gardens of tulips and daffodils. Return to Leiden in the afternoon to wander in the 16thC **Hortus Botanicus**.

Set the alarm for 6.30am on **Day 2** and take the bus to Aalsmeer to see the **flower auction** (see EXCURSIONS, page 200). Return to Amsterdam and wander in the **Hortus Botanicus**. Walk along the Amstel to the **Munttoren** and stroll through the flower market.

STRATEGIES FOR SUNDAYS

The Dutch like Sundays to be quiet days devoted to solemn family gatherings. Outsiders might find provincial towns rather too hushed, with few places open for lunch or even a coffee. Amsterdam and Rotterdam remain lively, but you might take advantage of the relatively peaceful roads to take a cycle trip (see CYCLE TRIPS, pages 201 to 203).

Amsterdam

Amsterdam: the glorious morass

Where else in the world could one choose a place
where all life's commodities and all the curiosities one could
wish for are as easy to find as here?
(Descartes — lived in Amsterdam, 1628-49)

With its tree-lined canals and delirious skyline, Amsterdam is one of the world's most beautiful cities. Yet it is imbued, too, with a defiant spirit bordering on anarchy. The most youthful city in the Netherlands, Amsterdam is untamed, and forever critical of the government in The Hague. Its unique atmosphere engulfs you the moment you arrive: jaunty barrel organs, screeching yellow trams, pigeons flapping, bicycles clanking over tram rails, taxis honking, a saxophone playing. Where else but in Amsterdam would you find such chaos?

The very siting of the city at the waterlogged delta of the Rhine is the sign of a stubborn character. "On a desolate marsh overhung by fogs and exhaling diseases," wrote the historian Thomas Macaulay, "a marsh where there was neither wood nor stone, neither firm earth nor drinkable water, a marsh from which the ocean on one side and the Rhine on the other were with difficulty kept out by art, was to be found the most prosperous community in Europe." A 17th century artist from Haarlem captured the essence of Amsterdam more briefly when he exclaimed: "O glorious morass!"

Each building in this glorious morass is supported on long piles (once wood, now concrete), which are laboriously hammered into the damp sand. Their peculiar building techniques once caused Erasmus to quip that Amsterdammers are like birds, living at the top of trees. Yet the foundations of these bird-houses are so sound that you may spend many months in the city blissfully unaware of their existence, until you happen to come upon a heap of sand, looking like a small beach, where the paving bricks have been dug up, or glimpse a building site where ancient gnarled tree trunks poke above the ground.

FROM FISHING TO EMPIRE-BUILDING

Legend has it that the city originated when the crew of a storm-tossed fishing boat followed their seasick dog onto dry land. Amsterdam duly adopted a coat-of-arms showing a boat with two fishermen and a dog on board. A more prosaic explanation, however, is that Amsterdam began, as its name suggests, at a dam on the river Amstel. Perhaps in deference to Dutch pragmatism, the old motif has been dropped, and the current coat-of-arms — which appears on everything from bridges to anti-parking posts (known affectionately as *Amsterdammertjes*) — features three crosses of Saint Andrew, the patron saint of fishermen.

This little fishing village built on sand turned into one of the world's greatest ports, the capital of a seaborne empire that extended across almost the entire globe, from the spice islands of the Far East to Manhattan. For Descartes, who lived and wrote in Amsterdam at the zenith of its power, it was the ultimate metropolis.

COMMODITIES AND CURIOSITIES

Amsterdammers turn to statistics to prove Descartes' point that their city is unlike any other. With a population of 700,000, the city boasts more than half a million bicycles; more than one thousand bridges; 2,500 houseboats (including one for stray cats), 1,500 cafés and 7,000 protected monuments.

Amsterdam became a storehouse of curiosities after the voyages of discovery to the East and West Indies in the early 17thC, when ships returned laden with unknown spices, rare botanical species, coffee beans, tobacco bales and furs.

The city is still crammed with strange and exotic curiosities: a floating flower market, a covered street hung with paintings, a doll doctor, three pet crematoria, a parking lot under the harbor, a royal palace standing on 13,659 wooden piles (a figure almost every Dutch person knows by heart), and an international airport built on a drained lake.

The N waterfront of the old city retains the mood of seafaring days, especially in remote corners such as Oude Schans, the Zandhoek and the Entrepôtdok. The modern port lies to the W of the city, but you can glimpse the busy shipping lanes from the deck of one of the free ferries that ply between Centraal Station and Amsterdam Noord.

For all that it is an exotic city, there is also an unmistakably Dutch flavor to Amsterdam's gentle life style and peaceful mood, recalling paintings by 17th century Dutch Masters such as Rembrandt, Ruisdael and Vermeer. This quiet mood, tinged with a certain nostalgia, can be felt most strongly in brown cafés on rainy Saturday afternoons, when the only sound to break the silence is the rustle of a newspaper.

A HAVEN OF TOLERANCE

Amsterdam has been famous since the 17th century for its tolerance of exiles, attracting successive waves of Jews, Huguenots and Armenians, who enriched the city with their skills and alien cultures. Descartes spoke for many exiles when he wrote, "In what other country can one enjoy such complete liberty?" — omitting to mention that he took advantage of this Dutch liberty to cohabit with his maidservant. Amsterdam is still famous for its tolerance; of homosexuality, street performers, brothels, squatters, soft drugs, almost everything — except for illegally parked cars, and tourists who stray onto cycle lanes.

Open-mindedness goes along with a zest for enlightened social experimenting that began with the 17th century Amsterdam improvers, who spent lavish sums building houses of correction (the Rasphuis for men and Spinhuis for women) and a palatial orphanage (now the Amsterdam Historical Museum).

The process of trial and error continues unabated today, despite several ill-fated gambles in the 1960s such as the "white bicycle scheme," which flopped after thieves spirited away the entire stock of free public bicycles, and the "white car scheme," when public electric cars were briefly to be seen crawling through town in search of a recharging station. The city presses on regardless in its search for utopian solutions, constructing lavish municipal housing in Nieuwmarkt and the Jordaan, and developing a public transportation network that combines efficiency with the best in Dutch design.

Despite its laid-back tolerance, Amsterdam is not a particularly easy city to inhabit. Apartments are cramped, bicycles regularly stolen and the hard drug problem has still to be beaten. But Amsterdammers, insisting on architectural harmony and low-density traffic, have fought hard over the years to preserve their city as a livable metropolis. They will devote boundless creative energy to every aspect of the city, be it defending a protected house or persuading clematis to take root in a sandy hole in the sidewalk.

The city is infected with their style and enthusiasm, crowded with sensations and teeming with radical ideas. You will come away perhaps chilled by the wind that frequently blows off the sea, or dismayed by the sex and drugs, but also stimulated and refreshed by the bright yellow daffodils, the painted bicycles, the mellow browns and golds of Rembrandt's paintings, the jaunty carillon bells, and, most of all, by the sheer exuberance of the Amsterdammers.

Basic information

Getting around

FROM SCHIPHOL AIRPORT TO AMSTERDAM
There is an underground rail station at Schiphol airport, situated on the main line from Amsterdam to Leiden, The Hague, Rotterdam, Antwerp and Brussels. Two separate lines run to Amsterdam, one to **Centraal Station** *(map 11 B6, 18mins)*, the other to **Zuid WTC** *(map 3 F3, 7mins)* and **RAI** *(map 3 F3, 10mins)* on the southern rim of the city. During the day there are four trains an hour on each line, and one train per hour runs through the night to Centraal Station only. *(For train information ☎ 06-8991121 (Dutch services); (020) 6202266 (international services); Mon-Fri 8am-10pm; Sat and Sun 9am-10pm.)*

PUBLIC TRANSPORTATION
The **GVB public transport information office** is located opposite Centraal Station *(☎ (020) 6272727, map 11 B6, open Mon-Fri 7am-10.30pm; Sat, Sun 8am-10.30pm)*.

BUSES
The smaller villages N of Amsterdam can be reached by regional buses *(streekbussen)*, operated by **NZH** from **Centraal Station** *(☎ 06-8991177, map 11 B6)*.

TAXIS
Taxis can be ordered by telephone *(☎ (020) 6777777)*, in which case they arrive almost immediately, or picked up at one of the taxi stands in the city, which are located at rail stations, hotels and near major sights and museums.
   Many destinations in Amsterdam can be reached using modern **Water Taxis** *(☎ (020) 6222181)*, which seat up to seven passengers. The cost is, of course, considerably higher than for an ordinary taxi.

GETTING AROUND BY BOAT
Amsterdam is an ideal city for those who like boat trips. Several companies run one-hour guided tours of the 17thC canals. Tours take place throughout the year except on those rare and remarkable days when the canals freeze solid. Despite the often banal commentary in four languages, an organized boat trip offers some fascinating glimpses of the canals. You might see a heron perched on an automobile, or a

houseboat decorated with garden gnomes, or an Amsterdammer carrying a double bass by bicycle. Should you spot an attractive café terrace, be sure to mark it on a map, or you may never find it again on foot.

Most tours begin opposite Centraal Station, many of them organized by **Holland International** *(Prins Hendrikkade ☎ (020) 6227788, map 11 C6)* and **Lovers** *(Prins Hendrikkade ☎ (020) 6222181 ♿ map 11 C6)*. One company, **Kooij** *(Rokin ☎ (020) 6233810, map 10 E4)*, sails from a pier near Spui, while the tours departing from opposite the Rijksmuseum, run by **Noord-Zuid** *(Stadhouderskade 25 ☎ (020) 6791370 Fx (020) 6754362, map 5 G3)* follow an interesting and unusual route. The boats of Noord-Zuid often have open decks at the back, which are pleasant on sunny days.

Two companies have recently introduced regular **water bus services**, rather like *vaporetti* in Venice. You can use the canal buses to get to most of the main sights by water. The **Museumboot** *(Stationsplein 8 ☎ (020) 6222181 Fx (020) 6259301, map 11 B6)* is a circle line with boats every 45 minutes stopping at Centraal Station, the Anne Frank Huis, Leidseplein, Leidsestraat/Herengracht, the Rijksmuseum, Waterlooplein and the Nederlands Scheepvaart Museum. **Canal Bus** *(Nieuwe Keizersgracht 8 ☎ (020) 6239886 Fx (020) 6241033, map 7 F7)* operates a similar circular service every 30 minutes. Each company sells a **day pass**, which gives unlimited travel on their services.

FERRIES

Two **free ferries** take pedestrians and their bicycles across the IJ to Amsterdam Noord, departing from behind Centraal Station. The **Buiksloterwegveer** runs to Buiksloterweg *(24-hour service)*, while the **Adelaarswegveer** provides a less frequent service to IJplein and Meeuwenlaan *(Mon-Sat 6.35am-8.50pm)*.

GETTING AROUND BY CAR

To paraphrase a famous New York slogan, don't even *think* of driving in Amsterdam. The picturesque streets and narrow bridges that are a delight to the cyclist and pedestrian make driving a nightmare. Drivers will find their way constantly blocked by road repairs, one-way streets and removal vans, while pedestrians and manic cyclists add to the general chaos.

Parking is also difficult; illegally parked cars may be wheel-clamped or towed away to a remote corner of the dock area. To make matters worse, cars with foreign number plates are often broken into, so never leave **valuables** inside the car.

The best thing to do is to park your car and travel by public transportation. Beyond Singelgracht, you can usually find safe parking in the street, but if you are staying within the canal area, you should park your car at the **Europarking** multistory garage *(Marnixstraat 250 ☎ (020) 6236694, map 9 E2)*. You can easily walk from here through the peaceful Jordaan to the city center, or take tram 7 or 10 for Leidseplein, or tram 17 for Dam and Centraal Station.

GETTING AROUND BY BICYCLE

You will sometimes see mothers on bikes weaving through the anarchic traffic with a beaming child perched on a front carrier, a crate of Grolsch beer strapped to the rear pannier and a dog on a lead trotting alongside. With its half million or so bikes, Amsterdam is undoubtedly one of the world's most bicycle-friendly cities, but two-wheeling visitors should still be cautious before venturing into the traffic.

The basic rules for cyclists in the Netherlands are set down on pages 36-37, but Amsterdam is, as always, a case apart. You must watch out for trams, speeding taxis and tourists who unwittingly stray onto cycle lanes. The city continues to be plagued by bicycle **theft**, and you must lock your bike securely. Prudent Amsterdammers spend more money on a lock than a bike, and they cycle around town equipped with lengths of chain that would secure an oil tanker. It is often worth paying a small sum to leave your bike at a *rijwielstalling* (guarded bicycle rack).

RENTING A BICYCLE

Centraal Station ☎(020) 6248391, map **11B6**
Amsterdam Amstel Station ☎(020) 6923584, map **4E4**
Amsterdam Muiderpoort Station ☎(020) 6923439, map **4D4**
Amsterdam Sloterdijk Station ☎(020) 6848409, map **3C1**
Take a Bike Amstelveenseweg 880-900, at main entrance to Amsterdamse Bos ☎(020) 6445473, map **1C3**
Koenders Rent Shop Utrechtsedwarsstraat 105 ☎(020) 6234657, map **6G5**
MacBike Nieuwe Uilenburgerstraat 116 ☎(020) 6200985, map **11E6** and Marnixstraat 220 ☎(020) 6266964, map **9E2**. Friendly service and helpful tips.

GETTING AROUND ON FOOT

The most peaceful areas for walking in the vicinity of Amsterdam are the woods near **Hilversum** and the dunes w of **Haarlem**. The 17thC city is ideal for ambling around on foot. Distances are never too great and the traffic is generally civil. It is worth planning routes to avoid busy roads such as Raadhuisstraat and Vijzelstraat. The best walking routes are along the quiet canals or down narrow cross-streets such as Staalstraat and Huidenstraat.

Useful addresses

TOURIST INFORMATION

VVV (tourist office)   Located opposite Centraal Station, at Station-splein 10   ☎(020) 6266444 ☒(020) 6252869, map **11**B6; write to Postbus 3901, 1001 AS Amsterdam. Open Easter-June, July, Aug daily 9am-11pm; Sept Mon-Sat 9am-11pm, Sun 9am-9pm; Oct-Easter Mon-Fri 9am-6pm, Sat 9am-5pm, Sun 10am-1pm, 2-5pm. There is a small VVV office at Leidsestraat 106 *(closed Sun Oct-Easter)*. Tourist offices outside Amsterdam usually close on Sunday.

American Express Travel Service   Damrak 66 ☎(020) 6262042, map **10**C5 and Van Baerlestraat 38 ☎(020) 6738550, map **5**I3). A valuable source of information for any traveler in need of help, advice or emergency services.

BANKS AND CURRENCY EXCHANGE

Banks in Amsterdam are open Monday to Friday 9am-4pm and sometimes later on Thursday (late-night shopping). Branches of the **Grens-wisselkantoor (GWK)** at **Amsterdam Centraal Station** *(☎06-0566 — free, map 11B6)* and **Schiphol airport** *(☎06-0566 — free, map 1C3)* stay open 24 hours.

TOUR OPERATORS

The following companies organize bus excursions in and around Amsterdam:

American Express   Damrak 66 ☎(020) 6262042, map **10**C5
Holland International   Rokin 54 ☎(020) 5512812, map **10**C5
Lindbergh   Damrak 26 ☎(020) 6222766, map **10**C5

WALKING TOURS

The enthusiastic and genial young graduates employed by **Artifex Travel** *(Postbus 50019, 1007 BA, Amsterdam ☎(020) 6208112 ☒(020) 6206908)* lead personalized walking tours for individuals and groups interested in Amsterdam's rich art and history. Reservations are made through the tourist office.

CYCLE TOURS

Yellow Bike *(Nieuwe Zijds Voorburgwal 66 ☎(020) 6206940 ☒(020) 6382125, map 10C5)* runs bicycle tours in English led by clued-up Amsterdammers (April to October). Regular $3\frac{1}{2}$-hour tour of Amsterdam (at 9am and 1pm) or $6\frac{1}{2}$-hour trip in the Waterland landscape (at 8.30am and noon).

AIRLINES

Aer Lingus   Heiligeweg 14 ☎(020) 6238620, map **10**E4
Air UK   Schiphol airport ☎(020) 6010633, map **1**C3
American Airlines   WTC, Strawinskylaan 1019 ☎(020) 6648686
British Airways   Stadhouderskade 4 ☎(020) 6852211, map **5**G2
British Midland   WTC, Strawinskylaan 1019 ☎06-0222426

Emergency information

EMERGENCY SERVICES
For **Police, Ambulance** or **Fire** ☎06-11.

HOSPITAL
The main hospital is the **Academisch Medisch Centrum** *(Meiberg-dreef 9* ☎ *(020) 5669111 for general inquiries or (020) 5663333 for the first-aid team).* Take the metro to Holendrecht.

MEDICAL EMERGENCIES
Doctors' and dentists' 24-hour service ☎(020) 6642111

ALL-NIGHT PHARMACIES
Pharmacies are open Monday-Friday 8am or 9am to 5.30pm. For information on weekend services and all-night pharmacies ☎(020) 6948709.

HELP LINE
SOS Telefonische Hulpdienst ☎(020) 6161666

LOST PROPERTY
If you have lost something on public transportation, go to the **GVB office** *(Prins Hendrikkade 108-114* ☎ *(020) 5514911, map 11 C6).*

EMERGENCY REPAIRS
Go to **Hakky** *(Spui 4, map 10 E4)* if you need a fast shoe repair service, or to the **Wentholt Luggage Repair Shop** *(N.Z. Kolk 4* ☎ *(020) 6243252)* if your suitcase bursts open. The friendly people at **MacBike** *(Nieuwe Uilenburgerstraat 116* ☎ *(020) 6200985, map 11 E6 and Marnixstraat 220* ☎ *(020) 6266964, map 9 E2)* will repair a damaged bicycle. Take your jammed camera to **Swank Shot Studios** (Spui). **Sneeuwwit** *(Oude Leliestraat 11, map 10 C4)* offers a careful dry cleaning service, while broken zips can be replaced at **Clements** *(Beulingstraat 3* ☎ *(020) 6229208).* If you pull a muscle while jogging, limp to the **Scandic Active Club** (see RECREATION, page 197), where the resident physiotherapist is trained to fix sprains.

Dan Air   Schiphol airport ☎(020) 6531125, map **1C3**
KLM   Metsusstraat 2-6 ☎06-8747747, map **5**H3, 24-hour service
Suckling Airways   Schiphol airport ☎(020) 6041499, map **1C3** (direct flights from Cambridge and Manchester airports in the UK)
Transavia   Schiphol airport ☎(020) 6046518, map **1C3**
TWA   Singel 540 ☎(020) 6262277, map **10F4**

BUSES AND YOUTH FARES
Magic Bus   Rokin 38 ☎(020) 6264434, map **10D5**
Budget Bus   Rokin 10 ☎(020) 6275151, map **10D5**
NBBS   Youth fares: Rokin 38 ☎(020) 6205071, map **10D5**

MAJOR LIBRARIES
British Council Library   Keizersgracht 343 ☎(020) 6223644, map **9**E3
Openbare Centrale Bibliotheek   Prinsengracht 587 ☎(020) 6265065, map **9**E3 (the central public library)
Rijksmuseum   Stadhouderskade 42 ☎(020) 6732121, map **5**H3 (reference books on art and artists; closed Saturday and Sunday)

PLACES OF WORSHIP
With a mere 4 percent of Amsterdammers regularly attending church, it is not surprising to find that most of the city's churches have been closed down, demolished, or converted into cultural centers. The **Nieuwe Kerk** on the Dam, officially the national church, is breezily used for temporary photography exhibitions and antique fairs, while the **Zuiderkerk**, where three of Rembrandt's children were buried, now contains nothing more spiritual than a permanent exhibition on town planning. Of the great old churches, only the **Oude Kerk** still has a Sunday service, although some of the smaller churches are more active.
Begijnhofkapel (Catholic)   Begijnhof 30 ☎(020) 6221918, map **10**E4. Usually open for prayer.
English Church (Anglican)   Groenburgwal 42 ☎(020) 6248877, map **10**E5.
English Reformed Church   Begijnhof 48 ☎(020) 6249665, map **10**E4. Scottish Presbyterian, in spite of its name.

CONSULATES IN AMSTERDAM
Many countries have a consulate in Amsterdam.
Austria   Weteringschans 106 ☎(020) 6268033, map **6**G4
Belgium   Drentestraat 11 ☎(020) 6429763, map **3**F3
France   Vijzelgracht 2 ☎(020) 6248346, map **6**G4
Germany   De Lairessestraat 172 ☎(020) 6736246
Italy   Herengracht 609 ☎(020) 6240043, map **7**F6
Japan   Keizersgracht 634 ☎(020) 6243581, map **6**F4
Spain   Frederiksplein 34 ☎(020) 6203811, map **5**I2
Switzerland   Johannes Vermeerstraat 16 ☎(020) 6644231, map **5**H3

United Kingdom   Koningslaan 44 ☎(020) 6764343
United States   Museumplein 19 ☎(020) 6645661, map **5**H3

POSTAL AND TELEPHONE SERVICES

The **Central Post Office** *(Hoofdpostkantoor PTT, Singel 250-256* ☎ *(020) 5563311, map 10D4 ⅙)* is just w of Dam, and is open Monday to Friday 8.30am-6pm (Thursday until 8pm) and Saturday 9am-noon.

International telephone calls, telegrams, fax and telex are handled by the **Telehuis** *(Raadhuisstraat 48* ☎ *(020) 6743654, map 10D4, open 24 hours)*. **Faxes** can be sent for collection at the Telehuis: send to Ⓕ𝔁(020) 6263871, indicating the name and telephone number of the recipient.

LOCAL AND FOREIGN PUBLICATIONS

The monthly *Uitkrant,* which is available free at the **Uit Buro** *(Leidse-plein 26, map 5F3)*, provides a comprehensive listing in Dutch of theater, dance, galleries, music and other events happening in Amsterdam. The VVV's fortnightly English guide *What's on in Amsterdam* is available free at tourist offices, hotels, etc. and lists selected events.

Amsterdam
planning and walks

Where to go

Amsterdam is a compact city with a distinctive pattern of canals and streets, which, once mastered, is never forgotten. The most pleasant area for exploring is the 17thC ring of canals, the GRACHTENGORDEL (canal girdle), which encloses the old city in a sweeping arc. The main canals, HERENGRACHT, KEIZERSGRACHT and PRINSENGRACHT, offer an endless parade of architectural styles from Renaissance to Post Modern, while the side streets, radiating from the center like the spokes of a wheel, contain many of Amsterdam's most interesting shops.

The main museums are located beyond here in the 19thC ring, which extends in a broad arc around the old city, whose boundary is marked by Singelgracht. The architecture in this area ranges from opulent to utilitarian, and the streets tend to lack the animation of the central area.

The 20thC ring and the outlying suburbs are of considerable interest architecturally, but are otherwise somewhat dull and suburban.

ORIENTATION
The following list gives an idea of the distinctive character of each of Amsterdam's different areas.

OUDE ZIJDE (Old Side — *map 10 C5-E5).* Between Damrak/Rokin and Kloveniersburgwal: Amsterdam's oldest, most historic area, packed with interest but becoming seedy N of the line of Damstraat-Oude Doelenstraat-Oude Hoogstraat, which marks the boundary of the red-light district.

NIEUWE ZIJDE (New Side — *map 10 C4-E4).* Between Damrak/Rokin and SINGEL: somewhat bleak due to the filling in of its canals, but still full of historic interest, especially around the Dam; still has a slightly dilapidated air N of Dam, even though the completion of several new hotels in the 1980s has revitalized the neighborhood.

JODENBUURT (Jewish Quarter — *map 11 E6-F6).* Waterlooplein and J. D. Meijerplein: melancholy relics of Amsterdam's once-flourishing Jewish community, interspersed with controversial modern architecture. With the completion of the Muziektheater (Opera House), the area has at last begun to recover from the bitter memory of the war, and streets such as Staalstraat and Oude Doelenstraat are increasingly fashionable.

GRACHTENGORDEL (Canal Girdle — *maps 10, 9, 5, 6, 7 and 8).* Amsterdam's great arc of canals: an area of outstanding architectural interest — every visit to this area reveals some new delight or detail.

JORDAAN *(map 9)*. w of PRINSENGRACHT: a baffling maze of streets and canals possessing a dilapidated charm that Amsterdammers find irresistible; jammed with small ateliers and businesses ranging from the bohemian to the bizarre, good brown cafés and intimate restaurants.

PLANTAGE *(map 7E7-F7)*. E of Waterlooplein: an unusual, almost forgotten area of the 17thC GRACHTENGORDEL, with parks, gardens, a zoo and elegant 19thC villas.

NAUTISCH KWARTIER *(map 4D4)*. E of Centraal Station: a windy waterfront area in the throes of redevelopment. The restored 18thC ship *Amsterdam* provides a focal point for a new maritime quarter, with old ships, harbor walkways, jaunty pavilions and cafés.

WESTELIJKE EILANDEN *(map 10A4-B5)*. N of Haarlemmerhouttuinen: a peaceful area of crumbling warehouses, canals jammed with old boats, and white wooden drawbridges; ideal for a gentle stroll on Sunday morning while waiting for the museums to open.

OOSTELIJKE EILANDEN *(map 11 C7)*. E of the SCHEEPVAARTMUSEUM: interesting maritime details and distinguished modern architecture.

OUD ZUID *(map 5)*. S of Singelgracht: the 19thC ring, opulent and prosperous around the VONDELPARK and RIJKSMUSEUM; somewhat dreary w of Hobbemakade and N of Overtoom.

NIEUW ZUID *(map 7)*. Around the Amstelkanaal: the 20thC ring, rich in Amsterdam School architecture of the 1920s and De Stijl buildings of the 1930s. A new business district has sprung up along the s edge of the city, especially around the World Trade Centre.

AMSTERDAM NOORD *(map 4C4)*. N of the IJ inlet: this isolated suburb is dominated by modern apartment blocks, but there are still a few attractive North Holland houses with bright green wooden facades, strung out along ancient dikes such as the Nieuwendammerdijk and Buiksloterdijk.

65

Organizing your time

On a short visit to Amsterdam, try not to cram in too much sightseeing. Visit one or two museums, of course, and take a boat trip on the canals, but you would be missing an important dimension of Amsterdam if you did not sample the quiet conviviality of a Dutch brown café or while away an hour or two exploring small shops and boutiques. It is generally a good idea to spend cold or wet days in museums, and hope for sunny weather to explore the canals.

Remember that most museums are closed on Sunday morning (with the exception of the ANNE FRANK HUIS) and all day Monday, with the exception of the STEDELIJK MUSEUM, AMSTERDAMS HISTORISCH MUSEUM, NIEUWE KERK, WILLET-HOLTHUYSEN MUSEUM and TROPENMUSEUM in Amsterdam, the Frans Hals Museum in HAARLEM and, during the summer, the Zuiderzee Museum in ENKHUIZEN (see EXCURSIONS). You may already have a clear idea of what you want to see in Amsterdam; if not, here are two suggested programs, for a two-day and a four-day visit.

TWO-DAY VISIT

- **Day 1**   Begin with a visit to the RIJKSMUSEUM, arriving early to enjoy the Dutch Masters before the crowds. While in this area, you might also visit the VAN GOGH MUSEUM or STEDELIJK MUSEUM. Have lunch on P.C. Hooftstraat. Take a boat trip from Stadhouderskade, and plan the afternoon to end in a brown café.
- **Day 2**   In the morning visit the AMSTERDAM HISTORISCH MUSEUM (Historical Museum), then, if it is open, the KONINKLIJK PALEIS (Royal Palace) and the NIEUWE KERK. Have lunch near the Dam and in the afternoon explore the area of canals to the w of Dam. End the afternoon with a visit to a *proeflokaal* (see introduction to CAFÉS). Sample a *rijsttafel* (Indonesian rice table) for dinner.

FOUR-DAY VISIT

- **Day 1**   Follow **Walk 1**, then take a canal-boat tour from Centraal Station. If you are not sure where to eat, take tram 4 to Rembrandtsplein and investigate the restaurants along Utrechtsestraat.
- **Day 2**   Visit the NEDERLANDS SCHEEPVAARTMUSEUM (Maritime Museum) in the morning, and walk down Nieuwe Herengracht to reach the AMSTEL. Lunch in the vicinity of Waterlooplein, then visit the REMBRANDTHUIS. Walk down Oude Schans to the Montelbaanstoren. If you are feeling adventurous, try reserving a table for dinner in one of the restaurants on Reguliersdwarsstraat.
- **Day 3**   Walk along Brouwersgracht and then turn off down Korte Prinsengracht to reach the Westelijke Eilanden (Western Islands). Take tram 3 to De Clercqstraat, then tram 13 or 14 to Westermarkt to visit the ANNE FRANK HUIS. In the afternoon, explore the JORDAAN, pausing in a brown café.
- **Day 4**   Select a trip out of Amsterdam (see EXCURSIONS). GOUDA is at its best on Thursday, ALKMAAR on Friday and UTRECHT on Saturday, while HAARLEM is the only town with much to offer on Monday. Most

small towns are decidedly bleak on Sunday, although the IJsselmeer ports of ENKHUIZEN and HOORN are always cheerful on windy, summer days.

AMSTERDAM ON SUNDAY

Amsterdam is by far the liveliest Dutch city on a Sunday, but it can still sometimes be forlorn in the rain. Most museums are closed on Sunday mornings, just when people need them most, although the **Anne Frank House** is open from 10am. Those who want to cycle in Amsterdam should find the quiet streets a blessing.

Spui is animated on Sunday mornings, when Amsterdammers and tourists flock to the **Athenaeum** newspaper shop *(Spui 14-16 ☎ (020) 6226248)* to choose from an international selection of Sunday newspapers. Several Sunday **markets** have recently started up, aimed mainly at tourists who are at a loose end. Local painters and potters set up stands around the 19thC bandstand on **Thorbeckeplein** *(Sun, noon-6pm)*, and on **Spui** *(Sun, 10am-6pm)*. If it rains, you can take shelter in the indoor market **De Looier** (see SHOPPING, page 190).

Concerts are held every Sunday morning in the **Koepelzaal**, an unusual 17thC Classical church (see NIGHTLIFE AND ENTERTAINMENT, page 168). However, if nothing else appeals, you can always take to the canals for a boat trip.

Walks in Amsterdam

WALK 1: THE OLD TOWN

*Allow 1hr. Maps **10** and **11**. Tram 1, 2, 4, 5, 9, 13, 14, 16, 17, 24, 25 to Dam.*
"Holland," observed the writer Ethel Portnoy, "is the smell of *patates frites* (French fries) mingled with jasmine." This jarring contrast provides a foretaste of Amsterdam's oldest quarter, where you find a perplexing mixture of beauty and ugliness.

The walk begins at the historic center of Amsterdam, the **Dam**, where the former **town hall** retains an aloof dignity amid a rather chaotic scene. Walk down **Rokin**, an elegant shopping street, and turn right down Wijdekapelsteeg. This leads to the **Renaissance gateway** of the **municipal orphanage**. Enter the leafy courtyard of the orphanage, which is an unexpected surprise after the crush of **Kalverstraat**, Amsterdam's busiest shopping street.

Turn left beyond the courtyard to reach the **Schuttersgalerij**, a unique public passage hung with 17thC paintings from the collection of the AMSTERDAMS HISTORISCH MUSEUM. Take the first right to enter the **Begijnhof**, a medieval religious community that has managed against all odds to retain an atmosphere of gentle piety. Leave by the passage between #37 and #38 to reach **Spui**, an animated square that became famous in the 1960s for Provo happenings and political protests.

Turn left and cross Rokin, pausing on the bridge across **Grimnesse-sluis** (a former sluice) to catch one of Amsterdam's most picturesque

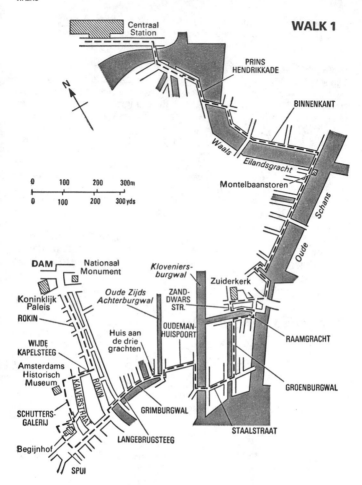

views, which includes the Renaissance **House on the Three Canals** (see illustration on page 19) and the tower of the Zuiderkerk. Walk down Langebrugsteeg to reach **Grimburgwal**.

Turn left down the second canal, Oude Zijds Achterburgwal, and then take the first right through the bookstore-lined passage Oudemanhuispoort to reach the canal Kloveniersburgwal. Turn right, then left across the bridge and straight ahead down Staalstraat. Then turn left down the canal Groenburgwal, which is splendidly terminated by the tower of the 17thC **Zuiderkerk**.

Turn right at the next canal, Raamgracht, then left again, to walk along the opposite side of the canal before turning right into Zanddwarstraat and right to enter the attractive **Zuiderkerkhof**. The houses here are built on replaceable rubber shock absorbers to deaden vibrations from the metro, which passes below. Leave this square by the **Renaissance gateway**, which once gave access to the Zuiderkerk churchyard. Turn right, then take the first left, passing a **gateway** that once belonged to the Amsterdam leprosy asylum. Descend the steps by the sluice (which is closed every night while the canals are pumped out) and walk around the canal to reach Oude Schans. Walk down to the **Montelbaanstoren**, and turn left along Binnenkant to reach **Centraal Station**, where there are trams that depart to most parts of the city.

WALK 2: CANALS AND THE RIVER AMSTEL
Allow 2hrs. Maps 10 and 11. Tram 1, 2, 5 to Spui.

"Have you noticed that Amsterdam's concentric canals resemble the circles of hell?" inquired the narrator in Albert Camus' *The Fall*. Other observers have responded more positively to Amsterdam's stately canals; "Nothing can be more pleasing," wrote John Evelyn in 1641, "being so frequently planted and shaded with the beautiful lime trees, which are set in rowes before every mans house." In recent years the canals have been the scene of fierce battles between developers and conservationists, yet the unique Baroque framework remains intact.

Begin at Spui and walk down Heisteeg to reach **Singel**, continue down Wijde Heisteeg to **Herengracht** and turn left on the far side of the canal. This takes you past a splendid row of **17thC gable houses**, interrupted by a remarkable **19thC palace** (#380-82). Turn right down Leidsegracht to reach an elegant area of **Keizersgracht**. Cross this canal and turn left to reach Leidsestraat, then continue along the next stretch of Keizersgracht. On reaching Nieuwe Spiegelstraat, turn left to return to **Herengracht**. This stretch of canal was much coveted by merchants in the late

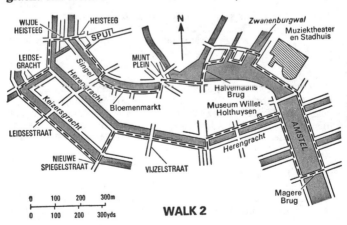

WALK 2

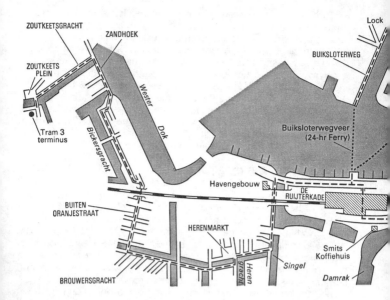

17th and 18thC and became known as *De Bocht in de Herengracht* (The Bend in Herengracht).

Turn right to reach Vijzelstraat and continue along Herengracht to the **Museum Willet-Holthuysen**. Then continue to the river Amstel, and turn right to reach the wooden drawbridge known as the **Magere Brug** (Narrow Bridge). Cross the bridge and turn left down the **Amstel**, past an interesting cross section of houseboats. Located on the bend in the Amstel is Amsterdam's controversial **Muziektheater** (Opera House) and **Stadhuis** (Town Hall), a curious combination that one acerbic Dutch critic attributed to "that cut-rate philosophy of two for the price of one that is so dear to the Dutch commercial soul."

Follow the Amstel on the opera house side, cross the bridge across Zwanenburgwal and turn left. Keep to the edge of the river and cross at the first bridge, the **Halvemaansbrug** ("Half-Moon Bridge"). Turn right, still following the Amstel, to reach the **floating flower market** on Singel, where the narrator in *The Fall* exclaimed: "How beautiful the canals are this evening! I like the breath of stagnant waters, the smell of dead leaves soaking in the canal and the funereal scent rising from the barges laden with flowers."

WALK 3: THE HARBOR
*Allow 2-3hrs. Maps **4**, **8**, **10** and **11**. Tram 3 to Zoutkeetsgracht.*
The peculiar charm of Amsterdam's port area was discovered by Vincent van Gogh during his stay here. "I like to wander through the old,

WALK 3

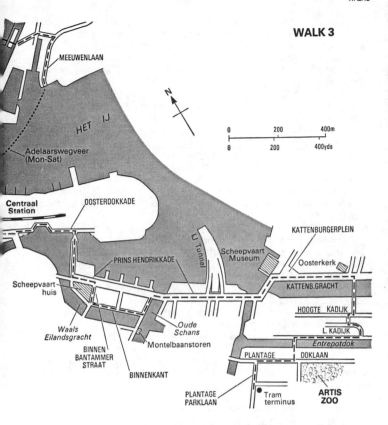

narrow and rather somber streets," he wrote, "with their shops occupied by chemists, lithographers and ships' chandlers, and browse among the navigation charts and other ships' supplies. I cannot tell you how beautiful the area is at twilight."

This walk follows in the footsteps of Van Gogh along the old harbor front, where there are still numerous echoes of Amsterdam's seafaring past.

From the tram terminus at Zoutkeetsgracht, cross the bridge to Zoutkeetsplein, a small square, and turn right along the canal to reach **Zandhoek**, an evocative corner of the old city rarely penetrated by tourists. Turn right along Zandhoek, cross the bridge and turn right onto **Bickersgracht**, a canal where boats, bridges and warehouses blend into a picturesque confusion. At the end of Bickersgracht, turn left, pass under the railway viaduct and continue straight ahead down Buiten Oranjestraat. On reaching Brouwersgracht, a canal lined with sturdy warehouses, cross the bridge, turn left and follow the canal.

73

Overlooking **Herenmarkt** — a small square on the N side of Brouwersgracht between KEIZERSGRACHT and HERENGRACHT — is the former headquarters of the **Dutch West India Company**, which established the Dutch colony of Nieuw Amsterdam on Manhattan, having bought the island from the Indians in 1626 for 60 guilders ($24). The company was not so astute in its other ventures, however, and almost went bankrupt in 1674.

Continue along Brouwersgracht to **Singel** and turn left. Cross the street and walk under the railway viaduct. On reaching the **Havengebouw**, whose 12th-floor restaurant enjoys a panoramic view of the port, turn right and walk along the quay to the pier marked *Buiksloterwegveer*, where you can take the **free municipal ferry** across the IJ to Amsterdam Noord to catch a glimpse of the port. You can then catch a second ferry (which only runs from Monday to Saturday) back to Centraal Station. To reach this ferry, walk down Buiksloterweg, take the first right to cross the **Noord Hollandsch Kanaal** at the lock, then turn right on reaching Meeuwenlaan.

After this brief detour, walk through Centraal Station, perhaps pausing for refreshment at **Smits Koffiehuis**, which overlooks Damrak, the last vestige of Amsterdam's oldest harbor, or the **1e Klas Café-Restaurant** (see CAFÉS, pages 162 and 160). Continue E along Oosterdokskade and turn right to reach Prins Hendrikkade. On the opposite side of the street is the splendid **Scheepvaarthuis**, with its row of mariners' heads gazing purposefully seaward. Turn right down the picturesque **Binnen Bantammerstraat**, then left along **Binnenkant**. The old harbor front once ran along the opposite side of Waalseilandsgracht, and the **Montelbaanstoren**, at the end of this canal, protected the NE corner of the city.

At Oude Schans, turn left, then right, to pass the **West India Company warehouses** at 's Gravenhekje and the **East India Company warehouses** at Prins Hendrikkade 176. After crossing the IJ-tunnel approach road, take the underpass to reach the NEDERLANDS SCHEEPVAART MUSEUM and the attractive cluster of 17thC houses on Kattenburgerplein. Continue E along Kattenburgerstraat to the 17thC Classical **Oosterkerk** and then cross the bridge opposite this church to reach **Hoogte Kadijk**, a former dyke. Go down the street that is almost directly straight ahead of you and turn left along Laagte Kadijk to discover the recently renovated **Entrepôtdok**, comprising some 84 warehouses named in alphabetical order after Dutch cities. Turn right to reach the bridge that leads to the terminus of tram 7.

WALK 4: SHOPPING IN AMSTERDAM
Allow 1hr. Maps 9 and 10. Tram 4, 9, 16, 24, 25 to Dam.

Amsterdam's past as a trading city is still much in evidence in the variety of shops stocked with exotic goods from all over the world. Some small businesses resemble private collections of rarities and many are worth visiting simply for their interiors.

Begin at the elegant department store **De Bijenkorf** (see SHOPPING, page 182) cross Damrak and walk down the narrow alley Zoutsteeg, then

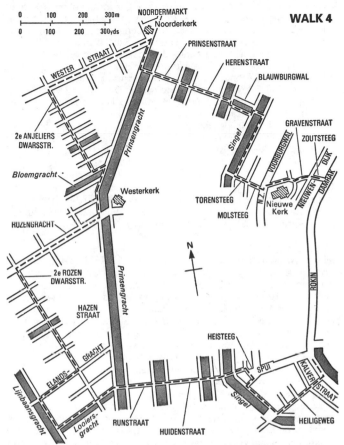

cross Nieuwendijk and continue down Gravenstraat. Some interesting **shops** are located around the NIEUWE KERK, including a few tiny premises surrounding the outside walls of the church. Cross Nieuwe Zijds Voorburgwal to visit the new **Magna Plaza** shopping center. Continue down Molsteeg, then cross Spuistraat and head down Torensteeg to SINGEL.

Turn right and walk down this canal, then cross the first bridge on the left and head down Blauwburgwal to reach the lively shopping streets **Herenstraat** and **Prinsenstraat**. On reaching PRINSENGRACHT, cross the bridge and turn right to reach **Noordermarkt** (see SHOPPING), scene of a bustling **flea market** on Monday mornings. Turn left along Westerstraat, a filled-in canal which on Monday is lined with stalls selling clothing. Turn left at Tweede Anjeliersdwarsstraat (one of many short

75

streets in the JORDAAN with uncommonly long names). Follow this street, which changes its name many times, until you reach an attractive canal, **Bloemgracht**; then turn left to reach Prinsengracht again. Turn right to reach Rozengracht, cross the street and turn right again to reach Tweede Rozendwarsstraat. This leads into **Hazenstraat**, one of the Jordaan's most buoyant shopping streets. At the end of Hazenstraat, turn right along **Elandsgracht**, a former canal that lost its sparkle when it was filled in during the 19thC. The indoor antique market **De Looier** *(Elandsgracht 109, open Sat-Thurs 9am-5pm)* sells old books, Art Nouveau vases, postcards, coins, records and toys.

At the end of Elandsgracht, turn left along Lijnbaansgracht, which marks the western limit of the 17thC city. Then take the first left down the canal **Looiersgracht**, where there is a small, chaotic, indoor flea market *(Looiersgracht 38, open Sat-Thurs 11am-5pm)*. Cross Prinsengracht and continue down **Runstraat** and **Huidenstraat**, which are lined with interesting, unusual shops of every description. Now continue down Heisteeg to reach **Spui**, good for bookstores, then head right down Singel, and left down Heiligeweg. Cross Kalverstraat and carry on straight ahead to reach the elegant shops on **Rokin**.

WALK 5: NIGHTLIFE

Allow 1-2hrs. Maps 5, 6 and 10. Tram 1, 2, 4, 5, 9, 13, 16, 17, 24, 25 to Centraal Station; or tram 9, 14 to Waterlooplein to avoid the red-light district.

Amsterdam's most celebrated nocturnal attraction is, of course, the **red-light district**, where prostitutes pose in seductive lingerie at the windows of 17thC gable houses, while the police stroll nonchalantly by. The walk described below includes an optional detour through this strangely surreal quarter of the city, where you should obviously proceed with a certain amount of caution and keep to the crowded streets. (Those who would prefer to stay clear of this area should begin the walk at the Muziektheater on Waterlooplein.)

Begin at **Centraal Station** and walk down **Damrak**. The red-light district lies E of here and can be reached by turning left down Oude Brugsteeg, left again at Warmoesstraat and then right into **Lange Niezel**. This street was favored in the Middle Ages by Amsterdam's richest merchants but, as the 17thC Amsterdam playwright Bredero was fond of reminding his audiences, "things can change," and Lange Niezel is now jammed with sex shops and cramped striptease joints.

On reaching the canal Oude Zijds Voorburgwal, turn right towards the OUDE KERK, Amsterdam's finest Gothic church, now encircled by brothels. Cross the canal by the bridge facing the church and walk straight ahead down Oude Kennissteeg, across Oude Zijds Achterburgwal and down Molensteeg. Then turn right down Zeedijk to reach NIEUWMARKT. This marks the limit of the red-light district.

To continue the walk, cross the market square, walk down Sint Antoniesbreestraat, and at the sluice turn right down Zwanenburgwal. Cross the bridge on the left and continue past the **opera house** (which looks its best at night) to the **Blauwbrug**, a stately bridge from which there is a good view of the **Magere Brug** (Narrow Bridge) outlined in

WALK 5

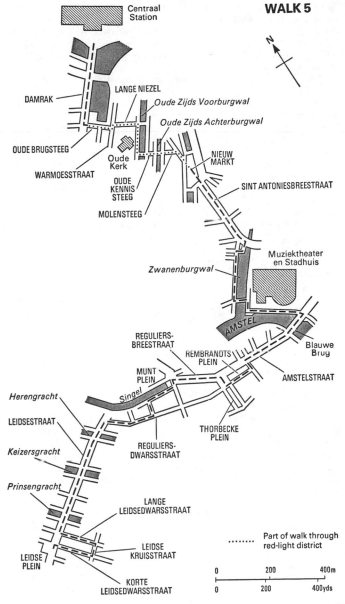

Centraal Station

DAMRAK

LANGE NIEZEL

Oude Zijds Voorburgwal

Oude Zijds Achterburgwal

OUDE BRUGSTEEG

Oude Kerk

NIEUW MARKT

WARMOESSTRAAT

OUDE KENNIS STEEG

SINT ANTONIESBREESTRAAT

MOLENSTEEG

Muziektheater en Stadhuis

Zwanenburgwal

AMSTEL

REGULIERS-BREESTRAAT

REMBRANDTS PLEIN

Blauwe Brug

MUNT PLEIN

AMSTELSTRAAT

Herengracht

Singel

LEIDSESTRAAT

THORBECKE PLEIN

Keizersgracht

REGULIERS-DWARSSTRAAT

Prinsengracht

LANGE LEIDSEDWARSSTRAAT

.... Part of walk through red-light district

LEIDSE KRUISSTRAAT

LEIDSE PLEIN

| 0 | 200 | 400m |
| 0 | 200 | 400yds |

KORTE LEIDSEDWARSSTRAAT

77

lights. Cross the Blauwbrug and continue straight ahead down Amstel-straat to reach **Rembrandtsplein**, lined with somewhat nostalgic-seeming cafés, such as the traditional brown café **De Populair** *(Reguliersbreestraat 51)*. This mood spills over into the topless bars on adjacent **Thorbeckeplein**, where even the striptease shows have an old-fashioned flavor.

Walk down **Reguliersbreestraat**, pausing to glance into the Art Deco lobby of the TUSCHINSKI movie theater, then cross over to SINGEL, walk down the left side of the canal and take the first left to reach **Reguliersdwarsstraat**. This is Amsterdam's most fashionable street at night, its restaurants always packed, its cafés spilling out into the street. On reaching **Leidsestraat**, turn left and follow the crowds. After crossing PRINSENGRACHT, turn left down Lange Leidsedwarsstraat, take the first right along a side street and then turn right again down Korte Leidsedwars-straat. This short detour provides a glimpse of some of Amsterdam's nightspots, ranging from crowded discos to highbrow jazz cafés.

End the evening in a peaceful brown café, such as **Eijlders** *(Korte Leidsedwarsstraat 47)* or **Pieper** *(Prinsengracht 424)*, or visit one of the smart new waterfront cafés near the **Amsterdam Lido**.

Tram rides

Amsterdam's extensive tram network can be used to reach many of the city's remoter sights. If possible avoid the rush hour (4.30-5.30pm). (For practical information on using public transportation, see GETTING AROUND on page 33.)

ROUTE 1: THE OLD CITY

Take tram 9 from Centraal Station to Mauritskade. Cross the street and catch tram 6 to Leidseplein, then change to tram 1, 2 or 5 to return to Centraal Station. The trip will take approximately $1\frac{1}{2}$ hours.

The first stage of this route provides a glimpse of Berlage's **Beurs** (see illustration on page 22), the DAM, Muntplein, the Art Deco TUSCHINSKI movie theater, Rembrandtsplein, the AMSTEL, Waterlooplein, the Syna-gogues and finally the TROPENMUSEUM. The second stage of the journey follows the outer edge of the 17thC city past several monumental build-ings. The last part of the trip takes you down a lively shopping street that crosses the main canals of the GRACHTENGORDEL, and past the ROYAL PALACE and the NIEUWE KERK.

ROUTE 2: ECCENTRIC ARCHITECTURE

Amsterdam's 19thC and 20thC rings are dotted with curious buildings in Neo-Gothic, Art Nouveau and Expressionist styles. Some edifices are merely quirky, but others in the Amsterdam School style represent a heroic, if ultimately unsuccessful, attempt to create a modern style. The following route by tram and on foot takes you to several unexpected buildings located off the beaten track.

Take tram 4 from Centraal Station to Victorieplein. Walk down Rijnstraat to Churchilllaan, turn right through the arcade and continue on to Waalstraat. Turn right to reach **P. L. Takstraat**, which begins on the far side of the Amstelkanaal. Walk down P. L. Takstraat, turn left down Burg. Tellegenstraat, left again along Willem Passtoorstraat and soon afterwards left into Thérèse Schwartzestraat, which leads to a small square. Leave the square at the opposite end and turn left to recross the bridge across the canal.

Return to Churchilllaan and take tram 12 to Roelof Hartplein. Walk down J. M. Coenenstraat and turn left into Harmoniehof. Return to Roelof Hartplein and take tram 3 or 12 to Overtoom. Walk back along 1^e Constantijn Huygensstraat to Vondelstraat and turn right to reach the **Vondelkerk**, where a path leads left into the VONDELPARK. Leave the park by the path beside the **Filmmuseum**. Follow Roemer Visscherstraat, turning left into Tesselschadestraat, then left along Vondelstraat. Take tram 1, 2 or 5 on Overtoom to return to Centraal Station. Allow 2 hours.

After crossing the major canals, the tram leaves the old city to pass through first the 19thC ring and then the early 20thC ring. At Victorieplein there is a solitary 1930s **skyscraper** by J. F. Staal and a robust statue of H. P. Berlage who planned Amsterdam Zuid. The short walk N leads through the remarkable **De Dageraad** housing scheme, from the early 1920s.

The next stage of the tour ends at **Roelof Hartplein**, designed as a ceremonial entrance to Amsterdam Zuid with some late Amsterdam School-style buildings dating from just before the Depression. J. F. Staal designed the block **Harmoniehof**, on the right-hand side of J. M. Coenenstraat.

The final short walk from Overtoom takes you past P. J. H. Cuypers' neo-Gothic **Vondelkerk** and other 19thC architectural delights of the Vondelpark area. Look out in particular for the astonishing row of houses at Roemer Visscherstraat 20-30a known as **De Zeven Landen** (The Seven Countries).

Sights and places of interest

Introduction

Unusually for such a fascinating city, Amsterdam can boast only a few of what could be considered major sights (the Rijksmuseum, the Van Gogh Museum and the Anne Frank Huis being the most notable). Its peculiar charm lies in the small details and unexpected curiosities that crop up all over the city. A selection of the most eccentric is given in CURIOSITIES on page 87. In addition, many are mentioned under the area descriptions and can be found in the INDEX.

USEFUL TO KNOW

Most museums in Amsterdam are closed on Sunday morning and all day Monday. See individual museums for opening times. Certain departments in the Rijksmuseum are occasionally closed because of staff shortages.

For the footsore, or those who seek a moment's respite from the hustle and bustle of the city, a few quiet spots in which to rest and regroup are mentioned in INTERLUDES on page 92. If the flat Dutch landscape becomes oppressive, select one of the opportunities to rise above it offered in VIEWPOINTS, page 123. Things to see on or near the canals and rivers that are so important a part of this unique city are spotlighted in WATER on page 125.

HOW TO USE THIS SECTION

In the following pages, Amsterdam's sights are arranged alphabetically, using English or Dutch names according to common English-speaking usage. The sights are classified by category on page 82.

Look for the ★ symbol against the most important sights and 🏛 for buildings of great architectural interest. Places of special interest for children ♣ and with outstanding views ⋐ are also indicated. For a full explanation of symbols, see page 7.

If you only know the name of a museum, say, in English, and cannot find it in the following A-Z, try looking it up in the INDEX. Some lesser sights do not have their own entries but are included within other entries: look these up in the index too.

Bold type is generally employed to indicate points of outstanding interest. Entries given without addresses and opening times are described more fully elsewhere: check the **cross-references**, which are in SMALL CAPITALS.

Amsterdam's sights A to Z

AIR MUSEUM   See AVIODOME.

ALLARD PIERSON MUSEUM
Oude Turfmarkt 127 ☎*(020) 5252556. Map 10E5* 🖼 ⅙. *Open Tues-Fri 10am-5pm; Sat, Sun, hols 1-5pm. Tram 4, 9, 14, 16, 24, 25 to Spui.*
The extensive archeological collection of the University of Amsterdam is located in a Neoclassical building that once belonged to the Nederlandsche Bank. The interior has been completely modernized, leaving only the curious 19thC lamps as a memento of the bank. The museum's collection includes unusual Coptic finds, a large selection of Greek relics and a number of objects from Crete and Cyprus. The museum occasionally organizes excellent temporary exhibitions on Classical themes.

AMSTEL
Map 7. Tram 9, 14, sneltram 51 or metro to Waterlooplein, or tram 6, 7, 10 to Oosteinde.
The meandering river Amstel, a remote distributary of the Rhine, once formed the main axis of the city, although now it is a tranquil backwater and a popular place for walks on Sunday afternoons.

The finest stretch is s from the 19thC bridge, the **Blauwbrug,** an attempt by the architect, W. Springer, to copy the Belle Epoque allure of Paris. Look to the s, toward the restored wooden drawbridge known as the **Magere Brug** (Narrow Bridge), which seems a more fitting symbol of Amsterdam's antique charm. An eccentric touch is added to the scene by the **barge** — constructed by the American artist, Victor Bulgar — which sits below the

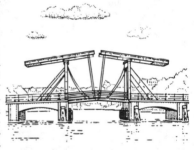

The **Magere Brug**

Blauwbrug like a raft that has floated in from the South Seas. On the right are several splendid mansions, including a sober **Doric house** built by Adriaen Dortsman at Amstel 216. On the opposite bank is the **Amstelhof,** a 17thC old people's home.

Overlooking a picturesque complex of sluices is the splendid **Theater Carré,** originally built as a circus in 1887. Continuing beyond the **Hogesluis** — another of Springer's opulent bridges — you pass the legendary **Amstel Hotel,** built in 1867. Some of its splendor rubs off on Weesperzijde, as can be seen in the **IJsbreker Café** (see CAFÉS, page 164). Cross the **Nieuwe Amstelbrug** — built in 1902 by Berlage — to reach the fairy-tale 19thC house complete with giant gnomes on the roof at Ceintuurbaan 251-55.

SIGHTS CLASSIFIED BY TYPE

MAJOR MUSEUMS
Amsterdams Historisch Museum ★
Anne Frank Huis
Het Rembrandthuis Museum
Rijksmuseum ★
Stedelijk Museum ★
Van Gogh Museum ★
OTHER MUSEUMS
Allard Pierson Museum
Aviodome ♣
Bijbels Museum
Electrische Museum Tramlijn ♣
Informatiecentrum Ruimtelijke
  Ordening
Joods Historisch Museum
Madame Tussaud Scenerama ♣
Nederlands Scheepvaart
  Museum ♣ ★
Nederlands Theater Instituut
NINT Technisch Museum ♣
Spaarpotten Museum ♣
Tropenmuseum ♣
PERIOD HOUSES
Amstelkring, Museum
Van Loon, Museum
Willet-Holthuysen, Museum
CHURCHES
Nieuwe Kerk
Oude Kerk ★ ◀€
Westerkerk ◀€
Zuiderkerk ◀€
OTHER SIGHTS
Begijnhof ★
Beurs van Berlage ▥

Heineken Brouwerij
Hollands Schouwburg
Koninklijk Paleis ★ ▥
Lapidarium
Normaal Amsterdams Peil
Schuttersgalerij
Tuschinski ▥
Waag
CANALS AND RIVERS
Amstel
Herengracht ★
Keizersgracht
Prinsengracht
Singel
DISTRICTS
De Dageraad public housing ▥
Grachtengordel ▥
Jodenbuurt ▥
Jordaan ★
Nieuwe Zijde
Nieuwmarkt
Oude Zijde
Spaarndammerbuurt ▥
Zandhoek
PARKS AND GARDENS
Amstelpark ♣
Amsterdamse Bos
Artis ♣
Hortus Botanicus
Vondelpark
SQUARES
Dam
Leidseplein
Spui

Continuing s takes you past the highly ornate neo-Renaissance **Ge-meentearchief**, which often exhibits prints from the city's archives. A short detour to the right, down Tolstraat, is the **Technical Museum NINT**, while opposite is the brilliantly revitalized **Cinétol** library, which was built by J. A. Brinkman and L. C. van der Vlugt in 1926 as a Theosophical Hall and later used as a movie theater. The modern interior is particularly striking.

Farther down the Amstel, a ceremonial effect is created by the twin blocks of Amsterdam School housing on the right, facing a bridge — the **Berlagebrug** — one of Berlage's last projects. From here, continue down the Amstel, past scenes sketched by Rembrandt, to reach the AMSTELPARK, or pick up a tram back to the center.

AMSTELKRING, MUSEUM

Oude Zijds Voorburgwal 40 ☎(020) 6246604. Map 11C6 ▨ *Open Mon-Sat 10am-5pm; Sun, hols 1-5pm. Tram 4, 9, 16, 24, 25 to Dam, then a 5min walk.*

This delightful museum is unfortunately located on a shabby patch of canal in the red-light district. Once safely inside, however, the visitor is plunged back into the Dutch Golden Age, with its sober virtues and solid furniture. The private foundation responsible for restoring this building has gone to great lengths to create the appearance of an Old Master painting, and the neat arrangements of fruit and casually discarded clay pipes give the impression that the owner has just stepped out to supervise the arrival of a consignment of spices from the East Indies. One of the house's most attractive rooms is the kitchen, which persuades light into its darkest corners by means of ingenious windows and gleaming tiles.

The house is full of unexpected surprises: windows in strange places, labyrinths of creaking staircases and a concealed priest's room in the belly of the building. But the biggest surprise is the bulky church constructed in the attic, which gives the house its memorable name: Onze Lieve Heer Op Zolder — Our Lord in the Attic.

The original owner was a Catholic merchant who built a clandestine church here after the outlawing of Catholicism by the Calvinist authorities in 1581. The museum contains an interesting map showing just how many of these ostensibly secret churches there were in Amsterdam in the 17th and 18thC. It also reveals the astonishing variety of religions practiced in the tolerant climate of Amsterdam. The present church — which extends over no fewer than three houses — was built in the 1730s. Its ingenious foldaway pulpit is a typical Amsterdam space-saving solution.

Looking from the upper windows toward the harbor, you can see the Baroque domes of **St Nicolaaskerk**, which the congregation of Onze Lieve Heer Op Zolder erected in the 19thC when the ban on the Catholic church was finally lifted. Religious enthusiasm waned almost completely during the 20thC and, sadly, the church is now used only for occasional services.

Facing the museum is a magnificent **neck gable** in Vingboons style dating from 1656. Fabulous dolphins wreathed with strings of pearls decorate the claw pieces, although few people in this part of Amsterdam take much interest in such detail.

AMSTELPARK

Europaboulevard. Map 3F3 ▣ ▬ ♣ ● *Open dawn-dusk. Tram 4 to Station RAI. On leaving the station turn right — the park entrance is just beyond the Novotel.*

This restful park on the s edge of the city near the RAI exhibition center contains an art gallery (**Het Glazen Huis**), a rosarium, Japanese garden, maze and sauna, as well as animals such as seals and donkeys.

AMSTERDAMS HISTORISCH MUSEUM (Amsterdam Historical Museum) ★

Kalverstraat 92 ☎(020) 5231822. Map 10E4 ▨ ♿ ▬ ✗ *Guidebooks in English, French or German can be borrowed. Open daily 11am-5pm. Entrances at*

Kalverstraat 92, St Luciensteeg 27, Nieuwezijds Voorburgwal 357, Gedempte Begijnensloot and Begijnhof. Tram 1, 2, 5 to Spui.

How did a tiny fishing village on the Amstel develop into one of the world's richest and most beautiful cities? What were Amsterdam's achievements and failings? How did its citizens live? Amsterdam's historical museum attempts to answer questions such as these by means of a fascinating collection of maps, portraits, utensils, clothes, globes, models, books, sculpture and topographic views.

The bustling, cosmopolitan spirit of Amsterdam is best seen in the various **views of the Dam** in the 17thC (rm 6), and the languid stillness of its great canals in the 18thC is reflected in the attractive **urban scenes** of Jan de Beijer and H. P. Schouten (rms 9, 10). The most remarkable **map** is Cornelis Anthoniszoon's 1544 woodcut showing the medieval city in minute detail (rm 1), while Amsterdam's finest moment is captured in H. C. Vroom's *Return of the Second East Indies Expedition* (rm 5), depicting the dramatic scene on the IJ, an inlet of the Zuider Zee, in 1599 as a flotilla of small boats (including a gondola) surround the four returning galleons. The painful, slow decline of the city is symbolized by the models of the unbuilt Nieuwe Kerk tower (rm 10), the paintings of the Napoleonic army entering Amsterdam (rm 16), the melancholy Impressionist works by Witsen and Breitner, and the scenes of the 1930s Depression and war years (rm 17).

An attic (rm 10a) houses a working 17thC **carillon** from the Munttoren. Visitors are invited to play on the wooden keyboard, which, with practice, will chime the carillon bells. You can then listen to recordings of music played on the four surviving 17thC carillons built by the brothers François and Pierre Hemony (in the Koninklijk Paleis, Oude Kerk, Zuiderkerk and Westerkerk).

The museum, which is housed in the splendid 17thC **municipal orphanage**, retains the **Regentenkamer**, a beautiful 17thC Classical room where the governors met. The small adjoining room commemorates one of the orphans, Jan van Speyk, who heroically blew up his ship during the 1830 Belgian revolt to prevent its falling into enemy hands.

Other interesting details include the original orphanage entrance — dating from 1581 — at Kalverstraat 92, and a collection of facade stones displayed along St Luciensteeg (including a delightful scene of the Montelbaanstoren, and a giant tooth).

AMSTERDAMSE BOS

Amstelveenseweg. Map 1C3 ☰ ➤ CN bus 170, 171, 172 from Amsterdam Centraal Station to Van Nijenrodeweg; for details of summer tram service, see ELECTRISCHE MUSEUM TRAMLIJN *on page 89.*

Amsterdam's largest park was built in the sw suburbs in the 1930s as an employment creation scheme. Although inspired by the Bois de Boulogne in Paris, the Amsterdamse Bos has an unmistakably Dutch flavor, with carefully segregated routes for cars, bicycles, horses and pedestrians. The park even includes an artificial hill (signposted *heuvel*). Notice also the distinctive **wooden bridges**, built in Amsterdam

School style by P. L. Kramer between 1937 and 1957. Another feature is a rowing racecourse, the **Bosbaan**, which was built for the 1928 Amsterdam Olympics.

The Amsterdamse Bos can also be reached on a bicycle, by following the Amstel to the café **Kleine Kalfje** (see EXCURSIONS, page 203), then turning right and following the cycle path along Kalfjeslaan, which leads straight into the park. There is a small cycle rental shop at the Van Nijenrodeweg entrance to the park *(Take A Bike, Amstelveenseweg 880-900 ☎ (020) 6445473)*, and canoes and water bicycles can also be rented (follow signs to *kano- en waterfietsen verhuur)*.

ANNE FRANK HUIS (Anne Frank's House)

Prinsengracht 263 ☎(020) 6264533. Map 9C3 ▨ *Open Mon-Sat 9am-5pm; Sun, hols 10am-5pm. Closed on Yom Kippur. Tram 13, 14, 17 to Westermarkt.*

During the Nazi occupation of the Netherlands, eight Jewish Amsterdammers hid for 25 months in the annex of this house near the WESTERKERK to avoid deportation to concentration camps. Among them was the 14-year-old schoolgirl, Anne Frank, who kept a diary recording her experiences in meticulous detail. Her observations ranged from complaints about the food to lyrical descriptions of the bells of the Westerkerk. Anne Frank and her family were eventually betrayed to the Germans and in 1945 she died in Bergen-Belsen concentration camp. Her diary was published in 1947 under the title *Het Achterhuis.*

The house has been kept in the same state as when the Franks were in hiding, and on the walls of the room occupied by Anne are photographs of Deanna Durbin and the British princesses, which she cut out of magazines, together with pencil marks indicating the growth of Anne and her sister.

Special exhibitions are organized by the Anne Frank Foundation to focus on contemporary manifestations of fascism, racism and antisemitism.

> From my favourite spot on the floor I look up at the blue sky
> and the bare chestnut tree, on whose branches little raindrops
> glisten like silver, and at the seagulls and other birds
> as they glide on the wind.
> (*The Diary of Anne Frank,* February 25, 1944)

ARTIS (Zoo)

Plantage Kerklaan 40 ☎(020) 5233400. Map 8F8 ▨ ⴲ ⇢ ⚘ *Open daily 9am-5pm. Tram 7, 9, 14 to Plantage Kerklaan.*

Natura Artis Magistra (Nature is the Teacher of the Arts) is the official title of Amsterdam's zoo, although it has always been known simply as Artis. It was opened in 1838 in a garden in the unfashionable E side of the city and grew to become one of the world's largest zoos.

Its delights include the reptile house, which is landscaped like a steamy jungle, a nocturnal house, an aquarium and a glass-walled seal pool. The owls peer out from a ruined city wall as in the paintings of Hieronymus Bosch. There is also a small farmyard, where children can wander freely among domestic animals.

Animals in Artis are given generous amounts of space, which does not leave a great deal for humans, and on weekends it can become somewhat crowded.

AVIODOME

Schiphol ☎(020) 6041521. Map 1C3 ▨ ✸ ➡ ♿ *Open May-Sep daily 10am-5pm; Oct-Apr Tues-Fri 10am-5pm; Sat, Sun noon-5pm. Train to Schiphol, then 10min walk.*

The Dutch national air museum is located near Schiphol airport in a futuristic dome, which shudders each time a Jumbo jet takes off. Some 20 historic aircraft and spaceships are on display, ranging from the Wright Brothers' fragile 1903 *Flyer* to the Spacelab, together with models and memorabilia. The salvaged fragments from the bomber of Captain McVie, a World War II pilot, whose last words to his crew were "No panic, don't forget the pigeons," are particularly haunting.

BEGIJNHOF ★

Spui. Map 10E4 ▣ *Begijnhof open dawn-dusk; Begijnhofkapel (Begijnhof 30) open 9am-5pm; Engelse Kerk (English Church, Presbyterian). Concerts Sat 8.15pm, Sun 3.15pm. Tram 1, 2, 5 to Spui. Disabled people are advised to use the side entrance on Gedempte Begijnensloot.*

The Begijnhof convent was founded by the Catholic sisterhood of Beguinages in 1346 near the s limit of the city, at a safe distance from the noise and confusion of the harbor. It is entered from the N side of Spui through a modest doorway that leads unexpectedly into an enchanting courtyard filled with birdsong — like a secret Garden of Eden in the center of the bustling city.

The sisters of this attractive religious order popular in the Low Countries took no vows but otherwise lived as nuns. The Mother Superior occupied the tall house at #26, and services were held in the charming Begijnenkerk, which dates from 1419.

After Amsterdam's conversion to Protestantism in 1578, the church was handed over to Scottish Presbyterians and, to their chagrin, renamed the English Church. Opposite, concealed behind a domestic facade, is the clandestine chapel built in 1665 for the Catholic Begijnhof residents, who had been allowed to retain their property after the Reformation. Both churches continue to coexist amicably.

Although most of the houses in the Begijnhof have 17th and 18thC facades, there is one splendid 15thC survival at #34, with a tarred wooden front and a simple spout gable. This is Amsterdam's oldest house, built with stone side walls to prevent the spread of fire. The small courtyard alongside contains several facade stones illustrating religious themes.

BEURS VAN BERLAGE 🏛

Damrak 279 ☎(020) 6265257. Map 10C5. Tram 4, 9, 16, 24, 25 to Dam.

H. P. Berlage's Koopmansbeurs (exchange) in Amsterdam (see illustration on page 22) is one of the key works of modern Dutch architecture. With its ornamental ironwork and tiled mosaics, the building originally provided a spectacular setting for the Amsterdam stock exchange. The brokers have now gone elsewhere, and the Beurs van Berlage is currently used for classical concerts and exhibitions.

BIJBELS MUSEUM (Bible Museum)
Herengracht 366 ☎(020) 6242436. Map 9E3 ☒ *Open Tues-Sat 10am-5pm; Sun, hols 1-5pm. Tram 1, 2, 5 to Spui.*
A somewhat evangelical collection of objects relating to the Old Testament is housed in two handsome canal houses built in 1662. The houses are worth a visit to look at the 18thC **spiral staircase** and the **ceiling** painted by Jacob de Wit with scenes from Classical mythology.

BOTANICAL GARDEN   See HORTUS BOTANICUS.

CURIOSITIES
Amsterdam is dotted with curious details that reflect the quirky humor of the Amsterdammers. You will almost certainly come upon some of them by chance — a barge festooned with garden gnomes, perhaps, or an artfully decorated tram — but some bizarre sights are permanent fixtures of the city. For example, there is the 19thC apartment block with twin gnomes playing handball on the roof *(Ceintuurbaan 251-5, map 7I6)*, the house with a church concealed in the attic (now the MUSEUM AMSTELKRING), and the row of seven 19thC houses illustrating seven different national styles of architecture *(Roemer Visscherstraat 20-30)*. Almost every apartment block and bridge designed in the style of the Amsterdam School is eccentric, but the facade of the **Scheepvaarthuis** *(Prins Hendrikkade 114)* is particularly remarkable for its sea monsters, sailing ships and protruding mariners' heads.

If you stand on Herengracht at the bridge over **Beulingsloot**, you will spy a white cat and mouse scrambling up the walls of opposite houses *(Herengracht 395 and 397, map 10E4)*. The city is teeming with curious sculptural details such as this, including the extraordinary lamp-posts on the 19thC **Blauwbrug**, incorporating ships' prows and imperial crowns; the sea monsters on the **bridges** near the AMERICAN hotel (see WHERE TO STAY, page 130), and the figures of an architect and mason at work on the roof of the RIJKSMUSEUM.

The Rijksmuseum contains untold curiosities, including a remarkable **dollhouse** in which each miniature chair or cup is made from the correct material. The STEDELIJK MUSEUM contains a most unsettling work called *The Beanery* — a dingy **Los Angeles bar** that you can walk inside — in comparison to which the waxwork figures in the MADAME TUSSAUD SCENERAMA seem harmless.

The restaurant of the AMSTERDAMS HISTORISCH MUSEUM contains large **wooden figures** of David and Goliath made in the 17thC for a permanent amusement fair. Peer behind Goliath to see the secret system of wires that once made his eyes blink.

A puzzling **sculpture** of a turtle supporting a Classical column on **St Antoniesbreestraat** *(map 11 D6)* celebrates the reconstruction of the neighborhood in the 1980s. Another enigmatic column on **Rokin** is a relic from the medieval pilgrimage chapel built on the site of the Amsterdam Miracle. You might find a modest **doorway** labeled **Manège** *(Vondelstraat 140)*, which leads into a vast Neoclassical hall with an iron roof built by A. L. van Gendt in 1881. Modeled on the Spanish Riding School in Vienna, the Hollandse Manège still features occasional riding displays.

Finally, Classical scholars might be amused by a sophisticated jest carved on a Neoclassical portal leading to the new casino *(Kleine Gartmanplantsoen, map 5 G3)*. The solemn Roman capitals spell out the words *Homo Sapiens Non Urinat in Ventum* (human beings do not piss in the wind).

DAM
Map 10D4. Tram 1, 2, 4, 5, 9, 13, 14, 16, 17, 24, 25 to Dam.
The main square in Amsterdam is named after the dam on the River Amstel built in about 1250 as a protection against floods. The Dam became the focus of the Dutch trading empire in the 17thC, with the old stock exchange (demolished) and the town hall (now the KONINKLIJK PALEIS or Royal Palace) together controlling a sizeable share of world commerce.

The square has largely lost its former grandeur. The Gothic NIEUWE KERK is no longer a church, and the former town hall lies empty for much of the year. Yet Dam continues to exude the vitality and glorious disorder of Amsterdam, with a constant flow of trams, bicycles, taxis and pedestrians. There is always something happening on Dam, whether it be *Kermis* (fairground), street theater, fire-eating, a street musician strumming *Blowing in the Wind*, a bagpiper rendering *Amazing Grace*, or a barrel organ playing *Tulips from Amsterdam*. The steps of the national war memorial are a favored meeting spot for young people, which the authorities reluctantly tolerate.

The endless flux of life on Dam can best be watched from the café terrace at the NIEUWE KERK, or the round window of the MADAME TUSSAUD SCENERAMA.

DE DAGERAAD PUBLIC HOUSING 🏛
s of the Sarphatipark. Map 3E3. Tram 4 to Lutmastraat.
This small patch of utopian public housing, built in bold Amsterdam School style from 1918-23 for De Dageraad (The Dawn) housing association, produces a thrilling impact in an otherwise rather dull area of Amsterdam Zuid.

The main axis of P. L. Takstraat, designed by P. L. Kramer, embodies the confidence of early 20thC socialism in its magnificently sculpted twin corner blocks standing sentinel over the street like a medieval city gate. Notice also the surging waves of roof tiles, the ornate hoist beams for lifting furniture into the houses, the sculpture by Hildo Krop and the heavily protective doorways.

Two secluded squares w and e of P. L. Takstraat — Thérèse Schwartzeplein to the w and Henriette Ronnerplein to the e — feature astonishing **mock-villas** (each containing eight apartments) built by Michel de Klerk for De Dageraad.

ELECTRISCHE MUSEUM TRAMLIJN (Electric Tramline Museum)
Haarlemmermeerstation, Amstelveenseweg 264 ☎*(020) 6737538. Map* **3***E2-F2*
🎦 ✳ *Open Apr-Oct Sun, hols only 10.30am-5.30pm; July-Aug Tues-Thurs, Sat
1-4pm; antique trams depart every 20mins, last ride 6pm. Tram 6, 16 to
Haarlemmermeerstation.*

A group of tram enthusiasts has built up a collection of some 60 antique trams from Amsterdam, The Hague, Rotterdam, Groningen,
Kassel and Vienna, and on summer weekends operates services from
the former Haarlemmermeer railway station to the AMSTERDAMSE BOS and
Amstelveen. The period detail is fastidiously maintained, to the extent
that the conductor is required to descend at each crossing to control
the traffic with a red flag.

GRACHTENGORDEL 🏛
Maps **5**, **6**, **7**, **8**, **9** *and* **10**. *Tram 13, 14, 17 to Westermarkt (early 17thC area);
tram 1, 2, 5 to Keizersgracht (mid-17thC); tram 16, 24, 25 to Keizersgracht
(Golden Bend) or tram 4 to Keizersgracht (Amstel area).*

Amsterdam's magnificent semicircle of canals and cross-streets (literally, the "canal girdle") was built under the ambitious "Plan of the
Three Canals" drawn up by the city carpenter Hendrick Staets in the
early 17thC. The three canals — HERENGRACHT, KEIZERSGRACHT and
PRINSENGRACHT — were built in two stages: initially from Brouwersgracht to Leidsegracht during the first half of the 17thC, and then from
Leidsegracht to the AMSTEL after 1665. The different periods can be
detected in the architecture: picturesque brick buildings such as the
Renaissance **Bartolotti House** (see NEDERLANDS THEATER INSTITUUT) in
the older part, and sober sandstone palaces such as the **Museum Van
Loon** in the final stretch. Subtle differences can also be discerned
between the aristocratic town houses on Herengracht ("The Gentlemen's
Canal"), the smaller middle-class dwellings on Keizersgracht ("The Em-
perors' Canal") and the modest artisan homes and workshops on
Prinsengracht ("The Princes' Canal").

The best introduction to the Grachtengordel is to take a **canal boat
tour**, since this shows the buildings as they were meant to be seen: from
the water. The tour also gives you an idea of the sights and areas that are
worth exploring in greater detail. To obtain a glimpse of a typical canal
house, visit the **Museum Willet-Holthuysen** or the **Nederlands
Theater Instituut**. It is also fascinating to view the canal web from
above, which is possible by climbing the **Westerkerk tower** *(summer
only)*, or by visiting the café-restaurant on the 6th floor of Metz & Co., at
Keizersgracht 455.

The tree-lined canals are also pleasant to walk along — particularly
on Sunday when there is scarcely any traffic. Don't try to cover too much
distance — Prinsengracht is 3.5km (2 miles) long, Keizersgracht 3km
(1¾ miles) and Herengracht 2.5km (1½ miles). Select a short stretch of canal
and take time to stop and look at the wealth of detail in gables, doorways,
staircases and decorated façade stones.

Be sure also to explore the cross-streets, which still fulfill their original
function as shopping streets. Between Raadhuisstraat and Leidsestraat is

the liveliest area of the Grachtengordel; the **Weteringbuurt** — between Spiegelgracht and Reguliersgracht — is the most peaceful and forgotten.

HEINEKEN BROUWERIJ

Stadhouderskade 78 ☎*(020) 5239239. Map* **6**H4 ✗*(compulsory, lasting 2hrs)* 🚻 ♨ ♿ *Open: mid-June to mid-Oct, Mon-Fri, tours at 9.30am, 11am, 1pm, 2.30pm; mid-Oct to Mid-June, Mon-Fri, tours at 9.30am, 11am. Closed Sat, Sun, hols. Minimum age 18 years. Tram 16, 24, 25 to Stadhouderskade.*

Heineken beer is no longer brewed in Amsterdam, but the company's giant brick brewery, built in the 1860s, has been preserved as a museum. The official guided tour takes in the granary, the brewhouse with its gleaming copper kettles, and the stables, which still accommodate the carthorses used to pull Heineken's ancient brewer's dray through the city.

HERENGRACHT ★

Maps **6**, **10**. *Tram 1, 2, 5 to Dam or Koningsplein, or tram 4 to Herengracht.*

No visit to Amsterdam would be complete without at least a glimpse of Herengracht, the inner canal of the 17thC GRACHTENGORDEL. Although the older section of the canal — from Brouwersgracht to Leidsegracht — is hardly distinguishable from the parallel sections of KEIZERSGRACHT and PRINSENGRACHT, the later stretch — from Leidsegracht to the AMSTEL — contains many of Amsterdam's most handsome 17th and 18thC town houses. These were built during the second phase of the canal web developments, when Herengracht was envisaged as an exclusive residential area from which many industries were banned, such as sugar refining (which was a notorious fire hazard), brewing (which produced unpleasant smells), and coopery (a noisy trade). Clearly the patrician families who moved here from the E side of the Amstel wanted to withdraw from the noise and smells of the trading city into an environment that was as rural as possible. Yet this absence of shops and warehouses produced a somewhat sterile atmosphere, not improved by the numerous banks and insurance companies that now occupy these houses.

Measuring about 2.5km (1½ miles), Herengracht can be walked from end to end without too much difficulty; if you have only a short time to spare, concentrate on the short stretches from Huidenstraat to Leidsestraat, and Leidsestraat to Vijzelstraat (the Golden Bend).

FROM BROUWERSGRACHT TO RAADHUISSTRAAT

The old end of Herengracht retains the flavor of the medieval city, especially on its E side, which was developed shortly after the construction of the 1585 city wall. Notice the curious sculleries attached to many of the corner houses, such as **Herengracht 1**. The most attractive relics from Herengracht's earliest period are the two warehouses **De Fortuyn** (Fortune) and **d'Arcke Noach** (Noah's Ark) at #43-45, probably dating from around 1600.

A much grander style of architecture begins to appear on the first bend in Herengracht, particularly the **Bartolotti House** at #170-72. This splendid Renaissance house, built by Hendrick de Keyser in 1617, is one of the finest facades in Amsterdam, and canal boats pause reverently on SINGEL to admire its jaunty red and white facade through the gap of Drie Koningenstraat. Its first owner was a brewer with the unremarkable name of Willem van den Heuvel, which he changed to the more catchy Guillielmo Bartolotti. The building now accommodates the NEDERLANDS THEATER INSTITUUT. Its rather more austere neighbor at **#168**, built in 1638 by Philips Vingboons, provides further accommodations for the museum. Notice the spectacular **coat of arms** in the **neck gable**, placed there by its first owner, Michiel Pauw, who in 1630 played a major role in the development of New York when he founded the colony of Pavonia, now Hoboken, New Jersey. Perhaps it was Pauw's self-important gable that prompted a later occupant of **#166** to adorn his cornice gable with the pious motto *Solo Deo Gloria* (Glory to God Alone).

FROM RAADHUISSTRAAT TO HUIDENSTRAAT

This section rambles along in a muddle of styles, with some fine 18thC gable tops to be seen on the w side, notably **De Witte Lelie** (The White Lily) at #274, with its ornate Louis XIV style balustrade rising to a crested top.

FROM HUIDENSTRAAT TO LEIDSESTRAAT

This beautiful stretch of Herengracht is best appreciated from the E side (where a few benches are provided). Philips Vingboons designed many of the houses on this bend, from the four dignified neck gables of the 1662 **Cromhouthuizen** at #364-70, to the Classical pilastered facade at **#386**, which, although built only one year later, represents a decisive break with traditional gables and provides a foretaste of the more formal styles that are to be seen in houses built in the 1660s and '70s.

The ornate confectionery in French Renaissance style at **#380-82** — seen by puritanical Amsterdammers as the last word in bad taste — was built by A. Salm in 1889 for a rich client who wanted to emulate the chic mansions of New York's 5th Avenue. Twin houses seem to have been popular when this stretch of Herengracht was developed, and at **#396-98** and **#409-11** are two pairs of 17thC neck gables known respectively as the "twin brothers" and "twin sisters." Notice also the twin at **#390-92**, built about 1665 with sculpture in the neck gable depicting a man and a woman mysteriously stretching a cord between them.

FROM LEIDSESTRAAT TO VIJZELSTRAAT

The legendary **Golden Bend**, which occupies this short stretch, comes as a slight disappointment. Although there are undoubtedly some magnificent houses — such as **#475**, built in the 1730s in a rich Louis XIV style — most houses of the 1660s and '70s present rather sober exteriors. Residences in this prime location include the **Andries de Graeff house** at #446, built for a prominent 17thC burgomaster; the **Huis van Deutz** at #450, designed by Philips Vingboons in 1663 for a banker; and the austere house by Adriaen Dortsman at **#462**, with its sculpture on the balustrade depicting the popular Dutch virtues of Welfare and Trade. **#476** was also built during the grim 1670s, but restyled in the 1740s to create one of Amsterdam's most elegant houses.

FROM VIJZELSTRAAT TO THE AMSTEL

The final stretch of Herengracht is somewhat less solemn and includes the four splendid neck gables at **#504-10**, whose claw pieces are decorated with dogs, mermaids and dolphins. Numbers **571-81** date from 1664, when four wealthy citizens reached the unprecedented decision to build four identical houses. The agreement did not apply to ornament, however, which is why the owner of **#579** was able to add the oversized figure of the Archangel Michael slaying a dragon, together with various other frivolous touches. The MUSEUM WILLET-HOLTHUYSEN is at #605.

HOLLANDS SCHOUWBURG

Plantage Middenlaan 24 ☎*(020) 6224308. Map* **7F7** ▨ *Open Mon-Fri 10am-4pm; Sat, Sun, hols 11am-4pm. Tram 7, 9, 14 to Plantage Kerklaan.*
A deeply moving memorial to the Jewish victims of the war, located in the roofless shell of the former theater where many were confined before being deported.

HORTUS BOTANICUS (Botanical Garden)

Plantage Middenlaan 2 ☎*(020) 6258411. Map* **7F7** ▨ *Open Apr-Sept Mon-Fri 9am-5pm; Sat, Sun, hols 11am-5pm; Oct-Mar closes 1hr earlier. Tram 9, 14 to Mr Visserplein; sneltram 51 or metro to Waterlooplein.*
This tiny botanical garden on the E side of the city, close to Waterlooplein, was established in 1682 for the cultivation of medicinal herbs. Many exotic species were shipped back from the Dutch East Indies, largely on the initiative of the East India Company director Joan Huydecoper.

Highlights of this beautiful garden — now owned by the university — include the palm houses and the ornamental ponds. The colors in August are particularly vivid.

INFORMATIECENTRUM RUIMTELIJKE ORDENING

Zuiderkerk, Zuiderkerkhof 72 ☎*(020) 6222962. Map* **11E6** ▨ *Open Mon-Fri 12.30-4.30pm; Thurs 6-9pm. Sneltram 51 or metro to Nieuwmarkt.*
Situated in the ZUIDERKERK, the information center of the department of town planning contains an extensive collection of maps, plans, photographs and models that illustrate Amsterdam's careful approach to urban planning. A large scale model of the IJ waterfront gives you an impression of the ambitious plan for Amsterdam's docklands, while a computerized information system provides data on many other interesting projects.

INTERLUDES

Amsterdam can sometimes be crushing and hectic, but there are many quiet spots in town where you can retreat from the crowds. By day, brown cafés are peaceful refuges for writing postcards, reading newspapers, warming toes, or planning walks. The city has a few well-placed benches where you can pause to admire the view or eat a sandwich. For the ultimate canal view, sit on one of the benches at the end of **Beulingstraat**, looking w down Leidsegracht. Another spot for lingering is found on **Brouwersgracht**, looking down Herengracht.

Anyone overwhelmed by the crowds on **Kalverstraat** should dive down the **alley** at Kalverstraat 92, which leads into two peaceful 17thC courtyards that once belonged to the city orphanage (now the AMSTER-DAMS HISTORISCH MUSEUM). Sit on the shady café terrace in the romantic *Jongensbinnenplaats* (Boys' Courtyard), next to the racks of wooden lockers where the orphans once kept their working clothes, or rest on one of the wooden benches in the rather grander *Meisjesbinnenplaats* (Girls' Courtyard).

Amsterdam's Protestant churches are normally locked, but you can find peace in the secret Catholic chapel in the **Begijnhof**. The **Vondel-park** does not offer much to those in search of silence, but the tiny **sculpture garden** behind the RIJKSMUSEUM is an enchanting and almost unknown retreat *(entrance on Hobbemastraat)*.

JEWISH HISTORICAL MUSEUM   See JOODS HISTORISCH MUSEUM.

JODENBUURT ▥
Map 11E6. Tram 9, 14 to Mr Visserplein; sneltram 51 or metro to Waterlooplein.
Until World War II, Amsterdam's Jewish quarter was located on the islands to the E of Oude Zijde. First to settle were the Portuguese and Spanish Sephardic Jews, who fled persecution in the late 16thC. They were followed in the 17thC by High German or Ashkenazi Jews, driven out of Poland and Germany.

Drawn by Amsterdam's unique mixture of religious tolerance and economic opportunity, Jews played a profound role in the development of the city, but the history of Jewish Amsterdam was brought to a terrible conclusion during the Nazi occupation, when some 70,000 Jews were deported from the city.

The entire area fell into ruin after World War II and later became the scene of controversial developments such as the IJ tunnel access road, the metro and the Stadhuis/Muziektheater complex, which together have destroyed much of the character of the old Jodenbuurt. Only recently has the area begun to show signs of revival, largely due to the highly imaginative municipal housing by the architects Aldo van Eyck and Theo Bosch. This area now contains some of the finest postwar Dutch archi-tecture, alongside the tragic remains of its Jewish past.

The main Jewish buildings to have survived are the synagogues overlooking J. D. Meijerplein. This square also contains the *Dokwerker* statue by Mari Andriessen, which commemorates the February 1941 dockers' strike held in protest at the persecution of the Jews. The N side of the square is dominated by the massive **Portuguese-Israelite Syna-gogue** *(☎ (020) 6253509, open Sun-Fri 10am-12.15pm, 1.30-4pm; closed Sat and Yom Kippur)*, built by Elias Bouwman in 1671-75. On the S side of the square are the two High German synagogues, the **Grote Shul** on the right, built in 1671 by Daniel Stalpaert, and the ornate **Neie Shul**, built in 1752 in Louis XIV style. The JOODS HISTORISCH MUSEUM now occupies these synagogues.

Jodenbreestraat and Sint Antoniesbreestraat, which connect Mr Visserplein with Nieuwmarkt, were devastated during the construction of the metro. The only relics of the old street are the twin neck gables at **Sint Antoniesbreestraat 64-72** (which are suspended from the modern buildings on either side), the splendid Classical **Pintohuis** built in 1651 for Isaac de Pinto at Sint Antoniesbreestraat 69, and the REMBRANDTHUIS.

JOODS HISTORISCH MUSEUM (Jewish Historical Museum)

Jonas Daniel Meijerplein 2-4 ☎*(020) 6269945* 🗷*(020) 6241721. Map* **7F6** 🔳
🚻 🅿 *Open daily 11am-5pm. Closed on Yom Kippur. Tram 9, 14, sneltram 51 or metro to Waterlooplein.*

The Jewish Historical Museum provides an insight into Jewish faith, the Jewish community in the Netherlands and the horrors of the Holocaust. The museum occupies an attractive complex of four synagogues, which have been sensitively converted using techniques pioneered by the Amsterdam Historical Museum, such as **overhead galleries** offering unexpected views, and a **street** through the museum (formerly an alley with the Yiddish name Sjoelgass). The museum **café**, situated in the smallest of the synagogues, offers kosher delicacies such as cheesecake and spicy ginger cake.

JORDAAN ★

Map **9**. *Tram 13, 14, 17 to Westermarkt.*

This area was developed to the w of Prinsengracht at the same time as the GRACHTENGORDEL. Its role in the 1609 Plan was that of a humble industrial quarter and, to cut costs, the majestic geometry of the great canals was abandoned in favor of a dense grid pattern with narrow canals cut E to W along the course of existing drainage ditches. This gives the Jordaan a logic quite different from the rest of the city, and even native Amsterdammers become lost when they venture w of Prinsengracht. It helps a little to know that the streets running N to S are usually called *dwarsstraten* (cross-streets) and numbered E to W as 1e, 2e and 3e (sometimes written *Eerste, Tweede, Derde),* so that 1e Laurierdwarsstraat is the most easterly street to cross Lauriergracht.

The Jordaan is still an industrial quarter — there are more than 900 small businesses registered within this compact area — but it is also a highly desirable residential area, which at first seems odd given the general air of shabby neglect and the fact that no fewer than seven of its eleven canals have been ignominiously filled in. What attracts people, especially students and artists, to the Jordaan is its vitality, and its mixture of innovative boutiques, galleries, restaurants and cafés. Perhaps this creative energy is a legacy of the 17thC, when numerous Huguenot refugees settled here after Louis XIV's revocation of the Edict of Nantes. There is even a theory that the name Jordaan is a corruption of the French word *jardin,* which seems particularly plausible given canals in the area with names such as Rozengracht (Roses Canal) and Lauriergracht (Laurel Canal).

The Jordaan is cut through the middle by the busy Rozengracht, where Rembrandt spent his final years. s of Rozengracht, the main shopping street is **Hazenstraat**, which is particularly good for unusual clothes. However, it is the area N of Rozengracht that is most lively, with the best shops on the cross-streets such as 1ᵉ Leliedwarsstraat and 1ᵉ Egelantiersdwarsstraat. There are also good brown cafés on almost every corner in this area, such as **'t Smalle** and **De Reiger**.

Bloemgracht was once called the Herengracht of the Jordaan, but now has a somewhat neglected air, apart from the splendid **trio of step gables** at #87-91, which was built at the rather late date of 1642 — long after the rest of Amsterdam had adopted Classical styles. The curious **facade stones** depict a man of the city, a man of the land and a man of the sea.

One of the special attractions of the Jordaan is its secretive *hofjes*, small almshouses founded by wealthy merchants in the 17thC. At Egelantiersgracht 105-141 is the intimate **St Andrieshofje**, which dates from 1615; its courtyard is generally open to the public. The nearby **Anslo's Hofje** at Egelantiersstraat 36-50 is a picturesque jumble of houses around three courtyards, reached through a small doorway on 2ᵉ Egelantiersdwarsstraat. Also open for visits is the much larger **Huiszitten-Weduwenhof** in Karthuizersstraat, built by city architect Daniel Stalpaert in 1650 as a home for impoverished widows.

Farther N at Lindengracht 149-63 is the **Suikerhofje**, established in 1670, with an inner courtyard open to visitors. Look out also for the witty **facade stones** nearby at **Lindengracht 53** (the Tangled Yarn) and **Lindengracht 55-57** (the Topsy-turvy World — this stone gives the date of construction upside down and the street name backward).

Two more *hofjes* can be discovered in the quiet NW corner of the Jordaan at **Palmgracht 20-26** and **28-38**.

KEIZERSGRACHT

Maps 5, 6, 9, 10. Tram 13, 14, 17 to Westermarkt; tram 1, 2, 4, 5, 16, 24, 25 to Keizersgracht.

Keizersgracht is the central of the three great canals forming the 17thC GRACHTENGORDEL. The early 17thC part — from Brouwersgracht to Leidsegracht — matches HERENGRACHT in grandeur, but the later section — from Leidsegracht to the AMSTEL — is much more modest, as many 17thC Herengracht residents bought up the adjoining lot on Keizersgracht to enlarge their gardens or build coach houses. The best stretches of Keizersgracht to explore are Brouwersgracht to Raadhuisstraat and Runstraat to Leidsestraat.

FROM BROUWERSGRACHT TO RAADHUISSTRAAT

The area from Brouwersgracht to Herenstraat contains mainly early 17thC buildings, including the lovely **Groenland Pakhuizen** (Greenland warehouses), at #40-44, where whale oil was stored in enormous 10,000-liter tanks.

Between Herenstraat and Leliegracht the 17thC architecture becomes rather more flamboyant. **Het Huis met de Hoofden** (The House with the Heads) at Keizersgracht 123 was built in 1622 by Hendrick de Keyser in a bustling Dutch Renaissance style, its six heads representing the Classical deities Apollo, Ceres, Mars, Pallas Athene, Bacchus and Diana.

Overlooking Leliegracht is a lofty **Art Nouveau building** designed by G. van Arkel in 1905 for an insurance company — the tile tableau at the top of the tower invests the insurance business with a rather far-fetched religious symbolism. Between Leliegracht and Raadhuisstraat is the **Coymans Huis** *(Keizersgracht 177),* a sober building in Dutch Classical style built a mere two years after the jaunty House with the Heads. Its reserved style found favor with the ruling elite, and the architect, Jacob van Campen, later won the competition to design the Town Hall (now the KONINKLIJK PALEIS) on Dam.

FROM RAADHUISSTRAAT TO LEIDSESTRAAT

Between Raadhuisstraat and Reestraat, walk on the E side in order to admire the buildings opposite — especially **Keizersgracht 209**, with its statue of Hope holding a basket of fruit. From Reestraat to Berenstraat, don't overlook **Keizersgracht 244-46**, a matching pair of houses laden with lavish Louis XIV-style cornices.

The stretch from Berenstraat to Leidsegracht is particularly rich in architectural interest. The **Felix Meritis building** at Keizersgracht 324 was erected in 1786 by a group of high-minded businessmen fired with the idea of spreading art and scientific knowledge. The society's name — Felix Meritis (Deservedly Happy) — says it all. The building has since had a varied history: it came into the hands of the Dutch Communist Party in 1946 and in the 1960s became one of Amsterdam's first experimental theaters.

Keizersgracht 319 has a dignified elevated neck gable built in 1639 by Philips Vingboons, whose brand of Classicism kept alive the flamboyant tradition established by Hendrick de Keyser. The small portal at **Keizersgracht 384** was the entrance to the former Stadsschouwburg (city theater), which a fire destroyed in 1772. **The Gilded Star** at #387 is another perfect example of the elevated neck gable style, built almost at the end of the Golden Age in 1668. **Keizersgracht 446** is a splendidly ornate Louis XIV style dwelling from the 1720s, which was at one stage occupied by the art collector Adriaan van der Hoop, whose treasures included Rembrandt's *The Jewish Bride.*

Overlooking Leidsestraat is a ponderous late 19thC building erected for the New York Life Insurance Company and later taken over by the furniture store Metz & Co. The **Rietveld penthouse** on the top floor provides a fascinating glimpse of the canal web from above. **Keizersgracht 508** is an appealing neo-Renaissance building with sculpture commemorating the 300th anniversary of the birth of the Dutch poet P. C. Hooft.

BETWEEN LEIDSESTRAAT AND THE AMSTEL

This stretch of Keizersgracht is essentially just a mews for the mansions on the "Golden Bend" of Herengracht. Examples of coach houses are at **Keizersgracht 481** and **485**. Any interesting buildings tend to be found on the W side — notably the splendid twins at **Keizersgracht 606-8** built in Louis XIV style in the 1730s. Also noteworthy are the twin houses by Adriaen Dortsman that form the VAN LOON museum. Almost directly opposite is the **Fodor Museum**, a center for contemporary art exhibitions.

KONINKLIJK PALEIS (Royal Palace) ★ 🏛

Dam ☎(020) 6248698. Map 10D4 🖼 ✗ Open June-Aug daily 12.30-4pm; Sept-May Wed 2-4pm or by appointment only. Tram 1, 2, 4, 5, 9, 13, 14, 16, 17, 24, 25 to Dam.

The Town Hall of Amsterdam — now a royal palace — was built at the high point of the Golden Age, when the city was ablaze with civic pride. In 1648, some 13,659 wooden piles were driven into the ground to provide a stable foundation, and 17 years later the building — although still unfinished — was proudly opened, the tireless poet Vondel producing a 1,500-line ode to celebrate the occasion.

The Town Hall, one of the glories of European Baroque architecture, so outstripped any other building in Holland that the Emperor Louis Napoleon fitted it out in 1808 as his palace, forcing the city dignitaries to shuffle off to the Prinsenhof on Oude Zijds Voorburgwal. The building is still occasionally used by the Royal Family, but most of the year it stands sadly dark and empty.

EXTERIOR

Amsterdam's Town Hall was designed in a severe Classical style by Jacob van Campen, whose use of sober yellow-gray Benthelm sandstone represents a decisive break with the bustling red brick and white stone facades of the early 17thC. To offset the stern appearance of Van Campen's Baroque box, the Antwerp-born sculptor Artus Quellien (or Quellinus) was appointed to decorate the building, and for 14 years he labored assiduously with a small army of assistants to create some of the most inventive sculpture of the 17thC.

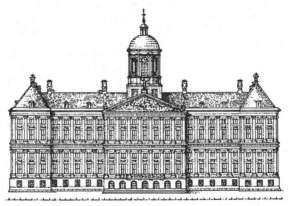

The highly moralistic **carvings** include the figure of **Peace** surveying Dam from the tip of the pediment. The motif of Peace recurs elsewhere as a reminder that the Town Hall was begun in the same hopeful year that the Treaty of Münster was signed, bringing to an end the horrors of the Eighty Years' War. The pediments are filled with magnificent Baroque sculpture depicting the Oceans (facing Dam) and the Continents (facing

97

Raadhuisstraat) paying homage to the Maid of Amsterdam. Quellien's painstaking decoration can only properly be appreciated through binoculars, or by examining the preliminary models displayed in the RIJKS-MUSEUM and AMSTERDAMS HISTORISCH MUSEUM.

"But where is the door?" visitors to the Town Hall often ask. The main entrance to this magnificent building is through a small concealed doorway at the right-hand side of the arcaded *avant corps*. The reason for this uncharacteristic modesty in an age dominated by pompous ceremony may have been the sobering experience of the Anabaptist uprising in 1535, when a group of religious fanatics stormed the old Town Hall.

BURGERZAAL

The pinched entrance contrasts with the magnificent Baroque drama of the lofty Burgerzaal at the top of the stairs. This vast assembly hall rises through four floors to create the most spacious interior in Amsterdam. The Maid of Amsterdam sits primly at the E end of the Hall, flanked by the figures of Strength and Wisdom, while above the entrance to the Council Chamber (**Schepenzaal**) at the W end, the figure of Atlas overlooks a sculptural group in which Justice, seated between Death and Punishment, treads Avarice and Envy underfoot.

The Burgerzaal floor is inlaid with three maps — two depicting the hemispheres and the third the heavens — across which Amsterdam's ruling elite once proudly walked in their black robes, deliberating policies with global repercussions.

GALLERIES

The council offices were located in the Galleries to the N and S of the Burgerzaal, reached through **arches** decorated with figures depicting the **four elements**: Earth, Water, Air and Fire. The different council offices are identified by some of Quellien's most imaginative work: Apollo, with his soothing lyre, guards the Chamber of Petty Affairs; Diana, goddess of hunting, unloads her booty at the entrance to the Treasury; Venus (who looks as if she is about to hurl an apple at Mars, the god of war) indicates the room in which marriages were registered; festoons hung with ink pots, wax seals and other symbols of bureaucracy flank the door into the City Secretary's Office; and a depiction of the Fall of Icarus once chastened debtors as they entered the Bankruptcy Court. It is worth poring over the fantastic wealth of erudite **sculpture**, which conceals delightful touches, such as the playful cherubs that adorn the two mantelpiece friezes in the Schepenzaal.

The **paintings** commissioned for the new Town Hall display a plodding moralizing tone, with none of the wit and imagination of Quellien's sculpture. Govert Flinck's *Solomon's Prayer for Wisdom* and Erasmus Quellien's *Amsterdam Glorified* in the Schepenzaal are heavily influenced by the surging Baroque of Rubens. The city magistrates' bias toward didactic bombast led to their rejection of Rembrandt's *Conspiracy of Claudius Civilis,* which they felt failed to exploit the full political potential of the revolt of the Batavians against the Romans.

As a souvenir of King Louis Napoleon's residence here in the early 19thC, the Royal Palace boasts an extensive collection of **Empire-style furniture**.

VIERSCHAAR

The heavily fortified ground-floor rooms of the palace are occupied by prison cells, the city bank vaults and the Vierschaar (Hall of Justice), where the death sentence was pronounced. This involved an elaborate baroque ceremony in which the condemned prisoner was brought before the city magistrates, who were seated on the long bench beneath the statues of four voluptuous **Caryatids** representing women in various states of remorse and anguish. The **panels** between the Caryatids are decorated with reliefs showing judicial incidents from the Bible and Classical mythology, while the **frieze** above bears grisly reminders of death. After the prisoner had been led into this exquisite tomb, the bronze doors, decorated with thunderbolts, skulls and a curling serpent, were closed and the death sentence solemnly pronounced.

LAPIDARIUM

Rijksmuseum garden, entrance on Jan Luijkenstraat. Map **5**H3 ⌑ *Open Tues-Sun 10am-5pm. Tram 6, 7, 10 to Spiegelgracht; tram 1, 2, 5 to Leidseplein.*
The formal garden behind the RIJKSMUSEUM contains a curious collection of old Dutch architectural fragments, which were rescued from buildings demolished in the 19thC.

The relics on display include a number of medieval and Renaissance **gateways** from different Dutch cities, the most impressive of which is the **Waterpoort** from Gorinchem, which has been neatly incorporated into the wall of the Rijksmuseum. An ornate 18thC **gateway** comes from one of the many country houses, now vanished, that once lined the Amstel, and a small **Rococo pavilion** from another villa is laden with old facade stones.

LEIDSEPLEIN

Map **5**F3. *Tram 1, 2, 5, 6, 7, 10 to Leidseplein.*
Once the site of a gate at the sw edge of the 17thC city, Leidseplein first began to assume a cultural role in the 18thC when the **Stadsschouwburg** (Municipal Theater) was rebuilt here. This was replaced in 1894 by an elaborate Renaissance confection by J. L. Springer.

Leidseplein received a further boost with the completion in 1902 of the elegant Art Nouveau **American Hotel**, designed by W. Kromhout. Café society began to develop in the grand **Café Américain** and in less pretentious locations such as **Eijlders** and **Reijnders** (see CAFÉS, page 159 and 162). In the 1960s Leidseplein became the territory of the "Pleiners" (who modeled themselves on English "Mods"), while the "Dijkers" (equivalent of the "Rockers") hung out around the Nieuwendijk.

Numerous movie theaters are found around Leidseplein, along with several alternative centers for the arts including the famous, if somewhat jaded, **Melkweg** (the Milky Way). There are also restaurants of every nationality, including an explosion of pizzerias and trattorias, which give the streets off Leidsestraat a distinctly Mediterranean ambience. Leidseplein never sleeps: after the cafés have closed, there is still plenty of action in the discos, nightclubs and piano bars.

MADAME TUSSAUD SCENERAMA

*Dam 20 ☎(020) 6229949. Map **10D4** ✱ Open daily 10am-6pm. Tram **1, 2, 4, 5, 9, 13, 14, 16, 24, 25** to Dam.*

The old Madame Tussaud's delighted visitors for some 20 years with its ghostly and grisly collection of lifelike wax models, including a wax attendant at the door (to which many a hapless visitor presented a ticket). The British owners eventually decided that the time had come to revamp and rename the institution, and a team of 500 craftsmen toiled for two years to convert the top three floors of the Peek & Cloppenburg department store into the Madame Tussaud Scenerama.

Many familiar faces from the original Tussaud's collection have been preserved, including Rembrandt in his atelier, Anne Frank penning her diary, and the Dutch royal family, but the wax attendant in the lobby has been replaced by a seductive Tina Turner. An elevator takes you up to the exhibition floors, where a five-meter-high animated figure representing Amsterdam Man descends amid puffs of liquid nitrogen smoke.

You are led by a disembodied voice (speaking Dutch and American English) through an impressive reproduction of a 17thC Amsterdam **street**, complete with 1,000 genuine brick paving stones, and across a bridge spanning a sizeable canal. The tour whisks you along at a cracking pace past a gruesome scene depicting the murder of the De Witt brothers in the Year of Disasters, and a handsome Vermeer-style interior with a woman playing a lute. The scenes are animated using the latest computer technology and special effects, including artificial smoke for a battle scene, cooking smells in a slum interior, and artificially chilled air to evoke a winter's day in the 17thC.

A revolving giant drum slowly reveals a wonderful **scale model** of 17thC Amsterdam with more than 10,000 miniature buildings precisely detailed. You can compare the model with the contemporary city by gazing through the huge round window pierced in the top floor, which offers a splendid view of the monocyclists and fire eaters on the Dam below.

NEDERLANDS SCHEEPVAART MUSEUM (Dutch Maritime Museum) ★

*Kattenburgerplein 1 ☎(020) 5232222 Fx(020) 5232213. Map **4D4** ✱ Open Tues-Sat 10am-5pm; Sun, hols 1-5pm. Bus 22, 28 from Centraal Station to Kattenburgerplein.*

The Dutch maritime museum is a must for anyone who loves ships, models of ships, figureheads, globes, maps, charts, sea battles or portraits of admirals. If you finally tire of room after room of rigged ships and stormy seas, you can gaze through the arched warehouse doors to the busy harbor where gray warships slide slowly past brightly painted houseboats, and the spires of Amsterdam look not unlike a 17thC painting.

In 1973 the museum moved to its present location in the former arsenal of the Amsterdam Admiralty. This stern Classical block, designed by Daniel Stalpaert in 1656, stands in splendid isolation on the edge of the Oosterdok. It was here that Amsterdam's warships were fitted with rigging and sails, and equipped with weapons, clothes and provisions for the long voyages to the East and West Indies. The gleaming brass pumps used to supply ships with drinking water can be seen in the courtyard, along with various war-damaged cannons.

The museum contains 30 packed rooms covering every aspect of navigation in the Netherlands, from Roman trade on the Rhine to surf-boarding. For those who find their interest flagging after 14 rooms, an escape route is helpfully signposted to the restaurant. The museum also provides a highly informative illustrated booklet in English.

One of the most interesting exhibits is the beautiful bottle-green and gold *trekschuit* (rm 5), a type of horsedrawn passenger boat used on the Dutch canal network from the 17th to the 19thC. The *trekschuit* offered a reliable but — as almost every traveler complained — agonizingly slow method of transportation. Travelers from Rotterdam to Amsterdam, for example, would spend 11 hours in the cramped and smoky cabin watching the flat Dutch fields slowly glide by.

Also worth seeing are the curious **Japanese paintings** of the 17thC Dutch trading post in the Bay of Nagasaki (rm 11), the tea clipper model (rm 15) and, in the same room, the melodramatic mementoes relating to the national hero **Van Speyk** (1802-31), who in the Belgian revolt of 1830 blew up his ship rather than allow it to fall into the hands of the rebels. Attractions that might interest children include the submarine periscope (rm 24), which gives a 360° view of the city.

The **Koningssloep** (royal sloop) on the ground floor is a magnificent barge built in 1816-18 for the Dutch King, with a gilded figure of Neptune poised at the prow. There are several other restored ships moored outside the museum including a herring drifter and a steam-powered icebreaker.

But the most remarkable vessel in the collection is the replica of the *Amsterdam,* an 18thC ship owned by the Dutch East India Company VOC that sank off the south coast of England in 1749. The excavation of the wreck (which lay near Hastings) has provided much of the data for the replica, together with old plans and ship models. The fastidious recon-struction, carried out by a team of 300 volunteers from 1985-91, is correct down to details such as furniture, hammocks and cannon.

The seldom-visited area around the Scheepvaart Museum is rich in maritime interest, with the imposing 1642 warehouses of the West India Company overlooking Oude Schans at 's Gravenhekje, the early 17thC East India Company warehouses at Prins Hendrikkade 176, Admiral de Ruyter's house at Prins Hendrikkade 131 and a splendid row of 84 18thC warehouses lined up along the Entrepôtdok (reached through the monumental gate on Kadijksplein). It is also possible to walk along the Entrepôtdok to reach the **Werf 't Kromhout** *(Hoogte Kadijk 147* ☎ *(020) 6276777, map 8E9, open Mon-Fri 10am-4pm),* where a num-ber of boats in various states of repair can be visited.

NEDERLANDS THEATER INSTITUUT (Dutch Theater Institute)
Herengracht 168 ☎*(020) 6235104. Map 10C4* ▨ ▬ *Open Tues-Sun 11am-5pm. Tram 1, 2, 5, 13, 14, 17 to Dam.*

Philips Vingboons' first neck gable house, located at Herengracht 168, is one of five handsome canal houses that comprise the Dutch Theater

Institute. Vingboons' 1638 house (pictured on page 20), built for the founder of the West India Company, Michiel Pauw, now contains a delightful theater museum. This organizes temporary exhibitions on theater, dance, mime, cabaret, film and television in the Netherlands, drawing on its fascinating collection of costumes, props, models, posters, recordings and videos. Background information is generally provided in English.

The interior, refurbished in Louis XIV style in the 1730s, is well worth a glance. It includes lavish **stucco decoration** in the hall by the sculptor Jan van Logteren, a fine **spiral staircase**, and two rooms decorated with **wall hangings** by the landscape artist Isaac de Moucheron, depicting scenes from the life of Jephthah, an Israelite judge who sacrificed his daughter in fulfillment of a vow.

NIEUWE KERK

Dam ☎*(020) 6268168. Map* **10**D4 ⬛ ⅄ ▣ *Open Mar-Dec daily 11am-5pm. Tram 1, 2, 4, 5, 9, 13, 14, 16, 17, 24, 25 to Dam.*

The Nieuwe Kerk on Dam is one of the few churches in the Netherlands that is open to the public — not as a church but as a lively social and cultural center, which includes a small bookstore and a brown café. At various times of the year, this huge whitewashed Protestant church is also used for exhibitions of paintings, photographs and antiques.

The Nieuwe Kerk has had an eventful history following its foundation in the 15thC as Amsterdam's second parish church. It burned down in 1421, 1452 and again in 1645, when it was accidentally set alight by a workman on the roof. After rebuilding the church to its former Gothic glory, the city council was browbeaten by the strict Calvinist burgomaster, Willem Backer, into building a **tower** at the w end to ensure that the church was not upstaged by the new Town Hall. "God's wrath must surely fall on a city that spends such treasure on the outward appearance of a worldly building," Backer darkly warned; but after his death and the outbreak of the First Anglo-Dutch War, the plan was quietly abandoned, leaving only the stump of the tower standing on N. Z. Voorburgwal. When the Town Hall was converted to a royal palace in the 19thC (see KONINKLIJK PALEIS), the Nieuwe Kerk was elevated to the national church of the Netherlands. Since then Dutch monarchs have been crowned here, including the current monarch, Queen Beatrix, in 1980.

The oldest part of the church is the **choir**, built of rough stone around 1400, while the **nave** was added in the 1430s in a "streaky bacon" style of alternating rows of brick and stone. A number of small shops have been built onto the side of the church, while on Gravenstraat there is an imposing Classical building of 1642, where poor relief was distributed.

The main feature of the interior is the magnificent **organ**, built in 1645. Jacob van Campen, the architect of the Town Hall, designed the casing to look almost like a Classical neck gable facade. Artus Quellien, who produced the Town Hall's sculpture, festooned the organ base with cherubs and musical instruments, while Jan Gerritsz. van Bronkhorst decorated the organ shutters with scenes from the life of David. The church also boasts a remarkable **pulpit** built by Albert Jansz. Vinckenbrinck in 1645-64 in a rich Mannerist style. The pulpit is illustrated with works of charity, while its large tester is adorned with a remarkably flamboyant tower.

On the former site of the high altar, the sculptor Rombout Verhulst erected a bombastic **tomb** to Admiral Michiel de Ruyter, who died while fighting the French at the Battle of Messina in 1676. A somewhat less pompous tomb by Verhulst for Admiral Jan van Galen, who died during the Battle of Leghorn, is to be seen on the N wall.

NIEUWE ZIJDE (New Side)
Map 10. Tram 1, 2, 5, 13, 17 to Dam.

This area, the "New Side," which extends w from Damrak and Rokin to SINGEL, mirrors the canal pattern of OUDE ZIJDE almost exactly. But its character is completely different due to the filling in of its canals in the 19thC, which lends a rather melancholy atmosphere. It is also very much more crowded, especially along **Kalverstraat** — Amsterdam's principal shopping street — which follows the course of the 13thC dyke along the w side of the Amstel. Less claustrophobic streets with interesting shops include St Luciensteeg, just N of the AMSTERDAMS HIS-TORISCH MUSEUM, and Gravenstraat, which bends around the back of the NIEUWE KERK. There is a **stamp market** on Wednesday and Sunday on N.Z. Voorburgwal just S of Dam and a cluster of **bookstores** between Spui and Dam, both of which add to the variety of Nieuwe Zijde.

The area around **Dam** is particularly animated, although the dignity of the ROYAL PALACE is somewhat marred by the Neo-Gothic pile of the former post office (now a shopping mall) at **N.Z. Voorburgwal 182**, whose turreted skyline led to its being ridiculed in a 19thC cartoon as "the pear mountain — an experiment in fruit architecture." N of Dam, notice the attractive group of houses at the **Blaeu Erf** (Blaeu's Yard) (*N. Z. Voorburgwal 87-99*), named after the printing works of the 17thC map-maker Jan Blaeu, which stood here. The picturesque 1633 Renaissance house at N.Z. Voorburgwal 75 is the **Makelaarsgildehuis** (real-estate agents' guild house), adorned with the stubborn motto "Freedom is not for sale at any price." Farther N at N.Z. Kolk 28 is the 1620 **Korenmetershuisje** (corn exchange).

To the S of Dam, N.Z. Voorburgwal passes the AMSTERDAMS HISTORISCH MUSEUM and leads to **Spui**, a particularly attractive square where the two canals of Nieuwe Zijde once converged. The BEGIJNHOF occupies the N side, while to the S is the 1787 **Maagdenhuis**, formerly a girls' orphanage. To the right is the 1633 **Old Lutheran Church**. The statue of a charming street urchin, **Het Amsterdamse Lieverdje**, was donated by a cigarette company and provided a popular target for 1960s demonstrations.

Voetboogstraat, which contains some unusual shops, leads S to the dramatic gateway of the **Rasphuis** at Heiligeweg 19, a model house of correction, set up in 1596, where men were put to work shaving a hard type of Brazilian wood used for dyeing. The **portal**, probably built by Hendrick de Keyser in 1603, shows the Maid of Amsterdam punishing two criminals above a rumination by Seneca: "It is virtuous to tame that which everyone fears."

NIEUWMARKT

Map 11D6. Sneltram 51 or metro to Nieuwmarkt.

One of the most fascinating areas of Amsterdam, Nieuwmarkt is particularly rich in sights associated with the Dutch painter Rembrandt van Rijn. To the s of the square, Nieuwmarkt, lies the university, and to the E a particularly beautiful area of silent, forgotten canals. The fringes of the red-light district impinge slightly on the w and N sides of Nieuwmarkt, but the seediness can easily be avoided.

Standing forlornly in the middle of the square is the WAAG (see illustration on page 124), a former city gate. Another relic of the medieval city wall is the **Schreierstoren** (Tower of Tears) at the N end of Geldersekade, named for the lachrymose women who, legend has it, would climb this tower to watch their husbands' ships depart.

Something of the former splendor of **Kloveniersburgwal**, which runs s from Nieuwmarkt to the Amstel, can be seen in the **Trippenhuis** at Kloveniersburgwal 29. This splendid Classical palace, modeled on the Town Hall on Dam, was built by Justus Vingboons in 1660-64 for the brothers Louis and Hendrick Trip, who achieved unprecedented domestic grandeur by concealing their separated dwellings behind a single facade. The most remarkable feature of the house is its two **chimneys**, modeled on cannons.

Other military emblems can be discerned in the **fresco** — a reminder that the Trip family was one of Europe's largest and most unscrupulous arms manufacturers, with no qualms about supplying both the Roundheads and Cavaliers during the English Civil War. In 1815 the separate dwellings were joined to house the Rijksmuseum for a time.

Amsterdammers are fond of pointing out the exceptionally narrow house at Kloveniersburgwal 26, known as the **Kleine-Trippenhuis**, which was supposedly built in 1696 for a family servant, using stone left over from the Trippenhuis.

The w side of Kloveniersburgwal is dominated by drab 19thC university buildings, but there are one or two hidden delights to be found down the side streets, such as the 1633 wine merchants' guild house (**Wijnkopersgildehuis**) at Koestraat 10-12, and the former offices of the Dutch East India Company at Oude Hoogstraat 24. This almost forgotten relic of Amsterdam's trading past contains a courtyard worth entering to view the exceptionally ornate 1606 Mannerist scrolled gable, built some four years after the foundation of the East India Company.

Continuing s on Kloveniersburgwal, you come to **#62**, with its rich sea imagery, and the stately **Poppenhuis** at #95, built by Philips Vingboons in 1642. Directly opposite is the E gate of the **Oudemanhuis**, which was once a home for old men, with sculpture by Anthonie Ziesenis added in 1786.

The **Doelen Hotel** overlooking the s end of Kloveniersburgwal is decorated with the two principal figures from Rembrandt's *Night Watch*, a reminder that this was the site of the tower in which the company of civil guards met. Furthermore, the Syndics of the Cloth Guild, whom Rembrandt painted in 1662, met in the **Lakenhal** on the nearby Groenburgwal. A last relic of the once flourishing linen trade on this island is

the **Saaihal** (serge hall), at Staalstraat 7, which was
built by Pieter de Keyser in 1641.

To reach the tranquil area E of Nieuwmarkt from
here, continue N along the quiet Groenburgwal
canal, turn right along Raamgracht, then left, following the Zwanenburgwal canal N to a picturesque lock, the **St Antoniessluis**.

Straight ahead is the **Oude Schans**, a canal that
obtains a certain grandeur from the **Montelbaanstoren**, a defensive tower on the E edge of the 16thC
city, which in 1606 was given an ornate spire by
Hendrick de Keyser. On the corner of Oude Schans
and Prins Hendrikkade are the imposing **warehouses** built in 1642 for the Dutch West India
Company, whose main trading interests were sugar
and furs.

Montelbaanstoren

Head w along Binnenkant to reach the magnificent **Scheepvaarthuis**, built for seven shipping
companies in 1912 by the Amsterdam School architects Johan van der
Mey, Michel de Klerk and P. L. Kramer. Notice the fantastic maritime
details decorating the outside of the building, such as whales, ships,
navigators' heads, mermaids, ocean deities and even rippling iron railings.

Walk around the outside of the Scheepvaarthuis and turn right down
the enticingly rural Buiten Bantammerstraat. Now cross the medieval-
looking Amsterdam School-style **bridge** and turn left to reach Lastage-
weg. This leads to the narrow canal Rechtboomsloot, where a right turn
leads to Kromboomsloot, a dark, silent and forgotten canal, where at **#22**
Amsterdam's Armenian community built a **Rococo church** in 1714.

NINT TECHNISCH MUSEUM

Tolstraat 129 ☎ *(020) 6754211. Map 7I7* 🔄 ♿ 💻 ✴ *Open Mon-Fri 10am-
5pm; Sat, Sun, hols noon-5pm. Tram 4 to Lutmastraat.*
Located in a former diamond-cutting factory in the 19thC district of
Amsterdam Zuid, the NINT technology museum is particularly geared
toward schoolchildren. The aim is to make science fun, and there are
countless push-button machines and models to demonstrate how
things such as magnets, electricity, cars and telephones work. The
explanatory notes are in Dutch, but this need not be a deterrent since
most children are quite content to dash from one working model to the
next, leaving their parents to puzzle over the theory.

NORMAAL AMSTERDAMS PEIL

Stadhuis, Amstel 1. Map 11E6 📷 *Tram 9, 14 or metro to Waterlooplein.*
Two plexiglass (perspex) columns of water in the new **Stadhuis** (town
hall) show the current North Sea tidal levels at IJmuiden and Vlissingen, perhaps to remind Amsterdammers that they live out their lives
much of the time below sea level. For dramatic effect, water surges into
a third plexiglass column to indicate the water level during the disas-

trous Zeeland floods of 1953. A bronze button mounted on a concrete pile in the basement indicates level zero in the Netherlands (the *Normaal Amsterdams Peil*, or Normal Amsterdam Level). A cross-section of the Netherlands on one wall indicates the perilously low situation of many parts of the Randstad, including Schiphol airport.

OUDE KERK ★

Oudekerksplein 23 ☎ *(020) 6249183. Map* **10D5** 🔲 *𝄞 compulsory for tower* ◄ *Church open Easter-Sept Mon-Sat 11am-5pm; Sun 1.30-5pm; Oct-Easter Mon-Sun 1-3pm; tower open June to mid-Sept Mon and Thurs 2-5pm, Tues and Wed 11am-2pm. Tram 4, 9, 16, 24, 25 to Dam, then 10mins' walk.*

Begun around 1200, burned to the ground in 1274 by the troops of Count Floris V, rebuilt as a hall church and then converted to a basilica around 1500, the Oude Kerk is Amsterdam's oldest and most fascinating church. Of particular interest to the visitor are the massive wooden vaulted **roofs**, the frescoed **columns**, the delightful **misericords** illustrating various traditional proverbs, the ornate **gravestones** of eminent Amsterdammers, and the 16thC stained-glass **windows** in one of the choirs, known as the *Nieuwe Vrouwenkoor,* depicting the life of the Virgin.

Dedicated to St Nicholas, patron saint of sailors, the Oude Kerk echoes Amsterdam's seafaring past in features such as the **Hamburgerkapel**, which was built in the early 16thC by Hamburg merchants living in Amsterdam. Ships appear everywhere: on the vaulted roof, on the various monuments to Dutch admirals who died in battle, on the small organ, and even crudely carved on the back of the wooden choir screen.

Rembrandt's wife Saskia, who died in 1642, is buried in a grave numbered 29K, near the small choir organ.

The Oude Kerk's famous large **organ** was built during 1738-42 by Johannes Caspar Müller; the small choir organ was recently replaced, although the decorative casing dates from the 17thC.

The Oude Kerk also boasts a 17thC **carillon** built by bell-maker François Hemony, which is played every Saturday from 4-5pm as Amsterdammers rush to finish their shopping.

The gracious Late-Gothic **spire**, built by Joost Jansz. Bilhamer in 1565, can sometimes be climbed to obtain a view of the old city.

OUDE ZIJDE (Old Side)
Map 10. Tram 4, 9, 14, 16, 24, 25 to Spui.

The "Old Side" runs E from Damrak and Rokin to Kloveniersburgwal, which marks the limit of the medieval city. This quarter consists of Warmoesstraat, formerly a dyke along the AMSTEL, and the two canals O.Z. Voorburgwal and O.Z. Achterburgwal, whose names literally mean before and behind the city wall.

As its name suggests, Oude Zijde is the oldest area of the city, and is packed with historic interest. Unfortunately, some of its finest buildings are buried in the red-light district, which lies to the N of the line formed by Damstraat, Oude Doelenstraat and Oude Hoogstraat. But venture only a few steps S of this demarcation line to discover the most tranquil and beautiful area of the city, with numerous old **gateways** richly adorned with symbolic sculpture and verse.

To see Oude Zijde at its best, turn off Rokin down the narrow Langebrugsteeg to reach Grimburgwal. Now head left down O.Z. Voorburgwal and walk to Oude Hoogstraat, then turn right and right again to return by O.Z. Achterburgwal.

Grimburgwal is a particularly pleasing corner of the medieval city at the convergence of three canals. Many of the narrow streets in this part of town provide reminders of former convents and monasteries in names such as Gebed Zonder End (Prayer Without End), a narrow lane that once divided two convents.

The view E of Grimburgwal is terminated by the **House on the Three Canals** (see illustration on page 19) at O.Z. Voorburgwal 249, an early 17thC step-gabled house built of rosy red brick trimmed with whitened sandstone.

Turning left down O.Z. Voorburgwal you can see the former **St Agnietenkapel** behind a jaunty 16thC Mannerist portal at O.Z. Voorburgwal 231. This 15thC chapel belonged to the convent of St Agnes, which, like many in medieval Amsterdam, adopted the rather relaxed rules of the Third Order of St Francis of Assisi. The building now houses the historical collection of the University of Amsterdam.

The S end of O.Z. Voorburgwal was dubbed "the velvet canal" in the 18thC because of the numerous rich merchants who settled here, putting up ornate facades such as **O.Z. Voorburgwal 237** and **#217**, with their exceptionally fine Louis XIV tops. At #197 is a former **Stadhuis** (Town Hall) designed in Amsterdam School style during the 1920s and incorporating on the s side of the courtyard the Classical **Admiraliteitsge-bouw** (Admiralty Office), built in the 1660s. The city council moved here in 1808 when Louis Napoleon established his Royal Palace in the Stadhuis on Dam.

At O.Z. Voorburgwal 300 is the **Stadsbank van Lening**, the municipal bank, which was established here in a rugged warehouse built by Hendrick de Keyser in 1616. The famous Dutch poet Joost van den Vondel (1587-1679) worked in the bank as a bookkeeper until he was 81. Notice in the alley to the right of the building the doorway with a relief by Hendrick de Keyser depicting a woman pawning her property at the bank. The bank building to the left of the warehouses, which was added in 1669, has a lengthy edifying poem above the entrance explaining the virtues of pawn banks.

The curious **Mannerist gate** to the right of the alley Enge Lombard-steeg formerly led to an inn whose name De Brakke Grond (The Brackish Ground) tells something of the terrain on which Amsterdam was built. Other revealing names near here are **Slijkstraat** (Slime Street) and **Rusland** (Rushes Land).

Amsterdam's involvement in the slave trade is recalled by the sculpture decorating the 1663 facade at **O.Z. Voorburgwal 187**, which depicts exhausted Black slaves and American Indians lying on tobacco bales.

To reach the OUDE KERK and the MUSEUM AMSTELKRING, you must venture N of Oude Doelenstraat into the fringes of the red-light district. Above the door of **O.Z. Voorburgwal 136** is a bust of Admiral Tromp and a scene from the Third Anglo-Dutch War of 1673.

Returning s by **O.Z. Achterburgwal**, you pass the attractive square, Walenplein, overlooked by the **Waalse Kerk** at O.Z. Achterburgwal 157. This chapel formerly belonged to a monastery and was given to the Walloon community in 1587. These French-speaking Protestants who had fled from the Spanish-occupied Southern Netherlands added a Mannerist gateway on Oude Hoogstraat and in 1647 a Classical entrance facing Walenplein.

At O.Z. Achterburgwal 185 is a dignified Classical building built in 1645 as the **Spinhuis**, a house of correction where women were made to spin wool as a form of therapy. Notice the ornate Ionic portal in Spinhuissteeg, which bears a moralistic motto by the poet P. C. Hooft telling visitors not to be alarmed by the punishments because their motivation is love and not revenge.

At the s end of O.Z. Achterburgwal are two more gateways, the **Oudemanhuispoort** and the **Gasthuispoort**.

PIGGY BANK MUSEUM   See SPAARPOTTEN MUSEUM.

PRINSENGRACHT
Maps 5, 6, 7, 9, 10. Tram 13, 14, 17 to Westermarkt; tram 1, 2, 4, 5, 16, 24, 25 to Prinsengracht.

"The Princes' Canal" is the outermost waterway of the 17thC GRACHTEN-GORDEL. Earmarked in the 1609 Plan for warehouses, workshops, churches, shops and artisan dwellings, the canal lacks the architectural splendors of HERENGRACHT and KEIZERSGRACHT, but offers instead a bustling blend of brown cafés, boutiques, art galleries and houseboats. It is rather tiring to walk the entire 3km (2 miles) of Prinsengracht, so limit yourself to short stretches, such as that from Brouwersgracht to Rozengracht or from Reguliersgracht to the AMSTEL.

FROM BROUWERSGRACHT TO NIEUWE SPIEGELSTRAAT

The intersection of Prinsengracht and Brouwersgracht offers fine views in every direction, which can be enjoyed from the traditional brown café **Papeneiland** or the newer, but just as brown, **'t Smackzeyl**. Proceeding s, one reaches **Noordermarkt**, a small square tinged with the shabby charm characteristic of the Jordaan, which lies just to the w. The unusual octagonal **Noorderkerk** was built as a Protestant church in 1620-23, probably by Hendrick de Keyser. Some curious little shops and cafés have taken root around the church; and at Prinsengracht 85-113 is the **Starhofje**, built in a rather utilitarian early 19thC style.

A much lovelier *hofje* is found between Noordermarkt and Westermarkt: **Zon's hofje** at Prinsengracht 159-71, built in 1765. The secluded courtyard is generally open to the public. Notice inside the impressive gateway with its facade stone showing Noah's Ark surrounded by a curious collection of animals. Beyond, the E side of the canal is dominated by 18thC warehouses, while the w side has numerous houses with 18thC shop fronts. Prinsengracht is not entirely mundane, however, and the frothy Rococo sculpture decorating the top of **Prinsengracht 126** is as lavish as anything on the more prestigious canals. Visit the brown café **De Prins** to enjoy the fine view down Leliegracht.

The ANNE FRANK HUIS is located at Prinsengracht 263, while nearby is the WESTERKERK. The French philosopher René Descartes spent the summer of 1634 living with a French schoolteacher at Westermarkt 6.

Between Westermarkt and Nieuwe Spiegelstraat, Prinsengracht assumes an amiable, although somewhat undistinguished character. The PULITZER HOTEL at Prinsengracht 315-31 (see WHERE TO STAY) made a unique contribution to architectural conservation when it restored a block of 24 gable houses to create a 250-room hotel. The **Pulitzer Art Gallery** is located within the complex. Other art galleries and chic restaurants have sprung up nearby, particularly in Reestraat.

FROM NIEUWE SPIEGELSTRAAT TO THE AMSTEL

The stretch of Prinsengracht between Nieuwe Spiegelstraat and Reguliersgracht is a touch more distinguished, and on the w side blends into the tranquil **Weteringbuurt**. At #855-99 is the **Duetzenhof**, an alms house established in 1695 by Agnes Deutz who, according to the inscription above the entrance, "exercised her love and faith as a comfort for the poor and an example to the rich" *(closed to the public)*.

Overlooking Reguliersgracht is the wooden **Amstelkerk**, which looks decidedly out of place in its urban setting. Erected in 1670 as a temporary Protestant church, it was intended to be replaced eventually by a much larger building on the Amstelveld. The plan was abandoned, however, leaving the Amstelveld with a rather sad appearance, enlivened only by the plant market held here every Monday. Opposite is a rare

109

19thC Neoclassical church, **De Duif**. The final stretch of Prinsengracht is a picturesque confusion of houseboats and gable houses drenched in wisteria.

HET REMBRANDTHUIS MUSEUM (Rembrandt House)
Jodenbreestraat 6 ☎*(020) 6249486. Map* **11E6** 🔲 *Open Mon-Sat 10am-5pm, Sun, hols 1-5pm. Tram 9, 14, sneltram 51 or metro to Waterlooplein.*

Rembrandt was only 33 years old when he bought this distinguished red-shuttered Classical house on the principal street of the JODENBUURT. He lived here from 1639-58, until financial difficulties forced him to move to a more modest house in the JORDAAN.

The main attraction of the museum is its extensive collection of some 250 **etchings** and **drawings** by Rembrandt. Many of these works illustrate biblical themes, while others show the gentle landscape of the river Amstel, which Rembrandt visited frequently after his wife Saskia's death. Perhaps the most delightful etchings, however, are those in the **mezzanine room**, showing Rembrandt's compassionate eye for beggars, street musicians, organ-grinders, rat-catchers and other 17thC figures. Another feature of the museum is an informative exhibition on etching techniques.

ROYAL PALACE   See KONINKLIJK PALEIS.

RIJKSMUSEUM ★
Stadhouderskade 42 ☎*(020) 6732121. Map* **5G3** 🔲 ♿ �](*Open Tues-Sat 10am-5pm; Sun, hols 1-5pm. Tram 6, 7, 10 to Spiegelgracht; tram 1, 2, 5 to Leidseplein.*

The national museum of the Netherlands houses a huge and diverse range of art works, of which its unrivaled collection of 17thC Dutch paintings is by far the most important. Established by King Louis Napoleon in 1808 along the lines of the Louvre in Paris, the Rijksmuseum collection was initially housed in the Royal Palace on the Dam, but later moved to the Trippenhuis on Kloveniersburgwal. Eventually the collection of paintings and decorative art grew too large for this canal house, and P. J. H. Cuypers was commissioned to build a new Rijksmuseum in the fashionable area of the 19thC ring near the Vondelpark.

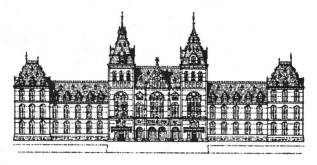

The intention was to have a building in Dutch Renaissance style, but Cuypers — a fervent Catholic — could not suppress his Gothic tendencies, and the building is imbued with an unmistakable medieval flavor with its Burgundian roofs and exuberant decoration. King William III was so upset at what he called "the monastery" that he refused to set foot in the building.

PLANNING A VISIT

If you have only a short time to spare, concentrate on the works of Rembrandt, Vermeer, De Hoogh and the other Dutch Masters. A useful introduction to the 17thC painting is the slide show (with English, French and German commentary), shown every 20 minutes in the Film Theater.

If time allows, set off to explore the neglected departments of the Rijksmuseum — Medieval Painting, Sculpture and Applied Art, Dutch History, 18th-19thC Dutch Painting and Asiatic Art — all of which offer delightful surprises.

The Rijksmuseum has two main entrances W and E of the tunnel. The W entrance is usually the more crowded, although either entrance gives access to the main collection of paintings. A quiet entrance at the rear of the building on Hobbemastraat takes you straight into the **Drucker Extension**, added in 1915 to house the growing collection of 18th-19thC paintings and Asiatic art. If you are meeting someone, be sure to specify at which of the three entrances.

EXTERIOR

The bustling architectural detail is best appreciated from the formal 18thC **garden** on Hobbemastraat, where you can admire tile tableaux depicting famous Dutch and Flemish artists, a relief showing Rembrandt at work on his *Staalmeesters* (above the tunnel entrance), and curious sculptures on the roof representing masons apparently at work on the construction of the museum.

SEVENTEENTH-CENTURY PAINTING

The glory of the Rijksmuseum is its collection of 17thC Dutch paintings (**rms 208-36**) and in particular its **Rembrandts (rms 221, 224, 229-30**). Pride of place is given to *The Company of Frans Banning Cocq and Lieutenant van Rutenburch*, which hangs in a room, custom-built in 1906, at the end of the Gallery of Honor. This large painting was commissioned in 1642 by a company of the civil guards to hang in their meeting hall at the end of Kloveniersburgwal. Later it became so covered with grime that it was mistaken for a night scene, thus acquiring the totally unjustified name *The Night Watch*. Now that the painting has been thoroughly cleaned it is possible to see the masterful way in which Rembrandt picks out details of expression and costume as the guards emerge dramatically from the building into a pool of sunlight.

The Rijksmuseum has a total of 18 Rembrandts spanning his working life, from an exquisite *Self Portrait* at the age of 22, before he moved from Leiden, to a troubled *Self Portrait as the Apostle Paul*, painted in 1661 after he had been forced to sell his house on Jodenbreestraat because of financial difficulties. His mastery of *chiaroscuro* (the Italian technique of mixing light and shade) is seen in the tender *Holy Family* in which Rembrandt sets the Nativity in the dark cellar of a Dutch house. Other portraits show his wife Saskia, his son Titus dressed in a monk's habit, and a woman who is presumably his mother as *The Prophetess Anna*. Rembrandt produced some of his most tender work toward the end of his life, such as his portrait of *The Wardens of the Amsterdam Drapers' Guild* and the haunting *Portrait of a Couple* (better known as *The Jewish Bride*), painted when he was 61.

Another highlight of the Rijksmuseum is its collection of paintings by the **Delft School (rm 222)**. The Delft artist **Johannes Vermeer** used strong light and bold colors to give an almost religious significance to quiet domestic scenes such as *The Kitchen Maid* and *Woman Reading a Letter*, and captured the warmth of Delft brick houses in *The Little Street*, which he painted from the window of his house looking across to the old people's home opposite. Pieter de Hoogh also painted tranquil domestic interiors in Delft and Amsterdam such as *Maternal Duty*, which is bathed in a mellow golden light, and *Interior with Women beside a Linen Chest*, and was particularly fond of the *doorkijk* — a view through several rooms to the outside.

The other paintings in the 17thC collection are arranged rather haphazardly. Saenredam's methodical studies of church interiors in Assendelft, Haarlem and Utrecht possess an almost mystical stillness, while his view of the old town hall of Amsterdam conveys its shabby charm. The merry domestic scenes of Jan Steen, such as *The Feast of St Nicholas* and the boisterous peasants of Adriaen van Ostade's *The Skaters,* might seem to belong to a more carefree world than Rembrandt, but the paintings had a deep moral purpose — for example, the eggshells casually strewn across the floor warn of the dangers of reckless indulgence. Even the still lifes of Heda and Claesz. contained hidden meanings, such as a fallen glass to symbolize death.

Frans Hals was less inclined to turn a painting into a sermon, and his *Wedding Portrait of Isaac Abrahamsz Massa and Beatrix van der Laen* is full of good humor, while the almost impressionistic *Merry Drinker* reflects the epicurean mood of Haarlem in the Golden Age. Amsterdam was a very serious and sober city by comparison, to judge from Werner van den Valckert's group portraits of the Governors and Governesses of the Amsterdam Leper Asylum. Even the figures in Bartholomeus van der Helst's *The Celebration of the Peace of Münster in the Headquarters of the St George's Guard, Amsterdam* do not seem to be enjoying themselves particularly. The feast is taking place in the guild's meeting hall on SINGEL, where the university library now stands. Notice also Van der Helst's unflattering portrait of Gerard Bicker.

The greatest landscape artist of the Golden Age was Jacob van Ruisdael, whose compellingly romantic *The Mill Near Wijk bij Duurstede* shows a heavily overcast sky threatening the small figures in the foreground. His uncle, Salomon van Ruysdael, favored a more placid landscape *(River Landscape with Cattle Ferry),* while Jan van Goyen's rural scenes were as shabby as Adriaen van Ostade's interiors. Least Dutch in character are the landscapes of Albert Cuyp, whose *River Landscape with Riders* is bathed in an Italianate golden hue.

MEDIEVAL PAINTING

The small medieval art collection (**rms 201-4**) contains several fine works by 15thC Northern Netherlandish artists, notably Geertgen tot Sint Jans and the Master of the Virgo inter Virgines (named after his most famous work). The subject matter is invariably religious, although the artists do not hesitate to dress the figures in sumptuous 15thC garments and include views of blue-roofed Burgundian cities in the background. The most appealing work is the Master of Alkmaar's *Seven Works of Charity*, a painting that has had more than its fair share of misfortune: the monks' faces were vandalized during the Iconoclasm and in later years damp caused further damage. Notice the modest figure of Christ in each of the scenes.

The arrival of the Renaissance in the Netherlands is marked by Jan van Scorel's *Mary Magdalene* (**rm 205**). His pupil Maerten van Heemskerck's *Erythraean Sibyl* is interesting for the hazy view of Delft in the background.

The excesses of Flemish Mannerism are illustrated by Joachim Bueckelaar's irreverent *Jesus with Martha and Mary*, while Joos de Momper's *River Landscape with Boar Hunt* conveys a breathtaking sense of space.

SCULPTURE AND APPLIED ART

The Rijksmuseum's vast collection of sculpture and applied art is spread across the three floors of the w wing. The collection is arranged chronologically: Medieval, Renaissance and Classical works on the first floor; 18thC works in Louis XIV and XV style on the ground floor; and finally Louis XVI, Empire and Art Nouveau pieces in the basement.

Among the medieval works (**rms 238-48**), the most important are the exquisite late 15thC sculptures by Adriaen van Wesel, who is regarded as the greatest Dutch sculptor of the middle ages (**rms 241-42**). The Flemish art of miniaturization is demonstrated by the incredible "devotional nut" (**rm 241**) carved by Adam Dirksz, which was designed to be carried on pilgrimages in a copper case inside a velvet bag. The melancholy sculpture of Northern Germany (**rm 245**) and the painfully honest Realism of the Southern Netherlands (**rm 246**) contrast with the rather placid vision of Dutch sculptors such as the Master of Koudewater.

The tormented Mannerism of the late 16thC is mainly represented by tapestries and furniture (**rm 250**), and the solemn temper of mid-17thC Dutch Classicism by the beautiful furnished room from a Dordrecht house (**rm 252**), the room of sculptures by Artus Quellien (**rm 258**), and the furniture designed by Philips Vingboons for the Huydecoper mansion on Singel (**rm 258a**). The remarkable **Chinese room** from Leeuwarden illustrates the Dutch fascination with Oriental art in the 17thC (**rm 261**).

Descend to the ground floor for the highly popular **dollhouses** (**rm 162, 175**), made in the 18thC with painstaking attention to detail.

The development of **Dutch interior design** from the early 18thC to the early 20thC can be followed in the furnished rooms: Louis XIV style emerging under William III (**rms 164-65** and **167-69**), the more delicate Rococo or Louis XV style appearing in the mid-18thC (**rms 173-76**, including the dollhouse in **rm 175**), and the cool and formal Louis XVI style developing toward the end of the century (**rm 179** and basement

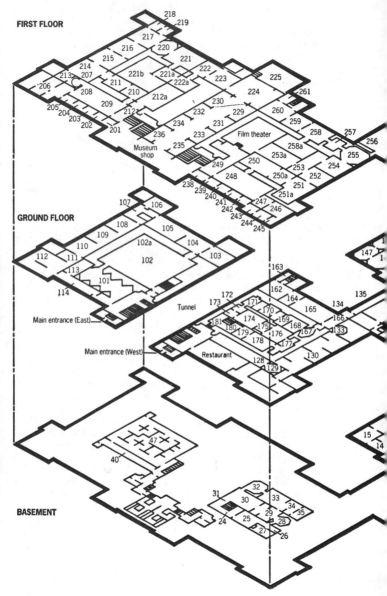

FIRST FLOOR

GROUND FLOOR

Museum shop

Film theater

Main entrance (East)

Tunnel

Main entrance (West)

Restaurant

BASEMENT

RIJKSMUSEUM FLOOR PLAN
Key to numbered rooms

FIRST FLOOR
Painting 15th-17thC
201 Geertgen tot Sint Jans
204 Lucas van Leyden
206 Mannerists
209-210 Frans Hals
211 Rembrandt
214 Ruisdael
216 Jan Steen

222 Vermeer
224 Night Watch
225 Foreign Schools
229-230 Rembrandt
Sculpture &
Applied Art I
15th-17thC
238-247 Middle Ages
248 Italy
249 Acquisitions
250 Renaissance
251a Treasure room

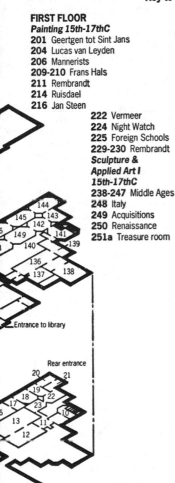

Entrance to library

Rear entrance

253 Glass & silver
253a Colonial art
254 Vianen & Lutma
255-257 Delftware
258 17thC Sculpture

GROUND FLOOR
Dutch History
101 Middle Ages & Revolt
102 Republic, East & West Indies,
 ship models
102a Everyday life
103-104 Sea battles against
 England
105 William III of Orange
107 Deshima, Sri Lanka
110 Battle of Waterloo
114 World War II
Print Room
128-133 Prints & drawings
Painting 18th-19thC
136-137 Cornelis Troost
139 Pastels
140 Miniatures
144-145 Romanticism
146-148 The Hague School
149 Amsterdam School
Sculpture & Applied Art II
138 Islamic art
162 Dollhouses
166 Lace
170-171 Meissen
177 Silver

BASEMENT
Asiatic Art
12 Indonesia
13-14 Japan
15-16 China
17-18 India
19-23 China
Study Collections
40 Tiles
47 Painting
Sculpture & Applied Art III
24 Glass
28 European porcelain
30 Textiles
32 Dutch porcelain
33 Empire
34 Art Nouveau

rms 25, 27 and 29). The gilded luxury of the Empire style was introduced during the French Occupation (**rm 33**), and a beautiful room in Art Nouveau style rewards those who manage to penetrate to the remotest corner of the museum (**rm 34**).

EIGHTEENTH TO NINETEENTH-CENTURY PAINTING

After the Golden Age, Dutch painting tumbled into whimsy. The pleasant little scenes of Cornelis Troost seem weak in comparison with the softly sensual pastels of the 18thC Swiss painter Jean-Etienne Liotard (**rm 139**). Perhaps the most interesting Dutch work of the period is Jan Kels' *The Writer* (**rm 142**), with its unmistakable hint of Vermeer.

Early 19thC painting (**rms 143-44**) was highly Romantic in flavor, as in the landscapes of Koekkoek and Nuijen and the highly atmospheric view of Amsterdam's *Raampoortje* by W. J. Troostwijk. A new sensibility entered Dutch painting in the second half of the 19th century when the artists of the Hague School, inspired by the French Barbizon painters, turned their attention to the dune and sea landscape of the Dutch coast (**rms 145-48**), producing placid scenes such as Anton Mauve's *Morning Ride on the Beach*. The Amsterdam Impressionists preferred to capture action and excitement in their work, as expressed in Breitner's thunderous *Horse Artillery*, or his *Bridge over the Singel at Paleisstraat, Amsterdam*, which reflects the feverish activity of late-19thC Amsterdam.

ASIATIC ART

The peaceful department of Asiatic Art (**rms 11-23**) contains some highly expressive examples of Indonesian art, such as the ferocious *Head of a Kala* and the exquisite *Head of Jatayu, King of the Birds*. Japanese art is represented by the miniature perfection of a birdcage, a smoking cabinet and a casket in the shape of a crane. Note also the whimsical painting of a *Fox in Festive Attire*. The more monumental character of Chinese art is illustrated by the 12thC wooden statue of *Avalokiteshvara*, while the 12thC Indian bronze of *Shiva, Lord of the Dance* is particularly impressive. Finally, look for the superb set of 12 Chinese cups from the Kangxi period, in which the months of the year are represented by different plants or flowers.

DUTCH HISTORY

The medieval history section (**rm 101**) unfortunately fails to come to terms with a potentially fascinating period, the most interesting exhibit being the set of panels of *The St Elizabeth's Day Flood,* showing the aftermath of the disastrous flood of 1421, which created the vast inlet s of Dordrecht known as the Hollands Diep. At the exit of the room is the bookchest that Hugo Grotius purportedly hid in to escape from Loevestein Castle. The religious quarrels that led to Grotius' banishment are the subject of the nearby painting by A. van de Venne, entitled *Fishing for Souls*.

The center of attention is the spacious **17thC square**, which fills the former E courtyard of the building. The extent of Dutch trading interests is illustrated by the series of six paintings of East India Company settlements, which originally hung in the company's Amsterdam head office on Oude Hoogstraat. Also of interest is the painting of *The Battle of the Haarlemmermeer* (1573) in which the Spanish fleet, based in pro-Catholic Amsterdam, defeated the Dutch rebels and captured Haarlem. The inland sea on which the battle occurred was drained in the 19thC and was later to become the site of Amsterdam's Schiphol airport.

The rooms that follow have an air of neglect. The most interesting room is devoted to Dutch trading links with China and Japan, and includes an intriguing Japanese painting showing scenes from the Dutch settlement on Nagasaki. Foreigners were forbidden to enter the city, so that the Dutch were confined to a small fan-shaped island in the bay of Nagasaki.

PRINT ROOMS

Interesting temporary exhibitions of prints from the Rijksmuseum's vast collection are found just beyond the restaurant (**rms 128-33**).

SCHUTTERSGALERIJ

Passage between Spui and St Luciensteeg. Map 10E4 ☎ *Open 10am-5pm. Tram 1, 2, 5 to Spui.*

A passage between two wings of the AMSTERDAMS HISTORISCH MUSEUM has been turned into a unique street gallery, the Schuttersgalerij (Guards' Gallery). The paved lane has doors at either end and a permanent guard, but you are free to use it as a public street. The brick walls are hung with large 17thC civic guard group portraits, including a work by Rembrandt's pupil Govert Flinck.

SINGEL

Maps 6 and 10. Tram to Centraal Station, Dam, Spui or Muntplein.

This canal marks the transition from the compact medieval city with its narrow streets, to the spacious and elegant 17thC canal web. From 1487 to 1585 it formed a moat on the w side of the city — Singel means literally a girdle — and the buildings on the inside of the canal therefore tend to be older and somewhat lower in height than those opposite. Nothing now remains of the medieval wall on Singel except for the brick base of the Munttoren.

Measuring slightly more than 1.6km (1 mile), Singel is one of the most pleasant canals for walking and has a variety of architectural styles.

NORTHERN END OF SINGEL TO RAADHUISSTRAAT

This end of the canal has a breezy, maritime flavor, with seagulls swooping and screeching around the Haarlemmersluis, one of the locks used to pump out the canals each night. One of Amsterdam's best-known fish stalls is located on the bridge — if the prospect of trying to down a raw herring tempts.

Het Spaanse Huis (The Spanish House) at Singel 2 is a ruggedly utilitarian step gable from the 1600s that was used both as a warehouse and home by a merchant named Cruywagen; the facade stone showing a wheelbarrow *(kruiwagen)* is a play on his name.

The view s is beautifully accented by the circular **Lutheran Church**, a grand Classical building designed in Doric style by Adriaen Dortsman in the 1670s on a somewhat cramped site. The church now serves as a rather splendid conference center for the Ramada Renaissance Hotel, and on Sunday mornings is used for concerts.

Several houses near the former harbor are adorned with sea imagery. The beautiful Rococo top of **Vriesland** at Singel 24 shows an 18thC sailing ship, while **Zeevrucht** (Fruit of the Sea) at Singel 36 boasts a superb Rococo centerpiece adorned with foamy waves. The **Poezenboot**, a refuge for stray cats, is located on a barge moored on this stretch of Singel.

Singel 7, which is no wider than a door, features in guided tours as the narrowest house in Amsterdam, although this is frankly a myth as it is merely the back door of a perfectly normal house. Another curiosity is **Singel 64**, which retains a 17thC step-gabled top although the lower part was given a facelift in the 18thC; this illustrates the casual way in which facades and parts of facades are regularly replaced.

Between Blauwburgwal and Torensteeg, **Singel 116** was affectionately dubbed "the house with the noses" after some friends of the 18thC owner offered to pay for the decoration of the claw pieces flanking the neck gable, provided that these included portraits of the owner and his two sons. The offer was taken up and these unflattering portraits were the result. The handsome **De Dolphijn** (The Dolphin) at Singel 140-42 was designed in a flamboyant Renaissance style by Hendrick de Keyser in the early 17thC. This jaunty house, with its double step gable, was later the home of Captain Frans Banning Cocq, the dashing character with the red sash who is seen leading the company of civil guards in Rembrandt's *Night Watch*.

One of Amsterdam's most sensitive modern buildings is Theo Bosch's **Faculteit der Letteren** (Literature Faculty), which fills almost an entire block, between Torensteeg and Raadhuisstraat. Those interested in architecture should enter the building to experience the structure's marvelous transparency.

FROM RAADHUISSTRAAT TO MUNTPLEIN

Singel, from Raadhuisstraat to Heisteeg, has a pleasing human scale, and the narrow alleys to the E are inviting to explore. Here you find antiquarian booksellers, wizened stamp dealers and old-fashioned tobacconists in cramped interiors that retain a medieval character. The most splendid house on this stretch is **Singel 288**, which ruffles its Rococo plumage like some exotic bird. The austere Art Deco **Bungehuis**, a 1930s office building now used by the university, looks on with stern disapproval. The beautiful facade stone *In de Vergulde Haringbuys* (In the Gilded Herring Boat) adorns **Singel 358**, where Rembrandt's son Titus lived for a time with his family. Also worth a glance is **Singel 390**, with reclining figures on the cornice and a highly ornate doorway. The Adam and Eve facade stone at **Singel 367** wittily recalls the apple market that formerly occupied this stretch of canal.

The final stretch of Singel, between Heisteeg and Muntplein, features several bold buildings, such as the soaring church **De Krijtberg** at Singel 446, which was built during the neo-Gothic fever of the 19thC to replace a clandestine Jesuit church. The 1633 **Old Lutheran Church** opposite looks quite dainty by comparison. The row **Singel 421-25** now accommodates the university library. The middle building, known as the **Bushuis** (Arsenal), is a manic Mannerist invention of 1606, which originally housed the armory of the guild of crossbow archers. The new library building to the right stands on the site of the meeting hall of this guild, whose group portrait by Bartholomeus van der Helst hangs in the RIJKSMUSEUM. The **Odeon** theater at Singel 460 occupies an attractive neck gable built by Philips Vingboons in 1662.

The final stretch of Singel is enlivened on one side by the **Flower Market**, which is overlooked by the ornate spire of the **Munttoren**, erected on the brick stump of a medieval tower by Hendrick de Keyser.

SPAARNDAMMERBUURT ▥

N of the Westerpark. Map 3C3. Bus 22 from Centraal Station to Zaanstraat; tram 3 to Haarlemmerplein.

In three separate housing units in NW Amsterdam dating from World War I, the Amsterdam School architect Michel de Klerk displays his full range of talents. On the W side of Spaarndammerplantsoen, a small square, is a 1914 row of houses with parabolic arches punctuating the skyline, while opposite is the more dashing row built for the Eigen Haard housing association in 1916, in which the familiar parabolas are combined with brick sculpture and vibrant colors. But it is the triangular block farther W on Zaanstraat, built in 1917 and nicknamed "The Ship," that shows the full force of De Klerk's creative gusto, with its surreal towers and billowy brick walls mixed with more traditional motifs of North Holland building style. Walk around it once to take in the wealth of detail, such as the distinctive chunky lettering and dramatic doorways, then peer into the courtyard to discover the small community hall, which has the air of a village church.

The Zaanhof, just W of The Ship, was built in 1918 by H. J. M. Walenkamp. Its vaguely medieval towers and pointed gables create the protective mood of a village, harking back to the semi-enclosed Begijnhofs. Just N is another quiet square, the Zaandammerplein, designed by K. P. C. de Bazel in his distinctive geometrical style and built in 1916-23.

SPAARPOTTEN MUSEUM

Raadhuisstraat 12 ☎(020) 5567425. Map 10D4 ▨ ♣ Open Mon-Fri 1-4pm. Tram 1, 2, 5, 13, 14, 17 to Dam.

An eccentric collection of some 12,000 piggy banks and money boxes from all over the world, ranging from beautiful terra-cotta models to horrendous modern kitsch.

SPUI

Map 10E4. Tram 1, 2, 5 to Spui.

The little square called Spui is one of the most genial spots in the city. Situated near the old university, the square has been the scene of whimsical political demonstrations since the Provo happenings in the 1960s. The curious statue of a city urchin, *Het Lieverdje,* was frequently daubed with slogans during the protests. Spui is more tame nowadays, and the ATHENAEUM bookstore (see SHOPPING, page 179) and **Café Luxembourg** are its main attractions.

STADHUIS   See KONINKLIJK PALEIS.

STEDELIJK MUSEUM ★
*Paulus Potterstraat 13 ☎(020) 5732737. Map **5H2** ☒ ☟ (entry for wheel-chairs at Van Baerlestraat 31) ╤ Open daily 11am-5pm. Tram 2, 3, 5, 12 to Van Baerlestraat.*

Amsterdam's municipal *(stedelijk)* museum of modern art looks decidedly old-fashioned from the outside, although the interior is ultra-modern. It was built in 1895 in a bustling neo-Renaissance style that was intended to counteract P. J. H. Cuyper's neo-Gothic RIJKSMUSEUM at the opposite end of Museumplein. Under its energetic postwar director Willem Sandberg the interior was whitewashed, while his successor Eddy de Wilde was even more ruthless and disposed of the reputedly hideous collection of period furniture that was bequeathed to the museum by its founder Sophia Augusta Lopez-Suasso. These sweeping measures, although somewhat unfair to Mrs Lopez-Suasso, have turned this old building into one of the most striking modern art galleries in Europe.

This dynamic approach means that nothing remains in the same place for very long in the Stedelijk. The best way therefore to approach the museum is to look first at the notice-board in the hall (rm 1) to find out about temporary exhibitions and events. Then pick up the free plan and monthly bulletin from the information desk (rm 15) to find out where the various collections are located. Photography is usually shown in rm 13, applied art and graphic design in rm 14, video art in the small sunken theater in rm 14, prints on the mezzanine floor (rm 114) and exhibitions of local art organizations in the new wing (rms 30, 130).

The permanent collection begins with a modest selection of late 19th and early 20thC paintings, with works by Cézanne, Monet, Chagall, Kandinsky and Matisse (including his large cut-paper work *La Perruche et la Sirène)*. But the main strength of the Stedelijk is its depth of coverage of more recent modern artists such as Appel, Dubuffet, De Kooning and Schoonhoven. The Stedelijk's aim — to show the development of a particular artist's style — is most effective in the case of its large Kasimir Malevitch collection, since Malevitch himself selected this series of paintings to show his development from Realism to Suprematism. His earliest paintings, dating from 1910, are splashed with bright colors in Impressionistic style; figures become more metallic in 1912 *(Taking in the Rye);* colorless abstraction appears in 1912-13 *(Head of a Peasant Girl);* Cubism in 1913 *(Desk and Room);* and finally, in 1915, Suprematism emerges triumphant.

Another important cluster of works covers the Dutch **De Stijl** group, who were clearly influenced by Malevitch. Both the painter Piet Mondrian and the architect Gerrit Rietveld strove to impose a framework of order on the freely-floating forms of Suprematism.

The Stedelijk's postwar collection begins with the **Cobra group**, whose first exhibition was held in the Stedelijk in 1959. Willem Sandberg was so taken with Cobra that he commissioned Karel Appel to decorate the walls of the original museum coffee shop (rm 15c).

Under Eddy de Wilde, the Stedelijk turned toward American trends of the 1960s such as Color Field Painting and Pop Art. The vandalized Barnett Newman painting *Who's Afraid of Red, Yellow and Blue?* is now back in the museum after a costly and controversial restoration. A chilling note is struck by Edward Kienholz's *Beanery* (rm 12), modeled on a sleazy bar in Los Angeles frequented by artists. You can enter the murky bar, squeezing past dusty waxwork dummies with clocks as faces, a strange and sinister experience.

The Stedelijk is the proud owner of a magnificent mechanical dance-hall organ, built in Antwerp in 1924 and restored and presented to the Stedelijk by the Amsterdam publishing house De Bezige Bij (The Busy Bee). As well as playing traditional tunes, **The Busy Drone** (as it was renamed) is used for performances of jazz, classical and contemporary music, including specially commissioned pieces by contemporary Dutch composers. Concerts are given in the *Aula* (rm 21a).

The restaurant, a popular meeting place for artists, overlooks an attractive sculpture garden that includes an eccentric invention by Tinguely.

TECHNOLOGY MUSEUM   See NINT TECHNISCH MUSEUM.

THEATER INSTITUTE   See NEDERLANDS THEATER INSTITUUT.

TOWN PLANNING INFORMATION CENTER   See INFORMATIECENTRUM RUIMTELIJKE ORDENING.

TROPENMUSEUM (Tropical Museum)
Linnaeusstraat 2 ☎*(020) 5688200. Map 8G9* 🖼 💺 ♣ ♿ *Open Mon-Fri 10am-5pm; Sat, Sun, hols noon-5pm. Tram 9, 10, 14 to Mauritskade.*
Devoted to the developing world and its problems, this museum is located on the E side of the 17thC moat, facing the grim Muiderpoort built in 1769-71. The building was constructed in 1916-26 to house the Dutch Colonial Institute and betrays an entrenched traditionalism in its anachronistic blend of Renaissance pear-shaped towers and Gothic beaver-tailed roofs. The lofty main hall with its cool arcades and color-ful majolica friezes of plants brings a certain tropical allure to bland E Amsterdam, and the occasional Indonesian *gamelan* or Andean flute concert adds an exotic flavor to a rainy Sunday afternoon.

The bias of the former Colonial Institute is evident in the sculpture depicting episodes from Dutch colonial history, and in an attempt to produce a more balanced view of the Third World, the building was purged of all derogatory exhibits in the 1970s and renamed the Tropen-museum. The museum is divided by continent, with Asia and Oceania on the first floor, and Africa, Latin America and the Middle East on the second floor.

Although the labels are all in Dutch, the collection is worth a visit simply for the visual delight of wandering through reconstructed streets from different Third World countries, and to peer into the dark, dusty interiors of shops and homes. Much of the audiovisual material is also in

121

Dutch, but the tape recordings of musical instruments are interesting.

The museum is constantly buzzing with exhibitions and activities, many of which are aimed at children. The basement theater, **Soeterijn** (☎ *(020) 5688500)*, specializes in films and plays relating to the Third World, while interesting programs of non-Western dance and music feature in the main hall.

TUSCHINSKI ▥

Reguliersbreestraat 26 ☎*(020) 6262633. Map* **6**F5 ▬ *Open 2-10pm. Guided tours July-Aug, Sun and Mon 10.30am* ▨ *Tram 4, 9, 14, 16, 24, 25 to Muntplein.*

Tuschinski looks as if it might have been abandoned after the filming of some early 20thC Hollywood epic. Its remarkable towers in particular seem to have been lifted straight out of D. W. Griffith's *Intolerance* and planted in this narrow Amsterdam street, while the interior, with its luxurious peacock carpets and dazzling Oriental decor, seems the perfect setting for a romantic scene between Gloria Swanson and Rudolf Valentino.

This lavish 1921 Art Deco movie theater was the dream of Abram Tuschinski, a Jewish emigré from Poland who later died in a concentration camp. The Cannon group now owns the six-screen complex and have carefully preserved the original style. Although the main lobby is accessible to the general public, only holders of tickets for a performance will be admitted to the rest of the building.

If visiting Tuschinski 1 — the most opulent of the interiors — it is worth paying the extra for a balcony seat to enjoy the full impact of the glamorous setting. Look out for occasional concerts on the cinema organ.

VAN GOGH MUSEUM ★

Paulus Potterstraat 7 ☎*(020) 5705200. Map* **5**H3 ▨ ⓗ ▭ *Open Tues-Sat 10am-5pm; Sun, hols 1-5pm. Tram 2, 3, 5, 12 to Van Baerlestraat.*

The museum was opened in 1973 to house the superb collection of some 200 paintings and 500 drawings bequeathed by Van Gogh's brother Theo to his son Vincent. The building, an uncompromising modern design by the Dutch *De Stijl* architect Gerrit Rietveld, is set in the small park between the RIJKSMUSEUM and the STEDELIJK. The spacious interior is particularly impressive.

The ground floor covers the years 1880-87. This includes the bleak paintings from the two years Van Gogh spent in the small Brabant town of Nuenen, culminating in his compassionate painting of *The Potato Eaters*. There are also a few hesitant Impressionist works from his Paris period.

The first floor covers the final three years of his life, from 1887-90 — a period of astonishing creativity. The paintings are arranged chronologically, following the dramatic changes that occurred after his move to Arles in Provence in early 1888. The spring blossom was one of the first things to catch Van Gogh's eye, then the beach at Les Saintes-Maries in the summer, and the harvest at La Crau in the month of June, 1888. But many of his finest works were painted after his admission to a sanatorium near

St-Rémy (following the well-known episode in which he cut off his ear): *Branch of Almond Tree in Blossom* and *Still Life: Vase with Irises*. A hint of the gloomy colors of Holland seems to creep back in *The Garden of the St Paul's Hospital in St-Rémy* and *Undergrowth*. Finally, there are the tormented landscapes painted during the last three months of his life while staying at Auvers-sur-Oise, including the bleak *Crows over the Wheatfield*.

The second floor of the museum is devoted to Van Gogh's collection of 19thC Japanese prints, mainly of actors and courtesans, whose tormented expressions perhaps influenced his later landscapes. The third floor contains further works by Van Gogh as well as a small collection of paintings by contemporaries of the artist, such as Emile Bernard and Toulouse-Lautrec.

VAN LOON, MUSEUM

Keizersgracht 672 ☎*(020) 6245255. Map* **6G5** ▨ *Open Sun 1-5pm, Mon 10am-5pm; ring bell to enter. Tram 16, 24, 25 to Keizersgracht.*

The museum provides a rare opportunity to penetrate behind the facade of a stately canal house and savor something of the everyday life of its inhabitants. The building and its twin at Keizersgracht 674 were built by Adriaen Dortsman shortly after the completion of this section of the GRACHTENGORDEL and illustrate the dry Classical style of the 1670s. The only touches of decoration are the four Classical deities on the balustrade, representing Minerva, Mars, Vulcan and Ceres.

One of the earliest occupants of #672 was Rembrandt's pupil Ferdinand Bol, who lived here until 1680. In 1884 the house was bought by the Van Loon family, who still own it. For those who enjoy piecing together family trees, the museum boasts some 50 portraits of family members, ranging from 17thC oil paintings of heroic Dutch rebels to sepia photographs from the 1920s, by which time the Van Loons had become solid pillars of respectability.

Previous generations have left their mark in other ways too, such as the initials of Abraham van Hagen and Catharina Trip that are worked into the staircase balustrade, and the monogram of Hendrik Sander in the master bedroom. The dilapidated Rococo moldings and chairs too frail to sit upon add to the mood of faded grandeur.

Perhaps the most splendid feature of the house is its formal garden, leading to a coach house disguised as a Neoclassical temple. Notice too the adjoining coach house, with its reclining statues and pretty clock tower buried behind the foliage.

VIEWPOINTS ◄€

The flat landscape of the Randstad sometimes creates a burning desire to get above roof level, but the opportunities to do so are rather limited. You can often climb the Classical tower of the **Westerkerk** to look down on the amiable muddle of the Jordaan, or ascend the winding stair in the **Zuiderkerk** tower to survey the new architecture in the former Jewish quarter. The **Oude Kerk** tower gives you a glimpse of the red-light district from a safe vantage point, while you get a fascinat-

ing view of the Dam from the **round window** on the top floor of
MADAME TUSSAUD SCENERAMA.

Twenty-three floors up, the **Ciel Bleu** restaurant and bar of the OKURA
HOTEL (see WHERE TO STAY) offers a sweeping view of the city's southern
quarter, while a window table in METZ & CO's **sixth-floor café** (see WHERE
TO SHOP) gives you a chance to look down on the canals from above.

One of the most intriguing viewpoints in the city is from the **bridge**
at the intersection of Reguliersgracht and Keizersgracht *(map 6 G5)*,
where you can count seven separate bridges receding into the distance,
illuminated with strings of lights on summer nights.

VONDELPARK

Stadhouderskade. Map 5 G1 🖸 🖲 *Tram 1, 2, 5, 6, 7, 10 to Leidseplein.*
Named after the prolific 17thC Amsterdam poet Joost van den Vondel,
the park is an extensive area of woods and lakes in the 19thC ring
between LEIDSEPLEIN and the RIJKSMUSEUM.

The park was designed in 1865 by the Dutch landscape architects J.D.
and L.P. Zocher, who abandoned the formal French garden style popular
in 18thC Holland, in favor of the more Romantic and irregular English style.

In the 1960s and '70s the Vondelpark became a famous hippie campground. Although such spontaneity is no longer tolerated, the Vondelpark still attracts large numbers of musicians, fire eaters, jugglers and the
like, and in the summer regular performances of music, theater and
poetry are given in the open-air theater in the middle of the park. As a
result the Vondelpark has lost its quiet English escapism, and has become
more like Central Park in New York.

In the summer months tea is served by the lakeside in the **Ronde
Blauwe Theehuis** (Round Blue Tea House), a daring modern building
of 1937 now looking a touch dilapidated. The café terrace of the **Filmmuseum** is a particularly enchanting place on a balmy summer evening

WAAG

Nieuwmarkt. Map 11 D6. Metro to Nieuwmarkt.
The dominant feature of Nieuwmarkt is the dusky medieval hulk of the
Waag, formerly a turreted city gate on the E edge of the city. When the
city expanded outward in the 17thC, the moat around the gate was
filled in and the building converted to a weigh house. Various local

guilds met in the upstairs
rooms, which were reached
by separate staircases in the
different towers.

The highly ornate **17thC
entrances** still survive: the
guild of artists used the door
decorated with the figure of
St Luke, while the masons'
entrance is distinguished by
a mason's head and tools.
Notice the tower with its

curious trial windows, which were painstakingly built by apprentices in order that they might qualify as master masons. The guild of surgeons, which used the door inscribed *Theatrum Anatomicum*, commissioned Rembrandt's famous early work *The Anatomy Lesson of Dr Tulp*, now hanging in the Mauritshuis in The Hague (see page 254).

The Waag once housed the Jewish historical museum, but now lies empty; various plans to rescue the moldering brick building have so far come to nothing.

WATER

Amsterdam is built around a web of intersecting waterways, of which the most important are the AMSTEL river, SINGEL, HERENGRACHT, KEIZERS-GRACHT and PRINSENGRACHT. Oil tankers, cruise ships and Rhine barges sail down the IJ river, which can best be seen from the free ferries (see GETTING AROUND, page 58).

The canals are increasingly used by tour boats, pedal boats, canal buses and pleasure craft. Some waterways, such as **Prinsengracht** and **Binnenkant**, are lined with old Rhine barges that have been converted into houseboats, and one barge opposite the Koepelzaal on **Singel** is now a home for stray cats.

Several important buildings in the city stand on islands, including Centraal Station and the NEDERLANDS SCHEEPVAART MUSEUM, while others float on the water, such as the **flower market** on Singel (see SHOPPING, page 190) and the **Sea Palace** Chinese restaurant in the harbor. The sluices are closed every night by turning a wooden wheel (between 7-8pm) to allow the canals to be pumped out. You can watch the operation being carried out at the sluice on the Amstel opposite Theater Carré or the Haarlemmersluis at the N end of Singel. But the most memorable event on the canals is the annual **Prinsengracht concert** (see CALENDAR OF EVENTS, page 48), when an orchestra performs on a flotilla of barges.

WESTERKERK

Prinsengracht 281 ☎(020) 247766. Map 9C3 ◄€ Church open mid-May to mid-Sept Mon-Sat 10am-4pm; tower open June to mid-Sept Tues, Wed, Fri, Sat 2-5pm. Tram 13, 14, 17 to Westermarkt.

When the architect Hendrick de Keyser was commissioned in 1620 to build a new Protestant church on the w side of the GRACHTENGORDEL, he showed his lingering loyalty to lofty Gothic proportions, although he had mastered all the details of the Italian Renaissance. So the building has a certain tension, especially in the six gables on the exterior.

De Keyser died in 1621, however, and the tower was completed by his son Pieter in a more strictly Classical style. Although Amsterdam had by then broken with its Habsburg past, it chose to top the tower with the imperial crown granted to the city by Maximilian I in 1489.

The **tower** features in several sketches by Rembrandt, who spent the last years of his life in a house on the Rozengracht, and is buried in the church. The tower, still the tallest in Amsterdam, can be ascended. The carillonneur climbs the tower every Tuesday to play from noon-1pm.

Westerkerk

The church has recently been restored, and several old shops built against the walls of the church are now let to jewelers, potters and other craftsmen.

WILLET-HOLTHUYSEN, MUSEUM

*Herengracht 605 ☎(020) 5231822. Map **7**F6 ☒ Open daily 11am-5pm. Tram 4, 9, 14 to Rembrandtsplein.*

This museum offers a rare opportunity to enter a handsome 18thC HERENGRACHT residence, albeit via the tradesmen's entrance. The first room encountered is therefore the kitchen, which conveys a convivial glow with its bright copper utensils and gleaming tiles decorated with exotic caged birds.

The upstairs rooms come as something of an anticlimax, with their sad gray and insipid green walls, limpid Louis XVI decoration and timid chiming clocks. Only the magnificent **blue room** at the front conveys any deep impression. The 18thC portraits, too, possess a pallid character, as if all the energy had drained out of Amsterdam, and these descendants of bold merchants and mariners had crept to this quiet stretch of Herengracht to fade away undisturbed.

The house and its collection of Delftware, glass and paintings were bequeathed to the city in the 19thC by Abraham Willet and his wife Louise Holthuysen, who died childless. The first curator of the museum was callous enough to write a sensational novel about the couple's unhappy life, and the wife's lonely death from cancer in a house filled with cats.

Looking from the upstairs windows of the house to the tree-lined canal below, the genius of the Plan of the Three Canals, which gave each house an almost rural setting, can be appreciated. The **rear garden**, in the formal french style of Daniel Marot, confirms one man's caustic observation that Dutch gardens are "scrawled and flourished in patterns like the embroidery of an old maid's work bag."

ZANDHOEK

*Map **3**C3. Tram 3 to Zoutkeetsgracht.*
To escape the crowds head for the three remote and almost traffic-free islands to the NW of Centraal Station, **Bickerseiland**, **Prinseneiland** and **Realeneiland**. With their quaint wooden bridges, wharves and tangle of ships' rigging, these islands preserve a 17thC seafaring flavor.

The Zandhoek, located on the most northerly, Realeneiland, contains a delightful row of 17thC merchants' houses. Further charm is added by the row of traditional sailboats moored along the harbor front, recalling 19thC photographs by Jacob Olie, who lived at Zandhoek 10.

South of here is Bickerseiland, once the property of the 17thC merchant Jan Bickers, which retains the atmosphere of a small village despite the redevelopment on the Westerdok side. Although most of the buildings on Bickerseiland are modern, they manage to suggest a 17thC scale, and the creation of a small urban farm along the harbor front has turned this into one of the most attractive corners of the city.

West of here lies Prinseneiland, which was given over in the 17thC to vast warehouses. Some of these hulks now lie empty and crumbling, while others have been given a new lease on life as apartments. At the SW tip of the island, overlooking Nieuwe Teertuinen, is a small artist's studio that once belonged to the 19thC Impressionist George Breitner.

ZOO   See ARTIS.

ZUIDERKERK
Zuiderkerkhof 72. Map **11E6** ◧ **𝒓** compulsory ◀€ Tower (entrance in Zandstraat) open June to mid-Oct Wed 2-5pm; Thurs, Fri 11am-2pm; Sat 11am-4pm. Tram 9, 14 to Waterlooplein; sneltram 51 or metro to Nieuwmarkt.

Completed in 1611 by Hendrick de Keyser, this was the Netherlands' first Protestant church. Although laden with Renaissance ornament, the design is still largely Gothic, as is seen in the octagonal tower with its pear-shaped top.

No longer used for services, the church now houses the INFORMATIECEN-TRUM RUIMTELIJKE ORDENING. The church tower can be climbed in the summer for a panoramic view of the renovated NIEUWMARKT.

Siena's famous main square inspired the layout of the **Zuiderkerk-plein**, which provides a pleasant spot to listen to the carillon concerts, given Thursday from noon-1pm.

Where to stay in Amsterdam

Making your choice

"You see it all below the level of the water, soppy, hideous, and artificial," complained Matthew Arnold on a visit to Holland in 1859, "and because it exists against nature, nobody can exist there except at a frightful expense, which is very well for the natives, who may be thankful to live on any terms, but disagreeable for foreigners, who do not like to pay twice as much as elsewhere for being half as comfortable." While this remark probably says more about Matthew Arnold as a traveler than Holland as a destination, there is a grain of truth in the accusation. Amsterdam's hotels are generally expensive for what they offer, although there are some comforting exceptions in each price category, such as the **SAS Royal**, **Pulitzer**, **Ambassade** and **Wijnnobel**.

RESERVATIONS

At busy times of the year, most hotels in Amsterdam are full, except for the very expensive luxury hotels. Good, modestly priced hotels are few and far between, so try if possible to reserve several weeks in advance. (A letter or fax written in English should be acceptable.) Periods to avoid, or for which you should reserve well in advance, are Easter, Ascension, Whitsun, All Saints Day (November 1) and Armistice (November 11).

The **Nationaal Reserverings Centrum** *(Postbus 404, 2260 AK Leidschendam* ☎ *(070) 3202600* Fx *(070) 3202611)* provides a free hotel reservation service throughout the Netherlands; you can reserve by letter, fax or telephone. If a last-minute reservation is unavoidable, try the hotel reservation services of the **VVV** (tourist office) at Schiphol airport or Centraal Station, although the standard of accommodations offered can be minimal. At Centraal Station, expect a 1-hour wait in the high season.

PRICE

The price categories quoted for each hotel in this book are intended as a rough guide to what you can expect to pay. There are five categories: cheap (▯), inexpensive (▥), moderate (▥), expensive (▥) and very expensive (▥). (See HOW TO USE THIS BOOK on page 7 for the approximate prices to which these refer.) Many branches of international hotel chains offer significantly lower rates on weekends or during the low season. Some hotels, such as the **Holiday Inn Crowne**

Plaza and the **Scandic Crown Victoria**, let children share their parents' room for no extra charge, which can represent a considerable saving for a family.

BREAKFAST
Traditional Dutch hotel breakfasts generally consist of fruit juice, cold meats, a boiled egg, sliced Gouda cheese, various types of bread and coffee. Breakfast is usually included in the price, especially in less expensive hotels. If not, however, it sometimes makes a pleasant change to slip out to a café for breakfast (see CAFÉS for suggestions) or to sample Sunday brunch Dutch-style at the **Amstel Hotel**.

A CHOICE OF STYLES
Representatives of most international hotel chains can be found in Amsterdam, including a **Hilton** in leafy Amsterdam-Zuid *(Apollolaan 138 1077 BG* ☎ *(020) 6780780* Fx *(020) 6626688)*, a **Holiday Inn Crowne Plaza** in the old town *(Nieuwe Zijds Voorburgwal 5 1012 RC* ☎ *(020) 6200500* Fx *(020) 6201173)* and a **Marriott** near Leidseplein *(Stadhouderskade 21 1054 ES* ☎ *(020) 6075555* Fx *(020) 6075511)*. These hotels guarantee travelers a high standard of service, but reflect scarcely any local character. For a room with a view of a canal, or a typical Dutch breakfast, or the sound of church bells, or the screech of gulls at dawn, or a late-night philosophical discussion, you must select one of the hotels described below.

LOCATION
Apart from price, a convenient location is usually the most important factor in choosing a hotel, so it is best to decide on where you want to stay first and then to pick the most suitable hotel in the area (see HOTELS CLASSIFIED BY AREA, page 131).

The most popular location is the **museum quarter**, close to the RIJKSMUSEUM, VAN GOGH MUSEUM, STEDELIJK MUSEUM, CONCERTGEBOUW and LEIDSEPLEIN. The VONDELPARK is also nearby for those who like to start the day with a brisk run. Hotels in this area are often situated in 19thC mansions in quiet streets with relatively easy parking.

For many people, however, a visit to Amsterdam would not be complete without staying in a historic house on one of the **canals**. Here, the main drawbacks are smallish rooms, steep staircases and impossible parking, but intrepid travelers are prepared to put up with these minor inconveniences for the pleasure of an oak-beamed roof over their heads and a view of a canal to wake up to. Of the canalside hotels, the **Ambassade**, **Pulitzer** and **Canal House** are the most captivating. Be prepared to pay a small extra charge for a room on the side facing the canal.

Another area worth considering is the **historic center**, which is convenient for reaching the main sights, while being close to Centraal Station — useful for those intending to make any excursions outside Amsterdam. A good hotel in this area does not come cheap and parking is again virtually impossible, although many larger hotels have their own garages.

Hotels in **Amsterdam Zuid** are popular with businessmen visiting the World Trade Center or RAI exhibition center, and are also close to suburban rail stations with frequent services to Schiphol airport, Leiden, The Hague, Delft and Rotterdam. The main drawback of the area is that it is rather far from the principal sights, and it is necessary to rely on taxis or trams.

The selection of hotels in this guide has been made not only to give a wide choice of price and location, but also with various other priorities in mind: atmosphere, hospitality, relative quiet, space and views. Addresses, telephone and fax numbers and nearest tram stops are given, as well as symbols showing which hotels are particularly luxurious (🏨) or simple (🏠), and which represent good value (♣). Other symbols show price categories, and give a resumé of the facilities that are available. See KEY TO SYMBOLS on page 7 for the full list of symbols.

Amsterdam's hotels A to Z

AGORA
Singel 462, 1017 AW ☎(020) 6272200 ⊠(020) 6272202. Map **6F4** ▢ to ▥
14 rms, 11 with bathrm 🆎 ⬤ 🆅🆂🅰 ♣ ▢
▱ Tram 1, 2, 5 to Koningsplein.
Location: On a canal near the flower market. A cheerful hotel with a tasteful breakfast room and pleasant, bright bedrooms furnished with a few antiques. The front rooms (slightly more expensive) overlook lively university buildings on the SINGEL canal.

AMBASSADE ♣
Herengracht 341, 1016 AZ ☎(020) 6262333 ⊠(020) 6245321. Map **10E4**
▥ 46 rms, all with bathrm 🆎 ⬤ 🆅🆂🅰 ⬤ 🆅🆂🅰
♣ ▢ ▱ ◄ Tram 1, 2, 5 to Spui.
Location: On an elegant canal, 5 minutes' walk from the Begijnhof. Those who rank romance and ambience above practical details such as parking garages and minibars should try for a room here. The fact that it is almost impossible to get one on short notice indicates that this hotel, located in a row of eight 17th and 18thC merchants' houses on Amsterdam's most elegant canal, has something special to offer. What you will enjoy here — as in no other Amsterdam hotel — is the pleasure of residing in a traditional canal house, furnished with a splendid

collection of antique clocks, chairs and paintings. Service is polite and efficient, and special features such as the comfortable lounge and exquisite breakfast room make this one of Holland's great small hotels.

AMERICAN
Leidsekade 97, 1017 PN ☎(020) 6245322 ⊠(020) 6253236. Map **5F3**
▥ 185 rms, all with bathrm ⇌ 🆎 ⬤ 🆅🆂🅰
🆅🆂🅰 ♣ ▢ ▱ 🏋 ☞ Tram 1, 2, 5, 6, 7, 10 to Leidseplein.
Location: On Leidseplein, surrounded by cultural attractions. This is the hotel for those who enjoy the bustle and action of the city. It is located in one of Amsterdam's most glorious Art Nouveau buildings, built in 1902 by Willem Kromhout. The hotel was modernized in the 1980s to keep abreast of the times, but the furnishings have been tastefully chosen to mirror the Art Nouveau élan of the architecture. The location is ideal for enjoying the cinemas, theaters and cafés around LEIDSEPLEIN. Amsterdam's nightlife can also be experienced in the hotel's elegant **Café Américain** (see CAFÉS).

AMSTEL INTER-CONTINENTAL 🏨
Professor Tulpplein 1, 1018 GX ☎(020) 6226060 ⊠(020) 6225808. Map **7G7**

HOTELS CLASSIFIED BY AREA

HISTORIC CENTER
Doelen Karena ▥
Europe ▥ ▦
Grand Hotel Krasnapolsky ▥ to ▥
Ramada Renaissance ▥
Rho ▢ to ▢
Roode Leeuw ▢ to ▥
SAS Royal ▥ ▦
Scandic Crown Victoria ▥
Schiller Karena ▥
Swissôtel Amsterdam Ascot ▥

CANAL RING
Agora ▢ to ▥
Ambassade ▢ ♣
Canal House ▢ to ▥
Estheréa ▥
Pulitzer ▥ ♣
Pullman Capitool ▥
Seven Bridges ▢ to ▢ ▰

Wiechmann ▢

MUSEUM QUARTER
American ▥
Barbizon Centre ▥
Engeland ▢
De Filosoof ▢
Mercure Arthur Frommer ▢
   to ▥ ♣
Holland ▢ to ▢
Museum ▢
Owl ▢
Piet Hein ▢
Terdam ▢
Toro ▢ ♣
Trianon ▥ ♣
Wijnnobel ▢ ♣

AMSTERDAM ZUID
Amstel Inter-Continental ▥ ▦
Okura ▥

▥ 79 rms, all with bathrm ▣ ⇋ ▣ ◉ ◉ ▥ ⌂ ♨ & ☐ ▱ ⬅ ♨ Tram 6, 7, 10 to Oosteinde; sneltram 51 or metro to Weesperplein.

Location: On the River Amstel, 10 minutes' walk from Waterlooplein. This grand palace hotel, which was built in 1867 by the dynamic entrepreneur Samuel Sarphati, is by far the most splendid place to stay in Amsterdam, with its magnificent entrance hall, impeccable service and beautiful floral displays. The hotel has recently been painstakingly restored throughout, in a bid to retain the loyalty of the monarchs, movie stars and pop singers who have stayed here in the past.

Perhaps the best time to experience the full grandeur of the Amstel Inter-Continental is at its Sunday Champagne brunch, which is served in the glittering **Spiegelzaal** (☐ *reservation essential, dress informal, Sun 11.30am-3pm; no admittance after noon).* The genteel service, live piano music and abundance of beautifully prepared dishes (salads, cold meats, fish mousses, soups, scrambled eggs, pâtés, breads and desserts) make this the perfect antidote to the Sabbatarian gloom of a Dutch Sunday.

BARBIZON CENTRE

Stadhouderskade 7, 1054 ES ☎(020) 6851351 ⬚(020) 6851611. Map **5G2**
▥ 242 rms, all with bathrm ⬌ ⇋ ▣ ◉ ◉ ▥ ♨ & ☐ ▱ ♉ ♨ Tram 1, 2, 5 to Stadhouderskade or 6, 7, 10 to Leidseplein.
Location: Overlooking Leidseplein. Art lovers who associate the name Barbizon with muddy brown and drab green landscape paintings may be wary about choosing to stay in the Barbizon Centre. However, the interior of this building — built in 1929 to accommodate Olympic athletes — has been expertly modernized in a style that thankfully bears little relation to the 19thC paintings of the Barbizon School. The bedrooms are well-equipped and tastefully furnished, and those at the front enjoy a view of the bright lights of LEIDSEPLEIN. For athletically inclined guests, the hotel has a fully-equipped health center, which includes a sauna, Turkish bath, gym and lounge.

CANAL HOUSE

Keizersgracht 148, 1015 CX ☎(020) 6225182 ⬚(020) 6241317. Map **9C3**
▢ to ▥ 26 rms, all with bathrm ▣ ◉ ◉ ▥ ⌂ ♣ ▱ ⬅ Tram 13, 14, 17 to Westermarkt.

131

Location: On a quiet 17thC canal, 5 minutes' walk from the Westerkerk. This small, friendly hotel situated in two historic canal houses is owned by an American couple who have furnished it throughout with antiques to re-create the mood of the Golden Age. Perhaps some would say they have gone too far, for even televisions are excluded from the bedrooms, but for those who appreciate silence (the hotel is probably the quietest on the canals) and a good night's sleep in a comfortable bed, the Canal House is ideal. Special features include a Victorian-style bar and an opulent breakfast room, once an insurance company's office. Rooms on the front, including a few attic hideaways, offer fine views, while those at the back overlook a peaceful garden, which is illuminated at night.

DOELEN KARENA

Nieuwe Doelenstraat 24, 1012 CP ☎*(020) 6220722* ⊠*(020) 6221084. Map* **10**E5 ▨ *86 rms, all with bathrm* ☵ AE ⊙ CD VISA ⬧ ⬦ □ 🏛 *Tram 4, 9, 14, 16, 24, 25 to Muntplein.*

Location: On the river Amstel, 2 minutes' walk from Muntplein and ideally situated for the opera house. It would be hard to find a better hotel from which to explore Rembrandt's Amsterdam, for this elegant 19thC Neoclassical building stands on the site of the medieval tower where Rembrandt painted the *Night Watch*. The event is recalled by the figures of Frans Banning Cocq and Lieutenant van Rutenburch high on the E wall and, in the depths of the building, by a fragment of wall (now a protected monument) on which the painting originally hung. Even the dark browns and golds of the furnishings evoke the mellow mood of a Rembrandt, while the attractive suite *(rm 515* ▨*)* offers a superb view down the canal Kloveniersburgwal to the WAAG, the former weigh house where *The Anatomy Lesson of Dr Tulp* was painted.

ENGELAND

Roemer Visscherstraat 30a, 1054 EZ ☎*(020) 6129691. Map* **5**G2 ▭ *27 rms,*

13 with bathrm AE VISA ⌂ *Tram 1, 2, 5, 6, 7, 10 to Leidseplein.*

Location: In a quiet street, 5 minutes' walk from the Rijksmuseum. A cheerful, inexpensive hotel decorated with vases of bright flowers, and offering breakfast in a pleasant room overlooking the back garden. The hotel occupies two of seven highly unusual 19thC houses built in distinctive European architectural styles.

ESTHERÉA

Singel 303-307, 1012 WJ ☎*(020) 6245146* ⊠*(020) 6239001. Map* **10**E4 ▨ *72 rms, all with bathrm* AE ⊙ CD VISA ⬧ □ 🖅 *Tram 1, 2, 5 to Spui.*

Location: On a 17thC canal, 5 minutes' walk from the Begijnhof. This very friendly hotel is conveniently located to explore the most beautiful area of the old city, and there is a frequent tram service that will take you to the main art museums. The rooms are well-equipped but small, and those at the front enjoy an attractive view of the SINGEL canal.

EUROPE 🏛

Nieuwe Doelenstraat 2-8, 1012 CP ☎*(020) 6234836* ⊠*(020) 6242962. Map* **10**E5 ▨ *100 rms, all with bathrm* ☐ ☵ AE ⊙ CD VISA ⬧ ♿ □ 🖅 ⚐ ≪ ♨ ♀ ⚗ ⌂ *Tram 4, 9, 14, 16, 24, 25 to Muntplein.*

Location: In the heart of Amsterdam, near the flower market. Founded in 1896, the Hotel Europe pampers its guests with every modern luxury, including one of the only hotel swimming pools in the city. From the outside, it is a merry bustle of late 19thC Renaissance details, but inside an elegant Neoclassical tone prevails, with pale yellow walls and Empire furnishings. Most of the rooms overlook the river Amstel, and probably the prettiest view is toward the MUNTTOREN, which is illuminated at night.

DE FILOSOOF

Anna Vondelstraat 6, 1054 GZ ☎*(020) 6833013* ⊠*(020) 6853750.* ▭ *25 rms, 18 with bathrm* ⊡ ♀ *Tram 1, 6 to Constantijn Huygensstraat.*

Location: near the Vondelpark. Ida Jongsma studied philosophy before she opened this small hotel in a 19thC building. Her enthusiasm is reflected in the naming of the hotel (The Philosopher) and the interior design. You may be put in the Philosophers Room or the Egyptian Room. The decor is elegant and spare, with occasional quotes from Goethe's *Faust* or Heraclitus to inspire guests. The air is especially thick with abstract discussion on Wednesday evenings, when the Dutch Association of Consultant Philosophers congregates in the hotel bar.

GRAND HOTEL KRASNAPOLSKY

Dam 9, 1012 JS ☎*(020) 5549111* ⒻⓍ*(020) 6228607. Map* 10D4 ▥ *to* ▥ *322 rms, all with bathrm* ▱ ⊟ ᴁ ⓞ ⓘⓓ ⱽⁱˢᵃ ✳ & ☐ ◨ ⚱ ♉ ☞ *Tram 4, 9, 16, 24, 25 to Dam.*

Location: On the Dam, 5 minutes' walk from Centraal Station. Named after the Polish emigré who built the hotel in 1883, the Krasnapolsky is a huge, bustling hotel on Amsterdam's main square, boasting a splendid 19thC cast-iron and glass **Winter Garden**, where breakfasts are served. The hotel has recently invested enormous sums to install modern conference facilities and new bedrooms, while adding a Japanese garden and a Dutch-style roof garden to relieve the monotony of endless corridors. As a result, the hotel is an intelligent choice for anyone staging a large conference (up to 2,000 delegates), but individual travelers may feel rather overwhelmed. The bedrooms are comfortable and modern, although some of them look out on dingy alleys.

HOLLAND

P. C. Hooftstraat 162, 1071 CH ☎*(020) 6764253* ⒻⓍ*(020) 6765956; for reservations* ☎*(020) 6831811* ⒻⓍ*(020) 6160320. Map* 5H2 ▥ *to* ▥ *67 rms, all with bathrm* ᴁ ⓞ ⓘⓓ ⱽⁱˢᵃ ▱ ✳ ☐ ◨ *Tram 2, 3, 5, 12 to Van Baerlestraat.*

Location: In a quiet street close to the Vondelpark. Like other hotels run by the AMS group (the TRIANON, MUSEUM and TERDAM), the Holland is an inex-

pensive but comfortable hotel, set in a quiet, yet convenient location.

MERCURE ARTHUR FROMMER ♣

Noorderstraat 46, 1017 TV ☎*(020) 6220328* ⒻⓍ*(020) 6203208. Map* 6G4 ▥ *to* ▥ *90 rms, all with bathrm* ☜ ⊟ ᴁ ⓞ ⓘⓓ ⱽⁱˢᵃ ▱ ✳ ◨ *Tram 16, 24, 25 to Prinsengracht.*

Location: In a quiet street of the Weteringbuurt, 5 minutes from the Rijksmuseum. This pleasant, comfortable hotel is situated in a tranquil corner of the city settled by Huguenot refugees in the late 17thC. Opened in the 1960s in a former complex of weavers' houses, the hotel was the brainchild of Arthur Frommer, indefatigable author of *Europe on $5 a Day.* Now owned by the French Mercure group, it is furnished in a style that attempts to recapture the glow of the Dutch Golden Age, although the addition of Colonial American trappings such as rocking chairs and reproduction oil lamps somewhat confuses the effect.

MUSEUM

P. C. Hooftstraat 2, 1071 BX ☎*(020) 6621402* ⒻⓍ*(020) 6733918; for reservations* ☎*(020) 6831811* ⒻⓍ*(020) 6160320. Map* 5G3 ▥ *115 rms, all with bathrm* ⊟ ᴁ ⓞ ⓘⓓ ⱽⁱˢᵃ ✳ ☐ ◨ *Tram 6, 7, 10 to Spiegelgracht.*

Location: Next to the Rijksmuseum. A comfortable hotel, run by the AMS group. Request a room overlooking the RIJKSMUSEUM to savor the delights of Cuypers' neo-Gothic style. (See also HOLLAND, TERDAM and TRIANON hotels.)

OKURA AMSTERDAM

Ferdinand Bolstraat 333, 1072 LH ☎*(020) 6787111* ⒻⓍ*(020) 6712344* ▥ *370 rms, all with bathrm* ☜ ⊟ ⊟ ᴁ ⓞ ⓘⓓ ⱽⁱˢᵃ ▱ ✳ ☐ ◨ ⟨⟨ ☀ ⚱ ☞ *Tram 12, 25 to Cornelis Troostplein.*

Location: Midway between RAI and the Rijksmuseum. Situated in the 20thC ring close to RAI and the beltway (ring road), this 23-story Japanese-owned hotel is ideal for business travelers who prefer not to get tangled up in the narrow inner-city streets. Not that you feel isolated in the Okura, for the city is spread out below, with some rooms overlooking the modern architecture of Amsterdam Zuid while others look N to the spires of the RIJKSMUSEUM and the cranes of the harbor. Another appealing feature of the Okura is its slightly Japanese flavor, from the shop in the basement selling *sake* to the beautiful **Yamazato** restaurant, which overlooks a miniature Japanese garden. But there are Western features as well, including the French cuisine of the **Ciel Bleu** restaurant on the top floor and the typically Dutch products that are on sale at the hotel's souvenir store.

OWL
Roemer Visscherstraat 1, 1054 EV ☎(020) 6189484 ☒(020) 6189441. Map **5**G2 ▥ *34 rms, all with bathrm* ⚏ ▣ ▨ ✦ ▢ ▨ *Tram 1, 2, 5, 6, 7, 10 to Leidseplein.*
Location: In a quiet street, 5 minutes' walk from Leidseplein. This quiet hotel, set in an elegant 19thC quarter, is conveniently placed for visiting Amsterdam's major sights. The bedrooms are pleasant, although small, and the breakfast room is bright and cheerful.

PIET HEIN
Vossiusstraat 53, 1071 AK ☎(020) 6628375 ☒(020) 6621526. Map **5**G2 ▥ *to* ▥ *27 rms, all with bathrm* ⚏ ▣ ▨ ▨ ▢ ▨ *Tram 2, 3, 5, 12 to Van Baerlestraat.*
Location: In a quiet street overlooking the Vondelpark, 5 minutes from the Stedelijk Museum. A small, friendly hotel situated in a 19thC house. The bedrooms are bright and comfortable, with modern prints and a vase of Dutch flowers. Some rooms have views of the park, but travelers on a limited budget can opt for one of the simpler, inexpensive rooms in the annex. With the VONDELPARK on its doorstep, this hotel is ideal for joggers.

PULITZER ♣
Prinsengracht 315-331, 1016 GZ ☎(020) 5235235 ☒(020) 6276753. Map **9**D3 ▥ *241 rms, all with bathrm* ▨ ▱ ⚏ ▣ ▨

▨ ▨ ✦ ▢ ▨ ◀◀ ▨ *Tram 13, 14, 17 to Westermarkt.*
Location: A canalside hotel, 5 minutes from the Westerkerk. No other hotel in Amsterdam manages to combine the romantic attractions of a canal residence with the modern facilities of a business hotel. The Pulitzer is situated in a block of twenty-four 17th and 18thC merchants' houses and warehouses that retain many picturesque details such as brick walls, oak beams and mezzanine floors.

It is part of the Pulitzer's policy to allocate guests their favorite rooms; to enjoy the graceful urban setting, it is worth asking for a room on KEIZERSGRACHT; or if you wish to listen to the birdsong and the gentle chimes of the nearby WESTERKERK, request a room that overlooks the rambling gardens.

Named after the founder of the Pulitzer Prize, the hotel (now part of the Italian-owned CIGA group) offers a highly cultured ambience. Guests can enjoy modern art exhibitions in the beautiful **Pulitzer Art Gallery** or occasional open-air concerts in the hotel gardens. But the event all of Amsterdam flocks to is the extraordinary concert given at the end of August by a small musical ensemble, performed on a flotilla of barges moored alongside the hotel (see CALENDAR OF EVENTS).

PULLMAN CAPITOOL
Nieuwe Zijds Voorburgwal 67, 1012 RE ☎(020) 6275900 ☒(020) 6238932. Map **10**D4 ▥ *148 rms, all with bathrm* ⚏ ▣ ▨ ▨ ✦ ᵭ ▢ ▨ ▼ ▨ *Tram 1, 2, 5, 13, 17 to Dam.*
Location: Just w of the Dam. One of several hotels that have sprung up in recent years in the historic center of the city, the Pullman Capitool is discreetly concealed behind the facade of a former printing works (dating from 1904). The furnishings are tasteful without being overly luxurious, and a sauna takes some of the misery out of winter tourism. Its location is ideal for sightseeing, although if you have a car, it could prove a disadvantage to be so centrally situated.

RAMADA RENAISSANCE
Kattengat 1, 1012 SZ ☎*(020) 6212223* ⓕ*(020) 6275245. Map* **10**C5 ▥ *425 rms, all with bathrm* ▬ ▣ ⇌ ⱯⒺ ⊙ ⓚ ▨ ⚡ ⚠ ▱ ♈ ⚓ *Tram 1, 2, 5, 13, 17 to Martelaarsgracht.*

Location: At the N end of Singel, 5 minutes' walk from Centraal Station. This luxury hotel is situated in a historic quarter of the old city, close to the harbor. The main feature that distinguishes the Ramada Renaissance from other large hotels in Amsterdam is its splendid collection of modern paintings and sculptures; there are about 1,000, including attractive works by the Dutch Cobra artists. The works decorate the lobbies, bars, the restaurant and the bedrooms of the hotel, so that a stay here can be a painless way to keep in touch with contemporary artistic trends.

RHO
Nes 11-23, 1012 KC ☎*(020) 6207371* ⓕ*(020) 6207826. Map* **10**D5 ▱ *to* ▱ *80 rms, all with bathrm* ▣ ⱯⒺ ⓚ ▨ ⚡ ▱ ▱ *Tram 1, 2, 4, 5, 9, 13, 14, 16, 17, 24, 25 to Dam.*

Location: Just off the Dam. The Rho hotel is situated in a curious building with an intriguing history. Originally an old Amsterdam music hall, it was bought in 1912 by the gold dealer H. Drijfhout (whose name still appears above the door). The historic building was converted into a hotel in 1989, and the spacious music hall now serves as a splendid breakfast room. The bedrooms — which come in various shapes and sizes — have elegant contemporary furniture and fabrics, and a Karel Appel print to add a splash of color.

ROODE LEEUW
Damrak 93-94, 1012 LP ☎*(020) 6240396* ⓕ*(020) 6204716. Map* **10**D5 ▥ *to* ▥ *78 rms, all with bathrm* ⱯⒺ ⊙ ⓚ ⚡ ▱ ▱ *Tram 4, 9, 16, 24, 25 to Dam.*

Location: Just off the Dam. This is a well-kept, old-fashioned hotel in a convenient and bustling location. The rooms at the front are particularly bright and well-proportioned, but suffer slightly from the throb of traffic. An airy breakfast room, small lounge and lively café terrace add to its charm.

SAS ROYAL ▥
Rusland 17, 1012 CK ☎*(020) 6231231* ⓕ*(020) 5208200. Map* **10**E5 ▥ *to* ▥ *247 rms, all with bathrm* ▣ ⇌ ⱯⒺ ⊙ ⓚ ▨ ⚡ ▱ ▱ ⚓ ♈ ◈ *Tram 4, 9, 14, 16, 24, 25 to Spui.*

Location: In the heart of the old city, 5 minutes' walk from the opera house. A row of 18thC gable houses has been incorporated into the fabric of the new SAS Royal Hotel in an entirely original manner. The traditional facades conceal an extraordinary seven-floor atrium with rampant tropical vegetation and a gurgling waterfall, standing on the site of an old church. To add to the confusion, the Scandinavian-owned hotel offers a choice of three bedroom decors: Dutch if you are looking for old-fashioned furniture and oak-beamed ceilings, Scandinavian for those who prefer modern pale wood furniture, or Oriental for guests seeking pure escapism. (Top-floor rooms tend to have the best views of the old town.)

The eclectic ambience is reflected, too, in the restaurants: **De Palmboom**, situated in a former tobacconist's shop with an Empire-style facade, serves New York-style pastrami rolls (made with seasoned smoked beef) and Danish Smørrebrød (open sandwiches), while the **Laxenoxen** restaurant offers freshly-landed Norwegian salmon or Scottish Angus Beef. A passage leads under the street to **Het Wapen van Amsterdam**, once a bible printing works, and now the hotel's gym and conference center. The hotel rents out a range of business facilities, including computers, faxes, portable phones and even an office. You can check out from your room via video, which keeps the lobby pleasantly quiet. Guests flying from Schiphol with SAS can check in their luggage at the hotel desk.

SCANDIC CROWN VICTORIA
Damrak 1, 1012 LG ☎*(020) 6234255* ⓕ*(020) 6252997. Map* **10**C5 ▥ *321*

135

rms, all with bathrm 🖼 ≋ AE 🔲 🔲 🗏
💲 ▢ *(CNN tv)* 🖼 ⬕ ⛵ ☂ ☞ 🚋 *Tram
or metro to Centraal Station.*

Location: Opposite Centraal Station.
The handsome Victoria Hotel, a relic of
the 1890s, has been renovated and expanded by the Swedish Scandic group.
Rooms are furnished in a sober modern
style, with mattresses made to exacting
Nordic standards. Ask to be put in the
Victoria Wing if you want to experience
a grand 19thC room.

With an eye to the business traveler,
Scandic has installed a business center
with computer, fax and photocopier,
while some bedrooms are equipped
with computer terminals. The day starts
off with a buffet breakfast that includes
seven types of cereal and six types of
bread, and ends, if you wish, with a dip
in the pool or a steamy sauna. You are
ideally placed here for trips by train or
bus from Centraal Station, but the neighborhood may be too frantic for some.

SCHILLER KARENA
Rembrandtsplein 26, 1017 CV ☎*(020)*
6231660 🖼*(020) 6240098. Map* **6***F5*
🛏 *95 rms, all with bathrm* ≋ AE 🔲 🔲
🗏 💲 ▢ 🖼 *Tram 4, 9, 14 to
Rembrandtsplein.*

*Location: Overlooking Rembrandts-
plein.* The Schiller was a favorite meeting place of Dutch artists in the years
before World War II, and it still retains
an artistic mood due to its remarkable
collection of 700 paintings by the former owner, Frits Schiller. One of the
prime virtues of this hotel, run by the
UK-based Forte Crest group, is its friendly
and efficient desk staff. However, the
bedrooms, crowded with standard
Crest gadgets such as a trouser press
and tea-making equipment, are somewhat characterless, although comfortable enough. Rooms at the front enjoy
a pleasing view of Rembrandtsplein,
although they can sometimes be noisy.

SEVEN BRIDGES 🏨
Reguliersgracht 31, 1017 LK ☎*(020)*
6231329. Map **6***G5* ▢ *to* 🛏 *11rms, 6
with bathrm. No charge/credit cards. Tram
4 to Keizersgracht.*

Location: On a quiet canal. A small
hotel, named after a viewpoint where
seven arched bridges can be counted by
diligent tourists. The rooms are basic,
but the laid-back atmosphere hits the
right spot with young Americans on
tight budgets. Reserve early and ask for
the garden room, or else one overlooking the canal.

SWISSÔTEL AMSTERDAM ASCOT
Damrak 95-98, 1012 LP ☎*(020)
6260066* 🖼*(020) 6270982. Map* **10***D5*
🛏 *110 rms, all with bathrm* ≋ AE 🔲 🔲
🖼 💲 ▢ 🖼 🚋 *Tram 4, 9, 16, 24, 25 to
Dam.*

*Location: On the Dam, 5 minutes' walk
from Centraal Station.* Businessmen
who once checked into large hotels on
the outskirts of Amsterdam are now rec-
ognizing the advantages of inner-city
locations, and several new hotels have
recently opened in the center of the city
to fill the gap. One of the best situated
is the Swiss-owned Ascot, which is just
around the corner from the ROYAL PA-
LACE, and close to shops, restaurants,
cafés and movie theaters. Getting
around town is effortless, as most trams
stop near the hotel, while excursions
can easily be made from Centraal Station, a 5-minute walk away. Rooms are
stylish and well-equipped, and although the hotel does not have parking
there is a 24-hour parking garage at the
nearby GRAND HOTEL KRASNAPOLSKY.

TERDAM 🏵
Tesselschadestraat 23-29, 1054 ET
☎*(020) 6126876* 🖼*(020) 6838313; for
reservations* ☎*(020) 6831811* 🖼*(020)
6160320. Map* **5***G2* 🛏 *60 rms, all with
bathrm* AE 🔲 🔲 🖼 ⛲ 💲 ▢ 🖼 *Tram
1, 2, 5, 6, 7, 10 to Leidseplein.*

*Location: In a quiet street, 5 minutes
from Leidseplein.* Occupying a 19thC
villa, this is the most distinctive of the
AMS-group hotels, with a lobby and bar
decorated in a style reminiscent of the
Vienna Secessionists of the early 20thC.
The bedrooms, however, are furnished
in the standard style of the AMS group,
which also owns the nearby HOLLAND,
MUSEUM and TRIANON hotels.

TORO ♣

Koningslaan 64, 1075 AG ☎*(020)*
6737223 ⨎*(020) 6750031. Map* **5**H1
▥ *22 rms, 20 with bathrm* ⅀ ⊡ ⊡ ⅥⅤ
⌂ ✿ ◻ ⊠ *Tram 2 to Valeriusplein.*
*Location: In a quiet street on the s side
of the Vondelpark, a short tram-ride
from Leidseplein.* This hotel in a bright,
elegant 19thC villa filled with plants and
flowers exudes a decidedly English air.
The bedrooms are spacious and comfortable (some of them have views of
the VONDELPARK), and the attractive
breakfast room is furnished with antiques and family portraits. This is an
ideal hotel for families, and parking in
the area is relatively easy by Amsterdam
standards.

TRIANON ♣

J. W. Brouwersstraat 3-7, 1071 LH
☎*(020) 6732073* ⨎*(020) 6738868; for
reservations* ☎*(020) 6831811* ⨎*(020)
6160320. Map* **5**H2 ▥ *55 rms, all with
bathrm* ▤ ⅀ ⊡ ⊡ ⅥⅤ ⌂ ✿ ◻ ⊠
Tram 3, 5, 12, 16 to Museumplein.
Location: Next to the Concertgebouw.
The Trianon is a conveniently located
hotel, which is furnished in the comfortable and unfussy style of the AMS
group. (See also HOLLAND, MUSEUM and
TERDAM hotels.)

WIECHMANN

Prinsengracht 328-330, 1016 HX ☎*(020)
6263321. Map* **5**F3 ▥ *36 rms, all with
bathrm* ◻ ⊠ *Tram 1, 2, 5 to
Prinsengracht.*
*Location: N of Leidseplein on the edge of
the Jordaan.* A well-situated hotel with
simple, modern rooms at a range of
prices, some enjoying a canal view. The
lobby and breakfast room are furnished
with antiques, and an impressive suit of
armor stands sentinel at the entrance.

WIJNNOBEL ♣

Vossiusstraat 9, 1071 AB ☎*(020)
6622298. Map* **5**G2 ▢ *12 rms, 1 with
bathrm. Tram 1, 2, 5, 6, 7, 10 to
Leidseplein.*
*Location: N in a quiet street overlooking
the Vondelpark, 5 minutes from the
Rijksmuseum.* This friendly, family-run
hotel is ideally suited for young people
or families on a limited budget. The
rooms are bright, clean and spacious;
those at the front enjoy a view of the
VONDELPARK and the golden glow of the
floodlit AMERICAN HOTEL at night. The
only drawbacks are the hotel's lack of a
breakfast room or private bathrooms,
but for those who can dispense with
such luxuries, this is one of the most
pleasant cheap hotels in the city.

Amsterdam: eating and drinking

Fashionable Amsterdammers enthuse wildly about the latest culinary trends, and flock to the restaurants reviewed in Dutch lifestyle magazines such as *Avenue*. New decor and exotic ingredients are prized above consistency. *Nouvelle cuisine* in minimalist settings has given way in the smartness stakes to lemon grass, carpaccio and beer stew. The most talked-about places in Amsterdam now are Thai, Philippine, Japanese and Belgian. Traditional Dutch restaurants have become unexpectedly popular, part of the city's current flirtation with its solid culinary heritage (described on page 41).

The Dutch eat their main meal in the evening, and have light lunches of cheese or ham rolls *(broodje kaas/ham)*, or bread with eggs and the inevitable cheese or ham *(uitsmijter kaas/ham)*. Those who want a more substantial midday meal may find the choice is somewhat limited. Near the art museums, try **Sama Sebo** for an Indonesian lunch, **Fong Lie** for Chinese dishes or **Mirafiori** for Italian cuisine. On Leidseplein, **Het Swarte Schaep** offers excellent French cuisine and **Manchurian** serves delicious Oriental dishes. Near the Dam, **Die Port van Cleve** provides sustaining Dutch food, and **Treasure** offers unusual Peking *dim sum* lunches. The **La Ruche** restaurant at De Bijenkorf (see SHOPPING) also has a wide range of dishes at moderate prices.

Travelers on a limited budget tend to head instinctively towards the sprawl of inexpensive Italian, Greek and Spanish restaurants s of Leidseplein. However, it is often just as inexpensive and sometimes more convivial to eat in cafés that offer meals (known as *eetcafés*). The menus are usually written on blackboards and the dishes are traditional and sustaining. The *dagschotel* (dish of the day) is usually nourishing, and good value. The main drawbacks of café eating are the noise and smoke, but for some this is part of the charm of such places. **Het Molenpad** has a friendly atmosphere, **De Jaren** has thrilling decor, while **Van Puffelen** consistently attains gastronomic heights (see CAFÉS for all three).

In our selection, addresses, telephone and nearest tram stops are given, and symbols showing which restaurants are particularly luxurious (⌂) or simple (⊖). Other symbols show price categories, charge/credit cards and any other noteworthy points. See KEY TO SYMBOLS on page 7 for the full list of symbols. Times are specified when restaurants are **closed**.

A number of restaurants are outstanding in their respective price categories. Examples are: **Dynasty** (Chinese ▥); **Het Stuivertje** (Dutch ▥); **Het Swarte Schaep** (French ▥ to ▦); **Sama Sebo** (Indonesian ▢ to ▥); and **Van Puffelen** (see CAFÉS ▥).

RESTAURANTS CLASSIFIED BY TYPE OF CUISINE

CHINESE
Dynasty ▨
Fong Lie ▨
Manchurian ▨
Treasure ▨
DANISH
Kopenhagen ▨
DUTCH
Keijzer ▨
De Knijp ▨
Die Port van Cleve ▨ to ▨
Sluizer ▨
De Smoeshaan ▨
Het Stuivertje ▨
Witteveen ▨
FISH
Bols Taverne ▨
Lucius ▨
Sluizer ▨
FRENCH
Christophe ▨
Ciel Bleu ▨ to ▨
L'Entrecôte ▨ to ▨
Excelsior ▨
Luden ▨
De Prinsenkelder ▨ to ▨
Sancerre ▨ to ▨
Sauvage ▨ to ▨
Het Swarte Schaep ▨ to ▨

Tout Court ▨ to ▨
De Trechter ▨
Warstein ▨
INDONESIAN
Cilubang ▨
Indonesia ▨
Kantijl & De Tijger ▨ to ▨
Sama Sebo ▨ to ▨
Speciaal ▨
Tempo Doeloe ▨
ITALIAN
Mirafiori ▨ to ▨
Tartufo ▨ to ▨
JAPANESE
Umeno ▨ to ▨
Yamazato ▨ to ▨
PHILIPPINE
At Mango Bay ▨
THAI
Klaas Compaen ▨
CAFÉS (see CAFÉS for descriptions)
Blincker ▨
De Engelbewaarder ▨
Frascati ▨
De Jaren ▨ to ▨
Het Land van Walem ▨
Het Molenpad ▨
Van Puffelen ▨

Amsterdam's restaurants A to Z

BOLS TAVERNE
Rozengracht 106 ☎*(020) 6245752*
▨*(020) 6204194. Map* **9D2** ▨ ▨ ▨
▨ *Closed Sun. Tram 13, 14, 17 to*
Westermarkt.
Situated in a beautifully restored 17thC
step-gable house, this restaurant is
named after the Pieter Bols distillery,
established near here in 1649. The ambience is warm and convivial, with
traditional wooden furniture and romantic 19thC marine paintings. Fish
features prominently on the menu, and
there are tempting combinations such
as poached monkfish, deep-fried sal-

mon trout and crayfish served in dill
sauce, or three filets of salmon trout
prepared in different ways and served
with Norwegian lobster sauce. The portions are enormous, the presentation is
careful, and the meal is brought to a
delightful conclusion by the chocolate
beans and small glass of Bols *crème de
cacao* liqueur that always accompany
the coffee.

CHRISTOPHE
Leliegracht 46 ☎*(020) 6250807. Map*
9C3 ▨ ▨ ▨ ▨ ▨ *Last orders 11pm.*
Closed lunch; Sun; Mon; most of Aug. Tram

139

13, 14, 17 to Westermarkt.

French-trained chef Christophe Royer has set new culinary standards in Amsterdam with his exquisite cooking based on old Mediterranean recipes. He is adept at using exotic ingredients such as saffron, figs, caviar, truffles and olives to reinvent classic French and North African dishes. Try the quail risotto with truffle juice or duck breast with olives to appreciate his serious commitment to good food. The interior of the canalside restaurant was once as original as the cooking, but the fashionably bare style proved too much for many people, and Christophe has had to redecorate in a rather traditional style with polished wood and mellow Art Deco lamps.

CIEL BLEU

Okura Hotel, Ferdinand Bolstraat 333 ☎*(020) 6787111* ⁙*(020) 6712344* ▥ *to* ▥ ♦ ⧉ ⒶⒺ ◉ ⒸⒹ ▥ *Last orders midnight. Closed lunch. Tram 12, 25 to Cornelis Troostplein.*

This French restaurant situated on the top floor of a 23-story Japanese hotel offers the twin attraction of a romantic view and delicate *nouvelle cuisine.* The set menus are well thought out and *flambéd* dishes are particularly well presented. The name "Ciel Bleu" should not be taken too literally: Dutch skies are seldom blue, and their fascination, as the 17thC landscape painters discovered, lies in dramatic cloud formations and sudden rainstorms. To enjoy the full spectacle, choose a bright, changeable day, and reserve a window table. But don't arrive too early in the summer, for the service here is so efficient that you may find yourself at the end of the meal long before the sun has gone down.

CILUBANG ✿

Runstraat 10 ☎*(020) 6269755. Map* **9E3** ▭ ⒶⒺ ⒸⒹ ▥ *Last orders 11pm. Closed lunch; Mon. Tram 1, 2, 5 to Spui.*

A short walk from spui, this tastefully decorated Indonesian restaurant offers a modest and inexpensive *rijsttafel.* Cilubang is popular with young people.

DYNASTY

Reguliersdwarsstraat 30 ☎*(020) 6268400* ⁙*(020) 6223038. Map* **6F4** ▥ ⒶⒺ ◉ ⒸⒹ ▥ ♨ *Last orders 11pm. Closed lunch; Tues; mid-Dec to mid-Jan. Tram 1, 2, 5 to Koningsplein, or tram 4, 9, 14, 16, 24, 25 to Muntplein.*

Situated amid a bevy of chic restaurants, Dynasty outshines them all with its sublime Thai and Cantonese cuisine, delighting the palate with rare herbs and unusual spices. Décor is equally exotic, with silk wall hangings and a curious arrangement of upturned parasols suspended from the ceiling. In summer, there is the added attraction of a garden terrace.

The menu is crammed with tempting dishes, such as *The Sixth Happiness* (duck, jellyfish, and century-old egg), *Phoenix and the Dragon* (duck and lobster on a bed of watercress with stir-fried mushrooms) and *Yunnan lamb* (lamb seasoned with Szechuan peppercorns and garlic). Perhaps the best option for the perplexed diner is *The Offering of the Emperor,* a combination dish of four exotic starters. The Dynasty is always crowded; early reservation is essential. It is sometimes easier to get a table at its sister restaurant MANCHURIAN on Leidseplein.

L'ENTRECÔTE ✿

P. C. Hooftstraat 70 ☎*(020) 6737776. Map* **5G2** ▭ *to* ▭ ⒶⒺ ◉ ⒸⒹ ▥ *Closed Sun; Mon; July. Tram 2, 3, 5, 12 to Van Baerlestraat.*

Following a simple formula that has proved highly successful in France, this glamorous Art Deco restaurant offers diners a straightforward choice of veal or steak, served in the Belgian manner with salad and French fries, and accompanied by either red Côtes du Rhône or white Burgundy house wine. This uncomplicated menu results in rapid service, which makes L'Entrecôte an ideal place to dine before going on to a concert at the nearby **Concertgebouw** (10 minutes' walk). If you decide to linger, however, you can choose from an extensive selection of imaginative desserts.

EXCELSIOR

Hotel Europe, Nieuwe Doelenstraat 2
☎*(020) 6234836* ℻*(020) 6242962. Map*
10E5 ▥ ℀ ⊡ ⊠ ▦ *Tram 4, 9, 14,*
16, 24, 25 to Muntplein.

Beautifully situated on the River Amstel, the restaurant of the EUROPE hotel is one of the most elegant places to eat in Amsterdam. The cooking strikes a balance between classic French dishes and *nouvelle cuisine,* with careful use of exotic ingredients such as truffles, vanilla, ginger and candied vegetables. Try the Bresse quails with candied endives, or duck with apple and vanilla followed by leg of duck in cabbage salad. There is a lengthy list of wines, including a good assortment of half bottles.

FONG LIE

P. C. Hooftstraat 80 ☎*(020) 6716404.*
Map 5H2 ▨ ℀ ⊡ *Last orders 10pm.*
Closed Mon; last three weeks in July. Tram
2, 3, 5, 12 to Van Baerlestraat.

An intimate Chinese restaurant offering delicate cuisine in a friendly atmosphere. The menu is small but tempting, and the dishes are brought to the table in the twinkling of an eye, making Fong Lie ideally suited for a quick lunch between art galleries or a light supper before a concert at the nearby **Concertgebouw.** One specialty of the house is *Tsjha Sioe Mai* (fried "butterflies").

INDONESIA ❧

Singel 550 ☎*(020) 6232035. Map 10F4*
▨ ℀ ⊡ ⊠ ▦ *Last orders 10pm. Tram*
4, 9, 14, 16, 24, 25 to Muntplein.

The illuminated tower on Muntplein provides a romantic backdrop to this first-floor Indonesian restaurant, which combines friendly, attentive service with traditional costumes and an opulent Neoclassical interior. *Rijsttafels* (including, somewhat exceptionally, one for vegetarians) are well-balanced and not too hot (apart from a few ferocious Balinese specialties).

KANTIJL & DE TIJGER

Spuistraat 291 ☎*(020) 6200994*
℻*(020) 6232166. Map 10E4* ▢ *to* ▢

℀ ⊡ ⊠ ▦ *Last orders 11pm. Tram 1,*
2, 5 to Spui.

A spacious Indonesian brasserie with polished wooden tables and waiters clad in fashionable black costumes, Kantijl is the ideal place to sample a single exotic Indonesian dish for lunch, although you can, if you want, order an entire *rijsttafel.* The menu is entirely in Indonesian, but the waiters explain everything in English. Most of the dishes are only lightly spiced, and specialties include grilled goat on skewers and satay. There are big tables for banquets and small ones for lone diners. A sister restaurant in The Hague shares the same philosophy.

KEIJZER

Van Baerlestraat 96 ☎*(020) 671441*
℻*(020) 6737353. Map 5H2* ▨ ℀ ⊡
⊠ ▦ *Closed Sun. Tram 3, 5, 12, 16 to*
Museumplein.

A conservative Dutch restaurant dating from 1903, patronized by musicians performing at the Concertgebouw. The house specialty is *sole à la meunière,* but you can also sample local delicacies such as Texel lamb and smoked IJsselmeer eel. The restaurant is tucked away at the back of a bustling café, which ensures a pleasant level of animation even when the restaurant is quiet.

KLAAS COMPAEN

Raamgracht 9 ☎*(020) 6238708. Map*
11E6 ▢ *Closed lunch; Sun. Tram 9, 14,*
sneltram 51 or metro to Waterlooplein.

This Thai restaurant — named after a 17thC Dutch seaman — is as dark and cramped as a ship's galley. There are few tables, but, perched at the bar, you can watch the cooks conjure up exquisite dishes featuring coconut and spices.

DE KNIJP

Van Baerlestraat 134 ☎*(020) 6714248.*
Map 5I2 ▨ ℀ ⊡ *Last orders midnight.*
Closed Sat lunch and Sun lunch. Tram 3, 5,
12, 16 to Museumplein.

While conductors and pianists performing at the Concertgebouw traditionally dine at **Keijzer,** the rest of the orchestra seems to prefer the more ca-

141

sual ambience of De Knijp. The interior has a slight *fin de siècle* mood, and the cuisine combines Dutch heartiness with a touch of traditional French flair. This is a useful restaurant to know about if you are staying in a hotel in Amsterdam's museum quarter.

KOPENHAGEN

Enge Kapelsteeg 1 (down alley at Rokin 84) ☎*(020) 6249376. Map 10E4* ▥ ▣ ▣ ▣ ▥ *Last orders 10pm. Closed Sun. Tram 4, 9, 14, 16, 24, 25 to Spui.*

A popular Danish restaurant, 5 minutes' walk from the Dam, decorated in a jovial nautical style that you will either love or hate. Kopenhagen's fish specialties are delicious.

LUCIUS

Spuistraat 247 ☎*(020) 6241831* ▣*(020) 6276153. Map 10E4* ▥ ▣ ▣ ▣ ▥ *Last orders 11pm. Closed lunch. Tram 1,2, 5 to Spui.*

This chic seafood restaurant on Spuistraat offers a wide choice of maritime delights, including salmon, oysters and mussels from northern waters and fresh bass and John Dory from the Mediterranean. The restaurant interior is fashionably frugal, with long wooden benches, and the menus are written up on large blackboards. Service is friendly and attentive.

LUDEN

Spuistraat 306 ☎*(020) 6228979. Map 10E4* ▥ *(brasserie) to* ▥ *(restaurant). No charge/credit cards. Tram 1, 2, 5 to Spui.*

Luden is divided into two parts, with an informal brasserie on one side and a more elegant restaurant next door. The layout is an almost exact copy of the successful sister restaurant in The Hague. You can sit on elegantly spartan wooden benches in the brasserie to eat a simple dish of pasta or fashionable *carpaccio* (thin slices of raw beef). Alternatively, you can order a three-course meal in a more opulent setting in the restaurant. The brasserie serves mainly Italian dishes, whereas the restaurant offers variations on New French Cooking.

MANCHURIAN

Leidseplein 10a ☎*(020) 6231330* ▣*(020) 6223038. Map 5F3* ▥ ▣ ▣ ▣ ▥ *Last orders 10.30pm. Closed mid-Dec to mid-Jan. Tram 1, 2, 5, 6, 7, 10 to Leidseplein.*

An Oriental restaurant decorated in delicate pastel colors and offering a range of exquisite dishes from the kitchens of Canton, Peking, Mongolia, Thailand and Indonesia. The crispy starters such as Cantonese *dim sum* and *Golden Triangle* (a spicy spring roll) are worth sampling. Manchurian is under the same management as its sister restaurant DYNASTY on the Reguliersdwarsstraat.

AT MANGO BAY

Westerstraat 91 ☎*(020) 6381039. Map 9B3* ▥ *No charge/credit cards. Closed lunch; Thurs. Tram 13, 14, 17 to Westermarkt, then a 10min walk N along Prinsengracht.*

A bright yellow facade on a drab street in the remote N Jordaan marks out a Philippine restaurant that is well worth the trek. Situated in the former front room of a gable house, At Mango Bay conjures up dusky tropical days with its huge bouquets of bright flowers and *trompe l'oeil* mural of a tropical beach. The cooking is based on the most delicate of ingredients, such as ginger, coriander and lime grass. Try the beef marinated in honey and soya sauce, or prawns simmered in coconut milk with spices. Cocktails come with cheeky names such as *Imelda's Shoes* and *Secret Swiss Bank Account* (referring to the excessive life-style of the wife of the former Philippine dictator).

MIRAFIORI ♣

Hobbemastraat 2 ☎*(020) 6623013. Map 5G3* ▥ *to* ▥ ▣ ▣ *Last orders 11pm. Closed Tues. Tram 1, 2, 5, 6, 7, 10 to Leidseplein.*

This staunchly traditional Italian restaurant is marvelously anachronistic with its marble stairway, thick linen tablecloths and signed black-and-white photographs of Italian celebrities of the 1960s. Italophiles will appreciate the traditional Italian cuisine, the patriotic wine list and the brisk *buon giorno* with which the manager greets his guests.

DIE PORT VAN CLEVE

Nieuwe Zijds Voorburgwal 178 ☎*(020) 6244860. Map 10D4* ☐ *to* ☐ *Tram 1, 2, 5, 13, 14, 17 to Dam.*

This cavernous dining hall is something of an Amsterdam institution. It was opened in 1870 behind the ROYAL PALACE and soon became famous for its steaks: so famous that it has been serving them up ever since. The cuisine, although certainly substantial, is presented with a touch of flair, and there is nothing quite like the thick *erwtensoep* (pea soup) to fortify you for a brisk walk along the canals.

DE PRINSENKELDER

Prinsengracht 438 ☎*(020) 6267721* ☒*(020) 6258986. Map 5F3* ☐ *to* ☐ ☐ ☐ ☐ ☐ *Last orders 10pm. Closed lunch; Mon. Tram 1, 2, 5 to Prinsengracht.*

This low oak-beamed 17thC warehouse cellar with its gleaming Delft tiles and shining brass pots calls to mind a Dutch Master painting of the Golden Age. The menu, however, is firmly based on the best principles of New French Cooking. You can expect to be offered inventive combinations of fish, and tempting desserts.

De Prinsenkelder shares kitchen space with the expensive and rather stuffy **Dikker & Thijs** restaurant *(Prinsengracht 444, 1st floor* ☐ *closed lunch, Sun, map 5F3),* which was set up in 1896 by a businessman (Dikker) and a chef (Thijs) fresh from Escoffier's school. The same group runs the adjoining **Brasserie Dikker & Thijs** *(Leidsestraat 84* ☐ *map 5F3),* where you can eat delicately poached salmon in tarragon sauce, or a simple sandwich. The brasserie boasts a growing collection of original paintings by modern artists, including cartoons by Simon Carmiggelt (a frequent guest at the Dikker & Thijs hotel) and a café table that was painted by the 1960s rebel Jan Cremer.

SAMA SEBO ♣

P. C. Hooftstraat 27 ☎*(020) 6628146. Map 5G3* ☐ *to* ☐ ☐ ☐ ☐ ☐ *Closed Sun; hols; mid-July for two weeks. Tram 1, 2, 5 to Leidseplein, or tram 6, 7, 10 to Spiegelgracht.*

This convivial Indonesian restaurant creates an exotic ambience with batik tablecloths, Indonesian masks and soporific background music. Sebo's *rijsttafel* may not be the biggest in town, but it is one of the most fragrant and refined, with sauces that are dark and full-bodied, but never too spicy. Dinner reservations should be made well in advance, although it is easier to squeeze in at lunchtime to sample inexpensive mini-*rijsttafels* based on rice *(nasi goreng)* or noodles *(bami goreng)*.

SANCERRE

Reestraat 28 ☎*(020) 6278794* ☒*(020) 6384599. Map 9D3* ☐ *to* ☐ ☐ ☐ ☐ ☐ *Last orders 10.30pm. Closed Sat lunch and Sun lunch. Tram 13, 14, 17 to Westermarkt.*

Three elegant 18thC shops have been run together to create this tasteful two-floor restaurant with bright pink tablecloths and contemporary paintings on the walls. Four set menus are offered, including a vegetarian one, and the cuisine is delicate and French. As might be anticipated, the wine list is strong on Sancerres, with a choice of ten whites, two reds and a rosé.

SAUVAGE

Runstraat 17d ☎*(020) 6270618. Map 9E3* ☐ *to* ☐ ☐ ☐ ☐ *Closed lunch. Tram 1, 2, 5 to Spui.*

Amsterdammers are thrilled by this small restaurant, which successfully combines their two passions — modern interior design and inexpensive eating. The cooking here is innovative without being minimal, and the menu features seasonal specialties such as game in winter. There are three set menus to choose from, numbering three, four or five courses. A typical meal might take the form of chicken broth with lemon and mint, followed by rabbit cooked in sage and bacon, rounded off with *Kai-*

serschmarren (a German specialty of shredded pancake with raisins and almonds) served with blackcurrant ice cream. The only drawback is that Sauvage is rather cramped, even by Amsterdam standards.

SLUIZER

Utrechtsestraat 43-45 ☎*(020) 6226376. Map 6F5* 🔲 🍴 *(fish restaurant)* AE 🔳 🔳 VISA *Last orders midnight. Closed Sat lunch; Sun lunch. Tram 4 to Keizersgracht.*
The two Sluizer restaurants — one offering Dutch food while the other specializes in fish — combine the conviviality of a brown café with well-prepared cuisine. The Art Deco fish restaurant is the more adventurous of the two, and offers a huge choice of fish (poached, fried or grilled), *coquilles Saint-Jacques, waterzooi* (a Belgian fish stew) and crab casserole. The service at Sluizer is friendly, and the menu invites customers who find the salmon too dry to send it back to the kitchen.

DE SMOESHAAN

Leidsekade 90 ☎*(020) 6250368. Map 5F2* 🔲 *Last orders 10pm. Closed lunch. Tram 1, 2, 5, 6, 7, 10 to Leidseplein.*
Attached to a small theater, De Smoeshaan preserves something of the artistic ambience of a brown café, while offering cuisine that is a shade more sophisticated. Specialties include *eendeborst met bosbessensaus* (duck breast in bilberry sauce), and *gevulde gerookte zeetongrolletjes* (filets of sole rolled and stuffed with smoked salmon). The restaurant serves generous portions and the set menu offered is excellent value. A simpler lunch menu is offered downstairs in the café **De Smoeshaan** (see CAFÉS).

SPECIAAL ♣

Nieuwe Leliestraat 142 ☎*(020) 6249706. Map 9C3* 🔲 *Last orders 11pm. Tram 13, 14, 17 to Westermarkt.*
The Speciaal is situated in a rather dingy street in the baffling JORDAAN. From the outside, the restaurant looks no larger than a boutique, but it opens out miraculously at the back into an attractive

bamboo-lined room with slowly revolving ceiling fans. A tropical heat builds up as the restaurant fills, and ziggurats of *rijsttafel* dishes are piled precariously onto the plate-warmers. As well as a choice of two *rijsttafels*, the menu offers an interesting selection of Indonesian meat, chicken and fish dishes. Although beer is the usual accompaniment to an Indonesian meal — helping to extinguish any unexpected explosions of spices on the palate — the Speciaal also offers a small selection of well-chosen wines.

HET STUIVERTJE ♣

Hazenstraat 58 ☎*(020) 6231349. Map 9E2* 🔲 AE 🔳 🔳 VISA *Last orders 11.30pm. Closed lunch; Mon. Tram 13, 14, 17 to Westermarkt.*
This friendly restaurant named after the Dutch 5ct coin is decorated in the style of a traditional brown café, while the accent is on cuisine with a slight French flavor. The clientele is unusually diverse and the restaurant is always bursting at the seams, so that a reservation is essential. The excellent steaks are particularly popular, but there is also a *dagschotel* (dish of the day) for the more adventurous. The hearty portions of vegetables and salads at Het Stuivertje are legendary, and the wine list is thoroughly researched.

HET SWARTE SCHAEP ♣

Korte Leidsedwarsstraat 24 ☎*(020) 6223021* 🔢*(020) 6248268. Map 5F3* 🔲 *to* 🔲 💳 AE 🔳 🔳 VISA *Last orders 11pm. Tram 1, 2, 5, 6, 7, 10 to Leidseplein.*
Until a few years ago there were several excellent French restaurants around Leidseplein, but one by one they have packed up and moved to the suburbs, leaving only one — the appropriately named "Black Sheep" — as a lonely outpost of good cuisine. The building dates from 1687, and is richly furnished with heavy dark wood and polished brass utensils. The cuisine combines the traditional virtues of the French kitchen with the best features of *nouvelle cuisine,* and offers superb steaks, duck and game, accompanied by vegetables

cooked to perfection. The old-fashioned courtesy of the waiters, the wide choice of set menus and the thick leather-bound wine list illustrate Het Swarte Schaep's serious commitment to good dining.

TARTUFO

Singel 449 ☎*(020) 6277175. Map* **10F4**
▢ *to* ▢ *AE* ◉ *Last orders 11pm.*
Closed Sat lunch and Sun lunch. Tram 1, 2, 5 to Koningsplein; or tram 4, 9, 14, 16, 24, 25 to Muntplein.

A friendly restaurant specializing in inventive pasta dishes such as tagliatelle with fresh salmon and chives in a cream sauce. Lunch is served in a cool, tiled kitchen with curious Post Modern triangular tables; dinners are eaten in the more formal upstairs dining area. The choice of either large or small portions at lunch is a welcome innovation.

TEMPO DOELOE

Utrechtsestraat 75 ☎*(020) 6256718. Map* **6F5** ▢ *AE* ◉ *Last orders 11pm. Closed lunch; late Jan–early Feb. Tram 4 to Keizersgracht.*

Don't let the refined décor and elegant porcelain in this small Indonesian restaurant deceive you into expecting delicate cuisine. The Javanese, Balinese and Sumatran dishes prepared by Don Ao from the island of Celebes make no concessions to the Western palate, and when a dish is described as *pedis* (sharp) it means just what it says. But for those attracted by hot spicy dishes, Tempo Doeloe is a must. The restaurant's specialties include the chili-strewn *nasi koening*, the *rijsttafel Istemewa*, the vegetarian dish and, to bring the meal to a soothing conclusion, the traditional Indonesian *spekkoek* (layered spice cake).

TOUT COURT

Runstraat 13 ☎*(020) 6258637. Map* **9E3** ▩ *to* ▩ *AE* ◉ ◉ *Last orders 11.30pm. Closed lunch; Sun; Mon. Tram 1, 2, 5 to Spui.*

Situated on a delightful street, this small, popular and bustling restaurant run by John Fagel offers French provincial cooking tinged with elements of *nouvelle cuisine*. This is not a restaurant for the conservative palate: the specialties are kidney, liver and brains, and the sauces tend to be rich. The portions are just right, the service is impeccable, and the set menus cater to every need from a light pre- or post-theater *souper* to a gastronomic extravaganza. Tout Court is one of the best-loved restaurants in Amsterdam, and it is advisable to reserve several days in advance to avoid disappointment.

TREASURE

Nieuwe Zijds Voorburgwal 115 ☎*(020) 6260915* ▣*(020) 6401202. Map* **10D4** ▥ *AE* ◉ ◉ ▨ *Last orders 10pm. Tram 1, 2, 5, 9, 13, 14, 16, 17, 24, 25 to Dam.*

The extensive menu of this friendly Chinese restaurant on Nieuwe Zijds Voorburgwal includes curiosities such as squirrel fish, Charlie Chaplin duck and a certain dish known as *Pun Fan Pei*, which the menu tantalizingly claims is "a mysterious Chinese dish indescribable in Western terms." The vast ten-course Peking or Szechuan banquets are particularly good value, but for more modest appetites Treasure offers a rare opportunity to sample Peking-style *dim sum* lunches. Very strongly recommended are the *Sze Pao Hsia*, which are prawn pouches wrapped in a crispy pancake.

DE TRECHTER

Hobbemakade 63 ☎*(020) 6711263. Map* **5I3** ▥ ▬ *AE* ◉ ◉ *Last orders 10pm. Closed lunch; Sun; Mon; mid-July to early Aug. Tram 16 to Ruysdaelstraat.*

De Trechter (called "The Funnel" because of its unusual shape) offers *nouvelle cuisine* at its most refined in an intimate interior that suggests the mood of a private dinner party. The service is friendly and attentive, and the exquisite dishes created by Jan de Wit are presented on attractive plates that harmonize with the cuisine. Delightful *amuse-gueules* appear at unexpected moments when interest might be flagging. Its consistent excellence ensures that this tiny restaurant is always full, and it is advisable to reserve well in advance in order to be sure of getting a table.

UMENO

Agamemnonstraat 27 ☎*(020) 6766089* ▢ *to* ▢ *Closed Wed. Tram 24 to Olympiaplein.*

This small, traditional Japanese restaurant near Olympiaplein offers fragrant, colorful dishes presented with consummate delicacy. Its businessmen's lunch, which is served at a breathtaking pace, is eagerly devoured by Japanese executives attending trade fairs at the RAI exhibition center, which is not far from here.

WARSTEIN ✿

Spuistraat 266 ☎*(020) 6229609. Map 10E4* ▢ Ⓐ Ⓒ Ⓥ *Last orders 10pm. Closed Mon. Tram 1, 2, 5 to Spui.*

Owned by the same dynamic duo as the BOLS TAVERNE on Rozengracht, Warstein is a restaurant with considerable vitality and culinary flair, and although it may make an occasional slight mistake, this is quickly forgiven. The restaurant's two-tier modern interior has the atmosphere of a Spanish hacienda, with flowers just about everywhere. Warstein offers a simple choice of five excellent 3-course menus; fish dishes are particularly interesting. Portions are enormous. The meal ends with a complimentary cup of coffee, served with a glass of water and a Bols liqueur.

WITTEVEEN

Ceintuurbaan 256-258 ☎*(020) 6624368* ▣*(020) 6712852. Map 6J4* ▢ Ⓐ Ⓒ Ⓒ Ⓥ *Last orders 11pm. Tram 3, 24 to Ferdinand Bolstraat or tram 12, 25 to Ceintuurbaan.*

A vast, handsome Old Dutch café-restaurant with wood paneling, red velvet walls and old paintings by minor Dutch artists. Amsterdammers of all ages flock here to enjoy the luxury of crisp white tablecloths and to be served by waitresses clad in formal black dresses. Traditional Dutch dishes featuring lamb, duck and sole are prepared with care and flair, to create a mood that becomes quite festive at times.

YAMAZATO

Okura Hotel, Ferdinand Bolstraat 333 ☎*(020) 6787111* ▣*(020) 6712344* Ⓥ ⬛ Ⓐ Ⓒ Ⓒ Ⓥ *Last orders 10pm. Tram 12, 25 to Cornelis Troostplein.*

Yamazato is situated in Amsterdam's only Japanese hotel, the OKURA on Ferdinand Bolstraat (see WHERE TO STAY). It offers a wide range of traditional Japanese dishes such as *sashimi* (raw fish), *tempura* (deep-fried delicacies) and seaweed soup. The restaurant is tastefully furnished and overlooks a miniature Japanese garden. The hotel also has a sushi bar and a *teppan-yaki* steak house, where steaks are grilled on large hot plates that are set into the tables.

KEY TO MAP PAGES

MAPS 7-11 : AMSTERDAM CITY

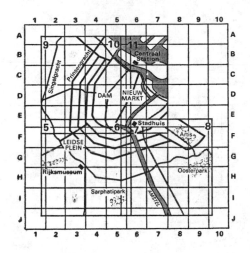

KEY TO CITY MAP SYMBOLS

- ▨ Place of Interest or Important Building
- ▬ Built-up Area
- ▨ Park
- ✝ Church
- ☾ Mosque
- ✡ Synagogue
- ⊞ Hospital
- ⓘ Information Office
- ⊠ Post Office (vvv)
- ⓞ Police Station
- ⌐ Parking Lot
- Ⓜ Metro Station
- 7▶ Adjoining Page No.

```
0        100      200      300m
0        100      200      300yds
```

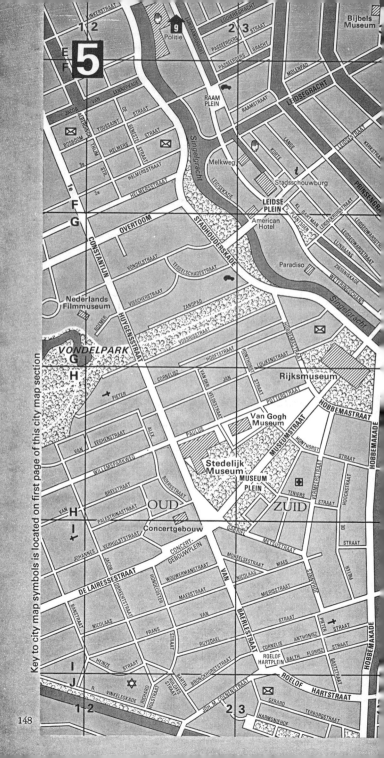

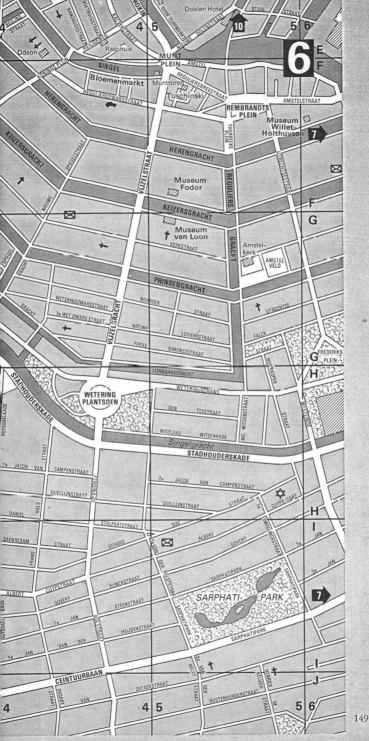

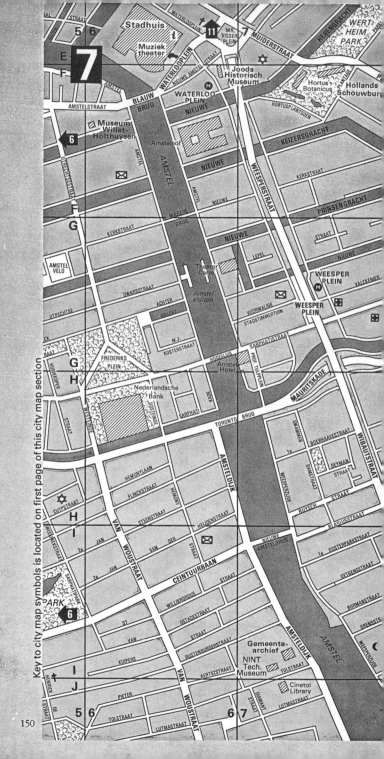

Key to city map symbols is located on first page of this city map section

150

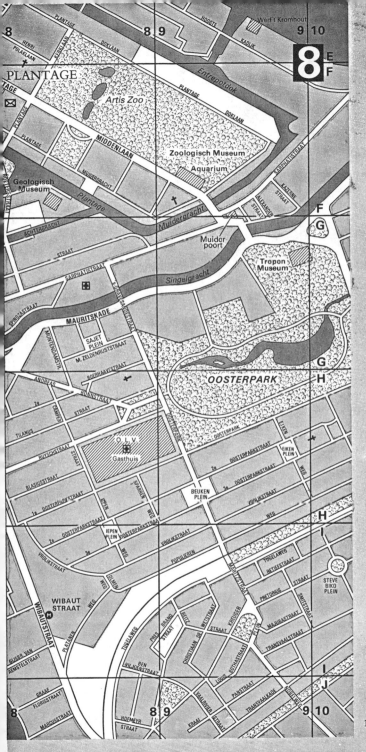

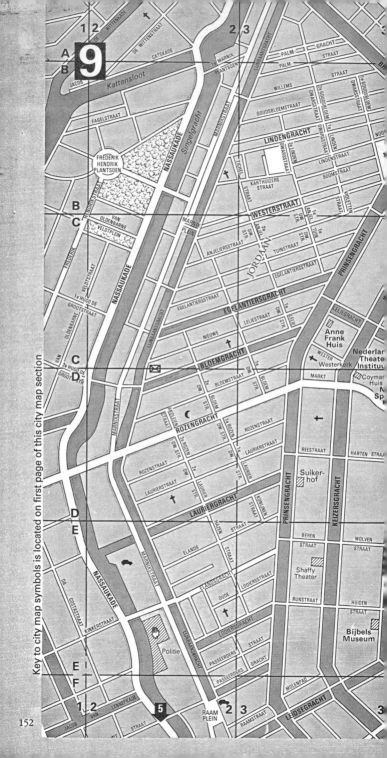

153

Key to city map symbols is located on first page of this city map section

Amsterdam's cafés

Amsterdam's cafés combine the comforts of London pubs with the bohemian spirit of Paris cafés; they are quiet places where you can linger over a coffee, read the newspaper, sample an exotic beer or ruminate on movies and fashions.

TRADITIONAL BROWN CAFÉS

Brown cafés take their name from their dark wood interiors and traditional furnishings; the atmosphere is enhanced by bare wooden floorboards that creak like the deck of a boat, wooden wainscoting, mustard-colored walls and a rather haphazard selection of tables and chairs. Many of these cafés have been in business since the 17thC, and their dark, candlelit interiors retain something of the atmosphere of a Golden Age painting. Occasionally, there is a hint of former splendor in an ornate lamp, coat hook or calligraphic detail, but the overwhelming mood is one of gentle decline. The nostalgic atmosphere is often rounded off by a group of men with oversized moustaches reminiscing about the good old days, which in Amsterdam can mean anything from the 1920s back to the 1640s.

The best brown cafés serve as a home away from home for Amsterdammers, many of whom live in cramped, dark apartments. They are places to linger over a beer *(pils)*, coffee *(koffie)* or soda water *(spa)* without feeling rushed. In all but the most brusque establishments, you can spend a long rainy afternoon reading a book from beginning to end without being disturbed. Some cafés even provide Dutch and foreign newspapers and a well-lit reading table. Most will offer filled rolls *(belegde broodjes)*, *uitsmijter* (a Dutch specialty of bread and ham or cheese, topped with fried eggs) and apple cake *(appelgebak)*, as well as traditional Dutch snacks such as *bitterballen* (meatballs) and various types of *worst* (sausage). Unless you only have one drink, it is customary to keep a running tab and pay for everything at the end.

The friendliest cafés in Amsterdam are generally the simply furnished places in the city center. Beyond SINGELGRACHT (the outer limit of the 17thC city) the cafés tend to become smothered in fussy domestic details such as frilly lace curtains in the windows and thick Persian carpets on the tables to protect them from beer stains.

MODERN CAFÉS

In the 1980s, young Amsterdammers made a decisive break with tradition when they began to frequent bright white architect-designed cafés with zinc tables, walls of mirrors and Post Modern architectural details. Although in the beginning these ultramodern cafés sent a shiver of dismay through the old brown cafés, they now seem to have settled into the fabric of the city and some — such as **De Blincker** — have even begun to acquire an endearing scruffiness.

One of the most exciting new cafés in Amsterdam is to be found on the sixth floor of the **Metz & Co.** department store (see SHOPPING, page 182). Reached via the tiny elevators or, for the energetic, by the ornate

19thC staircase, this spacious café offers a spectacular bird's-eye view of the city.

Amsterdammers currently favor a new generation of spacious and bustling cafés modeled on the "grand cafés" of the 19thC. Some of these establishments have no justification for describing themselves as "grand," but **De Jaren** and **Luxembourg** possess a certain splendor and cosmopolitan allure.

SPECIALIZED CAFÉS

Another recent trend is the emergence of specialized cafés. These include chess cafés such as **Het Hok** *(Lange Leidsedwarsstraat 134, map 5 F3)*, theater cafés and jazz cafés (see NIGHTLIFE AND ENTERTAINMENT), women-only cafés such as **Saarein** *(Elandsstraat 119, map 9 E2)*, specialized beer cafés such as **Gollem** *(Raamsteeg 4, map 10 E4)*, drugs cafés (which display a marijuana leaf on the window), punk cafés, gay cafés such as **April** *(Reguliersdwarsstraat 37, map 6 F4)*, and even a Belgian café, **De Brakke Grond**.

PROEFLOKALEN

An entirely different Amsterdam drinking institution is the *proeflokaal,* or tasting house. Originally these were attached to *jenever* (Dutch gin) distilleries and allowed customers to sample the product before they purchased a bottle. Although the licensing laws now prohibit them from selling *jenever* in bottles, the *proeflokaals* still retain the atmosphere of a shop rather than a café. These are ideal spots in which to have an apéritif, most being situated in attractive 18thC buildings in the old part of the city. Among the most genial *proeflokalen* are **De Drie Fleschjes**, behind the Nieuwe Kerk, **De Admiraal** and **Het Hooghoudt**.

One generally samples *jenever* — *jonge* (young), a clear liquid, or *oude* (old), with a yellow tint — served in miniature tulip-shaped glasses filled to the brim. Tempting specialties are *bessen jenever* (flavored with berries), *citroen jenever* (flavored with lemon), *taainagel* (a seamen's *jenever,* which translates as "tough as nails"), *korenwijn* (a strong malt liquor distilled with juniper berries), *brandewijn* (brandy wine) and *Beerenburg* (a herbal bitter invented by the Amsterdam spice merchant Hendric van Beerenburg).

There are also numerous specialties traditionally associated with festive occasions, such as *kandeel* (an egg punch served to a mother and guests after childbirth) and *Bruidstranen* ("bride's tears," served at weddings). *Boerenjongen* (farmer boy) and *boerenmeisje* (farmer girl) contain respectively raisins and apricots in *brandewijn,* and are traditionally given to children.

SHERRY AND WINE BARS

Amsterdam also has a number of specialized sherry bars, such as the friendly and informed **Continental Bodega** *(Lijnbaansgracht 246, map 5 G3)*. For a good selection of wines, try **Henri Prouvin** *(Gravenstraat 20, map 10 D4)*.

EETCAFÉS

An increasing number of Amsterdam's cafés, particularly some of the student brown cafés and modern cafés, have begun to offer complete meals at reasonable prices. The menu, which is usually chalked on a blackboard, often includes a dish of the day *(dagschotel)* and a vegetarian dish *(vegetarische schotel)*. The cuisine usually consists of solid and sustaining Dutch fare, although a few *eetcafés* such as **Van Puffelen**, **Frascati** and **Het Molenpad** offer a hint of French *nouvelle cuisine* at prices just slightly above those you can expect to pay for more standard fare. Food is generally ordered at the bar and tipping is not expected.

BREAKFAST AND BRUNCH

Amsterdam cafés generally do not open early in the day, and few places serve breakfast. If all else fails, you can eat at one of the major hotels, but the most panoramic place for a continental breakfast is the sixth-floor café at **Metz & Co** (see SHOPPING, page 182), where a quiet atmosphere is guaranteed at that time of day (9.30-11.30am). The most elegant Sunday brunch in Amsterdam is served at the **Amstel Hotel** (see WHERE TO STAY, page 131).

SANDWICH BARS

Most cafés serve *broodjes* and *uitsmijters,* and excellent kosher sandwiches can be obtained at **Sal Meijer** *(Scheldestraat 45* ☎ *(020) 6731313; closed Sat; tram 12, 25 to Scheldestraat).* Try also **Betty's Coffeeshop** *(Rijnstraat 75* ☎ *(020) 6445896; tram 4, 12, 25 to Victorieplein; open Sun-Fri 10am-9pm)* for delicious nonkosher Jewish pastrami sandwiches or blintzes, or **Caffé Panini** *(Vijzelgracht 3-5* ☎ *(020) 6264939, map 6 G4; tram 16, 24, 25 to Prinsengracht),* a modern Italian-style café offering *focaccia* (Tuscan bread) and *panini* (rolls) filled with Italian cheese or Parma ham. Despite its cramped interior, **Puccini** *(Staalstraat 21* ☎ *(020) 6265474, map 10 E5; tram 9, 14 or metro to Waterlooplein)* is favored by the young and fashionable. It serves excellent sandwiches and, for those not obsessed with the body beautiful, a wicked chocolate cake.

TERRACES

Amsterdammers flock to café terraces at the slightest hint of sunshine, to drink a fashionable Belgian *Hoegaarden Witbier.* They put out a few metal chairs in front of **Het Land van Walem** and **Het Molenpad**, both off Leidsestraat, to catch the afternoon sun, but most of the big café terraces are away from the 17thC canal ring. **De Jaren** has two terraces on the Amstel waterfront that catch the sun most of the day. The spacious terrace of **Café Dantzig**, in front of the opera house, is another alluring spot to bask in the sun. **Café Vienna**, which is located inside the opera house, has a sheltered terrace for windy days. **Café Kort** *(Amstelveld 12, map 6 G5, open Wed-Mon 11am-midnight),* situated in the basement of a wooden church on a rather forgotten square, has an attractive terrace dappled with sunlight. The **Lido** has a long waterfront terrace facing w. Several cafés nearby, such as **De Leidse Bocht**, have outdoor areas for watching the setting sun. The Vondelpark has a number of cafés with terraces, including **Café Vertigo** (attached to the Filmmuseum), which boasts a grand 19thC terrace overlooking a lake.

PÂTISSERIES

The austerity of Dutch Protestantism does not permit the guiltless consumption of gargantuan cakes and pastries that goes on in neighboring Germany and Belgium, but there are a handful of small cafés in Amsterdam where those with a sweet tooth can indulge their cravings. **Banketbakkerij Lanskroon** *(Singel 385, map 10 D4)* is an austere but friendly place to ingest a few hundred calories, whereas **Berkhoff** *(Leidsestraat 46, map 5 F3)* strives, with its house pianist, to create a more elegant ambience. (See also **Pâtisserie Pompadour** in SHOPPING, page 188.)

Cafés A to Z

DE ADMIRAAL
Herengracht 319 ☎*(020) 6254334. Map 10E4. Open Mon-Fri noon-midnight; Sat 5pm-midnight. Closed Sun* ☒ *open noon-3pm; 5-10.30pm. Tram 1, 2, 5, 13, 14, 17 to Dam.*

This unexpectedly spacious *proeflokaal* in a curiously stunted 19thC neo-Renaissance building is stacked to the ceiling with *jenever* kegs big enough to conceal a cow. It is the only *proeflokaal* in Amsterdam that invites one to linger, with sofas made from *jenever* kegs, candlelit alcoves hung with tapestries, and extravagant flower arrangements. Ranged along the bar are picturesque liqueurs produced by Amsterdam's last surviving independent distillery — **De Ooievaar** in the Jordaan — with intriguing names such as *Bruidstranen* ("bride's tears," a drink with tiny gold and silver leaves, traditionally reserved for weddings), *Roosje zonder doornen* ("rose without thorns," containing petals of four types of roses) and *Papagaaiensoep* ("parrot soup," which contains various types of nut).

AMÉRICAIN
Leidseplein 28 ☎*(020) 6245322. Map 5F3. Open Sun-Wed 11am-midnight;*

Thurs-Sat 11am-1am ☒ *Tram 1, 2, 5, 6, 7, 10 to Leidseplein.*

The **American Hotel** (see WHERE TO STAY, page 130) was designed by Willem Kromhout in 1902, combining elements of Venetian Gothic and Art Nouveau. The hotel café, which overlooks LEIDSEPLEIN, brought a new grandeur to Amsterdam with its vaulted ceilings, languid murals and exotic lampshades. Although service can be brusque and the prices steep, it is difficult not to be enchanted by the opulent interior of the Américain, with its softly evocative golden light.

DE BLINCKER
St Barberenstraat 7 ☎*(020) 6271938. Map 10E5. Open 10am-1am* ☒ *open 5-9pm. Tram 4, 9, 14, 16, 24, 25 to Spui.*

The dazzling two-tier interior of the Blincker looks like a cross between an oil refinery and a greenhouse. The café is attached to the **Frascati Theater** (see NIGHTLIFE AND ENTERTAINMENT, page 171) and tends to fill with avant-garde theater goers as the evening wears on. The masks and plaster noses attached to the wall provide a touch of whimsy and the Frascati theater's well-designed posters contribute lively touches of color.

DE BRAKKE GROND

Nes 43 ☎*(020) 6229014. Map* **10***E5.*
Open 10am-1am 🚃 *Tram 4, 9, 16, 24, 25*
to Dam.

This peaceful café is attached to the
Vlaams Cultureel Centrum (Flemish
Cultural Center), which exists to promote the culture of Dutch-speaking
Belgium. The café's contribution is to
offer a range of potent Belgian beers
in a somewhat formal modern Belgian
setting. Try the creamy-topped *Grim-
bergen* from the tap; or one of the many
bottled beers, each of which is meticu-
lously poured into its proper glass.
Duvel and *Wittekop* are pleasant light
beers, while *Geuze Lambiek* from the
Brussels area is a darker and sweeter
brew. The upstairs restaurant offers a
taste of the culinary culture of Belgium,
featuring several unusual dishes prepared in beer, as well as *waterzooi,* the
traditional fish stew.

DANTZIG

Zwanenburgwal 15 ☎*(020) 6209039. Map*
11*E6. Tram 9, 14 or metro to*
Waterlooplein.

A spacious café in a corner of the new
Stadhuis/Muziektheater complex,
Dantzig features a reading corner furnished with plump leather sofas and
bookcases. The broad **terrace** facing
the Amstel is packed out at the first hint
of spring.

DE DOFFER

Runstraat 12 ☎*(020) 6226686. Map* **9***E3.*
Open noon-1am. Tram 1, 2, 5 to Spui.

De Doffer is a popular student café
whose candles flicker invitingly into the
early hours.

DE DRIE FLESCHJES

Gravenstraat 16 ☎*(020) 6248443. Map*
10*D5. Open Mon-Sat noon-8pm; closed*
Sun. Tram 1, 2, 4, 5, 9, 13, 14, 16, 17,
24, 25 to Dam.

A convivial *proeflokaal* dating from
1650, De Drie Fleschjes (The Three Jars)
is located in a bell-gabled house behind
the NIEUWE KERK. The green and cream
wooden interior is softly lit by lamps in
old brass fittings, and a solitary candle

flickers romantically on top of the beer
tap. Occasionally, the bartender will ascend a stepladder to replenish a glass
from one of 43 padlocked casks, each
marked with the name of a local business. De Drie Fleschjes' regulars range
from organizations — such as the Rabo-
bank and the Air Force's 32nd Tactical
fighter Squadron — with their own private casks, to boisterous locals and students.

DE ENGELBEWAARDER

Kloveniersburgwal 59 ☎*(020) 6253772.*
Map **10***E5. Open 11am-1am* 🚃 *Tram 4,*
9, 14, 16, 24, 25 to Spui.

A gloomy brown café on the E side of
town with monstrous Amsterdam
School-style iron lamps casting pools of
soft light. De Engelbewaarder (The
Guardian Angel) maintains its reputation as a literary café with regular readings and exhibitions. On Saturday
afternoons, particularly peaceful in this
part of town, one can quietly read the
newspaper as the affable house cat
slumbers on top of the pinball machine;
on Sunday, however, jazz sessions
draw considerable crowds. Sustaining
café food and a tempting range of beers
make this one of Amsterdam's finest
brown cafés.

EIJLDERS

Korte Leidsedwarsstraat 47 ☎*(020)*
6242704. Map **5***F3. Open noon-1am. Tram*
1, 2, 5, 6, 7, 10 to Leidseplein.

A cozy brown café just off LEIDSEPLEIN
that hits exactly the right note as far as
most Amsterdammers are concerned.
Bartenders in long aprons provide a
touch of sophistication, but locals ensure that the elegance does not get out
of hand by piling their coats and scarves
on the wrought-iron lampstands. Once
the haunt of artists and poets, Eijlders is
still the place for frequent excellent
exhibitions of modern paintings.

FRASCATI

Nes 59 ☎*(020) 6241324. Map* **10***D5.*
Open Mon-Sat 10am-1am, Sun 5pm-1am
🚃 *open 5-11pm. Tram 4, 9, 14, 16, 24,*
25 to Spui.

The dark and dingy Nes, tucked away behind Rokin, is an unlikely setting for a café as smart as Frascati, with its burgundy-red walls and gleaming brass fittings. The café belongs to the **Frascati Theater** (see NIGHTLIFE AND ENTERTAINMENT, page 171), as does the astonishing **De Blincker**, which is just around the corner, and a rather arty crowd gathers here to read *Volkskrant* theater reviews, fill in applications for grant money and gorge on enormous slices of *appelgebak*. Frascati serves food until midnight.

HET HOOGHOUDT PROEFLOKAAL

Reguliersgracht 11 ☎*(020) 6255030.*
Map **6***F5. Open noon-8pm. Closed Sun* ☎
Tram 4, 9, 14 to Rembrandtsplein.
A dark 17thC warehouse cellar with walls lined with casks, and *jenever* distilling equipment dangling from the ceiling beams. Although it calls itself a *proeflokaal,* Hooghoudt is closer to a traditional brown café, and offers such comforts as a reading table and a simple menu. During the day, it is popular with bankers from nearby offices on HERENGRACHT; after dark it is a favorite stopping point for tours of the red-light district.

HOPPE

Spui 20 ☎*(020) 6237849. Map* **10***E4.*
Open 11am-1am. Tram 1, 2, 5 to Spui.
In most civilized cities Hoppe would probably be deemed a dive, but in nostalgia-prone Amsterdam it is a cherished memento of the Golden Age. Into Hoppe's smoke-choked sawdust-strewn interior pile a curious bundle of people, from professors of literature to unemployed seamen. The décor resembles a down-at-heel doctor's waiting room, and above the bar is a vast oil painting. The crush is almost always suffocating, although on sunny days it eases slightly as the hordes of drinkers spill out into the street, conversing in anything up to six languages.

DE JAREN

Nieuwe Doelenstraat 20-22 ☎*(020)*
6255771. Map **10***E5* ☎ *open daily*

10am-1am. Tram 4, 9, 14, 16, 24, 25 to Muntplein.
This is a former bank building, recently transformed into a spacious two-tier grand café, that appeals to young and old Amsterdammers alike. The interior is fashionably bare, while the waterfront terraces on both floors are constantly crowded on sunny days. Culinary offerings at De Jaren range from the excellent *broodjes* served in the café, to delicious Italian pasta dishes and fish, which are served in the evenings on the mezzanine floor. The impressively lengthy beer list includes Grolsch, Columbus (from Amsterdam's small 't IJ brewery) and that exquisite Belgian summer brew, Hoegaarden Grand Cru.

KARPERSHOEK

Martelaarsgracht 2 ☎*(020) 6247886.*
Map **10***C5. Open 7am-1am. Tram 1, 2, 5, 13, 17 to Martelaarsgracht.*
Amsterdammers are deeply fond of the scruffy, nostalgic Karpershoek, which has stood on the old harbor front since 1629. The café is conveniently close to **Centraal Station**, and its clock is set five minutes fast to ensure that regulars don't miss the last train to Purmerend or Paris.

1E KLAS

Centraal Station (spoor 2b) ☎*(020)*
6250131. Map **11***B6* ⬛ ⬛ ⬛ *Tram 1, 2, 4, 5, 9, 13, 16, 17, 24, 25 to Centraal Station.*
The handsome Neo-Gothic interior of the former first-class café-restaurant at Amsterdam's principal rail station has been painstakingly restored to its 19thC style. With its heavy, dark wooden furniture and mellow light filtering through stained glass windows, the interior evokes the warmth of a Breitner painting. There are newspapers on wooden handles for patrons to peruse, and the coffee is excellent. You can choose from a simple *uitsmijter* in the café or a more extensive meal in the brasserie. This is an excellent place to arrange to meet someone arriving by train.

HET LAND VAN WALEM

Keizersgracht 449 ☎*(020) 6253544. Map 5F3. Open 9am-1am* ══ *Tram 1, 2, 5 to Keizersgracht.*

You have to be up with the lark to get a seat in this furiously fashionable café with the busiest espresso machine in Amsterdam. Walem's unshakable success is the result of its quietly modern interior design, excellent food and coffee, wide stock of international newspapers and periodicals, friendly service, and rear garden complete with a classical teahouse. By noon the chances of finding an unoccupied seat are slim indeed.

LUXEMBOURG

Spui 22-24 ☎*(020) 6206264. Map 10E4. Open Sun-Thurs 10am-1pm; Fri, Sat 10am-2pm. Tram 1, 2, 5 to Spui.*

A handsome café with plump chairs and artfully distressed walls to create a fusty impression of antiquity, although Luxembourg has in fact only been around a few years. Best in the morning when you can quietly peruse the international press at the large reading table, or sit in the back room watching the boats go by; rather overcrowded by the late afternoon and nigh impossible on a Saturday.

HET MOLENPAD

Prinsengracht 653 ☎*(020) 6259680. Map 5F3. Open noon-1am* ══ *open noon-3pm, 6-8pm. Tram 1, 2, 5 to Prinsengracht.*

A quiet brown café on PRINSENGRACHT, where you can sit and read a book undisturbed, offering excellent café cuisine in friendly surroundings. The mill path *(molenpad)* that ran just s of here until it was swallowed up by the Fourth Expansion of 1609 is depicted in a painting by the window. The Molenpad puts on temporary exhibitions of contemporary art. Its minuscule terrace becomes impossibly crowded on sunny afternoons.

MORLANG

Keizersgracht 451 ☎*(020) 6252681. Map 5F3. Open Mon-Sat 9am-1am; Sun 10am-1am* ══ *Tram 1, 2, 5 to Keizersgracht.*

The ground floor and basement of this 18thC canal house have been attractively furnished in Post Modern style. With a fine view and creative menu, Morlang is a pleasant alternative to the overcrowded HET LAND VAN WALEM next door.

PAPENEILAND

Prinsengracht 2 ☎*(020) 6241989. Map 10B4. Open 11am-1am. Closed Sun. Tram 3 to Haarlemmerplein.*

A friendly brown café on the edge of the JORDAAN, occupying a 17thC step gable house blessed with a picturesque view of Brouwersgracht and PRINSENGRACHT. The café's name is inscribed in ornate calligraphy on the exceptionally tall windows, while the interior is evocative of a Dutch Old Master, with Delft tiles and antique brass hanging lamps. The view from the front window was captured by Breitner on a cold winter's day in 1901 in a painting that now hangs in the AMSTERDAMS HISTORISCH MUSEUM.

PIEPER

Prinsengracht 424 ☎*(020) 6264775. Map 5F3. Open noon-1am. Tram 1, 2, 5 to Prinsengracht.*

A snug old brown café on Prinsengracht possessing that nonchalant shabbiness that Amsterdammers assiduously cultivate in their cafés, dogs, bicycles and streets. The photographs and press cuttings on the wall remind one that this unassuming wooden interior is one of Amsterdam's most venerable institutions, and the soft light that falls through the stained-glass windows invokes an ache of mellow nostalgia in the most hardened of citizens. The steep descent to the WCs is quite giddying after a tot or two of Bols.

PILSERIJ

Gravenstraat 10 ☎*(020) 6250014. Map 10D5. Open noon-1am. Tram 1, 2, 4, 5, 9, 13, 14, 16, 17, 24, 25 to Dam.*

An exquisite re-creation of a *fin de siècle* interior in what was until recently a stationery store. The scratchy jazz recordings add to the outré mood, and the elegant room at the back seems to have been expressly designed for romantic assignations beneath the wispy hanging ferns.

DE PRINS

Prinsengracht 124 ☎*(020) 6461547. Map* **9***C3. Open 11am-1am ≡ open 11am-2pm, 6-10pm. Tram 13, 14, 17 to Westermarkt.*

Beautifully located in one of a series of 18thC gable houses at the w end of Leliegracht, De Prins' tall sash windows overlook a picturesque muddle of typical Amsterdam details. De Prins looks deceptively old, but is in fact a relative newcomer to the café scene. Its décor is somewhat bizarre. The breakfast of toast, egg, ham, cheese, *ontbijtkoek* (a gingerbread specialty), pumpernickel and currant bread makes a pleasant prelude to a Sunday morning stroll through the JORDAAN.

VAN PUFFELEN

Prinsengracht 377 ☎*(020) 6246270. Map* **9***D3. Open Mon-Fri 4pm-1am; Sat, Sun 4pm-2am ≡ open 6-10pm. Tram 13, 14, 17 to Westermarkt.*

The main reason that fashionable Amsterdammers flock to this brown café, located on the western rim of the main canals, is to sample the exceptional cuisine in the restaurant at the back. Here, you can eat delicate *nouvelle cuisine* at a fraction of the price charged elsewhere. In addition, the portions are more substantial than in some of the more precious French establishments, while the atmosphere is relaxed and lively. Expect to be served dishes such as guinea fowl stuffed with pistachio nuts, or lamb with honey and lemon.

DE REIGER

Nieuwe Leliestraat 34 ☎*(020) 6247426. Map* **9***C3. Open 9am-1am ≡ Tram 13, 14, 17 to Westermarkt.*

A brown café in the JORDAAN, popular with the students and artists who now make up a large part of the population of this former working-class neighborhood. Its selection of 19thC watercolors with sentimental titles such as *Betwixt*

the Hills and *A Peaceful Backwater* seems somehow not quite in keeping with the intense artistic milieu of the Jordaan. De Reiger opens earlier than most cafés of this genre, and is a pleasantly quiet place in which to pore over the newspapers.

REIJNDERS

Leidseplein 6 ☎*(020) 6234419. Map* **5***F3. Open 9am-1am. Tram 1, 2, 5, 6, 7, 10 to Leidseplein.*

A cheerful, old-fashioned brown café on LEIDSEPLEIN that attracts a fair cross-section of Dutch society, from wise-cracking billiards players who suddenly burst into sentimental song to glittering punks. The Dutch, despite their reputation for cleanliness, seem to prefer their cafés a little dingy, and Reijnders more than obliges with its smoke-stained walls and dusty old bottles above the bar.

SCHELTEMA

Nieuwe Zijds Voorburgwal 242 ☎*(020) 6232323. Map* **10***D4. Open 8am-11pm. Tram 1, 2, 5, 13, 14, 17 to Dam.*

A comfortable, creaking, brown café that has the battered look of an old suitcase. To add to its shabby charm, Scheltema, like a slowly sinking barge, is at least 1m (3 feet) below street level. Situated next door to the former offices of the newspaper *Algemeen Handelsblad,* Scheltema was the haunt of journalists until the major newspapers fled to the suburbs. The walls are still plastered with caricatures of well-known journalists and other memorabilia, and a few nostalgic scribblers retire here at the end of the day. The learned mood is enhanced by the handsome newspaper reading table planted firmly in the middle of the café.

SCHILLER

Rembrandtsplein 26 ☎*(020) 6249846. Map* **6***F5. Open 4pm-1am. Tram 4, 9, 14 to Rembrandtsplein.*

Schiller's dilapidated covered terrace on Rembrandtsplein may be disconcerting, but it is worth venturing behind the heavy curtain to discover one of

Amsterdam's most evocative Art Deco interiors, which looks like a Roxy movie theater about to be foreclosed. The ornate lamps that smear random patches of yellow light on the marble walls and the glittering mirrors create a sense of anticipation, although the only excitement these days happens when someone accidentally sits on the broken spring of a defeated sofa. The portraits of 1930s cabaret stars on the walls were painted by the café's former owner Frits Schiller.

'T SMACKZEYL

Brouwersgracht 101 ☎*(020) 6226520. Map 10B4. Open 11am-1am. Tram 3 to Haarlemmerplein.*

This beautiful café is located in a cheerful red-faced canal house overlooking a picturesque cluster of stately bridges and creaking boats. It is a perfect café to stroll to on a Sunday morning, to read the newspaper and watch the seagulls swoop around the ships' rigging, with the strains of Vivaldi gently playing in the background.

'T SMALLE

Egelantiersgracht 12 ☎*(020) 6239617. Map 9C3. Open 11am-1am. Tram 13, 14, 17 to Westermarkt.*

This café occupies an ivy-covered 18thC house in the s of the JORDAAN overlooking Egelantiersgracht. The interior — originally the distillery and tasting house of Pieter Hoppe — has been tastefully restored, and the golden light that filters through the stained-glass windows evokes the mellow hue of a Rembrandt painting. 't Smalle is especially attractive on dark winter evenings, with candles flickering at every table. The only drawback is that, as such a congenial place, it is almost invariably bursting at the seams.

SMITS KOFFIEHUIS

Stationsplein 10 ☎*(020) 6233777. Map 11B6. Open Mon-Sat 8am-8.30pm; Sun 9am-8.30pm* ═ *Tram 1, 2, 4, 5, 9, 13, 16, 17, 24, 25 to Centraal Station.*

Stepping out of Centraal Station into the cheerful confusion of trams, bicycles and street musicians, the first building to catch your eye is the ornate, wooden Smits Koffiehuis, formerly a tram station and now a tourist information office and café-restaurant. The attractive Old Dutch-style *koffiehuis* is an ideal place to catch your breath after a long journey or to meet friends off the train, and serves good coffee and reasonably priced food. In summer the café spills out onto a **floating terrace** overlooking the former harbor front.

DE SMOESHAAN

Leidsekade 90 ☎*(020) 6250368. Map 5F2. Open 10am-1am* ═ *Tram 1, 2, 5, 6, 7, 10 to Leidseplein.*

Actors and actresses gather in this very dark and simple brown café to launch new productions or mourn those that have died. There is a good and inexpensive café menu, and a slightly more expensive restaurant upstairs (see EATING AND DRINKING).

TISFRIS

St Antoniesbreestraat 142 ☎*(020) 6220472. Map 11E6. Open 11am-2am* ═ *open 6-9.30pm. Tram 9, 14 to Waterlooplein.*

Situated in Theo Bosch's Pentagon complex in the NIEUWMARKT district (where some of Amsterdam's best modern architecture can be found), this café is an intriguing modern design on three levels, with attractive views of canals through a multitude of windows. The food is above average.

IN DE WILDEMAN

Kolksteeg 3 ☎*(020) 6382348. Map 11C6. Open noon-1am. Closed Sun. Tram 1, 2, 5, 13, 17 to N. Z. Kolk.*

The Dutch Association for the Protection of Historical Monuments, which occupies a nearby 17thC corn exchange, should be proud of its local *bierproeflokaal* (beer-tasting house). Located in a medieval alley that is stubbornly resistant to change, In De Wildeman is a handsomely restored shop with lofty windows, wood-paneled walls and magnificent brass lamps. The neat rows of jars on the shelves behind the counter and the gleaming tiled floor create something of the air of a pharmacy, but the regulars generally take the chill off the place. Fashionable young Amsterdammers flock here to sample Rodenbach, De Koninck and other distinguished Belgian beers.

WILDSCHUT

Roelof Hartplein 1 ☎*(020) 6768220. Map 5/3. Open 9am-2.45am ☲ open noon-3.30pm, 6-10pm. Tram 3, 5, 12, 24 to Roelof Hartplein.*

The abandoned cinema fittings that decorate this café create a nostalgic 1930s interior reminiscent of the moody paintings of Edward Hopper. Art Deco lamps throw dim pools of yellowish light on antique theater seats, as languid vocalists sing husky songs of the 1930s in the background. The location is appropriate: Wildshut's curving plate-glass windows overlook Roelof Hartplein, that dazzling architectural showpiece of the late 1920s, which was intended as a prelude to the brave new world of Amsterdam Zuid. After a fortifying *uitsmijter*, perhaps washed down with a strong espresso, you might be ready to enjoy a stroll through the streets of fanciful workers' housing that lie to the s of here.

DE IJSBREKER

Weesperzijde 23 ☎*(020) 6653014. Map 7H7. Open 10am-1am. Tram 6, 7, 10, snel-tram 51 or metro to Weesperplein.*

This is an elegant *fin de siècle* café with mirrors, murals and slightly down-at-heel Art Nouveau lamps. The IJsbreker's excellent *warme chocolade* is wonderfully warming on winter days when the Amstel is frozen. The café is attached to a center for contemporary music (see NIGHTLIFE AND ENTERTAINMENT, page 168.)

Amsterdam: nightlife and entertainment

Amsterdam by night

Dutch towns can be sadly staid and lifeless after hours, due to the combination of unreliable weather and Protestant morals, but Amsterdam remains vibrant 24 hours a day. The tawdry delights of its famous red-light district are only a minor entry on the city's after-dark menu. Amsterdam's cultural venues, from concert hall to blues club, can boast programs to equal anything in Europe.

The main attractions for visitors are classical music at the **Concertgebouw**, opera and dance at the **Muziektheater**, cinemas, pop concerts and jazz cafés. The **Amsterdams Uit Buro** (*Leidseplein 26* ☎ *(020) 6211211* 𝗔𝗘 ◉ ◉ 𝘝𝘐𝘚𝘈 *map 5F3)* handles reservations for concerts, theater and dance, and publishes a monthly listing of events in the free *Uitkrant*. For mainstream, radical and fringe events, consult the monthly English-language listings magazine *City Life*.

Performing arts

The world's greatest orchestras give regular performances in Amsterdam's **Concertgebouw** and enthralling ballets are staged in the new **Muziektheater** (illustrated on page 168). But theater and music spill out into the streets of Amsterdam, and crowds will gather on the Dam or Leidseplein just to watch a mime act or listen to a wild poet. The tolerant spirit of Amsterdam favors an infinite variety of song, dance and drama. Some of it is official, but many performances happen spontaneously.

CARILLON CONCERTS

Amsterdam's 17thC carillon bells provide delightful background music as one wanders through the streets. The bells normally chime automatically every 15 minutes, but weekly recitals are given by professional players whose repertoire ranges from national anthems to nursery rhymes. Plan your day to be in the neighborhood of a church during a recital. Performances take place at the **Westerkerk** on Tuesdays from noon to 1pm, the **Zuiderkerk** on Thursdays from 10 to 11am, the **Munttoren** on Fridays from noon to 1pm and the **Oude Kerk** on Saturdays from 4 to 5pm.

CINEMA

Amsterdammers flock to the city's 40 movie theaters, which range in style from romantic Art Deco buildings to modern multiple-screen complexes. Films are almost always shown in the original language with Dutch subtitles, apart from children's matinees and movies marked *Nederlands gesproken* (Dutch spoken). Programs change on Thursday and most cafés display the current listings. For insomniacs, there are *Nacht-voorstellingen* (night screenings), beginning around midnight.

ALFA

Hirschgebouw, Leidseplein ☎*(020) 6278806. Map 5F3. Tram 1, 2, 5, 6, 7, 10 to Leidseplein.*

Four very comfortable theaters showing an interesting selection of international movies. The Alfa is tucked into the back of a former department store, which was modeled on Selfridges of London.

ALHAMBRA

Weteringschans 134 ☎*(020) 6233192. Map 7H6. Tram 4, 6, 7, 10 to Frederiksplein.*

This slightly down-at-heel Art Deco movie theater shows good foreign films.

BELLEVUE CINERAMA

Marnixstraat 400 ☎*(020) 6234876. Map 5F3. Tram 1, 2, 5, 6, 7, 10 to Leidseplein.*
Giant screens with Dolby stereo.

CINEAC

Reguliersbreestraat 31 ☎*(020) 6243639. Map 6F5. Tram 4, 9, 14, 16, 24, 25 to Muntplein.*

Duiker's 1934 functionalist answer to Tuschinski across the street. Notice the projectionist's room above the entrance.

CINECENTER

Lijnbaansgracht 236 ☎*(020) 6236615. Map 5F3. Tram 1, 2, 5, 6, 7, 10 to Leidseplein.*

A four-theater complex with an attractive café.

CITY

Kleine Gartmanplantsoen 13-25 ☎*(020) 6234579. Map 5F3. Tram 1, 2, 5, 6, 7, 10 to Leidseplein.*

A six-theater complex showing mainstream movies. The tower is all that remains of the original 1935 cinema designed by Jan Wils.

DESMET

Plantage Middenlaan 4a ☎*(020) 6273434. Map 7F7. Tram 7, 9, 14 to Plantage Kerklaan; sneltram 51 or metro to Waterlooplein.*

A small Art Deco movie theater with a program of avant-garde films and old favorites.

FILMMUSEUM

Vondelpark 3 ☎*(020) 5891400. Map 5G1. Tram 1, 2, 5, 6 to Eerste Constantijn Huygensstraat; tram 3, 12 to Overtoom.*

The avant-garde Filmmuseum is incongruously located in a grand pavilion that was built as a fashionable café in the heady 1880s. Movies shown here vary from vintage German Expressionism to W.C. Fields comedies.

KRITERION

Roetersstraat 170 ☎*(020) 6231708. Map 8G8. Tram 6, 7, 10 to Roetersstraat.*

Two-theater complex showing avant-garde movies hot from the Berlin or Venice film festivals. The Kriterion also has a very attractive café. The sort of movie theater that can be counted on to show *Death in Venice* at least once a year.

THE MOVIES

Haarlemmerdijk 161 ☎*(020) 6245790. Tram 3 to Haarlemmerplein.*

An attractive three-theater complex built in 1912 in Egyptian Art Deco style. The program offers a good selection of international movies, with an emphasis on Latin countries.

RIALTO

Ceintuurbaan 338 ☎(020) 6623488. Map 7I6. Tram 3 to Tweede van der Helststraat.
A two-screen theater showing avant-garde political movies. The Rialto also screens children's matinees on Wednesday and Saturday, which are normally in Dutch.

TUSCHINSKI

Reguliersbreestraat 26 ☎(020) 6262633. Map 6F5. Tram 4, 9, 14, 16, 24, 25 to Muntplein.
Amsterdam's most opulent Art Deco movie theater, with six screens showing international successes. (See SIGHTS, page 122).

CLASSICAL AND MODERN MUSIC

The obvious advantage of music is the absence of a language barrier, and Amsterdam offers a broad spectrum of styles from traditional opera to experimental modern music.

BETHANIENKLOOSTER

Barndesteeg 4-6 ☎(020) 6177500. Map 11D6. Sneltram 51 or metro to Nieuwmarkt.
Free concerts of classical and modern chamber music are held in the former nuns' dormitory of a restored 15thC convent on the edge of the red-light district. Friday at 12.30pm.

BEURS VAN BERLAGE

243 Damrak ☎(020) 6270466. Map 10C5. Box office open Tues-Sat 12.30-6pm. Tram 4, 9, 16, 24, 25 to Dam.
Concerts by the **Dutch Philharmonic Orchestra** (Het Nederlands Philharmonisch Orkest) and the **Dutch Chamber Orchestra** (Het Nederlands Kamerorkest) within the former 1903 stock exchange building designed by Berlage (pictured on page 22).

CRISTOFORI

Prinsengracht 583 ☎(020) 6268485 ⊠(020) 6272080. Map 9E3. Tram 1, 2, 5 to Prinsengracht.
Occasional piano recitals and chamber concerts in a salon above a piano shop.

CONCERTGEBOUW

Concertgebouwplein 2-6 ☎(020) 6718345. Map 5H2 [AE] [⊕] [●] [VISA] ⑤. Box office open 10am-3pm. Tram 3, 5, 12, 16 to Museumplein.
The elegant Classical Concertgebouw (concert hall) is home to Holland's foremost orchestra, the **Concertgebouw-orkest**, directed by Riccardo Chailly. Recently restored at enormous cost, the concert hall built in 1888 by A. L. van

Gendt boasts faultless acoustics. Watch out for special events such as the free lunchtime concerts (every Wednesday at 12.30pm in the intimate Kleine Zaal). Formal dress is not obligatory for Concertgebouw concerts, and younger people tend to wear colorful, casual clothes.

ENGELSE KERK

Begijnhof 48 (entrance on Spui) ☎(020) 6249665. Map 10E4. Tram 1, 2, 4, 5, 9, 14, 16, 24, 25 to Spui.
Evening concerts in a neat little church in the center of Amsterdam where the Pilgrim Fathers once worshiped.

HET MUZIEKTHEATER

Amstel 3 ☎(020) 6255455. Map 7F6 ⑤ Tram 9, 14, sneltram 51 or metro to Waterlooplein
With its view of the river Amstel, and its varied program of classical and modern opera and ballet, Amsterdam's Muziektheater (illustrated below), which opened in 1986, has brought renewed life to the former Jewish area of Amsterdam. Home to the national ballet (**Het Nationale Ballet**) and the Dutch opera company (**De Nederlandse Opera**), the Muziektheater also features performances by major foreign companies on tour. Free concerts of chamber music on Tues from 12.30-1pm in the intimate Boekmanzaal.

DE NIEUWE KERK

Dam ☎(020) 6268168. Map 10D4. Open Mon-Fri 9am-5pm. Tram 1, 2, 4, 5, 9, 13,

167

14, 16, 17, 24, 25 to Dam.
Occasional organ concerts.

OUDE KERK
Oude Kerksplein 1 ☎*(020) 6249183. Map*
10*D5. Tram 4, 9, 16, 24, 25 to Dam, then
a 5min walk.*
Occasional organ concerts are held in
Amsterdam's oldest (and coldest)
church.

KOEPELZAAL
Kattengat 1 ☎*(020) 6239896 Map* **10***C5.
Tram 1, 2, 5, 13, 17 to Martelaarsgracht.*
Sunday concerts by small ensembles at
11am in an unusual 17thC round Classi-
cal church.

STEDELIJK MUSEUM
Paulus Potterstraat 13 ☎*(020) 5732911.
Map* **5***H2 Tram 2, 3, 5, 12 to Van
Baerlestraat.*
Contemporary music concerts take
place on Saturday at 3pm, from Septem-
ber to June.

SWEELINCK CONSERVATORIUM
Van Baerlestraat 27 ☎*(020) 6647641
Map* **5***H2 Tram 2, 3, 5, 12 to Van
Baerlestraat.*

Free classical concerts by music students.

TROPENINSTITUUT
Mauritskade 63 ☎*(020) 5688500. Map*
8*G9. Tram 9, 10 to Mauritskade.*
Occasional performances of non-Western dance and music in the main hall of
the TROPENMUSEUM.

WAALSE KERK
Oude Zijds Achterburgwal 157. Map **10***D5.
Tram 4, 9, 16, 24, 25 to Dam, then a 5min
walk.*
Occasional chamber music concerts.

DE IJSBREKER
Weesperzijde 23 ☎*(020) 6681805. Map*
7*H7. Tram 6, 7, 10, sneltram 51 or metro
to Weesperplein.*
The photographs on the walls of the
IJsbreker café give an idea of what to
expect in this small concert hall specializing in contemporary music by Dutch
and international composers. The ascetic minimalism of much of the work
performed here seems almost a rebuke
to the opulent and eclectic 19thC architecture to be found nearby on this once-
fashionable stretch of the Amstel river.

The **Muziektheater**

CULTURAL INSTITUTES
As a major international city, Amsterdam has its fair share of cultural institutes, all of which act as a showcase for the cultures of their
various countries. **The British Council** *(Keizersgracht 343* ☎*(020)
6223644, map* **9***E3, tram 1, 2, 5 to Keizersgracht)* shows British films,
and the **Maison Descartes** boasts a bistro offering French *cuisine
bourgeoise* in a tiled kitchen *(Vijzelgracht 2* ☎*(020) 6224936, map*
6*G4, tram 16, 24, 25 to Prinsengracht)*. German movies are screened

at the **Goethe Institut** *(Herengracht 470* ☎ *(020) 6230421, map 6 F4, tram 16, 24, 25 to Herengracht)*. Occasional Italian cultural events are held at the **Istituto Italiano di Cultura** *(Keizersgracht 564* ☎ *(020) 6265314, map 6 F4, tram 1, 2, 5 to Keizersgracht)*, while the Flemish region of Belgium promotes Dutch-language theater and contemporary art at **De Brakke Grond** *(Nes 45 (020) 6266866, map 10 D5, tram 4, 9, 14, 16, 24, 25 to Dam)*.

JAZZ, BLUES, FOLK, ROCK, LATIN AND AFRICAN MUSIC

Eclectic Amsterdammers soak up sensual blues or melancholy folk in dark cafés that stay open long after the last tram has gone. The **Jazz-line** *(*☎*(020) 6267764)* gives recorded information (in Dutch) on forthcoming jazz concerts.

CAFÉ ALTO
Korte Leidsedwarsstraat 115 ☎*(020) 6263249. Map 5 F3. Open 9pm-2am (Fri, Sat to 3am). Tram 1, 2, 5, 6, 7, 10 to Leidseplein.*
This intimate, cosmopolitan jazz café offers a tranquil escape from the crowds thronging Leidseplein.

BAMBOO BAR
Lange Leidsedwarsstraat 64 ☎*(020) 6243993. Map 5 F3. Open 9pm-3am (Fri, Sat to 4am). Concerts begin 10pm. Tram 1, 2, 5, 6, 7, 10 to Leidseplein.*
Tropical décor, friendly atmosphere and live bands.

BIMHUIS
Oude Schans 73-77 ☎*(020) 6231361. Map 11 E6. Concerts Thurs-Sat at 9pm. Café open Mon-Thurs 8pm-2am; Fri, Sat 8pm-3am (Thurs-Sat 8pm-midnight, café open to ticket holders only). Tram 9, 14, sneltram 51 or metro to Waterlooplein.*
The Bimhuis is a bright, crisp jazz center on the E side of town, not far from the REMBRANDTHUIS. It was set up in the 1970s by the Professional Jazz Musicians' Union — *Beroepsvereniging van Improviserende Musici (BIM)* — in a former warehouse. Concerts are given from Thursday to Saturday in the spacious amphitheater, while informal workshops featuring new musicians take place from Monday to Wednesday. The café offers a good range of beers, cocktails and Indonesian snacks such as *lemper* (rice mixed with spiced meat) and *pisang goreng* (fried banana).

DE ENGELBEWAARDER
Kloveniersburgwal 59 ☎*(020) 6253772. Map 10 E5. Open 11am-1am. Tram 9, 14 to Waterlooplein; sneltram 51 or metro to Nieuwmarkt.*
This literary brown café draws crowds of eager fans to its jazz sessions every Sunday afternoon from 4-7pm. (See CAFÉS, page 159)

JOSEPH LAM JAZZCLUB
Van Diemenstraat 242 ☎*(020) 6228086. Open Sat 9pm-3am; Sun 9pm-2am. Tram 3 to Zoutkeetsgracht (terminus).*
Atmospheric Dixieland jazz club in a remote part of the old harbor, best reached by taxi.

DE KONINGSHUT
Spuistraat 269 ☎*(020) 6264276. Map 10 E4. Open 2.30pm-1am. Tram 1, 2, 5 to Spui.*
Piano music on Monday from 6-8pm in a jovial Brueghelian interior, with antique beer tankards, jawbones and other curious paraphernalia dangling from the roof beams.

KORSAKOFF
Lijnbaansgracht 160 ☎*(020) 6257854. Map 9 E2. Open Mon-Sat 11pm-3am. Tram 7, 10, 17 to Elandsgracht.*
This former blues café now reverberates to the sounds of hard punk rock bands.

MILES

Lijnbaansgracht 163 ☎*(020) 6268910.*
Map 9E2. Open Sun-Thurs 10pm-4am; Fri,
Sat 10pm-5am. Tram 7, 10, 17 to
Elandsgracht.

Reggae, rock and jazz concerts begin
most evenings around 10.30pm in this
dark dive at the w limit of the Jordaan.
The room at the back may bear an un-
easy resemblance to Edward Kienholz's
horrific *Beanery* in the STEDELIJK MUSEUM
(see SIGHTS, page 120), but the atmosphere is friendly and relaxed.

PIANOBAR LE MAXIM

Leidsekruisstraat 35 ☎*(020) 6241920.*
Map 5F3. Open 9pm-3am (Fri, Sat to 4am).
Tram 1, 2, 5, 6, 7, 10 to Leidseplein.

The essential piano bar for those who
like to sing along to golden oldies.

RUM RUNNERS

Prinsengracht 277 ☎*(020) 6274079. Map*
9C3. Restaurant open Sun-Thurs 4-11pm;
Fri, Sat noon-midnight. Tram 13, 14, 17 to
Westermarkt.

Rum Runners is a Caribbean restaurant,
where the food is given added spice by
the hot sounds of Latin American bands
on Sunday at 4pm.

THE STRING

Nes 98 ☎*(020) 6259015. Map **10E5**.*
Open 8pm-1am. Tram 4, 9, 14, 16, 24, 25
to Spui.

The String is an intimate folk and blues
café, where acoustic guitarists and jazz
pianists perform in front of a small but
discerning group of connoisseurs,
every night of the week from about
9.30pm.

MULTIPURPOSE/ALTERNATIVE CENTERS

The heady days of flower-power live on for a certain breed of Amsterdammer, as proven by the survival of these peaceful backwaters of
1960s idealism, featuring programs of pop, poetry and politics.

DE MEERVAART

Osdorpplein 205 ☎*(020) 6107393. Tram*
1 to Osdorpplein.

A modern cultural center in an attractive
garden city on the w edge of Amsterdam. Specialties include jazz, blues and
pop music, as well as poetry.

MELKWEG

Lijnbaansgracht 234a ☎*(020) 6241777.*
Map 5F3. Open Wed-Fri 7.30pm-12.30am;
Sat, Sun 4pm-1.30am. Closed Mon, Tues.
Tram 1, 2, 5, 6, 7, 10 to Leidseplein.

Occupying a large converted dairy off
Leidseplein, the Melkweg (Milky Way)
is a somewhat fossilized relic of the
1970s, where you can watch movies,
listen to live bands or buy soft drugs
from a quaint shop that resembles an
old-fashioned grocery store. Dance
groups frequently perform innovative
works in the **Fonteinzaal**, while solemn European theater is staged in the
Nieuwe Vleugel. Perhaps the most
evocative corner of the complex is the
tearoom on the top floor, which has the
languid atmosphere of a party that has

gone on too long. The Melkweg café
(decorated like a 1950s milk bar) stays
open during the day *(open Wed-Sun*
10am-6pm; entrance at Marnixstraat
405). However, at night the complex is
only accessible by means of an iron
drawbridge, which is to be found behind the Stadsschouwburg. Visitors
must buy a membership ticket at the
door, valid for one month.

PARADISO

Weteringschans 6-8 ☎*(020) 6264521.*
Map 5G3. Tram 1, 2, 5, 6, 7, 10 to
Leidseplein.

Famous since the Sixties, this 19thC church,
repainted black, is Amsterdam's main spot
for pop, rock, blues and reggae.

VONDELPARK

Map 5G1. Tram 1, 2, 5, 6, 7, 10 to
Leidseplein.

In the summer months, concerts, poetry
readings and plays are held in the Vondelpark, in the open-air theater close to
the round blue teahouse. This is a pleasant place to come on fine evenings.

THEATER AND DANCE

The notorious "tomato protest" in 1969, when the cast in a production of Shakespeare's *The Tempest* at the **Stadsschouwburg** was bombarded with tomatoes, signaled the end of conventional theater in Amsterdam. However, if you are interested in experimental, fringe drama and dance, Amsterdam has a flourishing alternative circuit, which features Dutch and foreign companies. A glance at the Uit Buro's files of reviews might give you an idea of what is being offered. Bear in mind that plays can be produced in Dutch, English, French or German.

KONINKLIJK THEATER CARRÉ

Amstel 115-125 ☎*(020) 6225225. Map* **7G6.** *Tram 6, 7, 10, sneltram 51 or metro to Weesperplein.*

Opened in 1887 as a circus, this imposing Dutch Renaissance building on the Amstel still occasionally features international circus troupes, as well as ballet, modern dance, theater and cabaret.

FELIX MERITIS

Keizersgracht 324 ☎*(020) 6231311. Map* **9E3** *Tram 13, 14, 17 to Westermarkt.*

A center of experimental drama, film and dance, located in the splendid 18thC Neoclassical temple of the *Felix Meritis* society. Brahms, Schumann and Grieg were among the 19thC Romantics who performed in this building, where now a stern Minimalist philosophy prevails.

FRASCATI

Nes 63 ☎*(020) 6235723. Map* **10E5** *Tram 4, 9, 14, 16, 24, 25 to Spui.*

Alternative theater, dance and music form the mainstay of the program at Frascati.

DE KLEINE KOMEDIE

Amstel 56-58 ☎*(020) 6240534. Map* **6F5.** *Tram 4, 9, 14 to Rembrandtsplein.*

Established in the 18thC as a French theater, De Kleine Komedie now features a mixed program of Dutch theater, cabaret and opera.

NIEUWE DE LA MAR

Marnixstraat 404 ☎*(020) 6233462. Map* **5F2.** *Tram 1, 2, 5, 6, 7, 10 to Leidseplein.*

Cabaret, musicals and mainstream Dutch theater.

SOETERIJN

Linnaeusstraat 2 ☎*(020) 5688500. Map* **8G9.** *Tram 9, 10 to Mauritskade.*

A pleasant, small theater attached to the TROPENMUSEUM and featuring unusual and often exotic programs of non-Western dance, music, theater and film.

STADSSCHOUWBURG

Leidseplein 26 ☎*(020) 6242311. Map* **5F3.** *Tram 1, 2, 5, 6, 7, 10 to Leidseplein.*

This gloriously ornate neo-Renaissance theater on Leidseplein, which was shaken to the foundations by the famous "tomato protest" of 1969, now offers an indecisive mixture of traditional and contemporary theater and dance.

STALHOUDERIJ

Eerste Bloemdwarsstraat 4 ☎*(020) 6202202. Map* **9D3.** *Tram 13, 14, 17 to Westermarkt.*

Amsterdam's resident English-language theater company. Expect radical plays and bare sets.

Nightlife

Amsterdam is a pulsating city at night, and the focus of entertainment and culture of all kinds is **Leidseplein**, where many of Amsterdam's theaters, cinemas, discos, clubs and cafés are located. **Rembrandts-plein** forms a second, somewhat less frenetic, hub of activity, with its movie theaters, bars and nightclubs.

Violence can erupt in any large city, and you should try to avoid dangerous situations after dark in Amsterdam. Keep to busy streets if you are alone and dive into the nearest café to phone for a taxi if you feel threatened.

BARS

Although bars may lack the Bohemian charm of brown cafés, they can be quiet and comfortable places for cocktails and conversation.

AMSTEL HOTEL BAR
Prof. Tulpplein 1 ☎*(020) 6226060. Map 7G7* 🆎 🔟 🔟 📳 *Open 9am-1am. Tram 6, 7, 10 to Oosteinde.*
A quiet place for a riverside drink. Live piano music lends a touch of romance to the setting.

CIEL BLEU
Okura Hotel (23rd floor), Ferdinand Bolstraat 333 ☎*(020) 6787111. Map 6J4* 🆎 🔟 🔟 📳 *Open 6pm-1am. Tram 12, 25 to Cornelis Troostplein.*
The Okura Hotel's 23rd-floor bar is the ideal place to sip cocktails and listen to the house pianist as the sun sinks behind the western suburbs.

CONTINENTAL BODEGA
Lijnbaansgracht 246 ☎*(020) 6239098. Map 5G3. Open Mon-Sat 3-11pm. Tram 1, 2, 5, 6, 7, 10 to Leidseplein.*
A cask-filled specialized sherry bar with a resident piano player who performs from 7-11pm.

PASTORIE
SAS Royal Hotel, Rusland 17 ☎*(020) 6231231. Map 10E5. Open daily 11am-1am (Fri, Sat to 2am). Tram 4, 9, 14, 16, 24, 25 to Spui.*
The bar of the SAS Royal hotel, located in a former parsonage, is furnished in a handsome Old Dutch style with wooden cabinets, gilt-framed mirrors and chandeliers. You can sit by the fire-place where the pastor once toasted his toes, and listen to the house pianist playing old favorites *(6-10.30pm)*. Exotic cocktails and fashionable Belgian beers are served by one of the best barmen in town; however, the Pastorie is worth a visit after dark if only to wander through the dramatically spotlit hotel atrium.

HARRY'S AMERICAN BAR
Spuistraat 285 ☎*(020) 6244384. Map 10E4. Open Mon-Thurs 5pm-1am; Fri, Sat 5pm-2am; Sun 9pm-1am. Tram 1, 2, 5 to Spui.*
This bar is Amsterdam's answer to the celebrated watering-hole of Americans in Paris. A selection of good cocktails is served.

LIBRARY BAR
Marriott Hotel, Stadhouderskade 19-21 ☎*(020) 6075555. Map 5G2* 🆎 🔟 🔟 📳 *Open noon-1am. Tram 1, 2, 5, 6, 7, 10 to Leidseplein.*
As its name suggests, the Library Bar of the Marriott Hotel is lined with old books, though the bias toward works by minor 19thC Dutch theologians may not be to everyone's taste.

PULITZER BAR
Keizersgracht 234 ☎*(020) 5235235. Map 9D3* 🆎 🔟 🔟 📳 *Open 11am-1am. Tram 13, 14, 17 to Westermarkt.*
This pleasant bar, which overlooks Keizersgracht, is decorated with 17thC maps and prints.

CASINOS

Casinos are viewed with some suspicion by the Dutch, and the country's gamblers are confined to the eight official establishments run by Holland Casinos. The Dutch would appear to be shaking off their inhibitions, however, and the new **Amsterdam Lido** *(Max Euweplein 62 ☎(020) 6201006, map 5G3, open 2pm-2am)* claims to be the largest in Europe. Behind the gleaming marble facade on the Singelgracht, there are roulette tables, a bingo hall, and ranks of gaming machines. The Lido has a smart restaurant and a cheaper waterfront brasserie for those who, after a trip to the tables, have rather less money to flaunt.

DISCOS

Discos in the **Leidseplein** area tend to be crammed to capacity with the under-30s, while older Amsterdammers prefer the more sedately sophisticated places to be found slightly off the beaten track. Some of Amsterdam's discos are, strictly speaking, private clubs and will only admit you, if at all, after you have purchased a temporary membership. Most discos do not really begin to swing until about 1am, after the cafés have closed.

BOSTON CLUB

Kattengat 1 ☎(020) 6245561. Map 10B5. Open 10pm-5am. Tram 1, 2, 5, 13, 17 to Martelaarsgracht.

Exclusive disco for mature swingers, in the basement of the Ramada Renaissance Hotel.

HOMOLULU

Kerkstraat 23 ☎(020) 6246387. Map 5F3. Open Sun-Thurs 10pm-4am; Fri, Sat 10pm-5am. Tram 1, 2, 5, 6, 7, 10 to Leidseplein.

Homolulu is a popular gay disco, with a restaurant.

JULIANA'S

Hilton Hotel, Apollolaan 138 ☎(020) 6737313. Open Sun-Thurs 10pm-4am; Fri, Sat 10pm-5am. Tram 16 to Emmastraat.

This elite discotheque, named after the former queen of the Netherlands, occupies a prime spot in the Amsterdam Hilton.

MAZZO

Rozengracht 114 ☎(020) 6267500. Map 9D3. Open Sun-Thurs 11pm-4am; Fri, Sat 11pm-5am. Tram 13, 14, 17 to Westermarkt.

Mazzo's wall-to-wall audiovisual entertainment makes it popular with Amsterdam's avant-garde artists, musicians and fashion designers, who arrive on old black bicycles from nearby ateliers in the Jordaan.

ODEON

Singel 460 ☎(020) 6249711. Map 10E4. Open Sun-Thurs 10pm-4am; Fri, Sat 10pm-5am. Tram 1, 2, 5 to Koningsplein.

In 1782 John Adams negotiated the first US loan to the Netherlands in this elegant 17thC neck gable house designed by Philips Vingboons. The building is now used as a discotheque and theatre. The stately *voorkamer* (front room), with its painted Baroque ceiling, is now a late-night bar.

36 OP DE SCHAAL VAN RICHTER

Reguliersdwarsstraat 36 ☎(020) 6261573. Map 6F4. Open Sun-Thurs 11.30pm-4am; Fri, Sat 11.30pm-5am. Tram 4, 9, 14, 16, 24, 25 to Muntplein.

Richter's decor of shattered mirrors and brick rubble is intended to suggest the aftermath of an earthquake measuring a theoretically impossible 36 on the Richter scale. Jazz on Sunday.

RED-LIGHT DISTRICT

Amsterdam has been famous since the 17thC for its red-light district, known as **De Walletjes** after the two canals, **Oude Zijds Voorburgwal** and **Oude Zijds Achterburgwal**, where most of the visible prostitution goes on. With a frankness that is perhaps unique to Amsterdam, sexily dressed women sit in the front windows of 17thC gable houses, with every pimple and dimple visible in the strong glow of red neon.

This superlative exhibitionism has turned Amsterdam's red-light district into a major tourist attraction, and large bus parties are taken on what are reassuringly called "guided and guarded tours" through the maze of gaudy streets, like Dante being led through the Inferno. Some people may find the sexual explicitness offensive, but there is perhaps also a lighter side to it all, as in the ghastly bad taste of the brothel furnishings, and the sex shop signs announcing with the simple honesty of a corner grocery store: "100 percent guaranteed porn." The women, too, have all the gifts of small entrepreneurs, and each "service" is performed at a fixed price.

Because of its popularity, the red-light district is fairly safe at night. If you do decide to visit it, however, keep to the crowded streets and, if you feel at all threatened, head into the nearest café.

Nightclubs featuring old-fashioned strip shows are mainly found on Thorbeckeplein; the statue of Thorbecke, who drafted the 19thC constitution of the Netherlands, discreetly faces away from the inviting neon signs.

Two amiable and approachable Dutch women recently opened a condom shop on the edge of the red-light district. Tasteful and tactful, the **Condomerie Het Gulden Vlies** (*Warmoesstraat 141, map 10D5, closed Feb*) stocks a wide range of sheaths, from the basic to the bizarre.

Amsterdam: shopping

Where to go

Famous for diamonds, antiques and tulips, Amsterdam also boasts numerous excellent fashion boutiques, jewelers and bookstores, together with specialized shops devoted exclusively to such items as toothbrushes, Indian jewelry, bottled beers, beads and herbs.

The main shopping area runs from Centraal Station to Muntplein, with large department stores strung along **Damrak** and **Rokin**, while smaller chain stores are located along **Nieuwendijk** and **Kalverstraat**. Nieuwendijk has a young, rebellious image, while Kalverstraat is slightly more exclusive. **P. C. Hooftstraat** maintains its upscale allure with grim determination. Its elegant clothes boutiques draw rich clients from the suburbs, who like to double-park their Mercedes in front of the shops. The former 19thC Post Office has been converted into the **Magna Plaza** shopping center *(Nieuwe Zijds Voorburgwal 182, map10 D4)* in the hope of luring smart shops back to the old center.

The true genius of Amsterdam shines through in the small, specialized boutiques that tend to be somewhat off the beaten track. One of the best areas to explore is the series of parallel streets running w from **Spuistraat** to **Prinsengracht**. These streets lead into the **Jordaan**, which contains a mixture of fashionable boutiques and run-down bric-à-brac shops.

TAX-FREE SHOPPING

People buying goods in the Netherlands may be entitled to a **refund** of the 20 percent sales tax (*b.t.w.* in Dutch) they have paid, provided that the goods cost more than Fl.890 and the buyer can show that the item was exported unused from the Netherlands almost immediately. Non-EC residents should obtain a *certificaat van uitvoer OB90* (export certificate) from the shop, which they should hand to the customs officer. This will be returned to the shop, which will then refund the tax to the customer.

For the present, residents of other EC countries taking goods out of the Netherlands merely require proof of importing the goods into the country of destination. This should be sent to the shop to obtain a refund of tax. Some shops, such as those at **Schiphol Airport**, will deduct tax on the spot. With the completion of the Single European Market at the end of 1992, tax-free shopping for EC citizens is expected to be phased out gradually.

ANTIQUES

Rokin is the main center for antique dealers, but there is also a cluster of less forbidding shops on **Nieuwe Spiegelstraat**, which runs from the Rijksmuseum to the Golden Bend on Herengracht. It is worth shopping around before making a major purchase, and obtaining a signed **certificate of authenticity** from the dealer.

AMSTERDAM ANTIQUES GALLERY
Nieuwe Spiegelstraat 34 ☎*(020) 6253371. Map 6F4* 🆎 🔂 🏧
Twelve antique dealers gathered under one roof, offering icons, dolls, 19thC paintings and pieces of 16thC Spanish armor.

JAN BEST
Keizersgracht 357 ☎*(020) 6232736. Map 9E3.*
This shop specializes in Art Nouveau and Art Deco lamps.

COUZIJN SIMONS
Prinsengracht 578 ☎*(020) 6232654. Map 6G4* 🆎 🔂 🏧
Antique dolls and toys are sold in a beautiful 18thC interior.

DEGENAAR EN BIJLEVELD
Nieuwe Spiegelstraat 45-60 ☎*(020) 6277774. Map 6F4* 🆎 🔂 🏧
Antique clocks, model ships and scientific instruments.

ITALIAANDER GALLERIES
Prinsengracht 526 ☎*(020) 6250942. Map 5F3* 🆎 🔂 🏧
Primitive and traditional Asiatic art, including Indonesian puppets.

E. KRAMER
Nieuwe Spiegelstraat 64 ☎*(020) 6230832. Map 6F4* 🆎 🔂 🏧
Dutch tiles and old clocks are the specialties here.

LEIDELMEIJER
Nieuwe Spiegelstraat 58 ☎*(020) 6254627. Map 6F4* 🆎 🔂 🏧
Leidelmeijer specializes in Art Nouveau and Art Deco objects. These include the distinctive Amsterdam School lamps that are a feature of so many of Amsterdam's brown cafés.

VAN OS & YU
Nieuwe Spiegelstraat 68 ☎*(020) 6220740. Map 6F4* 🆎 🔂 🏧
Mechanical music boxes are Van Os & Yu's stock-in-trade.

C. P. J. VAN DER PEET
Nieuwe Spiegelstraat 33-35 ☎*(020) 6235763. Map 6F4* 🆎 🔂 🏧
Japanese woodcuts and specialized books on Japan and China.

ART GALLERIES

There are more than 150 small commercial art galleries in Amsterdam, featuring a broad range of Dutch and international art. Many galleries are located close to the Rijksmuseum, along the streets and canals running from **Leidsestraat** to **Vijzelstraat**. Others are clustered around hotels such as the **Pulitzer**, which has its own gallery, and the **Ramada Renaissance**, which owns a superb collection of modern painting and sculpture. Events worth watching out for include **Kunst RAI** in June, when many Dutch and European galleries mount exhibitions at the RAI center, and the **spring art fair** in the Nieuwe Kerk, where several hundred major Dutch galleries exhibit works.

The *Uitkrant* (available free of charge from the Uit Buro at Leidseplein 26) provides a monthly galleries listing. Gallery owners lead unpredictable lives, and it is worth phoning to check that a gallery is open before visiting. Generally, major galleries open on Tuesday to Saturday from noon to 6pm. A few galleries are also open on Sunday.

ABN AMRO BANK

Vijzelstraat 68-78. Map 6G4. Tram 16, 24, 25 to Keizersgracht.

The construction of the overscaled ABN bank in the 1970s raised a storm of protest. The brutal architecture is now somewhat softened by an art gallery in the arcade, and neon-art installations set in the pavement. Another ABN Amro Bank, at nearby Rembrandtsplein *(map 6F5)* has a similar street gallery where the works of contemporary Dutch artists are displayed. The Dutch brewing giant, **Heineken**, displays its favorite artists in another street gallery *(Ferdinand Bolstraat at Quellijnstraat, map 6H4).*

AMAZONE

Singel 72 ☎(020) 6279000. Map 10B5. Open Tues-Fri 10am-4pm; Sat 1-4pm. Tram 1, 2, 5 to Martelaarsgracht.

A women-only gallery set up in the radical 1970s.

ANIMATION ART

Berenstraat 19 ☎(020) 6277600. Map 9E3. Open Tues-Fri 11am-6pm; Sat 10am-5pm AE ⬤ ⬤ VISA Tram 13, 17 to Westerkerk.

Original hand-painted celluloid stills from international cartoon films. For fans of Disney cartoon characters or Dutch duck Alfred J. Kwak.

ARTI ET AMICITIAE

Rokin 112 ☎(020) 6233508. Map 10E4. Open Tues-Sun noon-5pm. Tram 4, 9, 14, 16, 24, 25 to Muntplein.

A rather forbidding Neoclassical exterior conceals the opulent Neo-Gothic interior of this artists' club, established in 1839. You will have to befriend a member to enter the handsome English-style club rooms on the ground floor, but the white-walled galleries on the first floor are open to the public. Mondrian exhibited many of his early romantic paintings at Arti. The works on display now range from photography to fashion drawings.

ELISABETH DEN BIEMAN DE HAAS

Nieuwe Spiegelstraat 44 ☎(020) 6261012. Map 6F4. Open Mon-Sat 10.30am-5.30pm; Sun 1-5pm. Tram 6, 7, 10 to Spiegelgracht.

A pleasant gallery in the antiques district, specializing in landscapes by the Dutch Bergen School, as well as graphics by Cobra artists.

CANON IMAGE CENTRE

Leidsestraat 79 ☎(020) 6254494. Map 5F3. Open Tues-Fri noon-5.45pm; Sat 11am-4.45pm. Tram 1, 2, 5 to Prinsengracht.

A modern gallery spread across three floors of a corner building with a beautiful canal view. Temporary exhibitions are mounted of photographs by contemporary Dutch and international photographers. There is a specialized photography bookstore on the top floor.

COLLECTION D'ART

Keizersgracht 516 ☎(020) 6221511. Map 6F4. Open Tues-Sat 1-5pm. Tram 1, 2, 5 to Keizersgracht.

Major gallery, exhibiting works by Cobra artists such as Appel, and Abstract Expressionists including De Kooning.

'D EENDT

Spuistraat 272 ☎(020) 6265777. Map 10E4. Open Wed-Sat noon-6pm; Sun 2-6pm. Tram 1, 2, 5 to Spui.

A busy gallery specializing in international modern painting and ethnic art.

ESPACE

Keizersgracht 548 ☎(020) 6240802. Map 6F4. Open Tues-Sat noon-5.30pm. Tram 1, 2, 5 to Keizersgracht.

A gallery set up in the 1950s, displaying recent works by Cobra artists such as Corneille and Lucubert.

BARBARA FARBER

Keizersgracht 265 ☎(020) 6276343. Map 9D3. Open Tues-Sat 1-6pm. Tram 13, 14, 17 to Westermarkt.

Barbara Farber travels to the far corners of Europe and America to discover exciting new talents. Her Amsterdam canal house gallery, with its incongruous Old World Baroque ceiling, is often the first European gallery to show New York's avant-garde, coupled with the work of Latin American and European artists establishing their reputation.

GAMMA

Keizersgracht 429 ☎(020) 6230767. Map 5F3. Open Tues-Sat 11.30am-5.30pm. Tram 1, 2, 5 to Keizersgracht.

Painting, sculpture and graphics are shown here, including attractive examples of Lyrical Abstractionism.

LIEVE HEMEL

Vijzelgracht 6-8 ☎(020) 6230060. Map 6G4. Open Tues-Sat noon-6pm. Tram 16, 24, 25 to Prinsengracht.

The full title of this gallery, *Lieve hemel stoot je hoofd niet* (For goodness' sake don't bang your head), is not just another piece of Amsterdam whimsy, but an attempt by the gallery owners to avoid a devastating liability action brought by customers who stun themselves on the low lintel. Despite its hazards, however, this is a beautiful gallery in an atmospheric 17thC interior with low beams and precarious staircases, which specializes in contemporary Dutch Realist painting and sculpture.

MOKUM

Oude Zijds Voorburgwal 334 ☎(020) 6243958. Map 10E5. Open Tues-Fri noon-6pm; Sat noon-5pm, Sun 2-4pm. Tram 4, 9, 14, 16, 24, 25 to Spui.

A small gallery specializing in melancholy Dutch Surrealist works.

PETIT

Nieuwe Zijds Voorburgwal 270 ☎(020) 6267507. Map 10E4. Open Tues-Sat noon-5pm. Tram 1, 2, 5 to Spui.

Larger than its name suggests, Petit presents interesting Lyrical Realist paintings and sculpture on its three floors.

PULITZER ART GALLERY

Prinsengracht 325 ☎(020) 5235235. Map 9D3. Open daily 9am-10pm. Tram 13, 14, 17 to Westermarkt.

The Pulitzer Hotel's art exhibitions are held in a beautiful sunlit gallery that zigzags through the leafy garden, from the hotel entrance on Prinsengracht to the bar on Keizersgracht. Look out for other interesting galleries in the vicinity of the Pulitzer, particularly on **Reestraat**.

RA

Vijzelstraat 80 ☎(020) 6265100. Map 6G4. Open Tues-Fri noon-6pm; Sat 11am-5pm. Tram 16, 24, 25 to Prinsengracht.

This is an exciting gallery presenting a selection of modern experimental jewelry, with designs ranging from the bizarre to the outrageous.

SWART

Van Breestraat 23 ☎(020) 6764736. Map 5H2. Open Wed-Sat 2-6pm. Tram 2 to Jacob Obrechtstraat.

Dynamic gallery showing recent abstract art, along with video and sculpture.

DE WITTE VOET

Kerkstraat 149 ☎(020) 6258412. Map 6F4. Open Tues-Sat noon-5pm. Tram 1, 2, 5 to Prinsengracht.

Avant-garde ceramic vases and plates.

AUCTIONS

Watch out for *kijkdagen* (viewing days) advertised at the various auction houses. **Christie's** *(Cornelis Schuytstraat 57 ☎(020) 6642011)* and **Sotheby's** *(Rokin 102 ☎(020) 6275656, map 10E4)* both have branches in Amsterdam. **Van Gendt** *(Keizersgracht 96-98 ☎(020) 6234107, map 10C4)* specializes in books, prints and maps.

BOOKS AND NEWSPAPERS

Amsterdammers are prodigious linguists with highly cosmopolitan reading interests, and have no hesitation in picking up books in English, French or German. Their tastes are also highly eclectic, so that you can find almost any book, new or second-hand, in Amsterdam. Book-hunting is made particularly pleasurable by the wealth of attractive bookstores, mainly on the canal ring formed by Singel and Kloveniersburgwal.

ALLERT DE LANGE
Damrak 62 ☎(020) 6246744. Map 10C5.
A serious literary bookstore with a wide range of Dutch, English, French and German novels, together with excellent travel and art sections.

AMERICAN DISCOUNT BOOK CENTER
Kalverstraat 185 ☎(020) 6255537. Map 10E4.
Discount imported US novels, magazines and unusual subjects such as Japanese classics, gay fiction, body-building and sci-fi.

ARCHITECTURA & NATURA
Leliegracht 44 ☎(020) 6236186. Map 9C3 ▣
Every day that goes by, the piles of unsorted books seem to increase in this bookstore devoted to the owner's two consuming passions, architecture and the natural world. A must for all lovers of Frank Lloyd Wright or England's threatened hedgerows.

ATHENAEUM BOEKHANDEL & NIEUWSCENTRUM
Spui 14-16 ☎(020) 6233933. Map 10E4.
Beautiful 1904 Art Nouveau shop with a labyrinthine interior designed in the 1960s. Amsterdammers flock here on Saturdays to buy literature, be it in Dutch, English, French, Spanish or Latin. There is also a small section devoted to Dutch literature in translation. The adjoining newspaper store (☎(020) 6242972) is stocked with newspapers and magazines flown in from every corner of the world.

THE BOOK EXCHANGE
Kloveniersburgwal 58 ☎(020) 6266266. Map 10E5.

Well-organized secondhand bookstore devoted to English paperbacks and hardbacks.

CINÉ QUA NON
Staalstraat 14 ☎(020) 6255588. Map 10E5.
Film posters and new and secondhand books for movie buffs.

DE SLEGTE
Kalverstraat 48-52 ☎(020) 6225933. Map 10D4.
Remaindered books are kept on the ground floor, and a vast treasure trove of rare antiquarian books is displayed upstairs.

ERASMUS
Spui 2 ☎(020) 6230535. Map 10E4.
Art, architecture and antiquarian books.

INTERNATIONAL THEATER BOOKSHOP
Leidseplein 26 ☎(020) 6226489. Map 5F3.
Books and periodicals in seven languages on theater, ballet, opera, cabaret, circus and magic.

INTERTAAL
Van Baerlestraat 76 ☎(020) 6715353. Map 5H2.
The Dutch hunger for foreign languages is evident in this beautiful bookstore stocking textbooks, dictionaries, cassettes, videos and computer programs in about 120 languages, with titles ranging from *English for Bank Cashiers* to *Basic Tagalog for Foreigners and Non-Tagalogs*.

KINDERBOEKWINKEL
Eerste Bloemdwarsstraat 23 ☎(020) 6224761, map 9D3 and Nieuwe Zijds

179

Voorburgwal 344 ☎*(020) 6227741, map* **10***E4.*
A well-stocked children's bookstore where young readers are welcome to browse.

DE KOOKBOEKHANDEL
Runstraat 26 ☎*(020) 6224768. Map* **9***E3.*
His devotion to the joys of eating and drinking has earned Kookboekhandel owner Johannes van Dam the nickname "the pudding professor," and chefs and gourmets flock from all over the world to his well-stocked international cookbook store.

ROBERT PREMSELA
Van Baerlestraat 78 ☎*(020) 6624266. Map* **5***H2.*
Avant-garde art bookstore opposite the Stedelijk, specializing in art, architecture, graphic design, photography, ballet and fashion.

SCHELTEMA, HOLKEMA, VERMEULEN
Koningsplein 20 ☎*(020) 6267212. Map* **6***F4.*
Amsterdam's main university bookstore, with a wide range of novels, art books and textbooks in Dutch, English, French and German.

W. H. SMITH
Kalverstraat 152 ☎*(020) 6383821 Map* **10***E4.*
This helpful branch of the English bookstore chain occupies four floors with its vast stock of titles, from *Beowulf* to BBC books.

STRAAT ANTIQUAREN
Rosmarijnsteeg 8 ☎*(020) 6227904. Map* **10***E4.*
A good selection of secondhand English, French and German novels, movie magazines and French fashion magazines dating back to 1803.

CLOGS
Wooden clogs were once common footwear in the boggy regions of the Netherlands, but are now more commonly hung outside Dutch houses as plant holders.

DE KLOMPENBOER
Nieuwe Zijds Voorburgwal 20 ☎*(020) 6230632. Map* **10***C5.*
A cluttered downtown clog workshop with some battered rocking horses and even the odd chicken pecking in the wood shavings. Real clogs and kitsch souvenirs for sale.

'T KLOMPENHUISJE
Nieuwe Hoogstraat 9 ☎*(020) 6228100. Map* **11***E6.*
Lumpish Dutch wooden shoes, ranging from sturdy clogs to gaudy souvenirs. Some conventional footwear, too, including slippers, thick socks and health sandals.

COMPACT DISCS AND RECORDS
Amsterdam's specialized record stores cover classical, jazz and pop music, as well as more esoteric styles. **Fame** *(Kalverstraat 2* ☎*(020) 6382525, map* **10***D4* ▰ ▰ ▰ ▰ *)* is an exciting, modern compact disc store on several levels, with rock pumping out in one department as soothing classical music plays in the basement. It has some pop videos and cassettes, but no records. **Concerto** *(Utrechtsestraat 54-60* ☎*(020) 6235228, map* **6***F5)* stocks a large collection of classical and pop compact discs, plus some secondhand records in good condition. Jazz enthusiasts should browse amid the Art Deco furnishings in **Jazz**

Inn *(Vijzelgracht 9* ☎*(020) 6235662, map 6G4* 🆎 💳 *)*; its stock is now mainly composed of compact discs, but it retains a few classic vinyl recordings.

CRAFTS

Although the Netherlands is not renowned for crafts, you can find small workshops producing tasteful pottery or hand-made gifts in the Jordaan.

JEROEN BECHTOLD
Korte Leidsedwarsstraat 159 ☎*(020) 6249871. Map 5G3* 🆎 💳 💳 💳
Limited-edition modern ceramics.

DROOMDOOS
Oude Leliestraat 1 ☎*(020) 6201075. Map 10C4. Closed Mon, Tues.*
Unique hand-made boxes for jewels or love letters, decorated with reproductions of famous paintings by Van Gogh and Cézanne.

KLEIKOLLEKTIEF
Hartenstraat 19 ☎*(020) 6225127. Map 9D3* 🆎 💳 💳
A small potters' collective producing zany black and white ceramics.

DE VOETBOOG
Voetboogsteeg 16 ☎*(020) 6260169. Map 10E4* 🆎 💳
Small arts-and-crafts center exhibiting tasteful ceramics, postcards and watercolors.

DELFTWARE, GLASS AND CHINA

High-quality, hand-painted Delftware porcelain is still produced by **De Porceleyne Fles** in Delft.

FOCKE & MELTZER
P. C. Hooftstraat 65-67, map 5G3 and Kalverstraat 176, map 10E4 ☎*(020) 6642311 (for all branches)* 🆎 💳 💳 💳
Classic Delftware, merry Dutch tiles and Scandinavian and German glassware.

DE MUNT
Muntplein 12 ☎*(020) 6232271. Map 10E5.*
Situated in a dusky neo-Renaissance building next to the Munttoren, this shop stocks a good selection of high-quality Delftware, Makkum porcelain, tiles and dolls in traditional Dutch costumes.

R & R
Rusland 27 ☎*(020) 6268107. Map 10E5* 🆎 💳 💳 💳
Antique glasses for wine, champagne and *jenever*.

ROSENTHAL STUDIO-HAUS
Heiligeweg 49-51 ☎*(020) 6245865. Map 10E4* 🆎 💳 💳 💳
The committee of German experts that selects the items sold in Rosenthal shops is clearly biased in favor of clean-cut modern Scandinavian design, judging by the items that are on display, although they are also impressed with the zany New York ceramics of Dorothy Hafner.

DEPARTMENT STORES

Amsterdam has only a few large department stores, which are located mainly along **Damrak** and **Rokin**.

DE BIJENKORF
Damrak 90a ☎*(020) 6218080. Map* **10***D5*
AE ⊙ ⊙ VISA ⇌

The Bijenkorf (beehive) is Amsterdam's most fashionable department store, where next season's colors are reflected in the litter baskets, corkscrews, sofas and table napkins, as well as in the clothes and shoes. The first floor has been redesigned as a series of elegant boutiques devoted to Mondi, Mexx, Esprit and other labels. The Bijenkorf is also an excellent store for perfumes, chocolates, international newspapers and stationery. Its restaurant, **La Ruche**, is constantly dreaming up new and enticing offers, such as the popular "teatime buffet," while the hushed **Literair Café** (near the books and magazines department) is a delightful place to pause for coffee.

HEMA
Nieuwendijk 174 ☎*(020) 6234176, map* **10***C5 and Reguliersbreestraat 10* ☎*(020) 6246506, map* **6***F5.*

The Hema chain is a subsidiary of De Bijenkorf (see above) and stocks inexpensive clothes, brightly colored kitchen utensils and a limited range of good-value wines.

MAISON DE BONNETERIE
Rokin 142 ☎*(020) 6262162. Map* **10***E4*
AE ⊙ ⊙ VISA ⇌

With its glittering chandeliers and spacious interior, Maison de Bonneterie struggles to retain an old-fashioned elegance amid the brash modernity of Kalverstraat. Its fashions are rather conservative for Holland, especially in the men's department, although it has recently begun introducing more colorful and relaxed women's clothes alongside the traditional tweeds, tartans and cashmeres. Upstairs, there is a small golf shop.

METZ & CO.
Keizersgracht 455 ☎*(020) 6248810. Map*
5*F3* AE ⊙ ⊙ VISA ⇌

Metz & Co., founded in 1740 by a French draper from Metz, occupies a striking corner building laden with caryatids looking down balefully on the flux of Leidsestraat. In the early 20thC, Metz encouraged furniture and fabric designers such as Bart van der Leck and Sonia Delaunay, and in 1933 the architect Gerrit Rietveld was commissioned to design the rooftop exhibition **cupola** *(koepel)*, which he offered as an example of "the space which we need to preserve in our structures." This De Stijl addition offers a splendid view of Amsterdam, as does the striking Post-Modern **café** on the sixth floor, designed by Cees Dam. The other floors of Metz — which is now owned by Liberty of London — are devoted to modern furniture, fabrics, kitchen utensils and gifts. One of the world's great stores.

VROOM & DREESMANN
Kalverstraat 201 ☎*(020) 6220171. Map*
10*E4* AE ⊙ VISA ⇌

This is the Amsterdam branch of The Netherlands' main department store chain.

DIAMONDS

The diamond trade was introduced to Amsterdam by refugee Jews in the 16thC, and in 1908 the world's largest diamond, the "Cullinan," was cut in Amsterdam by the Asscher Company. Today Amsterdam is one of the world's most important diamond centers. Demonstrations of diamond polishing can be seen in most factories and diamond stores, and visitors are under no obligation to buy. Outlets include the **Am-**

sterdam Diamond Centre *(Rokin 1-5* ☎*(020) 6245787, map* **10**D5 ▣ ▣ ▣ ▣), Bonebakker *(Rokin 86-90* ☎*(020) 6232294, map* **10**E4 ▣ ▣ ▣ ▣) and Willem van Pampus *(Damrak 97* ☎*(020) 6382422, map* **10**D5 ▣ ▣ ▣). Coster *(Paulus Potterstraat 2-4* ☎*(020) 6762222, map* **5**H3 ▣ ▣ ▣ ▣) is where, in 1852, the Kohinoor (Mountain of Light) diamond was cut for the British Crown Jewels. Conveniently close to the RIJKSMUSEUM, Coster allows visitors to view diamond polishers at work.

FABRICS
Bold, brightly colored traditional materials imported from Latin America, Africa and Asia are popular in Amsterdam. Capsicum *(Oude Hoogstraat 1* ☎*(020) 6231016, map* **10**D5 ▣ ▣ ▣) is stocked with exotic fabrics from India, China, Japan, Africa, Thailand and Portugal, mostly handmade from natural fibers. The gentle Indian background music recalls the 1970s, as does Harold the Kangaroo's decorated column at the entrance.

FASHIONS
The fashionable Amsterdammer's wardrobe leans heavily toward casual, loosely fitting clothes in bright colors. Sizes tend to be generous, however, apart from Italian and French lines. Successful Dutch designers often make their home on **P. C. Hooftstraat**, while younger designers may have a boutique in the **Jordaan** or in the increasingly fashionable area of **Nieuwe Hoogstraat** and **Sint Antoniesbreestraat**. The fashion scene is explored under various headings on pages 183-7.

WOMEN'S CLOTHING
Amsterdam women like to dress in bold and bright styles. They wear warm, multilayered clothes for winter, and move into loose and light-hearted styles at the first hint of spring. Dutch shops tend to stock clothes mainly for tall women, but French or Japanese labels frequently come in smaller sizes.

AGNÈS B
Rokin 126 ☎*(020) 6271465. Map* **10**E4
▣ ▣ ▣ ▣
Agnès B has built up a strong following in recent years for her quietly sophisticated French designs, which use bright colors sparingly.

MARGA ALBERS
Sint Antoniesbreestraat 126 ☎*(020) 6223214. Map* **11**E6 ▣ ▣
A small but attractive collection for daring dressers, including some designs by Marga Albers herself.

JACQUES D'ARIÈGE
P. C. Hooftstraat 98 ☎*(020) 6710918. Map* **5**H2 ▣ ▣ ▣ ▣
Elegant, seductive clothing.

AZZURRO
Van Baerlestraat 17 ☎*(020) 6716804. Map* **5**H2 ▣ ▣ ▣ ▣
Glittery Italian clothes and shoes are Azzurro's stock-in-trade.

CARMINA
Prinsengracht 496 ☎*(020) 6247523. Map* **5**F3.

Theatrical costumes, drawings and curiosities.

COLOMBINE INSTANT WHITE
Nieuwe Hoogstraat 6 ☎*(020) 6231599. Map* **11***E6* AE ⊡ ⊡ VISA
Elegant, Parisian-style fashions by Colombine Sarrailhé.

GIN AND TONIC
Tweede Tuindwarsstraat 6 ☎*(020) 6267830. Map* **9***C3.*
Bright fashions from Britain.

FONG LENG
P. C. Hooftstraat 77 ☎*(020) 6738427. Map* **5***H2.*
Elegant, imaginative prêt-à-porter collection for younger women.

FRANK GOVERS
Keizersgracht 500 ☎*(020) 6228670. Map* **5***F3.*
Silk and velvet evening dresses in opulent Baroque styles by one of Holland's foremost designers.

'T HAASJE
Elandsstraat 121 ☎*(020) 6238507. Map* **9***E2* AE ⊡ VISA
Bright, tropical colors.

KENZO
Van Baerlestraat 66 ☎*(020) 6626253. Map* **5***H2* AE ⊡ ⊡ VISA
Creative Parisian designs.

HET KIMONOHUIS
Singel 317 ☎*(020) 6258882. Map* **10***E4*
Imported kimonos for Japanese nights.

MEXX
P.C. Hooftstraat 118 ☎*(020) 6750171. Map* **5***H2* AE ⊡ ⊡ VISA
Crisp Dutch fashions for flaunting and flirting.

LOOK-OUT KLEDING
Sint Luciensteeg 22 ☎*(020) 6277649, map* **10***E4 and Utrechtsestraat 91* ☎*(020) 6255032, map* **7***G6* AE ⊡ VISA
Attractive pullovers, Slippely T-shirts and the colorful fashions produced by Oilily of Alkmaar.

FRANS MOLENAAR
Jan Luikenstraat 104 ☎*(020) 6735373. Map* **5***H2.*
Elegant and, at times, eccentric dresses and shoes by Dutch designer Frans Molenaar.

PAUW
Heiligeweg 10 ☎*(020) 6244780, map* **10***E4; Leidsestraat 16* ☎*(020) 6265698, map* **5***F3; Van Baerlestraat 72* ☎*(020) 6717322, map* **5***H2; Beethovenstraat 82* ☎*(020) 6713299* AE ⊡ ⊡ VISA
Highly successful Amsterdam chain of fashion boutiques stocking elegant but casual clothes in rather large sizes. No two shops are the same, and there are also branches for men and children.

PUCK EN HANS
Rokin 66 ☎*(020) 6255889. Map* **10***D5.*
Sleek, simple, slightly futuristic Dutch designer clothes.

LIESBETH ROOYAARDS
Prinsenstraat 6 ☎*(020) 6265026. Map* **10***C4* AE ⊡ ⊡ VISA
Fashionably bare shop selling stylish, original designs.

SHEILA
Rokin 50 ☎*(020) 6265364. Map* **10***D5* AE ⊡ ⊡ VISA
Exclusive evening dresses by Sheila de Vries.

CLAUDIA STRÄTER
Kalverstraat 179-181 ☎*(020) 6220559, map* **10***E4 and Beethovenstraat 9* ☎*(020) 6736605* AE ⊡ ⊡ VISA
Elegant clothes in large sizes.

UNITED COLORS OF BENETTON
Heiligeweg 23 ☎*(020) 6269150, map* **10***E4 and P C. Hooftstraat 72* ☎*(020) 6795706, map* **5***G2.*
Italian chain store specializing in fashion knitwear in many colors.

EDGAR VOS
P. C. Hooftstraat 134 ☎*(020) 6626336. Map* **5***H2* AE ⊡ ⊡ VISA
Exclusive clothes at affordable prices for older women.

MEN'S FASHIONS

Amsterdam men are free to dress casually or formally as they choose. English tailored jackets and sturdy shoes appeal to some, but other, freer spirits turn up to work in loose trousers, pastel shirts and flamboyant ties.

BARBAS
P. C. Hooftstraat 140 ☎*(020) 6713537. Map 5H2* AE ✛ CB VISA
Baggy pants; chunky knitwear.

HERZOG
Heiligeweg 37 ☎*(020) 6273114. Map 10E4* AE ✛ CB VISA
Traditional clothes in an old-style interior.

MARTIJN VAN KESTEREN
Herenstraat 10 ☎*(020) 6256371. Map 10C4* AE CB VISA
A small shop that stocks a good selection of colorful shirts, ties and pants, together with some arty Italian woolens.

MATINIQUE
Kalverstraat 88-90 ☎*(020) 6237283, map 10E4 and Van Baerlestraat 6* ☎*(020) 6621739, map 5H2* AE ✛ CB VISA

Predominantly Italian and French fashions that are particularly appealing to young men.

NERO
Kalverstraat 134 ☎*(020) 6230003. Map 10E4* AE ✛ CB VISA
Attractive Italian fashions in adventurous colors.

NEW MAN MODE
P. C. Hooftstraat 116 ☎*(020) 6799319. Map 5H2.*
Casual styles for men are a feature of this shop.

PAUW
Van Baerlestraat 88 ☎*(020) 6646653. Map 5H2* AE ✛ CB VISA
Situated on Van Baerlestraat near the museum quarter, Pauw sells chic fashions for young men; also blazers and bankers' overcoats.

MEN'S AND WOMEN'S CLOTHING

Youthful men and women in Amsterdam tend to favor a studied nonchalance in the clothes they wear. Several shops specialize in fashions for both sexes, such as **Hartman en Hartman** *(Prinsengracht 176* ☎ *(020) 6248718, map 9D3* AE ✛ CB VISA *and P. C. Hooftstraat 38* ☎ *(020) 6710688, map 5G3* AE ✛ CB VISA *)*, which sells casual, attractive men's and women's fashions and accessories. **Obsession** *(Gasthuismolensteeg 5* ☎*(020) 6382770, map 10D4* AE ✛ CB VISA *)* stocks contemporary fashions by French and Italian designers, while **Sissy Boy** *(Kalverstraat 210* ☎ *(020) 6260088, map 10E4 and Van Baerlestraat 15, map 5H2* AE ✛ CB VISA *)* sells casual, loose-fitting clothes for men and women.

CHILDREN'S CLOTHING

Fashions for children feature colorful, fun clothes that are quite expensive: **Hobbit** *(Van Baerlestraat 42* ☎*(020) 6710502, map 5H2* AE CB VISA *)* sells bright clothing for teenagers; **Pauw** *(Van Baerlestraat 48* ☎*(020) 6731665, map 5H2* AE ✛ CB VISA*)* stocks expensive clothes for trendy toddlers.

185

JEWELRY

Traditional jewelers tend to be found along Kalverstraat, while avant-garde boutiques, specializing in brightly colored and highly imaginative designs, occupy tiny shops in narrow streets such as Grimburgwal.

HANS APPENZELLER
Grimburgwal 1-5 ☎(020) 6268218. Map 10E5 AE CD CD VISA

Elegant, expensive modern jewelry by one of Holland's leading designers, in a stylish interior.

BAOBAB
Elandsgracht 128 ☎(020) 6268398. Map 9E2.

Thea de Vegte has turned a nondescript shop in the Jordaan into an Aladdin's Cave packed with Oriental treasures. Her main interest is jewelry, but she has also brought back, from her Far Eastern travels, furniture, carpets and utensils, which are arranged in such a way that you might feel you are entering a Nepalese temple or a Javanese home.

JORGE COHEN
Singel 369 ☎(020) 6238646. Map 10E4 AE CD VISA

Exquisite jewelry made on the premises by Jorge Cohen, born in Argentina. Some pieces are inspired by the red-and-black décor of the Tuschinski movie theater, while others incorporate fragments of old jewelry found in Paris flea markets.

ANDRÉ COPPENHAGEN
Bloemgracht 38 ☎(020) 6243681. Map 9C3.

A huge selection of beads in different colors and sizes for crafting inexpensive homemade jewelry.

GRIMM
Grimburgwal 9 ☎(020) 6220501. Map 10E5 AE VISA

This small boutique specializes in low-cost avant-garde jewelry by young Dutch designers: light, colorful and delicately constructed objects showing traces of De Stijl and the 1950s. Ideal presents for a loved one on Valentine's Day.

NOVANTA NOVE
Keizersgracht 717 ☎(020) 6270797. Map 6F5.

This chic gallery stocks boldly innovative, often bizarre, jewelry, pottery and art.

SCHAAP EN CITROEN
Kalverstraat 1 ☎(020) 6266691, map 10D4 and Rokin 12 ☎(020) 6255666, map 10D5 AE CD CD VISA

Exclusive silver jewelry for wearing to the opera. The shop on Kalverstraat is a curious Expressionist work by Amsterdam School architect Th. Wijdeveld, while the Rokin branch shows a distinct De Stijl influence.

THE TURQUOISE TOMAHAWK
Berenstraat 16 ☎(020) 6257106. Map 9E3 AE CD CD VISA

Turquoise *Amsterdammertjes* (the local word for traffic posts) announce this unusual shop specializing in imported New Mexican and South American Indian jewelry and all kinds of other crafts.

SHOES AND LEATHER GOODS

Shoe fashions fluctuate wildly in Amsterdam. There are times when every person on Kalverstraat is wearing a different color of shoe, and times when the shoe stores sell nothing but black.

FRED DE LA BRETONIÈRE
Sint Luciensteeg 20 ☎(020) 6234152, map 10E4 and Utrechtsestraat 77, map

6F5 AE CD CD VISA
Exclusive leather shoes, belts and bags traditional and modern.

CANDY CORSON LEERATELIER
Sint Luciensteeg 19 ☎*(020) 6248061.*
Map 10E4 `AE` `◆` `◆` `VISA`
Attractive leather bags and accessories
in a range of colors.

CINDERELLA
Kalverstraat 177 ☎*(020) 6233617, map*
10E4 and Leidsestraat 86 ☎*(020)*
6265519, map 5F3.
Shoes wild, wonderful and weird.

KENNETH COLE
Leidsestraat 20-22 ☎*(020) 6276012.*
Map 6F4 `AE` `◆` `◆` `VISA`
Elegant handbags and shoes by New
York's cheekiest designer are on sale
here

DR ADAM'S
P. C. Hooftstraat 90 ☎*(020) 6623835.*
Map 5G2 `AE` `◆` `◆` `VISA`
Dr Adam's sells tough, attractive shoes
made to survive Amsterdam's notorious
sidewalks.

DUNGELMANN
Heiligeweg 2-6 ☎*(020) 6221866. Map*
10E4 `AE` `◆` `◆` `VISA`

Dungelmann sells a range of classic
shoes for both men and women.

HESTER VAN EEGHEN
Hartenstraat 1 ☎*(020) 6269212. Map*
9D3 `AE` `◆` `◆` `VISA`
Purses, wallets and briefcases in a rainbow of colors, designed by a young
Dutch woman in a small atelier below
the shop. Closed Monday.

JAN JANSEN
Rokin 42 ☎*(020) 6251350. Map 10E4.*
Astonishing fashion shoes in a remark-
able Post-Modern interior.

PISA
Van Baerlestraat 19 ☎*(020) 6710741,*
map 5H2 and Kalverstraat 14 ☎*(020)*
6245910, map 10D4 `AE` `◆` `◆` `VISA`
Smart Italian styles and classic English
walking shoes in a handsome interior.

SHOEBALOO
Koningsplein 7 ☎*(020) 6267993, map*
6F4 and P.C. Hooftstraat 80 ☎*(020)*
6712210, map 5G2.
Zany shoes in just about every color
imaginable.

FOOD AND DRINK
Holland produces interesting liquor, sturdy cheeses that travel well and
delicious chocolates — so the figure-conscious should beware. Good-
quality tea, coffee, cigars, Belgian bottled beers and French wines are
imported. Amsterdam has a number of specialty delicatessens that
stock everything the most demanding gourmand could desire.

BERKHOFF
Leidsestraat 46 ☎*(020) 6240233. Map*
5F3.
Homemade candies and cakes, and an
elegant *salon de thé*.

HENRI BLOEM'S
Gravenstraat 8 ☎*(020) 6230886. Map*
10D5.
Friendly and informed wine merchant.

BRINK'S WIJNHANDEL
Staalstraat 6 ☎*(020) 6233957. Map*
10E5.
Good choice of Dutch and foreign
beers; some wines and liquor.

CRABTREE & EVELYN
Singel 439 ☎*(020) 6224774. Map 10E4*
`AE` `◆` `VISA`
A restored 19thC apothecary shop provides a fitting backdrop to Crabtree &
Evelyn's nostalgic range of British natural products, such as herbal soaps, jams
and old-fashioned hard-boiled candies.

EICHHOLTZ
Leidsestraat 48 ☎*(020) 6220305. Map*
5F3.
An eclectic range of gourmet foods to
take home to friends, including Van
Houten cocoa, dark chocolates, aged
Gouda cheese and crisp honey waffles.

GEELS & CO.
Warmoesstraat 67 ☎(020) 6240683. Map
10D5.
An old-fashioned coffee and tea store
on the edge of the red-light district. A
tiny private museum upstairs *(open Fri,
Sat 2-5pm)* is crammed with antique
coffee-brewing equipment.

GODIVA
Hobbemastraat 13 ☎(020) 6735384. Map
5G3 [AE] [●] [●D] [VISA]
Sophisticated Belgian chocolates laced
with liqueurs.

P. G. C. HAJENIUS
Rokin 92-6 ☎(020) 6237494. Map **10**E4
[AE] [●] [●D] [VISA]
This famous tobacconist has the air of
an English gentlemen's club, with its
dark mahogany cabinets and gleaming
marble walls. Although you can buy a
simple pack of cigarettes here, the assistants are happiest when explaining
the merits of pipes or the temperament
of different cigars, including Hajenius'
famous *Grande Finale.*

HART'S WIJNHANDEL
Vijzelgracht 27 ☎(020) 6238350. Map
6G4 [AE] [●] [●D] [VISA]
A ravishing Art Nouveau interior stock-
ing a carefully chosen selection of
French wines at all prices, some tempt-
ing beers and a good collection of
Dutch liqueurs.

HOLTKAMP
Vijzelgracht 15 ☎(020) 6248757. Map
6G4.
Homemade truffles, moist Dutch apple
cake and other temptations.

JACOB HOOY & CO.
Kloveniersburgwal 12 ☎(020) 6243041.
Map **11**D6.
The heady aroma of spices and herbs
wafts across Nieuwmarkt from Jacob
Hooy, which has been curing Amsterdammers' aches and pains since 1743.
This doggedly old-fashioned shop
stocks some 600 spices and herbs in a
magnificent array of 19thC wooden
drawers and earthenware jars labeled in

Latin. Jacob Hooy also sells 38 types of
drop, a peculiar Dutch licorice delicacy.

ROBERT KEF
Marnixstraat 192 ☎(020) 6262210. Map
9D2.
Grocer with a good selection of imported French cheeses.

KEIJZER
Prinsengracht 180 ☎(020) 6240823. Map
9D3.
Tea and coffee store furnished in Old
Dutch Granny style.

BANKETBAKKERIJ LANSKROON
Singel 385 ☎(020) 6237743. Map **10**E4.
This superb German *Konditorei* (cof-
feehouse) is popular with local office
workers, who steal out in the afternoon
to tuck into giant slices of strawberry or
bilberry tart. Lanskroon also bakes
mouth-wateringly delicious early-
morning croissants.

LEONIDAS
Damstraat 11 ☎(020) 6253497. Map
10D5.
Leonidas sells sumptuous and exclusive
Belgian chocolates made with fresh
cream.

MEIDI-YA
Beethovenstraat 18 ☎(020) 6737410.
This specialty food store imports *sake,*
Kirin beer, exotic seaweeds and other
essentials of Japanese cuisine.

D'OUDE GEKROONDE
Huidenstraat 21 ☎(020) 6237711. Map
9E3.
Specialized beer store with some 500
types of bottled beer and a wide range
of matching glasses.

PÂTISSERIE POMPADOUR
Huidenstraat 12 ☎(020) 6239554. Map
9E3.
A portrait of Madame de Pompadour
looks down with smiling approval on
Arnold Reijers' 45 varieties of hand-
made confections, which can be sam-
pled individually in the exquisite Louis
XVI-style tea room.

SPIGA D'ORO
Spuistraat 60 ☎(020) 6273983. Map 10C4.
Fresh Romagna pasta in bright colors, and other Italian delicacies, in a corner shop propped up by wooden buttresses.

H.P. DE VRENG EN ZONEN
Nieuwendijk 75 ☎(020) 6244581. Map 10C5.
A traditional family distillery where they still prepare Dutch liquor according to old recipes, without any artificial additives. Buy a basic Oud Amsterdam *jenever*, or experiment with a specialized liquor such as the ruby-tinted *Roosje Zonder Doornen* (rose without thorns). The amber-coloured *Kus me snel* (kiss me quick) and the bright green *Pruimpje prik in* are alleged aphrodi-

siacs. *Maagbitter* is said to cure indigestion, while the *Heksen Elixir* (witches' elixir), flavored with honey and herbs, is an old wives' remedy for just about everything.

WATERWINKEL
Roelof Hartstraat 10 ☎(020) 6755932. Map 5J3.
Specialized shop selling bottled waters from more than 100 sources, ranging from Sweden to China.

WOUT ARXHOEK
Damstraat 23 ☎(020) 6229118. Map 10D5.
This small shop has a good selection of Dutch cheeses for export, not just Edam and Gouda, but delicacies such as the unusual *Friese nagelkaas* (Frisian clove cheese).

HOUSEHOLD ARTICLES
Amsterdammers have a taste for bizarre clocks, lamps and espresso machines.

STUDIO BAZAR
Reguliersdwarsstraat 60 ☎(020) 6220830. Map 6F5 AE ⊕ ⊙ VISA
A wide selection of kitchen utensils, ranging from dazzling chrome espresso machines from Italy to frivolous pickle picks from England and cress scissors from Denmark.

HET MAGAZIJN
Keizersgracht 709 ☎(020) 6222858. Map 6F5 AE ⊕ ⊙ VISA
Hi-tech kitchen accessories for yuppies.

DE WITTE TANDENWINKEL
Runstraat 5 ☎(020) 6233443. Map 9E3 AE ⊕ ⊙ VISA
An eye-catching display of dental accessories, ranging from serious tooth picks to novelty brushes.

ZWILLING
P.C. Hooftstraat 43 ☎(020) 6714220. Map 5G3 AE ⊕ ⊙ VISA
Serious cooks who want to slice millimeter-thin morsels of truffle go to Zwilling for German-made kitchen knives.

MAPS
The great voyages of discovery of the 17thC Dutch explorers would appear to have given their descendants an inexhaustible taste for travel, and specialized maps and guides can usually be found in Amsterdam.

A LA CARTE
Utrechtsestraat 110-112 ☎*(020) 6250679. Map* **7G6** 📷 💳
An international selection of travel books and guides, as well as a range of maps covering everywhere from New York's East Village to the planet Mars.

L. J. HARRI
Schreierstoren, Prins Hendrikkade 94-5 ☎*(020) 6248092. Map* **11C6.**
Sailing books, sea charts and nautical instruments in a 16thC tower covered with bronze plaques commemorating historic sea voyages.

PIED À TERRE
Singel 393 ☎*(020) 6274455. Map* **10E4.**
Crammed with detailed maps and guidebooks. Excellent if you are planning a cycling trip or walking vacation.

JACOB VAN WIJNGAARDEN
Overtoom 136 ☎*(020) 6121901. Map* **5G1.**
Amsterdammers seized with wanderlust instinctively make a beeline for this shop, whose specialized map collection covering virtually the whole world is crammed into one of Amsterdam's smallest shops.

MARKETS
Amsterdam's specialized markets are particularly fascinating, but it is also interesting to visit one of the many food markets, if only to witness the size of Dutch vegetables.

ANTIEKMARKT DE LOOIER
Elandsgracht 109 ☎*(020) 6249038. Map* **9E2.** *Open Sat-Wed 11am-5pm; Thurs 11am-9pm. Closed Fri.*
A sprawling indoor market on the edge of the Jordaan, where you can find everything from rusty scythes to street organs. Its claim to be an antiques market should not be taken too literally.

BLOEMENMARKT
Singel (between Koningsplein and Muntplein). Map **6F4.**
Amsterdam's spectacular floating flower market.

ALBERT CUYPSTRAAT
Albert Cuypstraat. Map **6I4.**
A crowded, cosmopolitan street market held on Monday to Saturday on a drab 19thC street, with specialized stalls selling everything from potatoes to champagne. People of many nationalities flock here to buy olives, fresh herbs, Indonesian spices, Dutch *nieuwe haring,* cheese, dates and ugly fish. The quirky touches of humor — such as

women's tights displayed on rows of dancing mannequin legs — are guaranteed to lift one's spirits on even the wettest of days. The shops along Albert Cuypstraat are just as fascinating, with their exotic foods and cheap jewelry for teenage nights on the town.

BOEKENMARKT
Oudemanhuispoort. Map **10E5.**
An unusual passage containing 18 tiny shops dating from the 18thC, most of which are occupied by antiquarian booksellers who keep rather irregular hours.

PLANTENMARKT
Amstelveld. Map **6G5.**
This colorful plant and seed market takes place early on Monday mornings from May to October, while the rest of Amsterdam is still fast asleep.

POSTZEGELMARKT
Nieuwe Zijds Voorburgwal (opposite Amsterdams Historisch Museum). Map **10E4.**

This makeshift stamp and coin market is held on Wednesday and Saturday, near numerous philately stores.

NOORDERMARKT
Noordermarkt. Map 9B3.
A crowded Monday flea market, which spills over into Westerstraat. On Saturday, a bird market is held here.

WATERLOOPLEIN
Waterlooplein. Map 7F6.
"Lying there were headless nails, toothless saws, bladeless chisels, locks without springs, keys without locks, hooks without eyes and eyes without hooks, buckles without prongs." This description of Amsterdam's flea market, penned by the writer Multatuli in the 19thC, still rings true today, although the atrocities of World War II robbed the market of its distinctive Jewish identity. Amsterdammers will tell you regretfully that its heyday is long past, but Waterlooplein is still a good place in which to hunt for second-hand clothes, old books, prints and other curiosities.

POSTCARDS
Specialized postcard stores stock a wide range of imaginative, witty and bizarre cards as an alternative to the ubiquitous tulips and windmills.

ART UNLIMITED
Keizersgracht 510 ☎*(020) 6248419. Map 5F3* 🆎 💳 💳
Art Unlimited publishes a huge range of postcards to suit every whim, including reproductions of Dutch paintings, Amsterdam bicycles, misty polder landscapes and eccentric Italian furniture. Look out for the series of postcards based on Theo van den Boogaard cartoons, including an ironic *Götterdämmerung* (named after Wagner's opera) showing the traffic chaos in front of the Muziektheater. Many of Art Unlimited's best works are available upstairs in poster format.

STATIONERY AND ART SUPPLIES
Amsterdam has a number of excellent shops selling all kinds of art supplies. Amsterdammers have a penchant for flamboyant stationery, which is the specialty of a number of shops.

VAN BEEK
Stadhouderskade 63-5 ☎*(020) 6621670. Map 6H4* 🆎
Artists' supplies store opened in 1895, with paintings by former customers, such as the Impressionist George Breitner.

'T JAPANESE WINKELTJE
Nieuwe Zijds Voorburgwal 177 ☎*(020) 6279523. Map 10D4.*
Imports the best of Japanese design, including calligraphic materials, origami paper, porcelain tea sets and kimonos.

VAN DER LINDE
Rozengracht 38 ☎*(020) 6242791. Map 9D3.*
This professional art supplier trades in the appropriate setting of the street where Rembrandt spent his last years.

POSTHUMUS
Sint Luciensteeg 25 ☎*(020) 6255812. Map 10E4.*

Elegant writing paper, *ex libris* labels, unusual monogram and pictogram rubber stamps and other printing equipment. Closed on Saturday.

TOYS, GAMES AND MODELS

Amsterdam has several well-stocked toy stores that appeal to adults and children alike. Dutch children grow up playing with the same toys as their peers elsewhere: Lego, Playmobil and Fisher-Price are sold in most shops, but Amsterdam is also an excellent hunting-ground for beautifully-crafted models.

AUTHENTIC MODELS HOLLAND
Nederlands Scheepvaart Museum, Kattenburgerplein 1 ☎*(020) 6246601. Map 4D4* AE ◯ ◯ ▥ *Open Thurs-Sat 10am-5pm.*
Modeling enthusiasts will find a wide range of finely detailed wooden ships, including IJsselmeer fishing boats, in the basement of the maritime museum shop.

CLADDER
Utrechtsestraat 47 ☎*(020) 6237949. Map 6F5.*
Make-up and carnival masks.

MATRIOSKA
Nieuwe Leliestraat 43 ☎*(020) 6221172. Map 9C3.*
Beautiful Russian dolls and other traditional handicrafts are sold in a Chekhovian interior complete with nostalgic family snapshots.

E. KRAMER POPPENDOKTER
Reestraat 18-20 ☎*(020) 6265274. Map 9D3.*
E. Kramer is an old-fashioned doll doctor, and his shop is crammed with dolls, puppets and soft toys, as well as a range of candles.

SPEELGOEDZAAK INTERTOYS HOLLAND
Heiligeweg 26 ☎*(020) 6221122. Map 10E4.*
Amsterdam's biggest toy store, offering everything from dolls to Danish lollipops. The model railway department on the first floor has a vast stock of trains, including the latest bright yellow Dutch models, plus accessories ranging from Old Berlin streetlamps to flocks of sheep.

TEKEN AAN DE WAND
Huidenstraat 6 ☎*(020) 6256241. Map 9E3.*
It is impossible not to smile as you squeeze gingerly among the dangling marionettes, swooping birds and exclusive kites in this enchanting toy store. Teken aan de Wand (literally "the writing on the wall") is a paradise for model builders, bird kite fanciers, Snoopy fans and anyone who enjoys good old-fashioned nuttiness.

VLIEGERTUIG
Gasthuismolensteeg 8 ☎*(020) 6233450. Map 10D4* AE ◯ ▥
Vliegertuig sells kites and boomerangs, and offers friendly advice to the novice on how to make them fly.

Amsterdam: recreation

Amsterdam for children

Amsterdam is a rather cramped city, with few parks or open spaces where children can romp around. Children brought up in Amsterdam therefore quickly adopt adult pursuits such as visiting cafés, theaters, cinemas and art galleries. For more traditional children's activities, it is often necessary to venture outside the city.

Parents with small children may have trouble finding places to change diapers. A few progressive Dutch museums, including the AMSTERDAM HISTORISCH MUSEUM and the BOYMANS-VAN BEUNINGEN MUSEUM in Rotterdam, now provide a table with a changing mat (sometimes signed *babyverzorging*). Elsewhere, department stores are usually adequate. The STEDE-LIJK MUSEUM provides rucksacks for carrying small babies.

PARKS AND ZOOS
Probably the top attraction for children in Amsterdam is ARTIS, a well-designed zoo with numerous indoor attractions, such as an aquarium and nocturnal house, to keep children amused on rainy days.

The best parks for children are the AMSTELPARK, with its miniature train, pony rides, farmyard, maze, mini-golf, seals and pancake house; and the AMSTERDAMSE BOS, which can be reached on summer weekends by the ELECTRISCHE MUSEUM TRAMLIJN from Haarlemmermeerstation.

Children might also enjoy a visit to one of the **children's farmyards** *(kinderboerderijen)* in Amsterdam. These unusual city farms are found at Artis, the Amstelpark, next to the Okura Hotel and on Bickerseiland.

MUSEUMS AND WORKSHOPS
The most interesting museums for children are MADAME TUSSAUD SCENER-AMA (waxwork figures), the SPAARPOTTENMUSEUM (piggy banks), the NEDERLANDS SCHEEPVAART MUSEUM (ship models), NINT TECHNISCH MUSEUM (push-button models) and the TROPENMUSEUM (reconstructed Third World villages). The Tropenmuseum also has a separate children's department, the **Kindermuseum TM Junior**.

Amsterdam children also seem to enjoy the modern art (and particularly the video shows) in the STEDELIJK MUSEUM.

THEATERS, MOVIES, CIRCUSES AND OTHER EVENTS
Children usually enjoy the spectacle of street theater, which flourishes in the summer months around LEIDSEPLEIN and in front of the KONINKLIJK

193

PALEIS on the Dam. The *Uitkrant* has a special section, *Jeugdagenda*, devoted to children's events in Amsterdam, while Dutch-speaking children can also dial the **Jeugdtheaterlijn** *(☎(020) 6222999)* for a chatty recorded message informing them of coming events.

The main venue for children's theater is **De Krakeling** *(Nieuwe Passeerdersstraat 1 ☎(020) 6245123, map 9 E3, tram 7, 10 to Raamplein)*. Most shows will be in Dutch, but occasionally there is mime or music.

Movies for children are regularly screened at the **Kinder Film Centrum** *(☎(020) 6228206)*, at the **Rialto** movie theater (see NIGHTLIFE AND ENTERTAINMENT). The weekly film listings include details of children's matinees *(kindermatinees)*. Most of these are dubbed into Dutch (indicated by the words *"Nederlands gesproken"*).

The **Amsterdams Marionettentheater** *(Nieuwe Jonkerstraat 8 ☎(020) 6208027, map 11 D6)* puts on occasional shows featuring traditional marionettes. Guided tours backstage let you into the secrets of the art *(Wed at 2pm, advance reservation required)*.

Occasional shows are also put on by **Elleboog**, the children's circus *(Passeerdersgracht 32 ☎(020) 6269370, map 9 E2, telephone reservation essential, tram 7, 10 to Raamplein)*.

BOAT TRIPS AND TRAM RIDES

Canal boat trips are always fun, and most operators have reduced rates for children. A more energetic way to explore the canals is by **canal bicycle** (see SPORTS, page 196). The less adventurous can also get to know the city by tram (see TRAM RIDES, page 78).

On summer weekends, old-fashioned trams run regularly to the Amsterdamse Bos (see ELECTRISCHE MUSEUM TRAMLIJN, page 89). A tourist tram also departs from Dam *(mid-Apr to Sept 10.30am-6pm, every 45mins)* on a 70-minute tour of the city.

WALKS

Certain areas of Amsterdam have details that might appeal to children, such as the **western islands** (see ZANDHOEK in SIGHTS, page 126), a quiet, almost traffic-free area of narrow wooden bridges and old boats. The center of the city is also packed with interesting details (see WALKS 1 and 3, pages 69 and 72), such as the facade stones on **St Luciensteeg** (see AMSTERDAMS HISTORISCH MUSEUM) and the curious **barge** moored near the Muziektheater on the AMSTEL.

Taking a trip on the **free ferry** that departs from behind Centraal Station can also be interesting.

CAFÉS AND RESTAURANTS

In Holland, children are welcome in cafés, where they enjoy *chocomel* (chocolate-flavored milk) and *warme chocolade* (hot chocolate). Among the cafés that might appeal to children are the **Américain** for its grand interior, **De IJsbreker** for delicious hot chocolate (see CAFÉS for both), and the café-restaurant of the AMSTERDAMS HISTORISCH MUSEUM, which contains 17thC wooden models of David and Goliath.

Some restaurants offer an inexpensive *kindermenu* (children's menu), which usually involves dishes designed to appeal to children, although they may horrify conscientious parents with their emphasis on French fries, ice cream and soda.

Amsterdam also boasts a children's restaurant, **Het Kinder Kookcafé** *(Oude Zijds Achterburgwal 193 ☎ (020) 6253257, map 10 E5, open Sat, Sun 3-6pm, reservation essential for Sat noon-2pm, tram 4, 9, 14, 16, 24, 25 to Spui)*, where meals are prepared under adult supervision by children aged 6-12 years. Although most of the diners are children, parents may, if they wish, accompany their offspring.

OTHER IDEAS

Children will probably enjoy climbing a church tower for a view of the city. The towers of the WESTERKERK, ZUIDERKERK and OUDE KERK are all open to the public.

Energetic parents with small children can rent bicycles with children's seats attached for short trips into the country.

Amsterdam has several swimming pools, of which the **Mirandabad**, with its slides and artificial waves, has the most to offer energetic kids: see SPORTS, page 198. If all else fails, treat your child to a present from one of Amsterdam's toy stores (see SHOPPING, page 192).

EXCURSIONS

Amsterdam is well located for excursions to surrounding towns with attractions that might appeal to children. The historic harbor towns N of Amsterdam are particularly exciting. From HOORN there are **steam trains** to MEDEMBLIK and **boat trips** on the IJsselmeer. Boats also ply between the ports of MONNICKENDAM, MARKEN and VOLENDAM, and there are scheduled ferry services across the IJsselmeer from ENKHUIZEN. The **Zuiderzee Museum** in Enkhuizen allows children to roam freely through the reconstructed streets and houses, and younger children might enjoy **Sprookjeswonderland** (a park dotted with scenes from fairy tales) on the N edge of the town. Finally, UTRECHT offers the **Nationaal Museum van Speelklok tot Pierement** (From Carillon to Barrel Organ) and the **Nederlands Spoorwegmuseum** (national railway museum).

See RANDSTAD TOWNS AND VILLAGES (page 276) for further details of these towns and cities.

Sports

Although the flat, watery and densely populated landscape around Amsterdam may seem unsuited to outdoor activities, it provides the ideal setting for cycling, sailing and sailboarding, all of which are popular. The main recreation areas for Amsterdam are the AMSTERDAMSE BOS to the SW for boating and cycling; the **Gaasperplas** to the SE for boating, wind-surfing and fishing *(metro to Gaasperplas);* and **Het Twiske** to the N for cycling, sailboarding, rowing, canoeing, horseback riding, walking and bird-watching (☎ *(02984) 4338, bus 91, 92 from Centraal Station).*

Rowboats, canoes, sailboards, sailing-dinghies and bicycles can all be rented at Het Twiske, at **Jachthaven De Roemer** (☎ *(02984) 4890).*

BICYCLING

Cycling through the bustling streets of Amsterdam can be a stressful experience, but to the N and S of the city are a number of quiet roads that are ideal for short excursions on two wheels (see ENVIRONS OF AMSTERDAM, page 200). The brochure *Cycling in Holland,* available from the **Netherlands Board of Tourism** (see BEFORE YOU GO, page 32, for addresses) contains practical advice for the cyclist, with information on recommended long-distance routes, and details of special vacation packages.

Self-guided cycling tours are organized by **Anglo Dutch Sports** *(30a Foxgrove Road, Beckenham, Kent BR3 2BD, UK* ☎ *(081) 650-2347* [Fx] *(081) 663-3371).* The routes are carefully planned to avoid busy roads, and arrangements can be made for transporting or storing baggage. One possibility is a fascinating nine-day tour of **Old Dutch Towns,** which takes in Dordrecht, Delft, Leiden, Gouda and the windmills at Kinderdijk. **Yellow Bike** *(Nieuwe Zijds Voorburgwal 66* ☎ *(020) 6206940, map 10 C5)* organizes a (much less strenuous) 30-kilometer guided bicycle tour from Amsterdam to Marken and the villages of Waterland.

BOATING

Canal bicycles *(grachtenfietsen)* for 2-4 people can be rented at five locations on the main canals. These are: LEIDSEKADE at the American Hotel; PRINSENGRACHT at Westermarkt; SINGELGRACHT at the Rijksmuseum; KEIZERSGRACHT at Leidsestraat; and the Schreierstoren. *(For all* ☎ *(020) 6265574, open 9am-7pm; summer 9am-11pm.)* Rowboats can be rented at the AMSTERDAMSE BOS and **Het Twiske**.

CANOEING

Canoes can be rented at the AMSTERDAMSE BOS and **Het Twiske**. For general information on canoeing on Dutch inland waters, contact the **Netherlands Canoe Association** *(Postbus 434, 1380 AK Weesp* ☎ *(02940) 18331).* Good maps can be obtained from **Jacob van Wijngaarden** (see SHOPPING, page 190).

FISHING

Information on fishing can be obtained from the **Netherlands Board of Tourism**, or from the **NVVS** *(Postbus 288, 3800 AG Amersfoort* ☎ *(033) 634924).*

SOCCER

The main soccer club in Amsterdam is **Ajax** *(stadium at Middenweg 401, map 4 E5; tram 9).*

HEALTH CLUBS

The **Scandic Active Club** *(in the Scandic Crown Hotel, Damrak 1-6* ☎ *(020) 6200522, map 10 C5)* is a roomy and quiet health club decorated with exclusive Karel Appel lithos. The center is equipped with the very latest training equipment, together with a sauna and small pool, and a professional physiotherapist is on the spot to provide advice. You buy a pass for one day or longer.

Bronzed Amsterdammers maintain the body beautiful at the **Splash Fitness Club** *(Kattengat 1* ☎ *(020) 6271044, map 10 B5).* One-day passes can be bought at the desk.

ICE-SKATING

Amsterdam's ice-skating rink is the **Jaap Edenbaan** *(Radioweg 64* ☎ *(020) 6949894).* A temporary ice rink is also set up on LEIDSEPLEIN in winter; if it remains cold for long enough you can skate on numerous frozen canals, ponds and lakes around the city. Take your cue from the natives.

RUNNING AND JOGGING

The **Vondelpark** is the best green space for a brisk jog or run in the morning.

SAILBOARDING

Holland's inland waters are ideal for sailboarding. The most popular areas close to Amsterdam are **Het Twiske; Gaasperplas** (SE Amsterdam); the AMSTERDAMSE BOS; the **Gouwzee** (off Monnickendam); the **Kinselmeer** (NE of Durgerdam); and the **Hoornse Hop** (off Hoorn). Contact the Royal Netherlands Watersports Foundation: **Koninklijk Nederlands Watersport Verbond** *(Postbus 53034, 1007 RA Amsterdam* ☎ *(020) 6642611).*

SAILING

A country with so much water obviously offers excellent opportunities for sailing. The brochure *Holland Watersports Paradise,* available from the **Netherlands Board of Tourism** (see page 32 for addresses), contains practical information and recommended itineraries.

Traditional sailing-boats with crew can be rented in Amsterdam — contact **Stichting Het Varend Museumschip** *(De Ruijterkade 106* ☎ *(020) 6270001, map 11 C7)* — or in Enkhuizen — contact **Zeilvaart Enkhuizen** *(Stationsplein 3, 1601 EN Enkhuizen* ☎ *(02280) 12424)*

Ex *(02280) 13737)*. Charts and almanacs can be bought from **L. J. Harri** (see SHOPPING, page 190).

SAUNA
De Kosmos *(Prins Hendrikkade 142* ☎ *(020) 6230686, map **11**D7, open Mon-Sat 10.30am-10pm)* is a friendly, mixed sauna with a small open-air pool.

SWIMMING
The most modern pool in Amsterdam is the **Mirandabad** *(De Miran-dalaan 9* ☎ *(020) 6428080)*, which has artificial waves and slides.

TABLE TENNIS, POOL AND SNOOKER
Homesick Americans are thrilled to discover real pool tables at the **Table Tennis and Pool Center** *(Keizersgracht 209* ☎ *(020) 6245780, map **9**D3)*. Their British counterparts are to be found bent over the snooker tables at the **Snookercenter Rokin** *(Rokin 28* ☎ *(020) 6204974, map **10**E4)*.

WALKING
The landscape around Amsterdam is more suited to cycling than walking, but there are attractive areas for gentle rambles in the dunes w of Haarlem *(train to Overveen)* and w of Castricum *(train to Castricum)*, and the woods s of Hilversum *(train to Hollandsche Rading)*.

Activities

AMSTERDAM FOR FREE

Amsterdam is not a particularly inexpensive city, but there are always a number of free events. Travelers on tight budgets should look out for the **free lunch concerts** announced in the *Uitkrant* (itself a free publication). You can catch *gratis* recitals by the **Netherlands Philharmonic Orchestra** or the **Netherlands Ballet Orchestra** in the Boekmanzaal of the **Muziektheater** *(Tues at 12.30pm)*. The **Bethanienklooster** has a free lunchtime concert on Fridays at 12.30pm, and the **IJsbreker** has the occasional free lunchtime performance of contemporary music. You might even catch a free performance given by the world-famous **Concertgebouworkest** at one of the weekly free concerts *(Wed 12.30-1pm)* in the Concertgebouw (for addresses, see NIGHTLIFE AND ENTERTAINMENT, page 165).

The exhibitions, lectures, films and concerts organized by the **Goethe Institut** and the **Istituto Italiano di Cultura** (see NIGHTLIFE AND ENTERTAINMENT, page 169) are often free of charge.

Those who cannot afford a boat trip on the canals might like to take a trip on one of the **public ferries** that cross the IJ from behind Centraal Station (see GETTING AROUND, page 58). Most museums charge an entry fee, but you can visit the free **exhibition on town planning** in the Zuiderkerk (see INFORMATIECENTRUM RUIMTELIJKE ORDENING), or stroll into the SCHUTTERSGALERIJ to look at the **17thC paintings of civic guards**. It also costs nothing to visit one of the city's **markets**, or to watch the bidding at an **auction** (see SHOPPING, page 176).

BIRD-WATCHING

The island of **Texel** (85km/53 miles N of Amsterdam, reached by ferry from Den Helder) is particularly famous for its bird life. For information, contact the **VVV** *(Groeneplaats 9, 1791 CC Den Burg (Texel)* ☎ *(02220) 14741* Fx *(02220) 14129)*.

CHESS

Chess is played in many cafés, particularly **Het Hok** *(Lange Leidsedwarsstraat 134, map 5 F3)*, just off Leidseplein.

YOGA AND MEDITATION

Yoga, meditation and lectures on non-Western philosophy are organized by **De Kosmos** *(Prins Hendrikkade 142* ☎ *(020) 6230686, map 11 D7)*.

Environs of Amsterdam

Some attractive and undisturbed villages lie within easy reach of Amsterdam, such as **Broek in Waterland** and **Edam** to the N, and **Ouderkerk**, **Abcoude** and **Breukelen** to the s. A few unlucky ones such as Marken and Volendam have become overwhelmed by tourism, but even they still retain a certain charm at quiet times of the year (see RANDSTAD TOWNS AND VILLAGES, page 276). The villages are set in attractive Dutch landscapes, such as **Waterland** to the N of Amsterdam and the area of **lakes** *(plassen)* to the s.

BULBFIELDS

Carolus Clusius laid the foundations of the Dutch bulb industry in the 17thC with his experiments in the breeding of rare varieties of tulip. The main bulbfields in Holland were developed on polderland between Leiden and Haarlem, where fields are magically transformed into vivid blocks of color in April and May. A train journey from Haarlem to Leiden is the simplest way to view the bulbfields, after which you can take a bus *(NZH 50, 51)* to **Keukenhof** ★ *(Stationsweg, Lisse* ☎ *(02521) 19034* 🖼 ♿ 🅿 🚮 *open late Mar/early Apr to late May 8am-6.30pm)*, a huge, landscaped flower garden packed with five to six million tulips, hyacinths and daffodils. It is also possible to drive or cycle through the bulbfields; maps in English are available at tourist offices.

FLOWER AUCTION

Mon A.M.

The Aalsmeer flower auction, **Verenigde Bloemenveilingen Aalsmeer** ★ *(Legmeerdijk 313* ☎ *(02977) 34567* 🖼 ♣ 🚮 *open Mon-Fri 7.30-11.30am; bus CN 171, 172 from Amsterdam Centraal Station)* offers an intriguing glimpse of the commercial side of the bulb industry. Some 11 million flowers and one million plants are sold daily in this vast complex covering an area equal to 55 soccer fields. Visitors proceed along an elevated catwalk, which offers a panoramic view of the sorting, auction and distribution areas. Although efficiency is the main aim of the operation, the auction also possesses an undeniable romance: porters cycle by with huge bunches of flowers or toss stray red roses to the spectators above.

ZANDVOORT

Amsterdam is well placed for getting to the sea at Zandvoort *(i School-plein 1, 2042 VD Zandvoort* ☎ *(02507) 17947* [Fx] *(02507) 17003, 30mins by train from Amsterdam Centraal Station; by car, on the N5)*. The town is rather dull, even suburban, and there is little to do except sit on the fine, sandy beach, where even on crowded summer days the atmosphere is friendly and relaxed. The extensive dunes behind the beach are pleasant for walking or cycling.

Cycle trips

Amsterdam is such a neat and compact city that it is possible to cycle from the center to the outer edge in about half an hour. For a first taste of biking in Holland, it makes sense to choose quiet countryside rather than busy city streets. Just N of Amsterdam lies a protected area of flat, watery fields with grazing cows and pyramid-roofed farmhouses buried in clumps of trees. The region — known as **Waterland** because of its numerous lakes and drainage ditches — is dotted with unspoiled villages such as **Broek in Waterland** and **Durgerdam**. The towns on the edge of the **IJsselmeer** (the name for the Zuider Zee after it was enclosed by a dyke in 1932) each possess a distinctive character, and although some have become swamped by tourism, others retain a traditional flavor far removed from the cosmopolitan bustle of Amsterdam. (See RANDSTAD TOWNS AND VILLAGES.)

Amsterdam offers the cyclist two simple and relatively traffic-free routes to reach the open countryside to the S and N of the city. The first follows the course of the raised dyke on the N side of the IJ to **Monnickendam**, 16km (10 miles) from Amsterdam; the second follows the winding river Amstel to **Ouderkerk aan de Amstel**, 10km (6 miles) from Amsterdam. There is also a pleasant route to the AMSTERDAMSE BOS.

ROUTE 1/WATERLAND

Beginning at Centraal Station, use the underpass to the E of the station to reach De Ruijterkade, then turn left to reach the free ferry across the IJ, which departs from immediately behind the station (signposted **Buiksloterwegveer**). Once across the IJ, follow Buiksloterweg, turn right at a sign to Het Twiske, then follow the path alongside the Noord Hollandsch Kanaal to reach the **Florapark**. At the end of the park, turn right along the **Buiksloterdijk**, an old dyke lined with typical North Holland houses. At the end, turn left through an underpass, then right to join the **Leeuwarderweg**. Follow this street to the traffic circle, then cross the road to join the Nieuwendammerdijk. This quiet street follows an old sea dyke eastward, becoming Schellingwouderdijk and then Durgerdammerdijk. Simply follow the dyke to reach the pretty former fishing village of **Durgerdam**. The dyke road then meanders along the water's edge to **Uitdam**, 6km (4 miles) from Amsterdam.

If your legs are beginning to ache by Uitdam, cut the journey short by turning left to **Zuiderwoude** and then **Broek in Waterland**, 6km (4 miles) from Uitdam. Otherwise, continue along the side of the dyke about 3km (2 miles) until you come to an intersection. From here take a short detour right along an artificial causeway to reach the picturesque but crowded village of **Marken**, or turn left and pedal for 5km (3 miles) to the unspoiled town of **Monnickendam**. Energy permitting, continue along the dyke road, ignoring the horrendous Volendam, to **Edam**, which is beautiful; then return by the main N247 (which has a cycle lane) to Monnickendam. Most people, finding Monnickendam quite far enough, return to Amsterdam via the lovely village of **Broek in Water-**

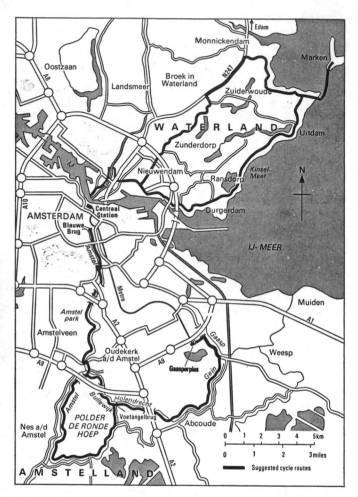

land, which is 3km (2 miles) by the main road. Here you can reward yourself with a pancake in **De Witte Swaen** (), a restaurant popular with cyclists. Once rested, return the 6km (4 miles) to Amsterdam by taking the underpass to reach the s side of the main road, then following signs to **Zunderdorp**. The route is marked *doorgaand verkeer* ("through traffic") and enters Amsterdam just beyond Zunderdorp. Follow the road straight ahead to return to Nieuwendammerdijk, then turn right to retrace the route back to the ferry. Allow 3 hours for the round trip to Broek in Waterland, 4 hours to Monnickendam and 5 hours to Edam.

ROUTE 2/AMSTELLAND

On warm Sunday afternoons, Amsterdammers set off down the Amstel in large family groups, with small children perched in baskets on the rear of a parent's bicycle, and grandparents following behind with folding chairs and fishing rods. The lure of the Amstel dates from the 17thC, when wealthy Amsterdammers built themselves country houses on the banks of the river. After the death of his wife Saskia in 1642, Rembrandt often wandered this route, sketching the landscape with a delicacy that seems more Japanese than European, and in the 19thC, the restful, watery landscape of Amstelland attracted many Dutch Impressionist painters.

Beginning at the **Blauwe Brug**, head down the left-hand side of the AMSTEL crossing the three main canals: HERENGRACHT, KEIZERSGRACHT and PRINSENGRACHT. On reaching Sarphatistraat, pass in front of the Amstel Hotel and through the underpass to reach Weesperzijde. Continue s past the Nieuwe Amstelbrug and cross the river at the **Berlagebrug**, with its distinctive red and black lampposts.

Continue down the w side of the Amstel and turn left just beyond the Rivierstaete office, following the red cycle sign to Ouderkerk. The quiet tree-lined road follows the Amstel all the way to **Ouderkerk aan de Amstel**, passing the cemetery Zorgvlied, the attractive AMSTELPARK (where cycling is prohibited) the octagonal **Rieker windmill** that formerly stood on the Rieker polder, a **statue of Rembrandt sketching**, and the café **Kleine Kalfje** (==).

On reaching the outskirts of Ouderkerk, turn left across the river, then immediately right and right again down Kerkstraat. On the left is the entrance to the **Portugees Israelitische Begraafplaats** (*Kerkstraat* ☒ *open dawn-dusk; closed Sat, Jewish hols),* a Jewish cemetery established in the 17thC and containing the exceptionally ornate, and romantically overgrown tombs of prominent Amsterdammers, many bearing Hebrew and Portuguese inscriptions. Male visitors should, out of courtesy, wear a cap, which can be borrowed from the **PIB Werkgroep office** (*Kerkstraat 7).*

For those who wish to venture beyond Ouderkerk, the best route to follow is along the river Bullewijk, which is reached by crossing the bridge at the end of Kerkstraat and turning left. On reaching the Voetangelsbrug, choose one of two routes: either straight ahead to follow a circular route around the polder **De Ronde Hoep** (the round hoop), which eventually leads back to Ouderkerk, a distance of 13km (8 miles), or left along the river Holendrecht to the village of **Abcoude**, which is 6km (4 miles) from Ouderkerk.

The energetic can continue N along the peaceful river Gein to **Weesp**, then follow the river Gaasp on the left-hand side (Provincialeweg) as far as the **Loosdrecht Dreef**. Turn left here and cycle through the **Park Gaasperplas** to reach the metro station Gaasperplas, which is 10km (6 miles) from Abcoude. You can then put your bicycle on the metro at a reduced fare and return to Centraal Station. Allow 2 hours for the round trip from Amsterdam to Ouderkerk and 4 hours for either one of the two longer trips.

Rotterdam

Europe's port

Rotterdam is not just Europe's, but the world's busiest port. An endless stream of ships from every continent lends an irresistible excitement to its sprawling waterfront. Bulky container vessels ease into the giant docks downstream of the city, while long convoys of barges sail up the broad River Maas, bound for the heart of the continent.

The visitor to Rotterdam cannot ever ignore the port, whose activities extend to every corner of the city. You will see aged gravel barges crammed into the Leuvehaven and Oude Haven, rusting East European cargo ships moored alongside the city park and sleek German cruise liners gliding past the geodesic dome of the Tropicana swimming pool.

Even in the heart of the city, the port makes its presence known through the proliferation of shipping firms, maritime insurers and churches for foreign seamen. One of the first sights a traveler will see on leaving the main rail station is an oil tanker superstructure planted in the middle of Kruisplein. Even the postwar architecture in Rotterdam, with its promenade decks and portholes, looks as if it was designed by a naval architect.

DESTRUCTION AND REGENERATION

Strategically located where the rivers Rhine and Maas enter the North Sea, Rotterdam can trace its origins almost as far back as can Amsterdam. The city was founded on the right bank of the Maas in the 13th century, and grew into one of the great ports of the Dutch maritime empire. However, virtually all traces of the old city have been erased, first by the course of 19th- and 20th-century progress, and then more brutally by the blitz of 1940, which provided a foretaste of the massive destruction of urban Europe in World War II. The St Laurenskerk, which miraculously survived the attack, stands as the only Gothic relic left in the old town. A 17th-century statue in front of the church represents the humanist scholar Erasmus, born in Rotterdam in 1466.

The bombed city has been restored so seamlessly that you are barely aware of the massive scale of the destruction in 1940. The Lijnbaan shopping center typifies the neat, shipshape style of Rotterdam in the Fifties, which set the tone for much of northern Europe's postwar architecture. The ruins may have been removed, but you can still feel something of the terror of May 14, 1940. On the windswept square next to the maritime museum, Ossip Zadkine's memorial shows an agonized figure reaching its arms to the sky in a gesture that combines fear and fury.

Rotterdam invested massive sums to build a new port to the west of the old town. Now Europe's principal harbor, it sprawls for some 37 kilometers (22 miles) along the Nieuwe Maas waterfront. Giant tankers pump crude oil into the huge storage tanks at the Europoort, while container ships unload vast tonnages of fruit, tea and tobacco at the Waalhaven docks.

BURSTING THE STRAITJACKET

In the triple alliance of Randstad cities, Rotterdam has traditionally been seen as the working partner, while The Hague housed the government and Amsterdam was home to the arts. But that stereotype has recently begun to collapse as Rotterdam breaks out of its straitjacket and improves its cultural image. A series of innovative new museums have been opened, devoted to shipping, architecture and ethnography, while the daring new architecture at Blaak and Leuvehaven has given Rotterdam one of the most exciting urban waterfronts in Europe.

Some of the developments are perhaps misguided, such as the flashy new skyscrapers on Weena, but Rotterdam remains one of the ultimate cities of the modern age. You will find its spirit best expressed in the metallic cafés buzzing with jazz, the experimental art shows at the Boymans-van Beuningen Museum, and the dizzying views from the Euromast and Promenade Overblaak. You may eventually find Rotterdam *too* modern, but you are bound to end up full of admiration for its energy and imagination.

Rotterdam has some excellent pictures in its Boymans Museum; but they are, I fancy, overlooked by many visitors. It seems no city in which to see pictures. It is a city for anything rather than art — a mercantile centre, a hive of bees, a shipping port of intense activity. And yet perhaps the quietest little Albert Cuyp in Holland is here, "De Oude Oostpoort te Rotterdam," a small evening scene, without cattle, suffused in a golden glow.
(E.V. Lucas, *A Wanderer in Holland*, 1905)

Basic information

Getting around

FROM THE AIRPORTS TO ROTTERDAM
Direct trains run from Schiphol airport to **Rotterdam CS** (45 minutes). Rotterdam has a small airport, **Zestienhoven** (☎ *(010) 4463455),* with business flights from many European cities. Take bus 33 from the airport to Centraal Station.

RAIL TRAVEL
There is an airline check-in desk at Rotterdam CS for passengers flying from Schiphol with KLM and certain other airlines. It might cut down the time you spend at the airport, though you still have to lug your baggage on the train (☎ *06-8991121 for information on domestic trains* ☎ *(010) 4117100 for international services).*

PUBLIC TRANSPORTATION
RET runs Rotterdam's extensive network of metro, trams and buses. The system of tickets is the same as elsewhere in the Randstad (detailed information on which is given on page 34).

The city has a modern and efficient metro system, which penetrates deep into the outlying suburbs. The two lines of the network run roughly E to W and N to S, and intersect at Churchillplein/Beurs. To buy tickets, and to pick up free maps of the metro network, go to the RET office on Stationsplein (facing Centraal Station). *(For information on timetables* ☎ *(010) 4546890.)*

TAXIS
Taxis can be ordered by telephone (☎ *(010) 4626060),* in which case they arrive almost immediately, or picked up at one of the taxi stands in the city, located at rail stations, major hotels, squares and near important sights.

GETTING AROUND BY BICYCLE
By the standards of a country that is a byword for bicycles, Rotterdammers are relatively reluctant cyclists. The city does have an extensive cycle lane network, but the traffic on many routes is heavy, which makes cycling a tough way to get around. Unless you are really dedicated to the bicycle, stick to trams and the metro in Rotterdam.

FERRIES
Stadsveer   ☎(010) 4601617. April to October 11am-6pm. This is a regular ferry service on the Nieuwe Maas; it stops at Leuvehaven, Willemskade, Katendrecht, Parkhaven (for the Euromast) and Charloisse Hoofd.

On-the-spot information

BANKS AND CURRENCY EXCHANGE
Banks in Rotterdam are open Monday to Friday 9am-4pm. The **Grens-wisselkantoor (GWK)** at Centraal Station (*☎(010) 4542219)* is open Monday to Saturday 7.30am-10pm; Sunday 9am-10pm.

POSTAL AND TELEPHONE SERVICES
The main post office in Rotterdam *(Delftseplein 31 ☎(010) 4542219)* is open from Monday to Friday 8.30am-9pm, and on Saturday 8.30am-noon.
  International telephone calls, telegrams, fax and telex are handled there. The dialing code for Rotterdam is **010**, which should be omitted when dialing within the city.

SHOPPING HOURS
Shops in Rotterdam are open normal Dutch hours, with an extension to 9pm on Friday *(koopavond)*.

GENERAL DELIVERY (POSTE RESTANTE)
Letters to be collected should be marked *poste restante* and sent to the **Hoofdpostkantoor PTT** *(Coolsingel 42 ☎(010) 4542220)*. These can be collected at the main post office: take identification. **American Express** *(Mient 92 ☎(010) 4330300)* offer the same service to their customers.

HARBOR TOURS
Rederij Rondvaart Waterstad   Leuvehaven ☎06-52738195. July-August daily; May, June, September, Tuesday to Sunday; April, October, Saturday and Sunday; March, November, December, Sunday only. Metro or tram 1, 3, 4, 6, 7 to Churchillplein/Beurs. This unusual tour of the Waterstad (waterfront) area of the city is conducted in a bright orange lifeboat.
Spido Havenrondvaart   Willemsplein ☎(010) 4135400. Tram 5 to Willemsplein or metro to Leuvehaven. Tours of the modern port, lasting from 75 minutes to one day. See SIGHTS AND PLACES OF INTEREST, page 225, for further details.
Stoomvaart Buitenmuseum   Leuvehaven ☎(010) 4048072. April to September, Sunday only 11am-4pm; sailings (lasting 45 minutes) on the hour. Metro or tram 1, 3, 4, 6, 7 to Churchillplein/Beurs. Tour of the river in an old steam tug.

Emergency information

EMERGENCY SERVICES
For **Police**, **Ambulance** or **Fire** ☎06-11

HOSPITAL
The main hospital is the **Academisch Ziekenhuis** *(Dr Molewaterplein 40* ☎*(010) 4639222).*

MEDICAL EMERGENCIES
Doctors' 24-hour service ☎(010) 4115504; dentists' 24-hour service ☎(010) 4552155.

ALL-NIGHT PHARMACIES
Pharmacies are open Monday to Friday 8am (or 9am) to 5.30pm. For information on weekend services and all-night pharmacies ☎(010) 4110370.

HELP LINE
SOS Telefonische Hulpdienst ☎(010) 4362244.

LOST PROPERTY
If you have lost something on public transportation, go to the **RET office** on Stationsplein *(*☎*(010) 4546655).*

BUS TOURS

The tourist office organizes regular bus tours of Rotterdam. The 2-hour tour begins and ends at the tourist office at Coolsingel 67 *(Apr-Sept only, 1.30pm)*. Tickets must be bought beforehand at the tourist office in Centraal Station or on Coolsingel.

AIR TOURS

Kroonduif Air Rondvluchten   Heathrowbaan 4, Luchthaven Rotterdam ☎(010) 4157855. Flights above Rotterdam harbor in a Cessna light plane for up to 3 passengers.

Useful addresses

TOURIST INFORMATION
The main **tourist office** is at Coolsingel 67 (☎ *06-34034065* Fx *(010)*
4130124, open Mon-Thurs 9am-5.30pm; Fri 9am-9pm; Sat 9am-5pm;
Sun (Apr-Sept only) 10am-4pm).
   The tourist information booth at Centraal Station is open longer hours
(Apr-Sept daily 9am-11pm; Oct-Mar, Mon-Sat 9am-5.30pm; Sun 10am-
10pm).

AIRLINES
KLM   Coolsingel 18 ☎(020) 6747747.

MAJOR LIBRARIES
The **Gemeentebibliotheek** *(Hoogstraat 110* ☎*(010) 4338911, metro*
to Blaak) is the largest city library in Europe. It is a superbly designed
edifice similar to the Pompidou Center in Paris, but less crowded. Take
the escalator to the sixth floor for the view, or browse in the periodicals
room.

CHURCH SERVICES
Eendrachtskerk   Eendrachtsweg 46 ☎(010) 4136980. Catholic.
Engelse Kerk   Pieter de Hoochweg 133 ☎(010) 4764043. Church of
England.
Schotse Kerk   Schiedamse Vest 119 ☎(010) 4124779. Church of
Scotland.

Rotterdam: planning and walks

Orientation

Leveled in an air raid in World War II, the **Binnenstad** (city center) was rebuilt from scratch in a sensitive modern style. There are almost no old buildings left, apart from the 1935 **Boymans-van Beuningen Museum**, the **St Laurenskerk**, and the 17thC **Historisch Museum Schielandshuis**, which turns up unexpectedly amid a cluster of modern offices. The focus of life in the city has shifted from the old church to the modern **Lijnbaan** shopping center. You are likely to sleep, eat, shop and go out after dark in the Binnenstad, but you will have to go farther afield in search of museums and parks.

The **Waterstad** (waterfront), s of Centrum, was long neglected, but in recent years some remarkable new buildings have appeared. The new **maritime museum** and **Imax Theater** have brought a new vitality to the **Leuvehaven**, while the eccentric buildings at **Blaak** provide an improbable backdrop to the old barges moored in the **Oude Haven**. The **Tropicana** swimming pool is yet another dazzling addition to the urban waterfront. You can now eat in a range of waterfront cafés and restaurants, but you will find only a few hotels in the Waterstad.

The **Stadsparken** (city parks), w of the center, is an area of large parks and leafy 19thC avenues. Several major museums are found here, including the **Boymans-van Beuningen**.

Kralingen, NE of the center, is an elegant district with parks and villas. You might come out here on a warm day to wander in the woods of the **Kralingse Bos**, or visit the exotic **Arboretum Trompenburg**.

The outlying suburbs contain exemplary modern architecture, but little else to tempt outsiders. But the vast **Haven** (port), stretching w along the river, is a fascinating area to explore. You can take a boat trip, rent a plane, or follow a route for drivers.

The traveler who tires of modern Rotterdam can take refuge in the more traditional Dutch townscape at **Delfshaven**, w of Stadsparken. Or you can go out to the old town of **Schiedam**, w of Delfshaven, just beyond the city limits but easily reached by a city tram.

Organizing your time

It is wise, as in any other city, to plan a schedule in advance. The following are suggested one-day and two-day visits.

ONE-DAY VISIT
- Visitors with just a day to spare might visit the BOYMANS-VAN BEUNINGEN MUSEUM in the morning, and eat lunch in the museum restaurant or the nearby **Old Dutch** (see EATING AND DRINKING, page 229).
- In the afternoon, take a Spido **boat tour** of the port.

TWO-DAY MODERN ARCHITECTURE VISIT
Day 1
- On day 1, follow the waterfront walk in the morning.
- Spend the afternoon in the Blaak quarter. Visit the KIJK KUBUS and the Gemeentebibliotheek.

Day 2
- Go to the new NEDERLANDS ARCHITECTUUR INSTITUUT in the morning and eat lunch in the restaurant.
- In the afternoon, look at the **Lijnbaan** shopping center, and stop for coffee at **Café de Unie**.

STRATEGIES FOR SUNDAYS
The **Leuvehaven** tends to be animated on Sundays with people taking boat trips or wandering along the waterfront. During the summer *(May-Sept, 11am-5pm),* a street market is organized along **Schiedam-sedijk**, with stalls selling naive paintings, old books and antiques.

A walk along the waterfront

A walk along the old harbor front from the Euromast to Blaak takes you past some of the most impressive new buildings in Rotterdam. Allow 3 hours.

Beginning at the EUROMAST, walk through the park to the river and turn left along Parkkade and Westerkade, where large cruise liners and sailing ships still occasionally berth. Turn left down Rivierstraat and right along Calandstraat, which is flanked by some impressive 19thC warehouses. Turn left on Veerhaven to Westplein. The building at **Westplein 5**, with its tiled paintings of steamers, is one of a number of imposing shipping offices in the vicinity. **Café Loos** is a good place to stop for coffee. Continue down the E side of Veerhaven past a remarkably elegant Greek Revival terrace, which is terminated by the delicate pastel-colored MUSEUM VOOR VOLKENKUNDE (Museum of Ethnography).

Beyond the SPIDO quay, where tours of the harbor begin, turn left along Leuvehaven, past the Imax Theater and the clutter of **maritime relics** on the quayside, which belong to the MARITIEM BUITENMUSEUM.

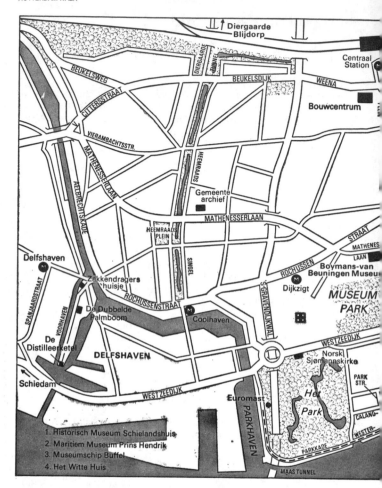

The modern MARITIEM MUSEUM PRINS HENDRIK sits like a ship at the end of the quay, with the 19thC MUSEUMSCHIP BUFFEL moored alongside. Now turn right across the deserted Plein 1940, which is dominated by Ossip Zadkine's impressive **monument** *De verwoeste stad* (The Destroyed City), erected in 1953 as a memorial to those who died in the 1940 bombardment. Turn right down Wolfshoek. A brightly painted **totem pole** presented by the port of Seattle stands strangely on the waterfront. Now turn left along Wijnhaven and walk under the bridge. The Art Nouveau landmark **Het Witte Huis** (The White House), which overlooks the Oude Haven, was Europe's tallest building at the time of its comple-

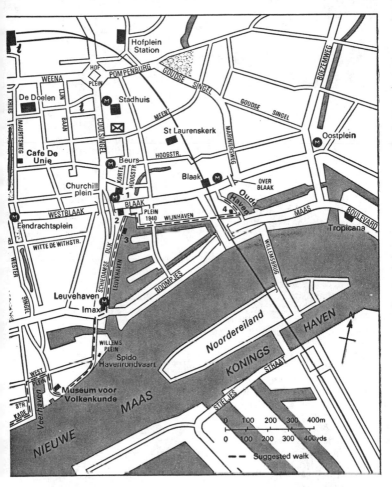

tion in 1898. Turn right down Geldersekade and left along the Koningsdam quayside to admire the miscellaneous collection of old Rhine barges put together to form the **Openlucht Binnenvaart Museum** (Open-air Museum of Inland Shipping). To glimpse the giant barges that currently ply Europe's inland waterways, cross the busy road on the right. From the **Willemsbrug**, you get a spectacular view of the river and the city waterfront.

Back at Oude Haven, cross the iron bridge and walk down Spaansekade to a cluster of attractive cafés overlooking the harbor. You can reach Blaak metro station from here on the elevated **Promenade Overblaak**.

Sights and places of interest

The main attractions in Rotterdam were once limited to the Boymans-van Beuningen Museum, Spido harbor tours, the Euromast and the zoo, but the city has recently invested heavily in museums and other tourist attractions. Major new sights include the **Maritiem Museum Prins Hendrik**, the **Imax Theater** and the **Tropicana** swimming complex. The main area to have benefited is the **Waterstad** quarter, where several disused harbors, such as Oude Haven and Leuvehaven, are now bustling with museum repair yards and excursion boats.

USEFUL TO KNOW
Most museums in Rotterdam are closed on Mondays. See individual museums for opening times.

Rotterdam's modern architecture is softened by a sprinkling of witty works of art, some of which are described in CURIOSITIES on page 219. Peaceful retreats from the crowds and bustle of the city are described in INTERLUDES, page 221. For ways of obtaining a panoramic view of Rotterdam's dramatic modern skyline, see VIEWPOINTS, page 225.

HOW TO USE THIS SECTION
In the following pages, Rotterdam's sights are arranged alphabetically, using English or Dutch names according to common English-speaking usage. The sights are classified by category on page 218.

Look for the ★ symbol against the most important sights and 血 for buildings of great architectural interest. Places of special interest for children ♣ and with outstanding views ◀€ are also indicated. For a full explanation of symbols, see page 7.

If you only know the name of a museum, say, in English, and cannot find it in the following A-Z, try looking it up in the INDEX. Some lesser sights do not have their own entries but are included within other entries: look these up in the index too.

Bold type is generally employed to indicate points of outstanding interest. Entries given without addresses and opening times are described more fully elsewhere: check the cross-references, which are in SMALL CAPITALS.

Rotterdam's sights A to Z

ARBORETUM TROMPENBURG
Honingerdijk 64 ☎*(010) 4141479* 📷 *Open Mon-Sat 9am-5pm. Tram 3 to Hoflaan.*
An exotic collection of some 3,000 varieties of trees and shrubs, all carefully labeled, forms one of the secret delights of Rotterdam. The first trees were planted in 1820, while the English-style w garden was added by Jan David Zocher in 1870.

BOYMANS-VAN BEUNINGEN MUSEUM ★
Mathenesserlaan 18-20 ☎*(010) 4419400* 📷 & 💷 *Open Tues-Sat 10am-5pm; Sun, hols 11am-5pm. Metro to Eendrachtsplein, or tram 5 to Witte de Withstraat.*
The Boymans-van Beuningen Museum is named after F. J. O. Boymans, who bequeathed his art collection to the city of Rotterdam in 1847, and D. G. van Beuningen, who added further works in 1958. Over the years, the museum has developed into one of the most important in Europe, and is particularly renowned for its ancient and modern art, ceramics and industrial design. The building is rather confusing, consisting of an old wing opened in 1935, with a distinctive tower beckoning like a lighthouse, and a new wing added in 1972.

The best place to begin is the department of old paintings, which is reached from the circular lobby in the old building (take the staircase from rm 39). The collection of **Early Netherlandish Painting** is exceptional, and includes Pieter Bruegel the Elder's fearsome *Tower of Babel*, which contains a wealth of fine detail. Boymans also boasts several works by Hieronymus Bosch (rms 3-4), ranging from two exquisite miniature portraits to the *Prodigal Son* and the *Wedding at Cana*, the latter filled with delightful details such as the concealed onlookers. Jan van Scorel's *Young Scholar in a Red Cap* is an impressive example of humanist portraiture, while Pieter Aertsen's *Christ in the House of Martha and Mary* is a striking example of Dutch Mannerism.

The museum's director in 1935 had the inspired idea of displaying the collection of **Dutch Masters** in a series of intimate rooms modeled on 17thC painting cabinets (rms 6-10). These contain works by Pieter Saenredam, including his view of the now-vanished Mariakerk in Utrecht, and a number of genre paintings such as Gerrit Dou's *The Quack* and Jan Steen's heavily symbolic *Fortunes can change (Soo gewonne, soo verteert)*.

Be sure not to miss the room devoted to **Rembrandt and his pupils** (rm 11), containing Rembrandt's affectionate portrait of his son Titus at his desk, and a self-portrait by Rembrandt's most gifted pupil, Carel Fabritius.

An extensive collection of small-scale works by **Rubens** (rm 15) includes an unusual series of seven scenes from the life of Achilles.

The **Van der Vorm collection** should on no account be missed (rms 19-24). As well as offering further fine examples of Dutch 17thC painting, it can boast works by Courbet, Corot, Sisley and Monet, and a small collection of 19thC Dutch painting, including Breitner's exquisite *The Earring*.

The Boymans' collection of **20thC painting** (rms 25-31) is not well known, although it contains a major collection of **Surrealism**, including paintings by Dalí, Magritte and Ernst, and two bizarre rooms given over to Broodthaers and Duchamp. Picasso, Klee and Kandinsky are also represented.

The collection of **decorative art and industrial design** on the ground floor is also worth a glance. It includes a fascinating collection of glazed tiles from Persia, Spain and the Low Countries (rm 45) and a delightful 15thC tiled floor from Naples (rm 51). The ceramics collection is also extensive, ranging from vibrant Italian majolica (rm 41) to contemporary works (rms 47-48). Another highlight is the unusual collection of household utensils from the Middle Ages to the 18thC, many of which feature in paintings on display in the museum. The industrial design collection includes eccentric examples of the Post Modern Italian school. The stylish museum store sells some fashionable black objects of modern design, plus art books and postcards.

When the weather is fine, the **café terrace** overlooking the museum garden is perhaps the most idyllic spot in Rotterdam. The **ornamental pool** is also a pleasant place to linger, with Claes Oldenburg's giant *Screw Arch* lending a surreal touch to the setting.

DE BUFFEL
Leuvehaven 1 ☎*(010) 4132680* 🚇 *(entrance fee for MARITIEM MUSEUM PRINS HENDRIK includes visit to De Buffel)* 🚻 *Open Tues-Sat 10am-5pm; Sun, hols 11am-5pm. Metro or tram 1, 3, 4, 6, 7 to Churchillplein/Beurs.*
The turret-ram *De Buffel* (Buffalo) lies permanently moored next to the maritime museum. This trim iron vessel was built for the Dutch navy in 1868 and converted in 1896 to a barracks ship. The officers' quarters are furnished in a plush Neoclassical Victorian style, and include a

spacious captain's suite and an officers' Long Room, which exudes something of the air of an exclusive London dining club. The ship has a small exhibition of working steam engines, models and charts.

CAFÉ DE UNIE �
Mauritsweg 35 ☎*(010) 4117394* 🍺 ═ *Open Mon-Thurs 8am-midnight; Fri, Sat 8am-1am; Sun 10am-midnight. Tram 3, 4, 5 to Mauritsweg.*
A fashionable boulevard café built in 1924 by J. J. P. Oud and destroyed during the bombardment of 1940, De Unie was rebuilt in 1986 on a nearby site as a café-restaurant and cultural center. Its red, blue and yellow facade was modeled on Mondrian's abstract paintings of the 1920s.

CURIOSITIES
Rotterdam is dotted with witty works of art that lend a touch of humor to the modern city. On leaving Centraal Station, you will see a **mock ship's deck** that serves as a private club, and on Oldenbarneveltplaats a curious **twisted lamp-post** designed by Cor Kraat *(at the corner of Karel Doormanstraat)*. One wall of the ONTDEKHOEK is decorated with an overscaled reproduction of the 1930 **school report** of Bob den Uyl, a Rotterdam novelist. The bizarre architecture at **Blaak** has given rise to several witty nicknames. Piet Blom's houses on columns are informally known as "The Blaak Forest," while the Blaaktoren skyscraper has been dubbed "The Pixie Hat" on account of its pointed roof.

DELFSHAVEN
Metro to Delfshaven, or tram 4, 6 to Spanjaardstraat.
The tiny port of Delfshaven was founded by the city of Delft in 1389 and remained within its jurisdiction until 1825, when it was granted independent status, only to lose it again 61 years later to Rotterdam. Two decorated gable stones mounted on the wall of the 17thC **Zakkendragershuisje** (House of the Guild of Grain Porters) recall that in its heyday Delfshaven was an important whaling and herring-fishing port. Yet its main claim to fame is that it was from here that the Pilgrim Fathers departed for America in 1620. Their ship, the *Speedwell,* proved unseaworthy, however, and they put into Plymouth some days later, before setting sail again on the *Mayflower.*

Situated in a handsome 19thC warehouse, the historical museum **De Dubbelde Palmboom** *(Voorhaven 12* ☎ *(010) 4761533* 📷 ⓔ 🍺 *open Tues-Sat 10am-5pm; Sun 1-5pm)* contains interesting relics relating to local trades such as peat-cutting, shipbuilding and *jenever* distilling. Excellent information sheets are available in English.

Like all dead ports, Delfshaven possesses a somewhat desolate atmosphere, although the recent extension of the metro line may inject new life into this picturesque corner of Rotterdam.

DIERGAARDE BLIJDORP
Van Aerssenlaan 49 ☎*(010) 4673131* 📷 🍺 ✿ *Open daily 9am-5pm. Tram 3 to Diergaarde Blijdorp.*

This sensitively planned zoo designed in the 1930s contains an unusual mixture of modern and exotic buildings in a romantically landscaped setting. Major attractions include tigers, seals and birds of paradise. The **Henri Martinhuis** is interesting for its nocturnal animals and for the nonchalant acrobatics of the gibbons. There is an attractive café terrace and a good adventure playground for children.

EUROMAST ★

Parkhaven 20 ☎*(010) 4364811* 🖼 ♿ ⬛ ♣ ◀€ *Open mid-Mar to mid-Oct 10am-7pm (Space Tower 10am-6pm); mid-Oct to mid-Mar 10am-6pm; Jan and Feb weekends only. Tram 4, 9 to Maastunnel.*

Rotterdam's tallest building, the 176m (560-foot) Euromast offers splendid views of the port, with large ships heading down the Maas, helicopters flitting across the city and streams of cars disappearing into the Maastunnel. The lower part of the tower rises to 100m (320 feet) and was built by H. A. Maaskant for the 1960 Floriade. It is capped with a distinctive crows' nest incorporating two **restaurants** with sloping windows that allow you to gaze straight down the funnels of ships. The **Space Tower**, added after the Euromast had been ousted from its position as tallest building in the Netherlands, incorporates a slowly **revolving drum** that ascends to the top of the mast, offering a magnificent view to anyone brave enough not to have their eyes firmly shut.

HAVEN (Port) ★

The sheer size of Rotterdam's port reduces everything else in Holland to Lilliputian proportions. Although it can no longer claim to be the world's largest port, it is still by far the busiest, handling almost 300 million tonnes of goods annually. The port stretches downstream of the city for some 37km (22 miles) and occupies about one half of the area of Rotterdam.

Some 32,000 sea-going ships berth in the harbor every year and 180,000 inland barges depart up the Rhine or Maas for destinations deep

in the heart of Europe. Rotterdam's **Europoort** is the world's main oil terminal, while the **Eemhaven** ranks as the largest container terminal in the world. You learn a host of other vital statistics about the port during the fascinating SPIDO boat trips, while those with a car can delve deeper into the vast port installations by following the signposted *Havenroute.*

The **Schielandshuis**

HISTORISCH MUSEUM SCHIELANDSHUIS 🏛

Korte Hoogstraat 31 🕾*(010) 4334188* ▱ *Open Tues-Sat 10am-5pm; Sun, hols 1-5pm. Metro or tram 1, 3, 4, 6, 7 to Churchillplein/Beurs.*

Rotterdam's historical museum occupies the only Golden Age building in the city to survive the 1940 bombardment (pictured opposite). The Schielandshuis was built in 1662-65 to house the powerful organization responsible for maintaining the dikes and polders in Schieland district. The handsome Dutch Classical building now contains a modest collection of old dollhouses, period rooms, paintings and films of the bombardment. Dutch prints selected from the famous Atlas van Stolk collection are occasionally exhibited.

IMAX THEATER

Leuvehaven 77 🕾*(010) 4048844* ▱ ✱ ♿ *Screenings Tues-Sun at 1pm, 2pm, 3pm, 7pm, 8pm, 9pm. Metro or tram 4 to Leuvehaven.*

This state-of-the-art movie theater on the waterfront shows special "Imax" films on a giant domed screen, to create an exceptionally lifelike realism. The films are mainly documentaries with Dutch commentary, but headphones can be rented to pick up a simultaneous English translation.

INTERLUDES

Not many churches are regularly open in Rotterdam, but you can often dive into the restored **St Laurenskerk** to escape the crowds. Take a brisk stroll along the waterfront next to HET PARK to unwind, or sit in the garden of the BOYMANS-VAN BEUNINGEN MUSEUM for a moment of quiet contemplation. For a complete escape, take the tram to the ARBORETUM TROMPENBURG and wander among the ancient cedar trees.

KIJK-KUBUS 🏛

Overblaak 70 🕾*(010) 4142285* ▱ *Open Apr, May and Oct-Dec, Tues-Fri 10am-5pm, Sat, Sun 11am-5pm; June-Sept Mon-Fri 10am-5pm, Sat, Sun 11am-5pm; Jan-Mar, Fri-Sun 11am-5pm. Metro to Blaak.*

The extraordinary housing complex dubbed *Het Blaakse Bos* (The Blaak Forest) was designed by the Amsterdam architect Piet Blom to provide a hint of the Ponte Vecchio in Rotterdam. Built on top of a bridge straddling a main road, the

Kijk-Kubus

221

bizarre dwellings take the form of tilted cubes on concrete columns. The *Kijk-Kubus* is open as a showhouse to allow inquisitive visitors to see the challenges involved in living in a building with sloping walls. The effect is rather giddying, and the problem of where to put the piano seems insoluble. But the project is still inspiring, and the exhibition of photographs and plans illustrates Blom's painstaking approach to architectural design.

KRALINGSE BOS

NE of central Rotterdam. Metro to Voorschoterlaan, then bus 42 (circular route through the woods); or walk from the metro down Rozenburglaan (5mins).
The Kralingse Bos is a vast area of woodland where Rotterdammers like to go to ramble, cycle, run, ride horses, picnic and walk their oversized dogs. The woods surround a large **lake** known as the Kralingse Plas, where you can sailboard, sail and swim.

Those without a car can reach the woods by taking the metro to Voorschoterlaan and then walking down the leafy Rozenburglaan. At the Kralingse Plas, you will see a series of wooden bridges with white iron railings, which take you across a number of **islands** to the E shore of the lake. A 5-minute walk along the waterfront brings you to two **windmills**. One of them, the *Molen De Ster (demonstrations on Wed 9am-noon, 1-4pm* 🔲 *)*, was once used to grind snuff and spices.

You can wander off into the woods to the E of here in search of a pancake house, or picnic at the edge of the lake. You can walk or run around the entire lake on footpaths, a total distance of 4.5km (2.7 miles).

MARITIEM BUITENMUSEUM LEUVEHAVEN

Leuvehaven 50-72 ☎*(070) 4048072* 🔲 *Open Mon-Sat 10am-4.30pm; Sun 11am-4.30pm. Metro or tram 1, 3, 4, 6, 7 to Churchillplein/Beurs.*
The Leuvehaven quay has become an open-air maritime museum, with cranes and repair yards sprawling along the waterfront. Occasional exhibitions are organized in the bright red lighthouse *Het Lage Licht (open Tues 1-4pm, Sun 11am-4pm* 🔲*)*. You can watch the 1917 sailing ship *Ooster Schelde* being repaired, or stroll along iron catwalks inside the repair sheds (enter at street level).

MARITIEM MUSEUM PRINS HENDRIK

Leuvehaven 1 ☎*(010) 4132680* 🔲 ▪ ✦ *Open Tues-Sat 10am-5pm; Sun, hols 11am-5pm. Metro or tram 1, 3, 4, 6, 7 to Churchillplein/Beurs.*
Holland's oldest maritime museum, founded by the seafaring Prins Hendrik in 1852, occupies a striking modern building overlooking the animated Leuvehaven. The museum recently created a series of dioramas illustrating the evolution of the harbor from the 15thC to the present day, with various special effects including medieval street noises. As well as displaying a fascinating assortment of maps, globes, paintings and ship models, the museum has a small fleet of 19th-20thC barges and steam tugs moored in the harbor (see MARITIEM BUITENMUSEUM LEUVEHAVEN and DE BUFFEL). The attractive **Museumcafé** is situated in a glass-walled angle of the building resembling the bow of a ship.

NEDERLANDS ARCHITECTUUR INSTITUUT (Dutch Architectural Institute)
Scheduled to move in early 1993 from Westersingel 10 to the Museumpark
☎*(010) 4361155* 📠*(010) 4366975* 💷 ▭ *(Museumpark building only). Open Tues-Sat 10am-5pm; Sun 11am-5pm. Tram 1, 3, 4, 5, 7 (old building); tram 5 to Witte de Withstraat (new building).*

The Dutch Architectural Institute stages stimulating and accessible exhibitions on Dutch architecture and planning based on its vast archives of 19th and 20thC drawings, photographs and models. The institute will be based from 1993 in an innovative building in the Museumpark designed by Jo Coenen, which will feature exhibition rooms, a library, an architecture bookstore and a restaurant with a lakeside terrace.

DE ONTDEKHOEK
Pannekoekstraat 55 ☎*(010) 4143103* 📠 *Open Tues-Sat 10am-5pm* ✦ 💷
Metro or tram 1, 3, 6, 7 to Station Blaak.

Kids and parents flock to this animated children's laboratory located in the old city library. Aimed at ages 4-14, the Ontdekhoek teaches young people essential technical skills. They can build a miniature dike, develop photographs, construct a wall using real mortar, fry chips, or milk a wooden cow.

OUDE HAVEN
Metro or tram 1, 3, 6, 7 to Station Blaak.

Devastated by a Nazi air raid in 1940, Rotterdam's old harbor area, the Oude Haven, now contains some of the most remarkable modern architecture in the Netherlands, including the pyramidal **Gemeentebibliotheek** (public library), which offers superb views of the city from the upper floors. Designed by the Van den Broek and Bakema Bureau, it shows obvious similarities to the Pompidou Center in Paris, particularly in the tangle of bright yellow ventilation ducts at the rear.

Farther s is a remarkable cluster of tilted cubic houses on poles designed by the Amsterdam-born architect Piet Blom (see KIJK-KUBUS). A number of avant-garde fashion boutiques have opened up in this futuristic environment, and various cafés line the attractive wharfside.

HET PARK
Tram 4 to Ziekenhuis Dijkzicht

The park below the Euromast — known simply as Het Park — was landscaped in a 19thC Romantic English style by J. D. and L. P. Zocher. Its most curious feature is the **Norsk Sjømannskirke**, a church for Norwegian seamen, with brightly painted carvings and a remarkable slate roof. Stop for coffee in **Zochers'**, a tranquil mansion in the park.

ST LAURENSKERK
Grotekerkplein ☎*(010) 4131494. Metro or tram 1 3, 6, 7 to Station Blaak.*

Gutted in World War II, the St Laurenskerk (Grote Kerk) remained a blackened shell for many years, but it has now been superbly restored to its Gothic glory. The wooden roof has been rebuilt and repainted, and the spectacular scarlet and gilt organ is back in working order *(concerts on Thurs 12.45-1.15pm)*. An exhibition of photographs includes scenes of the church in ruin in 1940, while the tomb of Cornelis de Wit in the s aisle evokes a more glorious era in Dutch history with its Neptune figure and sea battle scene.

SCHIEDAM
Map 2E2. w of central Rotterdam. Train to Schiedam-Rotterdam West, or (better) tram 1, 6 to Koemarkt (15mins from central Rotterdam) **i** *Buitenhavenweg 9* ☎*(010) 4733000* Ⓕⓧ*(010) 4736695.*

Schiedam is an atmospheric old Dutch port with moldering brick warehouses overlooking dark canals, and wooden bridges that still occasionally get cranked open to let a barge pass. The town is now virtually part of Rotterdam, but the old quarters have scarcely changed since the 18thC. Schiedam — like DELFSHAVEN — offers a refuge for those who find Rotterdam too relentlessly modern, but as yet it has scarcely been discovered by tourists.

The town was founded in the 13thC at the mouth of the River Schie. Once an important fishing port, it became famous throughout 18thC Europe for its *jenever* (sometimes called Geneva, or Hollands gin), a white spirit flavored with *jeneverbessen* (juniper berries). In its heyday, the town boasted more than 400 distilleries, but the local *jenever* industry is now dominated by a few large firms. Schiedam developed into a major grain port to supply the local *jenever* industry, and 14 huge *stellingmolens* (tower windmills) were built on the town ramparts to grind the corn. Five **18thC windmills** are still standing on the old city moat to the w of the town (Noordvest). Allegedly the largest windmills in the world, they rise impressively above the roofs of the old town.

The main sights in Schiedam are almost all linked to the *jenever* industry. Begin at the Koemarkt tram halt, and turn down **Lange Haven**, an attractive old canal with 18thC merchants' houses, a mackerel smokehouse and several abandoned distilleries. Turn left across the first iron drawbridge and down Walvisstraat to reach the windmill *De Walvisch* (the whale), built in 1724. A small shop on the ground floor sells flour, *speculaas* biscuits and old-fashioned Dutch boiled candies *(open Tues-Fri 1.30-5pm, Sat 10am-1pm)*.

Return to Lange Haven and turn left to reach the Dam. The 18thC Classical **Korenbeurs** (corn exchange) overlooks an attractive old lock with iron bridges. Turn left down Korte Haven to reach another massive 18thC windmill, **De Drie Koornbloemen** (the three cornflowers), which is still used for grinding cattle feed. Turn right along the Noordvest waterfront to look at the **Molen De Vrijheid** (freedom windmill), built in 1785, where corn is still regularly ground. It is sold to traditional bakeries in Rotterdam and The Hague, or taken across the road to the distillery **De Tweelingh** (the twins). When the windmill is open *(Sat only, 9am-4pm)*, you can climb several sets of steep steps to reach the wooden platform below the sails.

A short distance farther is the windmill **De Noord** (the North), claimed to be the highest in the world. A restaurant now occupies the first three floors of the windmill, and the sails still occasionally turn. The fifth windmill, *De Palmboom* (the palm tree), was until recently a ruin, but it has been carefully reconstructed.

Walk to the end of Noordvest, past several small distilleries, and turn right along the Schie waterfront to reach the *Zakkendragershuisje,* a compact brick guild house erected in 1725 for the porters who unloaded the sacks of grain shipped to Schiedam. Turn left along Oude Sluis to reach the Dam. Cross the bridge and walk down the lane to Hoogstraat, the main shopping street, and turn left to look at the **Stadhuis** (town hall) and **Oude Kerk**. Retrace your steps to reach the **Stedelijk Museum** *(Hoogstraat 112; open Tues-Sat 10am-5pm; Sun, hols 12.30-5pm).* A basement room contains various mementoes of the *jenever* industry, including scale models, drinking glasses and a vast collection of miniature gin bottles gathered from the most unexpected places.

SPIDO HAVENRONDVAART

Willemsplein ☎*(010) 4135400* 🖾 💻 ✱ ◁ᔕ *Tours last 75mins, daily Apr-Sept 9.30am-5pm, every 30-45mins; daily Mar, Oct at 10am, 11.30am, 1pm, 2.30pm; daily Nov-Feb at 11am and 2pm. Tram 5 to Willemsplein.*

The best way to see Rotterdam's modern port area is to take a Spido boat trip down the Nieuwe Maas, past an unending stream of tugs, dredgers, tankers, yachts, submarines, liners and barges. The tour boats also enter some of the docks, revealing ships in dry dock and mountains of containers. The basic tour lasts $1\frac{1}{4}$ hours, which is probably enough for most people, but enthusiasts can book a whole-day excursion, which takes in the Europoort refineries and the giant concrete dams of the Deltawerken.

TROPICANA

Maasboulevard 100 ☎*(010) 4020700* 🖾 ⚌ 💻 ✱ *Open Mon-Fri 10am-10pm; Sat 10am-6pm; Sun 10am-7pm. Lockers controlled by a smart card, which you use to enter and leave the complex. Additional fee for visits of more than 4 hours. Metro or tram 3, 6, 7 to Oostplein.*

A spectacular modern swimming complex situated under an enormous glass dome beside the River Maas. Exhilarating water attractions including wave machines, water chutes, artificial rapids and hot whirlpools are set amid a mock tropical landscape of rocky ravines and narrow bridges. The complex includes a shallow pool for toddlers, a sauna and several bars. Tropicana is romantically illuminated after dark, and you can float around in the outdoor pool beneath the stars as barges glide past on the River Maas.

VIEWPOINTS

The EUROMAST provides an all-embracing view of Rotterdam and its port from the deck 104m (343 feet) up. Less dizzying, but equally captivating, is the view of the ST LAURENSKERK and the modern city from the sixth floor of the **Gemeentebibliotheek** *(open to the public without formalities).* Walk to the S end of the **Promenade Overblaak** for an unexpected view of the Oude Haven, or cross the Willemsbrug to

Noordereiland for a sweeping view of the city skyline. If the gleaming modernity of central Rotterdam gets too much, take the tram out to SCHIEDAM, where you can sit on a bench on Dam gazing at the dark waters of the old lock.

VOLKENKUNDE, MUSEUM VOOR

Willemskade 25 ☎*(010) 4111055* ▨ ⚎ *Open Tues-Sat 10am-5pm; Sun, hols 11am-5pm. Metro to Leuvehaven or tram 5 to Westplein.*

Rotterdam's museum of geography and ethnography occupies a distinguished Neoclassical building, which was originally the clubhouse of the Royal Netherlands Yacht Club. The museum devotes considerable space to its temporary exhibitions, in which themes such as travel, festivals and ceremonies are treated with a combination of curiosity and concern. The restaurant's exotic Caribbean menu is worth investigating.

WATERSTAD

s of central Rotterdam. Metro to Leuvehaven or Blaak.

The old maritime quarter of Rotterdam lost much of its vitality after the giant modern docks downstream were dug, but it has recently become the setting for some of the boldest architecture in the Netherlands. The Waterstad, as it is now known, stretches along the Maas waterfront from the EUROMAST to TROPICANA. Several new museums have opened on the quayside, including the MUSEUM VOOR VOLKENKUNDE and the MARITIEM MUSEUM PRINS HENDRIK. New cafés and restaurants are clustered around old docks such as OUDE HAVEN and Leuvehaven.

Modern information signs have been set up along the waterfront describing the history and architecture of the area. Information on current events is provided by street video monitors. The waterfront walk (page 213) takes you past the outstanding sights of the quarter.

Rotterdam: where to stay

Making your choice

Rotterdam lost all its grand old hotels in World War II, and the traveler now has little choice but to stay in a modern skyscraper. The **Hilton International** *(Weena 10 ☎(070) 4144044)* is a safe bet for wary travelers, but the hotels down by the waterfront give you more of the feeling of being in a port.

LOCATION

Those looking for an inexpensive hotel should explore the quarter behind Centraal Station, where several small hotels such as **Bienvenue** and **Holland** occupy 19thC canalside houses. The setting might almost be Amsterdam, and yet you are close to the center of Rotterdam.

Not everyone with business in Rotterdam will want to stay in the modern city, and it is worth remembering that the tranquil old town of **Delft** is just 15 minutes from Rotterdam Centraal Station by train. You can easily spend the night in a canalside hotel in Delft, and yet be in central Rotterdam for a 9am meeting.

USEFUL TO KNOW

The price categories quoted for each hotel are intended as a rough guide to what you can expect to pay. There are five categories: cheap (▢), inexpensive (▢), moderate (▥), expensive (▦) and very expensive (▦). (See page 7 for the approximate prices to which these refer.) As Rotterdam is mainly a business destination, large hotels often drop their rates significantly on weekends. It can be worthwhile phoning around to check out special offers, or even gently haggling.

Rotterdam's hotels

BIENVENUE
Spoorsingel 24, 3033 GL ☎*(010) 4669394* 🖷*(010) 4677475* ▢ *10 rms, 8 with bath/shower* 🆎 ⊙ ⊙ 🖭 *Tram 9 to Proveniersplein.*
Location: On a quiet canal, 10 minutes' walk from Centraal Station. An inexpensive hotel behind the rail station, attractively furnished in a crisp, modern style. The stairs are steep, but you are rewarded with a rare glimpse of a canal from the breakfast room.

HOLLAND
Provenierssingel 7, 3033 ED ☎*(010) 4653100* 🖷*(010) 4670280* ▢ 🆎 ⊙

▣ ▥ *Tram 3, 5, 9 to Provenierssingel.*
Location: 10 minutes' walk from Centraal Station. An inexpensive and pleasant canalside hotel within walking distance of the station.

INNTEL

Leuvehaven 80, 3011 EA ☎*(010) 4134139* ▣*(010) 4133222* ▥ *to* ▥
150 rms ━ ⇌ ▣ ▣ ▣ ▥ ✻ ▢ ◹
◖ ▨ ⚲ ⛵ ⚥ Metro or tram 4 to Leuvehaven.
Location: Central Rotterdam on the Leuvehaven quayside. This modern blue-glass hotel in the heart of Waterstad (the maritime quarter) caters to romantic souls who want a view of Rotterdam's river from their bedroom window. You get a particularly good view of the waterfront from the sizeable swimming pool located on the top floor. The buffet breakfast features various types of meat and cheese, and eight types of bread. The IMAX THEATER adjoins the hotel, while the maritime museum and the SPIDO pier are just a few minutes' walk away. Rates tend to drop sharply on weekends.

PARKHOTEL

Westersingel 70, 3015 LB ☎*(010) 4363611* ▣*(010) 4364212* ▥ *to* ▥

199 rms ▣ ⇌ ▣ ▣ ▣ ▥ ✻ ▢ ◹
▨ ⛵ ⚥ Metro to Eendrachtsplein.
Location: Central Rotterdam. Probably the most interesting of Rotterdam's large business-class hotels, with sauna, fitness center and art gallery. It is close to the city center and the BOYMANS MUSEUM; shops, restaurants and cafés are all within walking distance.

SAVOY

Hoogstraat 81, 3011 PJ ☎*(010) 4139280* ▣*(010) 4045712* ▥ *94 rms* ⇌ ▣ ▣ ◖ ▥ ✻ ▢ ◹ Metro to Blaak.
Location: 10 minutes' walk from Blaak. A pleasantly furnished modern hotel not far from the architectural razzmatazz of Blaak.

SCANDIA

Willemsplein 1, 3016 DN ☎*(010) 4134790* ▣*(010) 4127890* ▥ *49 rms* ⇌ ▣ ▣ ▣ ▥ ✻ ▢ ◹ ▨ ⚲ Tram 5 to Willemsplein.
Location: On the Maas waterfront. For incurable romantics who thrill to the sight of ships sailing downstream and to the sound of foghorns booming in the night, the modern Scandinavian-style Scandia is one of the few hotels overlooking the river. Spido boat tours leave from opposite the hotel.

Rotterdam: eating and drinking

Where to eat

Rotterdam is a hard-working city that does not have much time for the pleasures of eating out. Such good restaurants as there are concentrate on providing businessmen with *nouvelle cuisine* delicacies to nibble as they negotiate the terms for a shipment of crude oil. Service is efficient and fast, but the atmosphere is sometimes rather formal.

Those in search of traditional Dutch ambience will find it only with difficulty. The **Old Dutch** restaurant offers roughly what you would expect from the name. As befits an international port, Rotterdam is dotted with foreign restaurants offering Indonesian *rijsttafels,* Hungarian goulash or even traditional English cooking. Many Rotterdam restaurants depend so heavily on business customers that they close for the entire weekend.

Rotterdam's restaurants

CHALET SUISSE
Kievitslaan 31 ☎*(010) 4365062* ☒*(010) 4365462* ⬚ *to* ▥ 🚭 ⚹ ⊕ ⊚ ⚼ *Last orders 10.30pm. Closed Sun. Tram 6.*
A mock Alpine chalet on the edge of the city park, where you can feast on fondue and other Swiss specialties. The garden makes an idyllic retreat in the summer.

DEWI SRI
Westerkade 20 ☎*(010) 4360263* ⬚ ⚹
⊕ ⊚ ⚼ *Last orders 10.30pm. Closed Sat lunch, Sun lunch. Tram 5 to Westplein.*
A waterfront restaurant for inexpensive Indonesian dishes, including two *rijsttafels* (order the Sumatran at your peril).

OLD DUTCH
Rochussenstraat 20 ☎*(010) 4360344* ☒*(010) 4367826* ⬚ *to* ▥ 🚭 ⚹ ⊕ ⊚ ⚼ *Closed Sat, Sun, hols. Metro to Eendrachtsplein.*

An old whitewashed farmhouse furnished with handsome antiques, where you can eat an inexpensive *stamppot* (stew) in the brasserie or splash out on quails in the adjoining restaurant. Popular with businessmen who feel the need occasionally to escape from the incessant modernity of their city. In summer you can dine on the terrace under giant parasols.

PARKHEUVEL
Heuvellaan 21 ☎*(010) 4360530* ☒*(010) 4367140* ▥ 🚭 ⚹ ⚹ ⊕ ⊚ ⚼ *Closed Sat lunch, Sun. Tram 4, 9 to Maastunnel.*
A stylish, modern restaurant overlooking the River Maas, offering highly inventive cooking and faultless service.

RADÈN MAS
Kruiskade 72 ☎*(010) 4117244* ☒*(010) 4119711* ▥ ⚹ ⊕ ⊚ ⚼ *Closed Sat lunch and Sun lunch. Tram 1, 3, 4, 5, 7 to Kruisplein.*

Exquisite Indonesian dishes in a sumptuous setting.

ZOCHERS'
Baden Powelllaan 12 ☎*(010) 4364249* ▢

Tram 4, 9 to Maastunnel.
An artfully romantic café-restaurant situated in an 18thC villa in Het Park. Sunday brunch, with classical music, is served from 11am.

Cafés

Nostalgic brown cafés, their walls covered with faded photographs of old liners, are concentrated along the **Oude Binnenweg**. But the progressive spirit of Rotterdam is better expressed by its modern cafés such as **Dudok** *(Meent 88, open 8am-1am, metro to Stadhuis),* a spacious, fashionable café near the stock exchange, designed in a spare modern style, with white walls and black tables. You can eat breakfast, or munch a pastrami roll for lunch. Dinner is served on the mezzanine floor.

Down by the waterfront, **Loos** *(Westplein 1* ☎*(010) 4117723)* is an airy and artful café, with paintings by young Rotterdam artists. The **Doelencafé** *(Schouwburgplein 53)* is a bustling modern café in the heart of the city, where jazz bands occasionally play. **Radio Café Rijnmond** *(Delftsestraat 23* ☎*(010) 4144820)* is another fashionable café tucked away in a quiet street near the station. Head w along Nieuwe Binnenweg to discover **Dizzy** *('s-Gravendijkwal 127* ☎*(010) 4773014, open Mon-Sat from 8am; Sun from 10am),* a spacious jazz café with a secluded garden for sultry summer evenings.

A cluster of fashionable cafés has sprung up recently around the **Oude Haven**, with terraces that run down to the waterfront on summer days. The café **De Spaanse Poort** *(Haringvliet 637, metro to Blaak)* offers an interesting list of some 46 types of beer, as well as simple, inexpensive meals.

EETCAFÉS
Young people, and others with limited resources, should investigate the *eetcafés,* where you can eat thick Dutch steaks, Italian pasta, or even French dishes at reasonable prices. Another advantage of *eetcafés* is that they tend to be open on weekends. Eating at **Dudok's** mezzanine restaurant *(Meent 88)* is enjoyable just for the buzz of voices coming from the café below. **Lux** *('s-Gravendijkwal 133* ☎*(010) 4762206)* offers excellent, inexpensive Italian cooking, with a summer terrace to complete the Mediterranean atmosphere. Other stylish modern cafés that have good kitchens are **Dizzy** *('s-Gravendijkwal 127* ☎*(010) 4773014),* and **Radio Café Rijnmond** *(Delftsestraat 23* ☎*(010) 4144820).*

For an inexpensive lunch while shopping, try the restaurant **La Ruche** in De Bijenkorf (see SHOPPING, page 235). If you arrive early, you might even get a window table with a view of the modern pavement sculpture by Naum Gabo.

BREAKFASTS

Large hotels such as the Hilton and the Park will serve you breakfast even if you are not staying there, but you can begin the day in a more local setting by breakfasting at **Dizzy** or **Radio Café Rijnmond** (see opposite). **Zochers'** (see opposite) offers Sunday brunch with chamber music in its decadent Classical interior *(from 11am)*.

TREATS

Prim ladies from Kralingen join stockbrokers and students for coffee and cake in the crowded **Konditorei** within the Bijenkorf *(Coolsingel 105, ground floor)*. You pick your cake from the display cabinet, as in Germany.

The evocative Art Deco **IJssalon La Venezia** *(Passage 1, Schiedam* ☎ *(010) 4267106, tram 1, 6 to Koemarkt)* opened in 1934 in a covered arcade. The Passage, as it was called, is now rather dilapidated, but the ice cream shop still tempts the faithful with its homemade Italian ice cream.

I think one may see barges and canal boats in greater variety at Rotterdam than anywhere else. One curious thing to be noticed as they lie at rest in the canals is the absence of men. A woman is always there; her husband only rarely. The only visible captain is the fussy, shrewish little dog which, suspicious of the whole world, patrols the boat from stem to stern, and warns you that it is against the law even to look at his property.

(E.V. Lucas, *A Wanderer in Holland,* 1905)

Rotterdam: nightlife and entertainment

Rotterdam by night

Rotterdam is mostly rather quiet after dark, but there are lively places for those in the know. Rotterdammers are particularly passionate about contemporary film, dance and jazz. Pick up a free copy of the current *Punt Uit Agenda* at the tourist office for a full listing (in Dutch only) of concerts, theater and sporting events. The tourist office at Coolsingel 67 also handles ticket reservations for plays and concerts.

BALLET

Exciting modern dance groups regularly perform at the **Rotterdamse Schouwburg** *(Schouwburgplein 25 ☎(010) 4118110 &)*. Expect explosive performances from the innovative **Scapino Ballet Rotterdam**.

BARS

The old bars down by the waterfront are perhaps best left to the natives, but you can still get a whiff of the sea at **Melief Bender** *(Oude Binnenweg 134)*, a big brown bar filled with nostalgic black-and-white photographs of transatlantic liners. This Rotterdam institution is now more than a century old, and retired dockers rub shoulders with maritime insurance brokers in a genial crush of bodies.

CASINO

The one and only legal casino in Rotterdam is scheduled to move from the Hilton Hotel to the new Rotterdam Plaza on Weena in 1992. Dress smartly and take your passport along. **Holland Casino Rotterdam** *(Weena ☎(010) 4147799 & ⇌ ♈ minimum age 18, open 2pm-2am)*.

CLASSICAL MUSIC

The **Rotterdam Philharmonic** is based at **De Doelen** *(Schouwburgplein 50 ☎(010) 4132490)*. Small ensembles perform in the restored **St Laurenskerk** every Thursday *(12.45-1.15pm)*. Modern chamber music gets an occasional airing in the **Zaal De Unie** *(Mauritsweg 34 ☎(010) 4113412)*.

DISCOS

When the weekend comes around, young Rotterdammers cram into discos featuring all styles of dancing and decor. The **Harbour Jazz**

Club *(Delftsestraat 15* ☎ *(010) 4114958)* has dancing on weekends, while the young and hip pack the big dance floor at **Nighttown** *(West-kruiskade 26* ☎ *(010) 4364020)*, where Dutch bands often perform. The daring can skate on ice to disco music at the **IJshal Weena** on Saturday evenings (see SPORTS, page 237), and roller skaters can spin to the latest pop hits on Saturday evenings at the **Energiehal** *(Energieweg 5* ☎ *(010) 4375527)*. Discos tend to be open on Friday and Saturday 10pm-5am, Sunday 10pm-4am, though the dance floors often remain deserted until after midnight.

JAZZ AND BLUES CONCERTS

Some of the friendliest night-spots in Rotterdam are the jazz cafés such as **Dizzy** *('s-Gravendijkwal 127* ☎ *(010) 4773014, concerts Tues 10pm, Sun 4pm)*, **Doelencafé** *(Schouwburgplein 53* ☎ *(010) 4148688)*, and the **Harbour Jazz Club** *(Delftsestraat 15* ☎ *(010) 4114958, concerts Fri-Sun)*. Jazz and blues also feature occasionally on the program at **Theatercafé Plan-C** *(Slepervest 1* ☎ *(010) 4124352)*.

MOVIES

The good, the bad and the awful from Hollywood are regularly screened at **Cinerama**, a five-theater complex *(Westblaak)*. The four screens at **Lumière** *(Lijnbaan 45)* are generally devoted to major US movies. The three-screen **Calypso** complex *(Mauritsweg 5)* and the two-screen **Alhambra** occasionally offer a thoughtful US film, but the sole cinema in town that regularly screens movie classics, plus modern European and Japanese works, is **Lantaren/Venster** *(Gouvernestraat 129* ☎ *(010) 4364998)*.

PLAYS AND MUSICALS

The **Rotterdamse Schouwburg** *(Schouwburgplein 25* ☎ *(010) 4118110* ♿*)* is the city's main theater, staging modern European plays in Dutch by various touring companies. The **Luxor Theater** *(Kruis-kade 10* ☎ *(010) 4138326)* features Dutch cabaret acts and occasional Broadway musicals in Dutch or English.

ROCK AND POP CONCERTS

International rock groups and singers perform to huge audiences in the **Ahoy'** complex *(Zuiderparkweg 20-30* ☎ *(010) 4812144, metro to Zuidplein)*.

Rotterdam: shopping

Where to go

The shops in Rotterdam are less varied than those of Amsterdam, but you will find a number of boutiques selling the best European fashions, shoes, books, postcards and avant-garde furniture. If you live only a short air journey away, before you go home pick up a big bunch of Dutch tulips, or whatever else is in season, at **Bloemenhal Ollefers**, outside Centraal Station *(open Mon-Sat 8am-8pm; Sun 9am-6pm)*.

Major shops are concentrated on the **Lijnbaan**, an attractive vehicle-free shopping street running for some 2km (1 mile) from Weena to Westblaak. Several fashionable brand names have branches here, including **Esprit** *(Lijnbaan 75)* and **United Colors of Benetton** *(Lijnbaan 63)*. The eight-floor **Donner** *(Lijnbaan 150* ☎*(010) 4132070)* is Rotterdam's biggest and best-stocked bookstore.

Other international names have branches in the cross-streets, such as **Scapa of Scotland** *(Kruiskade 61)* and **Kookai** *(Van Oldenbarnevelt-straat 117)*. Dutch designer **Puck & Hans** *(Oldenbarneveltstraat 119)* sells daring clothes for dining and dancing.

Several established European fashion houses including Mondi and Escada have outlets on **Karel Doormanstraat**, but you have to head some distance from Lijnbaan to find original or outrageous fashion. **Oude Binnenweg** and its continuation **Nieuwe Binnenweg** are for more adventurous shoppers. Flamboyant shoes are stocked at **Dr Adams** *(Oude Binnenweg 132* 🆎 🔲 🔲 🔲 *)*.

A cache of daring Rotterdam fashion designers struggle to survive on the windy **Promenade Overblaak**, amid some of the most bizarre modern architecture in Europe. Women who need something smart and shimmering should visit **Dorien David Design** *(Overblaak 84* 🆎 🔲 🔲 🔲 *)*, which stocks exclusive dresses by Rotterdam designer Dorien Bregman. The card shop **Art à la Carte** *(Overblaak 86)* has a big range of postcards of new Rotterdam architecture.

An unexpected row of smart boutiques can be found on the nearby Mariniersweg. **Portaal** *(Mariniersweg 315)* sells exclusive lines by young Dutch designers. **Oilily Store** *(Mariniersweg 309)* stocks baggy and bright clothes by Dutch designers for children and women.

Finally, you might want to check out the new shopping malls on Weena, such as **Rotterdam Plaza**, envisaged as a dazzling atrium with elegant boutiques and cafés. Some Rotterdammers remain skeptical about the architecture, however, which lacks the finesse of the Lijnbaan.

DEPARTMENT STORES

Head for the stock exchange skyscraper on Beursplein to find the city's biggest department stores. The **Bijenkorf** *(Coolsingel 105* ☎*(010) 4117400* 🆎 🔾 🔾 🆅) is by far the smartest department store in town. The air is awash with the seductive smell of perfume, and the interior design is impressive. The Bijenkorf can be relied on to have wearable clothes in next season's styles for men and women. You will find a good selection of contemporary English fiction in the book department.

Vroom & Dreesmann *(Hoogstraat 185)* is the place for necessities such as folding umbrellas and ballpoint pens.

MARKETS

A vast street market takes place in the streets around the *Gemeentebibliotheek* (public library) at **Blaak** *(Tues, Sat 9am-5pm, metro or tram 1, 3, 6, 7 to Station Blaak)*. Stalls selling vegetables, clothes, cassettes and tools are crammed along Hoogstraat and Mariniersweg. Locals huddle around the Bram Ladage vans (normally parked outside the library and on Oude Binnenweg) to eat steamy chips (French fries) out of paper cones. Nearby **Nieuwe Markt** is the place to go for old tables, mirrors, chandeliers, Art Deco lamps and ornaments.

Philatelists and book-collectors rummage for rarities at the **stamp, coin and book market**, which enlivens the bleak square in front of the St Laurenskerk *(Grote Kerkplein, Tues, Sat 9.30am-4pm, metro or tram 1, 3, 6, 7 to Station Blaak)*.

Stalls selling jewelry, pottery and other crafts animate the broad sidewalks around the **stock exchange** *(Beursplein, Tues, Fri, Sat, metro or tram 1, 3, 4, 6, 7 to Churchillplein/Beurs)*.

GALLERIES

Rotterdam is the only large city in the Randstad without a 17thC school of painters, but several interesting and provocative artists work in the city today. Exhibitions of paintings, photography and sculpture are staged at about 20 galleries in the city, but interesting works can sometimes be seen in cafés, hotels, banks, libraries and hospitals.

The most prestigious exhibitions take place in the galleries clustered around the BOYMANS-VAN BEUNINGEN MUSEUM. The **Witte de With** *(Witte de Withstraat 50* ☎*(010) 4110144* 🔾 *open Tues-Sun 11am-6pm)* is a spacious gallery staging provocative exhibitions of architecture, art, photography, video and design. The gallery regularly publishes thick art books in English, and is slowly acquiring its own permanent collection of sculpture and street installations. **Galerie Perspektief** *(Eendrachtsweg 21* ☎*(010) 4145766, open Tues-Sat noon-5pm)* specializes in current photography and publishes its own magazine.

Several Rotterdam artists have taken refuge in the old quarter of Delfshaven, and a cluster of galleries can be found on the Voorhaven waterfront. Look for Dutch prints and modern ceramics at **Galerie Aelbrecht** *(Aelbrechtskolk 2* ☎*(010) 4771637, open Tues-Sat noon-6pm; Sun 1-5pm)*.

Rotterdam: recreation

Rotterdam for children

Rotterdam's port is a thrilling place for older children to explore. They can go up the **Euromast** by high-speed elevator, board a **Spido boat** for a tour of the modern docks, roam around the **maritime museum** (MARITIEM MUSEUM PRINS HENDRIK), or look at the old cranes and steam tugs in the **open-air maritime museum** (MARITIEM BUITENMUSEUM). The **Ontdekhoek** is an imaginative science laboratory where children aged 4-14 can try simple (and safe) experiments.

The **Imax Theater** has *Kindermatinees* (daily, 11am and 4pm), at which Disney cartoon films are shown on its giant screen, but some children may not be old enough to face the terror of Mickey Mouse projected onto a screen equal in size to 800 television sets. Conventional cinemas often have children's matinees, almost always dubbed into Dutch.

Rotterdam has a modern **zoo** (DIERGAARDE BLIJDORP) which will keep children entertained for a day. The best park for children is **Plaswijkpark** *(C.N.A. Looslaan 23* ☎ *(010) 4181836* ◪ *open daily 9am-5pm, tram 4)*, which has kangaroos, monkeys, pony rides, mini-golf and a maze. The formal park stands on the edge of a lake, the **Bergse Achterplas**, NE of the center, where you can rent rowboats. The **Kinderboerderij De Kraal** *(Lagepad 60, open daily 9am-4pm* ◪ *bus 42)* is a city farm where children can touch the animals. Situated in the Kralingse Bos, it is a long trip for those without a car or bicycle.

The nearest beach is the **Strandbad**, on the W shore of the Kralingse Plas. The North Sea port of **Hoek van Holland**, 26km (15 miles) W of Rotterdam, has a long beach with soft sand.

Sports

Rotterdam is surrounded by several large recreational areas. The most convenient for visitors based in central Rotterdam is the Kralingse Bos, which has an inland beach, a sailing and windsurfing school, and extensive woods for walking.

BOATING

Rowboats can be rented at **Plaswijkpark** to explore the islands in the Bergse Achterplas, to the NE of the city center *(C.N.A. Looslaan 23* ☎ *(010) 4181836* ◪ *open daily 9am-5pm, tram 4)*.

BOWLING

Rotterdammers enjoy the camaraderie of ten-pin bowling at several venues. **Engels Kegelbaan**, opposite Centraal Station (*Stationsplein 45 ☎ (010) 4119551*), has six lanes.

CYCLING

Bicycles can be rented at **Rotterdam Centraal Station** (☎ *(010) 4126220)* or **Dordrecht station** (☎ *(078) 146642)*. The same rental conditions apply as for other parts of the Randstad (see page 36). Bicycles can be taken free of charge on the Rotterdam metro on Saturday and Sunday only. Within the city, the most interesting excursion is to follow the cycle paths in the **Kralingse Bos**. The meandering **dike** along the **Lek** river forms an attractive rural cycling route through old towns such as **Schoonhoven**, which has an unusual museum of gold, silver and clocks (*open Tues-Sun noon-5pm)*.

HORSEBACK-RIDING

The **Rotterdamse Manege** (*Kralingseweg 120 ☎ (010) 4526838)* is a large riding school on the edge of the Kralingse Bos. Experts can follow a riding trail in the nearby woods.

ICE SKATING

Ice skaters practice during the winter at the **IJshal Weena** (*Schaatsbaan 41-45, next to Centraal Station ☎ (010) 4110850)*. Skates are available for rent.

ROLLER SKATING

When the weather is dry and mild, you can roller skate outdoors at the **Gemeentelijke Rolschaatsbaan** (*Ratelaarweg 2 ☎ (010) 4125395)*.

RUNNING AND JOGGING

The meandering paths in **Het Park** are ideal for an early-morning run, or you can follow the quays along the **Nieuwe Maas** waterfront from the Euromast to Blaak. The more energetic can run a circuit of 4.5km (3 miles) around the silent **Kralingse Plas** (see KRALINGSE BOS).

SAILBOARDING AND SAILBOATS

The **Kralingse Plas** is ideal for sailing and wind-surfing. Boats and equipment can be rented at **Zeilcentrum Henk van Gent** (*Plaszoom 350 ☎ (010) 4121098)*, next to the windmill *De Ster*.

SAILING SHIP

Traditional brown-sailed fishing boats can be chartered by groups for one day or longer from **Hollands Glorie** (*Haringvliet 619, 3011 ZP Rotterdam ☎ (010) 4115880)*.

SOCCER

The main soccer team in Rotterdam is **Feyenoord**, based at Feyenoord stadium (*Olympiaweg 50 ☎ (010) 4195711)*.

WALKING

Rotterdammers ramble in the beech woods of the **Kralingse Bos**, an extensive wood enclosing a large lake, to the NE of the central Rotterdam *(metro to Voorschoterlaan, then a 5-minute walk down Rozenburglaan).*

Activities

FREE ACTIVITIES

You can wander free of charge along the **Leuvehaven quay** to inspect the old cranes and barges displayed at the **open-air maritime museum** (MARITIEM BUITENMUSEUM). Temporary exhibitions at the **Nederlands Architectuur Instituut** are normally free, as is entry to the **Voorlichtingscentrum Het Nieuwe Rotterdam** (New Rotterdam Exhibition Center). This exhibition center, above the IMAX THEATER, displays models of tram halts and sewers, and screens a **video** depicting one day in the life of Rotterdam *(Schiedamsedijk 128, 6th floor* ☎ *(010) 4129265* ▣ *open Tues-Fri 10am-5pm; Sat, Sun 11am-5pm).* You can wander into the lobby of the new **Delftse Poort** insurance office complex, opposite Centraal Station, where there is a **free gallery** featuring temporary exhibitions of contemporary art from the MUSEUM BOYMANS-VAN BEUNINGEN collection.

Choirs and chamber orchestras perform free **concerts** at the **St Laurenskerk** every Thursday, while **jazz concerts** at the **Doelencafé** cost nothing more than the price of a *pils.*

Environs of Rotterdam

The nearest old towns to Rotterdam are **Delft** (see page 278), **Dordrecht** (see page 283) and **Gouda** (see page 289). The downstream region to the W of the city is dominated by oil refineries and docks, but just to the E of Rotterdam lies an unexpectedly rural area of dairy farms and canals.

KINDERDIJK

One of the most photographed sights in the Netherlands is the concentration of 19 **windmills** along the Molenkade at Kinderdijk, which was formerly used to drain the Ablasserwaard polder. The **Bezoekmolen**, which means "visitors' windmill" (☎ *(01859) 14118)*, is open from April to September, Monday to Saturday 9.30am-5.30pm. You can see all the windmills with their sails turning, Saturdays in July and August *(1-5.30pm),* and on **Nationale Molendag** (National Windmill Day — see CALENDAR OF EVENTS, page 45); all of the windmills are floodlit during the second week of September.

The name Kinderdijk (child's dike) comes from the legend that a child was found nearby floating in a basket, following the devastating St Elizabeth's Day flood in 1421.

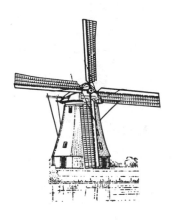

The Hague

The Hague: dignity and diplomacy

The Hague is Hampton-Court turned into a large town.
(William Hazlitt, *Notes of a Journey
through France and Italy*, 1826)

Much admired in previous centuries for its elegant avenues and extensive parks, The Hague (Den Haag) still retains some of its former grandeur in the quarters around the royal palace and the Scheveningse Bosjes. With a population of under half a million, The Hague is a modest and somewhat staid city dominated by government departments, embassies and multinational companies. To visitors looking for the anarchy of Amsterdam or the glittering modernity of Rotterdam, it *can* seem somewhat dull, yet The Hague has its own appeal, with its air of quiet elegance and sober restraint.

The Hague owes its existence — and its curious Old Dutch name of 's-Gravenhage ("at the count's hedge") — to a medieval hunting lodge of the Counts of Holland, built in the 13th century in the depths of the forests fringing the North Sea. A modest town grew up around the Oude Kerk to the west, to serve the needs of the court. The Hague was never formally granted municipal privileges or enclosed by a wall, so that it technically remained a village, albeit a "most divertissant, and noble Village," as John Evelyn wrote after a visit in 1641.

This "noble village" assumed an increasingly important role in Dutch politics following a meeting there in 1586 by the States General of the new Dutch Republic. The representatives of the original seven provinces opted for The Hague, rather than Amsterdam or Rotterdam, as a neutral meeting ground, acceptable to all. Thus it was a lack of qualities in The Hague that led to it becoming the seat of Dutch government (although Amsterdam is the official capital). The present-day parliament meets in a modern complex adjoining the Binnenhof, once the main courtyard of the count's residence. The state opening of parliament takes place in the heavily restored medieval Ridderzaal.

The art of diplomacy was perfected in this detached and dignified city, and several historic international conferences were hosted there, including the Hague Peace Conferences of 1899 and 1907, which tried with little success to halt the drift toward war in Europe. The Vredespaleis (Peace Palace) was built in The Hague in 1913 to provide a permanent forum for settling international disputes, and the International Court of Justice, sometimes called the World Court, now meets there to adjudicate in disputes between nation states.

THE HAGUE, THEN AND NOW

The Hague in the 19th century was an elegant city that aspired to the manners and culture of Paris. Luxurious department stores, shopping arcades and grand hotels were erected, of which only a few mementoes, such as the Hotel Des Indes and the Passage shopping arcade, remain. Literature flourished at the time, and a group of Dutch Impressionist painters coalesced to form the Hague School. The luminous

Scheveningen seascapes of Mesdag and the melancholy portraits of Israels are among the secret delights of The Hague's Gemeentemuseum.

Any visitor to The Hague today is likely to notice an atmosphere tinged with nostalgia. It has been through a rough patch in recent years, when overscaled offices were erected for government departments or multinational corporations, and huge highways driven through the heart of the city. The normally careful Dutch were blind to the destruction of The Hague until it was almost too late, and the citizens now look upon their battered city with a mixture of sadness and rage. Go into any bookstore in town and you will come upon a selection of local history studies with titles such as *Den Haag, Toen en Nu* (The Hague, Then and Now), which juxtapose photographs of the old and the new city. The faded photographs of *toen* (then) show the canals, elegant streets and villas that no longer exist, while photographs of *nu* (now) illustrate mainly ugliness and dereliction.

There might be another reason for the atmosphere of nostalgia in The Hague, as it was here that many Dutch colonials put down roots after being thrown out of the colony of Indonesia in 1945. They settled in large, 19th-century villas close to the dunes, and continued to feast on fiery *rijsttafels* in the many Indonesian restaurants that opened in The Hague after World War II. Many of the settlers have never properly come to terms with exile on the rainswept North Sea coast, and The Hague, however elegant, could never compare with the idyllic life in Batavia (now Jakarta).

The adjoining coastal town of Scheveningen has shared much the same lot as The Hague. Once an elegant 19th-century resort, it has been relentlessly remolded into a glitzy modern town, designed to compete with Mediterranean destinations. Women in ostentatious furs parade their shaggy black dogs along the promenade in winter, and on hot summer days stroll topless, and deeply tanned, by the water's edge. Locals flock here on Sundays to escape the grim silence of The Hague, although the glamorous atmosphere sometimes seems as fake as the suntans. If it all gets too much, you can escape briefly into the mellow hauteur of the Kurhaus Hotel for a coffee in the restored concert hall. Or head along the promenade to the old port to watch the fish being landed at first light.

The Hague has begun to change in recent years as more young people move in to take up jobs in the government. You will now find branches of fashionable Amsterdam shops and restaurants in the Passage and around the Oude Kerk, and cosmopolitan cafés where once there were only seedy bars. Aware of the city's tarnished image, the local council recently launched a plan to improve the culture and conviviality of The Hague. The construction of the new Stadhuis (town hall), Danstheater, and parliament building have certainly boosted the city's recovery, and the old quarters have become more animated after dark and on Sundays. The Hague has hung onto several great assets which set it apart from other Dutch cities: the woods where the Counts of Holland once hunted, the windswept dunes of the Hague Impressionists, and the solemn intimacy of the Mauritshuis picture gallery. The Hague may never be as effervescent as Amsterdam, but it may well please those who come to Holland in search of quiet Dutch dignity.

The Hague: basic information

Getting around

FROM SCHIPHOL AIRPORT TO THE CITY
Direct trains run from Schiphol airport to **Den Haag CS** (Centraal Station) every 30 minutes. Be careful not to take the direct train to **Den Haag HS** (Holland Spoor) station, which will deposit you in one of the town's more gloomy quarters. If you happen to blunder onto the wrong train, change at Leiden station for Den Haag CS, or take a train from HS to CS.

RAILWAY TRAVEL
There is an **airline check-in desk** at Den Haag CS for passengers flying from Schiphol with KLM and certain other airlines. It might cut down the time you spend at the airport, although you will still have to lug your baggage on the train (☎ *06-8991121 for all information on train travel).*

PUBLIC TRANSPORTATION
The Hague has an excellent tram and bus network run by **HTM** *(for information on timetables ☎ 06-8991121).*

TAXIS
Taxis can be ordered by telephone (☎ *(070) 3907722),* in which case they arrive almost immediately, or picked up at a taxi stand, located at rail stations, major hotels, squares and important sights.

BANKS AND CURRENCY EXCHANGE
Banks in The Hague are open Monday to Friday 9am-4pm. The **Grenswisselkantoor (GWK)** at Centraal Station is open Monday to Saturday 8am-9pm and Sunday 9am-9pm (☎ *(070) 3471231);* the branch at Den Haag HS station is open Monday to Saturday 8am-8pm and Sunday 9am-5pm (☎ *(070) 3890832).*

SHOPPING HOURS
Shops in The Hague are open normal Dutch hours, with an extension to 9pm on **Thursday** *(koopavond).* Many shops in Scheveningen, especially around the Kurhaus, are open extended hours *(mid-Mar to mid-Oct Mon-Sat 9am-10pm and Sun 10am-10pm; mid-Oct to mid-Mar Mon-Sat 9am-6pm and Sunday 10am-6pm).*

POSTAL AND TELEPHONE SERVICES

The main **post office** in The Hague *(Kerkplein* ☎ *(070) 3653843)* is open Monday to Friday 8.30am-7pm (8.30pm on Thursday); Saturday 9am-4pm. Go there for international telephone calls, telegrams, fax and telex. The dialing code for The Hague is **070**, which should be omitted when dialing within the city.

TOURIST INFORMATION

The **VVV** (tourist office) is located opposite Centraal Station *(Babylon shopping complex, Koningin Julianaplein 30* ☎ *(070) 3546200; write to: Postbus 17224, 2502 CE Den Haag. Open Apr to mid-Sept Mon-Sat 9am-9pm; Sun 10am-5pm and mid-Sept to Apr Mon-Sat 9am-6pm).* The tourist office in the Palace Promenade shopping mall in **Scheveningen** *(Gevers Deynootweg 1134)* opens roughly the same hours.

GENERAL DELIVERY (POSTE RESTANTE)

Letters to be collected should be marked **poste restante** and addressed to the **Hoofdpostkantoor PTT** *(Kerkplein* ☎ *(070) 3845845).* These can be collected at the main post office; remember to take some form of identification with you. **American Express** *(Venestraat 20* ☎ *(070) 3469515)* offers the same service to card-holders.

Emergency information

EMERGENCY SERVICES
For **Police, Ambulance** or **Fire** ☎ 06-11

HOSPITAL
The most central hospital is **Westeinde** *(Lijnbaan 32* ☎ *(070) 3889393)*

MEDICAL EMERGENCIES
Doctors' service (day) ☎ (070) 3455300, (night) ☎ (070) 3469669; Dentists' 24-hour service ☎ (070) 3974491.

ALL-NIGHT PHARMACIES
Pharmacies are open Mon-Fri 9am-5.30pm. For information on weekend services and all-night pharmacies ☎ (070) 3451000.

HELP LINE
SOS Telefonische Hulpdienst ☎ (070) 3454500

LOST PROPERTY
If you have lost something on public transportation, go to the **HTM office** *(Dynamostraat 10* ☎ *(070) 3429201).*

The Hague:
Planning and walks

Orientation

The Hague has a compact **old town** *(Centrum)* surrounded by extensive woods and suburbs. The **Binnenhof**, at the E end of Centrum,
marks the heart of the government quarter, while the **Groenmarkt**, to
the w, is the focus of commerce. Centrum is a pleasant area to explore
on foot, with its royal palaces, churches, stately avenues, museums,
hotels, restaurants, shops and cafés.

The city becomes more diffuse in the outlying quarters. Distances are
generally too great to cover comfortably on foot, and cycling is not always
wise, so you will inevitably have to master the city's tram network. The
Zeeheldenkwartier (Sea Heroes Quarter) lies immediately N of Centrum, taking its name from the many streets in the area named after 17thC
Dutch admirals. The broad avenues of 19thC villas shelter many government offices and embassies, and the main attractions for the traveler are
several museums.

A large area of woods, the **Scheveningse Bosjes**, separates the
Zeeheldenkwartier from the elegant **Statenkwartier** (States-General
Quarter), where the street names tend to commemorate 17thC Dutch
political leaders. Business visitors are likely to find themselves taking a
tram out here to get to the **Congresgebouw**, a modern conference
center, while tourists will step off one stop sooner to go to the **Gemeentemuseum**.

The seaside resort of **Scheveningen** runs along the coast N of the
Statenkwartier. The old fishing port partly survives, with crooked lanes
lined with cramped 19thC fishermen's houses, but most of Scheveningen
has been turned into a modern vacation resort. With its sandy beaches
and windswept dunes, Scheveningen can be invigorating and romantic,
but it gets somewhat too crowded for comfort in the summer.

The suburbs to the S of Centrum are rather staid, and the main reason
for venturing there is to visit Constantijn Huygens' country house at
Voorburg.

STRATEGIES FOR SUNDAYS

The Hague is often uncomfortably quiet on Sundays, as most of the
local population is either at the beach or having coffee and cake with
relatives. Your best bet is to stroll down the **Lange Voorhout**, where a
market takes place in the summer (see SHOPPING, page 270). Dive into
Café Schlemmer if you feel the need for a friendly face, or wander

into the **Pulchri Studio** (see SHOPPING, page 270). Take the tram to Scheveningen if you want crowds and noise, or, as a last resort, take the train to Amsterdam.

EVENTS
The main event every year is the **North Sea Jazz Festival**, a friendly and sprawling festival held in mid-July, which brings together some of the biggest names in jazz. It is held in the **Congresgebouw**, a building designed in the 1960s by J. J. P. Oud in his distinctive nautical style *(for further information, write to Postbus 87840, 2508 DE, Den Haag* ☎ *(070) 3502034* Ⓕⓧ *(070) 3512832).*

A walk through The Hague –

The most rewarding area of The Hague to explore lies between the Binnenhof and Javastraat. Broad tree-lined avenues and fashionable boutiques on cobbled lanes give this area an elegant allure. The walk takes in the royal palace, the parliament building and the superb collection of 17thC paintings in the Mauritshuis. Allow 1 hour.

From Centraal Station, walk down Herengracht and continue along Lange Poten, pausing, if you wish, at the **Wiener Konditorei** *(Korte Poten 24)* for coffee and Viennese *Sachertorte*. Turn right at the square Plein to reach the handsome MAURITSHUIS, then go left through the 17thC gate to penetrate the courtyard of the **Binnenhof**, home to the Dutch government.

On the other side of the courtyard, turn left, and walk around the building along Hofweg, stopping to admire the new TWEEDE KAMER (second chamber) building on the left, designed with a vast glass front to convey a spirit of open government. Cross Hofweg and enter the **Passage**, an elegant 19thC glass-roofed arcade. Turn right at the rotunda and, on Gravenstraat, left to reach the 16thC Renaissance **Stadhuis**, which was once the town hall. Go down the street between the town hall and the Late Gothic **St Jacobskerk** *(open mid-May to mid-Sept Mon-Sat 11am-4pm)*, then continue straight ahead down **Oude Molstraat**, a narrow, winding street with bookstores, cluttered antique stores and a curious **museum** devoted to the **Haagse Hopje** (see page 253). Turn right onto Molenstraat, and left up Noordeinde to peer through the iron railings at the restored 17thC **Paleis Noordeinde**, built in Dutch Classical style by Jacob van Campen and Pieter Post. Facing it is a small mock-Gothic **art gallery** built in the 19thC by the Anglophile King William I.

Retrace your steps and turn left along Heulstraat to reach Kneuterdijk. The somewhat overbearing **Paleis Kneuterdijk** on the left *(NW corner of Kneuterdijk)* was built in 1717 by Daniel Marot. King William I bought the house in 1816, and lived there with his Russian wife Anna Paulovna. On the right, at **Kneuterdijk 6**, stands the handsome Classical house of the Raadspensionaris Johan de Witt, who in 1672 was murdered by a mob incensed by the French invasion of the Netherlands.

247

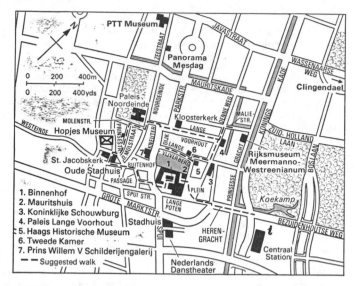

1. Binnenhof
2. Mauritshuis
3. Koninklijke Schouwburg
4. Paleis Lange Voorhout
5. Haags Historische Museum
6. Tweede Kamer
7. Prins Willem V Schilderijengalerij
– – Suggested walk

Cross Kneuterdijk and head down the **Lange Voorhout**, a beautiful tree-lined avenue with broad lawns that in early spring are carpeted with yellow and lilac crocuses. The last surviving **step gable** in The Hague, at **Lange Voorhout 6**, was built in 1618 for the state ordnance officer. Cannons were stored in the choir of the nearby **Kloosterkerk**. Notice the former **Koninklijke Bibliotheek** (Royal Library), at **Lange Voorhout 34**, built by Daniel Marot as a five-bay-wide town house in 1734-38 and extended on both sides by Pieter de Swart in 1761.

A short detour left down **Vos in Tuinstraat**, then right along **Maliestraat**, leads to an unexpectedly picturesque spot where two canals meet. Unfortunately, this charm does not extend very far in any direction, and so, having taken in the wisteria-drenched houses, retrace your steps and continue straight ahead down the short arm of the L-shaped Lange Voorhout.

The reserved Classicism of Pieter de Swart is evident in the house he built in 1760-64 for the banker John William Hope at the E end of Lange Voorhout (now the **Paleis Lange Voorhout**, owned by the royal family), and in the unfinished palace he designed for Princess Caroline van Nassau in 1760, which is now the **Koninklijke Schouwburg** (*Korte Voorhout 3*).

At the S end of Lange Voorhout, turn right to reach the **Lange Vijverberg**, a pleasant chestnut-lined avenue that borders the Hofvijver.

The Hague: sights and places of interest

The foremost sights in The Hague are concentrated around the Hof-vijver. A walk along the water's edge takes you past the Mauritshuis, the Gothic Ridderzaal, the Bredius Museum and several smaller museums located in handsome old brick houses.

A second string of sights and places of interest runs along the fringes of the Scheveningse Bos, an extensive wood to the N of the old town. Hordes of schoolchildren spill out of buses to visit Madurodam, Omniversum and the Museon, while adults stroll around the Gemeentemuseum and the Vredespaleis. Finally, you can head out to the jaunty coastal resort of Scheveningen to eat fried fish or sunbathe on the vast sandy beach.

USEFUL TO KNOW
Most museums in The Hague are closed on Mondays. See individual museums for opening times.

The visitor who tires of gray suits and *gravitas* should be aware that there is another side to this dignified city. A short selection of CURIOSITIES, from the antique to the bizarre, appears on page 251. There is no shortage, either, of green spaces in which to compose the spirit and rest the feet; a number are described in INTERLUDES, page 253. For a selection of places from which you can obtain a bracing view of the North Sea, see VIEW-POINTS, page 258.

HOW TO USE THIS SECTION
In the following pages, The Hague's sights are arranged alphabetically, using English or Dutch names according to common English-speaking usage. The sights are classified by category on page 250.

Look for the ★ symbol against the most important sights and 🏛 for buildings of great architectural interest. Places of special interest for children ✿ and with outstanding views ◀€ are also indicated. For a full explanation of symbols, see page 7.

If you only know the name of a museum, say, in English, and cannot find it in the following A-Z, try looking it up in the INDEX. Some lesser sights do not have their own entries but are included within other entries: look these up in the index too.

Bold type is generally employed to indicate points of outstanding interest. Entries given without addresses and opening times are described more fully elsewhere: check the cross-references, which are in SMALL CAPITALS.

SIGHTS CLASSIFIED BY TYPE

MUSEUMS
Museum Bredius
Rijksmuseum Gevangen-
  poort
Haags Gemeentemuseum 🏛 ★
Haags Historisch Museum
Hopjes Museum
Huygens Museum
  Hofwijk
Mauritshuis, Koninklijk Kabinet
  van Schilderijen 🏛 ★
Museon ✸
PTT Museum
Schilderijengalerij Prins
  Willem V
Rijksmuseum Meermanno-
  Westreenianum

Rijksmuseum H.W.
  Mesdag

BUILDINGS
Passage
Ridderzaal 🏛
Tweede Kamer
Vredespaleis

OTHER SIGHTS
Cinemotion
Clingendael
Madurodam ✸ ★
Omniversum ✸
Panorama Mesdag ★
Scheveningen ✸
Westbroekpark

BREDIUS, MUSEUM
Lange Vijverberg 14 ☎*(070) 3620729* 📷 *Open Tues-Sun noon-5pm. Tram 12 to Tournooiveld.*
An 18thC mansion houses the private collection of Abraham Bredius, former director of the Mauritshuis. Those who share Bredius's passion for 17thC Dutch painting can admire portraits by Rembrandt, landscapes by Cuyp and brothel scenes by Steen, beautifully displayed in an 18thC merchant's house.

CINEMOTION
Palace Promenade, Scheveningen ☎*(070) 3556162* ✸ *Screenings daily from 11am-10pm. Minimum age 6. Tram 1, 7, 8, 9 to Gevers Deynootplein.*
For those who find OMNIVERSUM'S three-dimensional film technology too tame, the Cinemotion cinema offers a thrilling simulation of flight on state-of-the-art hydraulic seats. The brief ride is not for the faint-hearted or the impoverished.

CLINGENDAEL
Wassenaarseweg 🚗 🚌 *Open dawn-dusk. Japanese Garden open early May to mid-June 9am-8pm. Bus 18 from Centraal Station to Laan van Clingendael.*
Located in the grounds of the Van Brienens' 18thC country house, Clingendael is one of the most attractive parks in The Hague, with its mass of rhododendrons in the star-shaped **Sterrebos**, its **Rosarium** and an 18thC **Old Dutch Garden** (Oud-Hollandse Tuin). But its greatest glory is the **Japanese Garden** (Japanse Tuin), which is open to the

public for a mere six weeks every year while the azaleas and cherry trees are at their best.

This enchanting miniature garden, begun in the early 20thC, is correct in every detail, from the stone lanterns placed in symbolic settings beside the winding paths, to the striking red lacquered bridge across the pond. Every corner of the garden cries out to be photographed, but the view through the Moon Window of the replica Tea House is the most picturesque.

CURIOSITIES

The **Schilderijengalerij Prins Willem V** is a rare example of an 18thC picture gallery, while the **Panorama Mesdag** has survived as one of the last intact examples of a panoramic painting. But the model of the submarine **Nautilus** on Scheveningen pier has the most mesmerizing aura. Inspired by Jules Verne's science fiction fantasy *Twenty Thousand Leagues Under the Sea,* or more probably by Walt Disney's 1954 movie of the book, the replica is, if not 20,000 leagues, then quite some distance *above* the sea, occupying a concrete bunker on one of the pier's satellites.

A short slippery walk leads to the metal ship, which floats in an artificial sea stocked with plastic fish. Amid a clutter of Victorian steam pipes and ornate iron railings, you glimpse surreal waxwork models of Captain Nemo and his crew, or, through a porthole window, spy an octopus attacking a small boat. Nautilus is a strangely romantic spot, and lovers often flirt in the shadows, seduced perhaps by the delectable dark mystery of a fabricated submarine floating in an artificial sea.

THE HAGUE GOVERNMENT QUARTER: KEY 1 Museum Bredius **2** Haags Historisch Museum **3** Mauritshuis **4** Koloniën (Pvd A party) **5** Justitie (CDA party) **6** Tweede Kamer **7** Ridderzaal **8** Eerste Kamer ⇒ Entrance

HAAGS GEMEENTEMUSEUM 血 ★

Stadhouderslaan 41 ☎*(070) 3381111* 🚗 🅿 *Open Tues-Sun 11am-5pm. Tram 10 to Stadhouderslaan.*

The fascinating and diverse collection of The Hague's municipal museum is housed in an attractive building designed by H. P. Berlage in 1935. The ivy-clad brick walls and ornamental lily ponds are particularly picturesque, while the interior possesses a certain ceremonial grandeur, especially in the **Erezaal** (Hall of Honor) above the main entrance, where Eric Orr's remarkable *Light Space* highlights the awesome dimensions of Berlage's design. The Gemeentemuseum's glass cabinets and lamps were also designed by Berlage, who died shortly before the building was completed.

The ground floor is mainly devoted to applied art and includes some intriguing Spanish and Italian apothecaries' jars, examples of Chinese porcelain and a magnificent 18thC dollhouse. The **five rooms** furnished in 18thC styles *(stijlkamers)* are also worth a glance, particularly the exquisite **Japanese room**, rescued from a house that was demolished to make way for the VREDESPALEIS. For many, the most interesting feature of the Gemeentemuseum is its extensive **collection of musical instruments**, ranging from a 14thC wooden flute dredged up from a moat to a remarkable 19thC Viennese pyramid piano, lavishly adorned with Egyptian motifs. It is also worth seeking out the **Nederlands Kostuummuseum**, which has an engaging gallery of fashions covering everything from 18thC corsets to 20thC punk clothing.

The layout of the upper floor, devoted to the museum's collection of 19th and 20thC painting, is quite baffling; it is easy to miss large sections of the collection. The best rooms to begin with are those devoted to **19thC Romantics** such as Wijnand Nuijen and early Impressionists such as Jan B. Jongkind. Be sure not to miss Monet's vibrant *Quai du Louvre* or his much later, almost abstract, *Glycine,* painted in the 1920s in his garden at Giverny.

The collection of works by the **Hague School** contains attractive seascapes such as Jacob Maris' *Bomschuit* and J. H. Weissenbruch's *Strandgezicht,* which capture the breezy atmosphere and silver-gray light of the Dutch coast. There is also an excellent collection of Impressionist works by George Breitner, including a view of the Zandhoek in Amsterdam, a startling cavalry charge and the exquisite painting entitled *Red Kimono* (1893).

A room is devoted to **Jan Toorop**, a Dutch artist who tried various modern styles before settling into a rather tormented Symbolism.

The museum's collection of **Mondrian** paintings spans the full range of the artist's diverse styles, and includes some early landscape paintings of the river Gein and the dunes at Domburg. There is also a series of tree studies that show his development from the style of late Van Gogh, as seen in *Red Tree, 1908,* to complete abstraction, as in *Composition: Trees II.* The museum also has works by **Theo van Doesburg**, including a painting whose diagonal lines threw Mondrian into a rage. Finally, don't miss the atmospheric **Dijsselhofkamer**, an Art Nouveau room dating from 1895.

HAAGS HISTORISCH MUSEUM
Korte Vijverberg 7 ☎*(070) 3646940. Open Tues-Sun noon-4pm. Tram 12 to Tournooiveld.*

Overlooking the Hofvijver, the **Sebastiaansdoelen** was built in 1636 by Arend van 's-Gravesande as an assembly hall for the guild of archers. The handsome Classical building is now home to The Hague's historical museum. The displays are rather timid compared to those in Amsterdam's historical museum, but you may find the urban landscapes and plans illuminating. The front room overlooking the pond has some fascinating paintings of the Hofvijver, showing the archery range that once stood on the waterfront.

HOPJES MUSEUM
Oude Molstraat 20 ☎*(070) 3924567* 🖾 *Open Tues-Sat 10am-5pm* 🚊 *Tram 3 to Grote Kerk.*

This is a strange little museum devoted entirely to the **Haagsche Hopje**, a caramel-flavored boiled candy that is native to The Hague. Visit the museum café to sample a Hopje, and maybe buy a tin to take home.

HUYGENS MUSEUM HOFWIJK
Westeinde 2, Voorburg ☎*(070) 3872311* 🖾 🚶 *Open Wed, Thurs, Sat, Sun 2-5pm. Tram 10, or train to Voorburg Station.*

Hofwijk was a country retreat on the river Vliet belonging to the politician, poet and scientist Constantijn Huygens (1596-1687), who helped Rembrandt gain a number of major commissions. The house, an elegant Classical box, was designed by Huygens with help from Jacob van Campen.

Suburban sprawl has swallowed up most of the estate, and the throb of traffic destroys the idyllic atmosphere. Yet the interior, with its tiled kitchen and intimate library, retains the charm of the Golden Age.

The museum contains memorabilia such as portraits, letters, scientific instruments and books, including Huygens' 2,824-line poem in praise of Hofwijk, and his plan for a broad, straight boulevard between The Hague and Scheveningen (now the Scheveningse Weg).

On leaving Hofwijk, turn right to reach Voorburg's attractive main street, **Herenstraat**, which is assumed to be the old Roman road that led to the settlement of Forum Hadriani. The main sights in Voorburg are the 15thC church, the handsome Renaissance double step gable of **Swaensteyn**, a former inn, and the pleasant park **Vreugd en Rust**, designed by the 19thC landscape gardener J. D. Zocher.

INTERLUDES
Take a break from exploring the city and retreat to the **Haagse Bos**, opposite Centraal Station, where you can wander along the meandering streams and look at the deer penned up in the **Koekamp** reserve. The **Paleis Tuin**, behind Paleis Noordeinde, is a useful little garden to take refuge in. Go to WESTBROEKPARK to smell the roses or to CLINGENDAEL to unwind amid Japanese temples and gurgling water.

MADURODAM ★
Haringkade 175 ☎*(070) 3553900* 🚍 ♿ *(signposted route for wheelchairs)*
🚃 ✶ 🚗 🚤 *Open daily Apr-May 9am-10.30pm; June-Aug 9am-11pm; Sept 9am-9.30pm; Oct-early Jan 9am-6pm. Tram 1, 9 to Madurodam.*

Founded in memory of a Dutch soldier who died in Dachau concentration camp, the miniature town of Madurodam has been assembled with painstaking attention to detail. Because Madurodam is intended to reflect every aspect of Dutch society, the models include not only historic buildings, trains, airplanes and ships, but also a **sewage works**, an **automobile accident** and a **nudist beach**. Large multinational corporations such as Shell and Unilever have donated models of their own head offices to provide a true, if rather uninspiring, vision of contemporary Holland. The miniature vegetation is carefully selected to enhance the realism, and at night the entire town is ablaze with some 50,000 miniature lamps.

MAURITSHUIS, KONINKLIJK KABINET VAN SCHILDERIJEN 🏛 ★
Korte Vijverberg 8 ☎*(070) 3654779* 🚍 *Open Tues-Sat 10am-5pm; Sun, hols 11am-5pm. Tram 3, 7, 8 to Centrum.*

A visit to the Royal Picture Gallery in the Mauritshuis is doubly delightful, since its superb collection of 17thC Dutch Masters is housed in an architectural gem dating from the Golden Age.

The Mauritshuis was commissioned by Johan Maurits, a popular governor of the ill-fated Dutch settlement in Brazil. It was built on the edge of the Hofvijver by Jacob van Campen in 1633-44 in a mixture of mellow brown brick and yellow-gray sandstone that epitomizes the quiet contentment associated with the Golden Age.

The collection is particularly renowned for its **Rembrandts**, including two self-portraits: the rather haughty *Self-portrait as a Young Man*, painted around 1629 when Rembrandt was still living in Leiden, and the quietly resigned *Late Self-portrait,* painted shortly before his death. The museum also possesses Rembrandt's first major commission, *The Anatomy Lesson of Dr Tulp,* painted in 1632 — one year before the Mauritshuis was begun — to hang in the surgeons' hall of the WAAG in Amsterdam.

Equally remarkable are the two paintings by **Vermeer**: the astonishingly tender *View of Delft,* painted in an uncertain moment between sunshine and rain, and the snapshot-like *Head of a Girl.*

The Mauritshuis also boasts 13 paintings by **Jan Steen**, illustrating his delight in providing compact moral tales enhanced with touches of bawdy humor. The most boisterous scene illustrates the old Dutch adage, "The way you hear it is the way you sing it" — a warning against children imitating their parents — in which Steen includes himself offering a clay pipe to a child.

Other popular works are **Jacob van Ruisdael**'s *View of Haarlem* and **Paulus Potter's** remarkably realistic *Young Bull;* but possibly the most endearing painting in the collection is the *Goldfinch* painted by Rembrandt's ill-fated pupil **Carel Fabritius**, who was killed in a gunpowder explosion in Delft in 1654. Many of his works perished in the disaster, and others, which had been bought by the Czar of Russia, were lost in a shipwreck, leaving only eight surviving. Although the accent of its collection is on 17thC Dutch paintings, the Mauritshuis also contains several works by **Flemish Primitives**, such as Rogier van der Weyden's *Lamentation,* and paintings by Holbein and Rubens.

MUSEON

Stadhouderslaan 41 ☎*(070) 3381338* 🚇 ♿ 💻 ✳ 🚃 *Open Tues-Fri 10am-5pm; Sat, Sun, hols noon-5pm. Tram 10 to Stadhouderslaan.*

The Museon is the catchy new name for the former Museum of Education, which was founded in 1904 as a progressive science museum for children. The attractive new building was designed by Gerardus Quist to harmonize with Berlage's GEMEENTEMUSEUM, and the interior design creates just the right sense of adventure. The main subjects covered are geology, biology, physics, history, ethnology and human rights, and each section is packed with exhibits such as a Bedouin tent, a prehistoric shelter and a model of the Rhine.

OMNIVERSUM

President Kennedylaan 5 ☎*(070) 3545454* 🚇 ♿ 💻 ✳ 🚃 *Screenings Tues-Thurs on the hour 11am-4pm; Fri-Sun, hols on the hour 11am-5pm and 7-9pm. Commentary in Dutch only. Tram 10 to Stadhouderslaan.*

View the PANORAMA MESDAG first, then visit Omniversum to see an attempt, dating from around 100 years later, to achieve a similar illusion of three-dimensionality on a two-dimensional surface. Omniversum uses a giant domed cinema screen, similar to that of a planetarium, as well as a computer and a vast array of loudspeakers, to create a highly convincing sensation of movement. The films regularly screened are mainly documentaries on themes such as space travel (scenes involving flight are particularly stomach-churning).

PANORAMA MESDAG ★

Zeestraat 65 ☎*(070) 3642563* 🚇 🎨 ✳ *Open Mon-Sat 10am-5pm; Sun, hols noon-5pm. Tram 7, 8 to Mauritskade.*

The Panorama Mesdag, one of the few surviving 19thC panorama paintings in the world, is a 120m (400-foot) long and 14m (45-foot) high circular view of the village of Scheveningen and the North Sea coast, seen from the **Seinpostduin** (a dune). Its main fascination is its uncanny realism, which is achieved by creating a three-dimensional *faux terrain* between the viewing platform and the canvas, so that there appears to be no dividing line between the painting and the viewer. The Panorama Mesdag is famous not merely for its technical virtuosity, but also for its artistic merit. It was painted in 1881 by the Dutch marine artist H. W. Mesdag, assisted by his wife (who painted the village of Scheveningen), Th. de Bock (responsible for the sky and dunes), and the Amsterdam Impressionist G. H. Breitner, who painted the cavalry and artillery on the beach.

The viewing platform incorporates Mesdag's sketching cylinder, and a set of peepholes at the exit provides a glimpse behind the scenes. The museum also contains a small collection of seascapes by Mesdag, together with a permanent exhibition on the panorama phenomenon that was a feature of the 19thC.

PASSAGE
Entrances at Hofweg 5-7, Spuistraat 26-28 and Buitenhof. Tram 3 to Graven-straat.

The Neo-Renaissance Passage was built in the 19thC in a bid to mimic the elegant covered arcades of Brussels and Paris. Three glass-roofed passages lined with shops meet at a vaulted rotunda. Despite its architectural grandeur, the arcade has never really been a roaring success. The opening of a new hotel in the Passage has helped to revitalize the building, however, and some fashionable shops, selling smart shoes and clothes, have recently opened up there.

PRINS WILLEM V, SCHILDERIJENGALERIJ
Buitenhof 35 ☎*(070) 3182487* 🎦 *Open Tues-Sun 11am-4pm. Tram 7, 8 to Kneuterdijk.*

Founded in 1773 by Prins Willem V, this unusual art gallery was the first public museum in the Netherlands. It is perhaps most interesting as a curiosity, as it retains its 18thC appearance; the walls of the long gallery and small antechamber are covered from floor to ceiling with paintings.

The 130 or so paintings in the collection are mainly 17thC Dutch and Flemish works, showing familiar subjects such as church interiors, still lifes, prim towns and romantic landscapes. The smaller paintings are difficult to appreciate in this setting, and it takes a huge work such as Bloemaert's *Marriage of Peleus and Thetis* (1638) to catch one's attention. W. van Haecht's strange treatment of *Alexander the Great Visiting the Studio of Apelles* shows a gallery similar to that of Prins Willem V.

PTT MUSEUM
Zeestraat 82 ☎*(070) 3624531* 🖼 ♿ 🍴 *Open Mon-Sat 10am-5pm; Sun, hols 1-5pm. Tram 7, 8 to Vredespaleis.*

The recently-modernized Postmuseum is concealed behind a white Neoclassical facade near the PANORAMA MESDAG. The museum charts the development of post and telecommunications in the Netherlands, from the slow horse-drawn boats known as *trekschuiten* to modern fiber optics. The exhibits include a beautiful reconstructed post office, a collection of mail boxes, delivery vans, a sorting machine, radios, telephones and a huge international stamp collection.

RIDDERZAAL 🏛
Binnenhof 8a ☎*(070) 3646144* 🖼 𝄇 *compulsory. Open Mon-Sat 10am-4pm (also Sun noon-4pm July-Aug). Tram 3, 7, 8 to Centrum.*

Begun in the 13thC by Count William II and completed by his son Floris V, the Ridderzaal is the oldest and most imposing building of the Binnenhof complex. During the Middle Ages, the Binnenhof served as an administrative center for the provinces of Holland and Zeeland, and after the Revolt of the Netherlands it became the seat of government of the new Republic.

Restored in the 19thC, the Ridderzaal remains the symbol of Dutch government, although it is only used on ceremonial occasions such as the state opening of parliament. Everyday government business is conducted in the surrounding buildings of the Binnenhof and the adjoining TWEEDE KAMER complex.

RIJKSMUSEUM GEVANGENPOORT
Buitenhof 33 ☎(070) 3460861. Open Apr-Oct, Mon-Fri 10am-4pm; Sat, Sun 1-4pm; Nov-Mar Mon-Fri 10am-4pm ✗ (compulsory, on the hour). Tram 3, 7, 8 to Centrum.
The former 14thC gatehouse of the Count's castle has been fastidiously restored as a somber museum of torture instruments.

RIJKSMUSEUM MEERMANNO-WESTREENIANUM
Prinsessegracht 30 ☎(070) 3462700 ▣ Open Mon-Sat 1-5pm. Ring bell for entry. Tram 1, 9 to Zuid-Hollandlaan.
This striking Neoclassical town house contains an extensive collection of antiquities and rare books, begun in the 18thC by Gerard Meerman and extended by Baron van Westreenen in the 19thC. Interesting temporary exhibitions on contemporary book design are organized by the **Museum van het Boek**, which was established in 1960. The interior of the building is worth a glance, both for the delightful 18thC rooms on the ground floor, and the 19thC museum and library above.

RIJKSMUSEUM H. W. MESDAG
Laan van Meerdervoort 7f ☎(070) 3635450 ▣ Closed for restoration until early 1994. Ring bell for entry. Tram 7, 8 to Vredespaleis.
While the crowds push to see the spectacular PANORAMA MESDAG, the home and private collection of the marine painter H. W. Mesdag is a must for anyone interested in the quiet, meditative landscapes of late 19thC French and Dutch artists. Closed for major refurbishment, it is expected to reopen in early 1994, but visitors would be wise to check.

The top floor of the museum is devoted to Mesdag's collection of paintings by the Romantic Barbizon School, the largest collection of works by this group outside France. It includes landscapes by Millet, Daubigny, Corot and Courbet. The rest of Mesdag's collection concentrates on the artists of the Dutch Hague School, including Israels, Roelofs, Willem and Jacob Maris, Bosboom and Mesdag himself. These artists depicted the dunes, polders and sea near The Hague in the same melancholy dark browns and greens favored by the Barbizon artists.

SCHEVENINGEN
⚘ Tram 1, 7, 8, 9 to Gevers Deynootplein.
Originally a fishing village dating back to the 15thC, Scheveningen became one of Europe's most fashionable resorts in the late 19thC, due largely to its proximity to The Hague. Of the old Scheveningen, which Baedeker's 1905 guidebook dubbed "the most fashionable watering-place in Holland," scarcely a trace remains, apart from the recently-restored **Kurhaus**, with its famous frescoed **Kurzaal**. But the *fin de*

siècle elegance is marred by a brash explosion of modern shops and apartments, which are Scheveningen's way of competing with Mediterranean resorts.

The old pier at Scheveningen was demolished long ago, to be replaced by the modern concrete **Pier Scheveningen** *(Strandweg 1 ☎(070) 3543677)*, which has several satellite islands at its far end. There is a windswept tower to climb, a coral exhibition, some slot machines that bleep forlornly, and a restaurant decorated in a tacky nautical style. Only the replica **Nautilus** is interesting, with its antiquated iron fittings, ghostly organ music and mechanized fish (see CURIOSITIES, page 251).

TWEEDE KAMER
Hofsingelplein. Tram 3, 7, 8 to Centrum. See plan on page 251.
The directly-elected Tweede Kamer (Second Chamber) of the Dutch parliament traditionally debated in a comfortable Neoclassical ballroom, built by Stadholder William V shortly before he was forced to flee from the invading Napoleonic army. The 150 members of parliament are due to move in late 1992 to a new assembly room designed by P. B. de Bruijn, which features a sweeping glass frontage designed to symbolize open government. You can watch elected representatives from the street, or sit in the large public gallery.

The 75 provincial representatives of the Eerste Kamer (First Chamber) continue to gather in the 17thC assembly room of the States General.

VIEWPOINTS ◀€
Stand on the **Seinpostduin** at Scheveningen to discover what remains of the panoramic view of Scheveningen represented in the PANORAMA MESDAG, or climb the winding **tower** at the end of Scheveningen pier for a wonderfully romantic view of the North Sea far below.

VREDESPALEIS
Carnegieplein 2 ☎(070) 3469680 ■ Open Mon-Fri ⚹ (compulsory) at 10am, 11am, 2pm, 3pm; also 4pm May-Aug. Tram 7, 8 to Vredespaleis.
The Hague was the scene of the first international peace conference in 1899, which was held in the splendid if somewhat unsuitable Oranjezaal of the Huis ten Bosch, whose vast Baroque murals depicted the military exploits of Frederik Hendrik. It was later decided to set up a permanent court of arbitration in The Hague, and the Scottish-born steel magnate Andrew Carnegie donated a million pounds for the construction of a peace palace. .

The French architect Louis Cordonnier won the competition for the design of the palace with a grandiose eclectic pile that originally included four corner towers. But even Carnegie could not afford to sponsor such splendor and the palace was eventually built with only one tower, giving it a decidedly lopsided appearance.

The interior is an intimidating display of opulence, and contains various unusual items donated by member states of the United Nations such as wood paneling, chandeliers and tile tableaux. Perhaps the most delightful items are the fountain in the courtyard, which was donated by

Denmark, and the Japanese wall hangings. The most impressive gift, however, is the main staircase of the Vredespaleis, which was given by the city of The Hague.

Begun in 1907, the Vredespaleis was completed just before the outbreak of World War I put an end to its noble aspirations. The guided tour takes in the Permanent Court of Arbitration and the International Court of Justice, which was added in 1922.

WESTBROEKPARK

Kapelweg, Scheveningen *Open 9am-1hr before dusk. Tram 1, 9 to Nieuwe Duinweg.*

This romantic landscaped park in the Scheveningse Bosjes, just N of Madurodam, is famed for its **Rosarium** of some 20,000 roses, which are at their peak from about July to September. At other times of year, you can wander in the herb garden or admire the sculptures dotted among the shrubs.

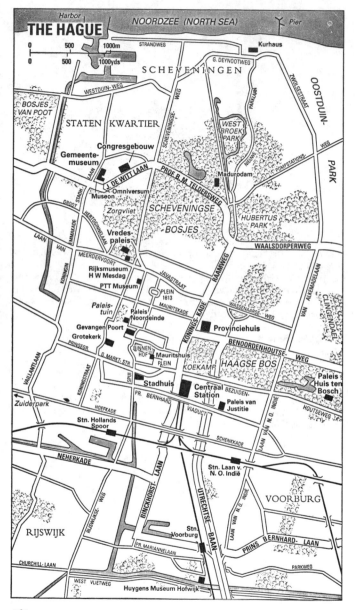

THE HAGUE

Harbor

NOORDZEE (NORTH SEA)

Pier

0 — 500 — 1000m
0 — 500 — 1000yds

STRANDWEG

Kurhaus

SCHEVENINGEN

G. DEYNOOTWEG

WESTDUIN- WEG

ZWOLSESTRAAT

OOSTDUIN-

BOSJES
VAN POOT

STATEN KWARTIER

SCHEVENINGSE WEG

PARKLAAN

WEST
BROEK
PARK

NIEUWE

PARK

WEG

Congresgebouw

Gemeente-
museum

J. DE WITT LAAN

PROF. B. M. TELDERSWEG

Madurodam

POMPSTATIONS-

Omniversum

Museon

Zorgvliet

SCHEVENINGSE

BOSJES

HUBERTUS
PARK

STADH.

GROOT

HERTOGINNELAAN

Vredes-
paleis

WAALSDORPERWEG

LAAN VAN

EMMAKADE

KONINGIN

MEERDERVOORT

RAAMWEG

Rijksmuseum
H W Mesdag

JAVASTRAAT

WASSENAARSE- WEG

VAN ALKEMADELAAN

CLINGENDAEL

PTT Museum

PLEIN
1813

MAURITSKADE

Paleis-
tuin

Paleis
Noordeinde

KONINGS- KADE

Provinciehuis

Gevangen Poort

Grotekerk

PRINSEGR.

BINNEN-
HOF

G. MARKT- STR.

Mauritshuis

PLEIN

BENOORDENHOUTSE- WEG

VAILLANTLAAN

KONINGINSTRAAT

SPUI

KOEKAMP

HAAGSE BOS

Paleis
Huis ten
Bosch

Zuiderpark

Stadhuis

PR. BERNHARD

Centraal
Station

BEZUIDEN-

HOUTSEWEG

HOEFKADE

VIADUCT

Paleis van
Justitie

LAAN VAN N.O. INDIE

Stn. Hollands
Spoor

SCHENKKADE

NEHERKADE

BINCKHORST- LAAN

RIJSWIJK- SE WEG

UTRECHTSE- BAAN

Stn. Laan v.
N. O. Indië

LAAN VAN N.O. INDIE

VOORBURG

Stn.
Voorburg

PR. MARIANNELAAN

PRINS BERNHARD- LAAN

PARKWEG

CHURCHILL- LAAN

WEST VLIETWEG

Huygens Museum Hofwijk

260

The Hague: where to stay

Making your choice

Only a few international chains are represented in The Hague, such as **Novotel**, **Pullman** and **Mövenpick**. Several of the city's large hotels retain an old-fashioned appeal. **Des Indes** is the grandest of the old-style hotels, but the **Kurhaus** in Scheveningen has a definite edge for those who want the best modern facilities combined with a sea view. Travelers looking for something less expensive should avoid the city center, and consider one of the less pricy Scheveningen hotels.

The Hague's hotels

BEL PARK
Belgischeplein 38, 2587 AT ☎*(070) 3505000* ▭ *to* ▭ *12 rms* ▣ ▢ ▱ ⅋
Tram 1, 9 to Stevinstraat.
Location: 10 minutes' walk from the beach. A friendly, comfortable hotel situated in a quiet Art Nouveau villa. The hotel offers rooms in a range of prices, from elegant suites to simple attic rooms.

DES INDES
Lange Voorhout 54, 2514 EG ☎*(070) 3632932* Fx*(070) 3451721* ▨ *77 rms* ▬ ▭ AE 🕾 ⊚ ▨ ⬥ ▢ ▱ ⬗ ⅋
Tram 12 to Tournooiveld.
Location: In the town center, near the Mauritshuis. Des Indes is one of the last souvenirs of The Hague's glittering past, its name an evocation of French elegance and colonial grandeur. Built in 1859, it was converted to a hotel in 1881. The spy Mata Hari frequented Des Indes in the years before World War I and the ballerina Anna Pavlova died here of pleurisy in 1931 after a performance at the nearby theater. Despite its fame, Des Indes remains a discreet hotel, which is a popular choice with visiting diplomats.

NOVOTEL
Hofweg 5-7, 2511 ΛΛ ☎*(070) 3648846* Fx*(070) 3562889* ▨ *106 rms* ▬ ▭ AE ⊡ ⊚ ▨ ⬥ ▢ ▱ ⬗ ⅋ *Tram 3 to Gravenstraat.*
Location: In the town center, near the Mauritshuis. The Novotel chain attracts cost-conscious business travelers by offering standard rooms furnished in a modest but tasteful style. The Hague's Novotel has the added allure of a location within the PASSAGE, a 19thC glass-roofed arcade, just opposite the new Dutch parliament building.

PARKHOTEL
Molenstraat 53, 2513 BJ ☎*(070) 3624371* Fx*(070) 3614525* ▭ *to* ▨ *114 rms* ▬ AE ⊡ ⊚ ▨ ▢ ▱ ⅋
Tram 3 to Grote Kerk.
Location: In the center of the old town. The Parkhotel is one of the few hotels in The Hague to retain something of a traditional Dutch atmosphere. The flavor of old Holland is most obvious in

the breakfast room, with its stained glass windows and gleaming chandeliers. The bedrooms are furnished in a comfortable, traditional style. There is no restaurant, but you hardly need one in this neighborhood, which has no shortage of restaurants and lively bars.

PULLMAN CENTRAL

Spui 180, 2511 BW ☎*(070) 3636700* 🔲*(070) 3639398* ▥ *159 rms* ▱ ➡ 🔤 ◉ ◎ ▨ ✦ 🔲 ▱ ⚌ ⟡ ⅋ *Tram 1, 8, 9, 10, 12 to Spui.*

Location: 5 minutes from the Mauritshuis. The Pullman offers standard business-class rooms in a modern glass building towering over the Danstheater. Progressive Dutch architects aren't too keen on this arrogant style, but it has injected new vitality into the neighborhood. Stay here if you prize comfort and a parking lot above conviviality.

STEIGENBERGER KURHAUS

Gevers Deynootplein 30, 2586 CK Scheveningen ☎*(070) 3520052* 🔲*(070) 3500911* ▥ *231 rms* ➡ ◉ 🔤 ◉ ◎ ▨ ✦

🔲 ▱ ⟨⟨ ⚌ ⟿ ⟡ ⅋ ▦
Tram 7, 8 to Gevers Deynootplein.
Location: In Scheveningen, facing the North Sea. The Kurhaus is one of Holland's grand hotels, a relic from the days when Scheveningen was a chic spa resort. Saved from demolition a few years ago, the Kurhaus has been given a new lease on life by the careful addition of modern facilities such as a financial center and fully-equipped conference rooms, but the center of attraction is still the magnificent **Kurzaal**, with its frescoes of sea nymphs. Because the Kurhaus now caters mainly for business visitors, its rates can drop markedly on weekends.

SWEELINCK

Sweelinckplein 78, 2517 GL ☎*(070) 3608058* 🔲*(070) 3460310* ▥ *10 rms* 🔲 *Tram 10 to Laan van Meerdervoort.*
Location: An elegant quarter N of the center. A quiet hotel overlooking the stately Sweelinckplein — a must for those who enjoy the whimsicalities of 19thC eclectic architecture.

The Hague: eating and drinking

Dining out in The Hague

Because of its links with the former Dutch colonies in the Far East, The Hague boasts numerous excellent Indonesian restaurants offering exotic *rijsttafels*. The Hague is also well-known for its fish, which is landed at Scheveningen.

In recent years, several successful Amsterdam restaurants have opened up sister establishments in The Hague, including **Sauvage** and **Royal Dynasty**. The migration has not been only in one direction. Three acclaimed restaurants in The Hague — **Kantijl & De Tijger**, **Luden** and **Radèn Ajoe** — have opened up branches in Amsterdam.

EETCAFÉS

The Hague has several brown cafés where you can eat an inexpensive *dagschotel* amid a convivial crowd of students and artists. **De Paraplu** (*Bagijnestraat 9*) serves steaks, grilled plaice and other honorable Dutch dishes.

Describing itself as a "*café-tabac animé,*" **Schlemmer** (*Lange Houtstraat 17* ☎ *(070) 3609000; café open Mon-Tues 9.30am-8pm, Wed-Sun 9.30am-1am; restaurant (▢) closed Mon dinner, last orders 9.30pm*) was launched some years ago to provide The Hague with a lively literary café. It has succeeded in creating a warm theatrical decor, with its thick velvet curtains draped across the windows. The atmosphere is relaxed, and the conservatory overlooking the garden is particularly romantic. The kitchen does an inexpensive *dagschotel,* or you can drop in for Sunday brunch (*11am-3pm*).

The Hague's restaurants

CHARCOAL
Denneweg 130 ☎*(070) 3659788* ▢ 🆑
🔲 🔲 📧 *Last orders 11pm. Tram 1, 9 to Zuid-Hollandlaan.*
This informal restaurant is filled with a rather battered collection of wooden furniture. As its name suggests, excellent charcoal-grilled steaks are its specialty.

GAROEDA
Kneuterdijk 18a ☎*(070) 3465319* ▢ 🆑
🔲 📧 *Closed Sun lunch. Last orders 11pm. Tram 7, 8 to Kneuterdijk.*
Delicate and fragrant Indonesian dishes are served in an airy upstairs restaurant overlooking the elegant Lange Voorhout. The waiters wear colorful Javanese clothes, while the customers

are rather drab by comparison in their dark business suits. Garoeda opened in 1949, 4 years after Indonesia proclaimed independence, and its *rijsttafel* remains a firm favorite with nostalgic colonial administrators.

GOLDEN DUCK

Dr Lelykade 29, Scheveningen ☎*(070) 3541095* ▢ ▣ ▣ ▣ ▣ *Closed Tues. Tram 10, 11 Doornstraat.*
An unexpected cluster of restaurants occupies the former fish auction shed overlooking Scheveningen's harbor, including the excellent **Golden Duck**, where you can watch the sun set while experimenting with the cuisine of Canton, Peking or Szechuan.

HAVENRESTAURANT

Treilerdwarsweg 2, Scheveningen ☎*(070) 3545783*
▢ ▣ ▣ ▣ ▣ *Last orders 7.30pm. Closed Sun. Tram 11 to Duinstraat.*
Locals cram into this plain restaurant overlooking the harbor to enjoy fish landed by Dutch trawlers that very morning. The portions are huge, and prices are considerably lower than elsewhere in town, but last orders are strictly 7.30pm, so you may have to eat your plate of fried plaice in a hurry.

KANTIJL & DE TIJGER

Prinsestraat 110 ☎*(070) 3654398* ▢ *to* ▥ *No cards. Tram 3 to Grote Kerk.*
This is a spacious brasserie with modern decor offering authentic Indonesian cooking at affordable prices. Young bohemians and sober lawyers flock here to sample specialties such as *saté oedang* (prawns fried on skewers).

LUDEN

Frederikstraat 36 ☎*(070) 3601733* ▢ *(brasserie) to* ▢ *(restaurant)* ▣ ▣ ▣ ▣ *Closed Sat lunch, Sun lunch. Tram 1, 9 to Dr Kuyperstraat.*
Luden introduced The Hague to an innovative style of dining by opening a restaurant and brasserie in two adjoining 19thC houses. The formula was so successful that they opened a second restaurant in Amsterdam. You can eat

cheaply at almost any time of the day in the brasserie, which is furnished with old pine dressers and stocked with contemporary art and architecture magazines. Or you can pay slightly more to eat in the French-style restaurant.

PARADOX

Prins Hendrikstraat 53 ☎*(070) 3456736* ▢ *Last orders 8.45pm. Closed lunch and Mon. Tram 3 to Van Speijkstraat.*
An imaginative variety of vegetarian dishes are served in an elegant and quiet interior reminiscent of a winter garden.

RADÈN AJOE

Lange Poten 31 ☎*(070) 3644592* ▢ *(lunch) to* ▥ ▣ ▣ ▣ ▣ *Closed Sat lunch, Sun lunch. Last orders 10pm. Tram 3, 7, 8 to Centrum.*
Close to the Binnenhof and popular with politicians, Radèn Ajoe is a luxurious Indonesian restaurant with a long menu, strong in seafood and vegetable dishes and offering a range of overflowing *rijsttafels*. The quick lunch is good value for those without the time to linger over an Indonesian banquet. Food and presentation are equally impressive in its sister restaurant in Scheveningen, **Radèn Mas** (*Gevers Deynootplein 125* ☎*(070) 3545432* ▢ ▣ ▣ ▣ *last orders 10.30pm)* .

ROYAL DYNASTY

Noordeinde 123 ☎*(070) 3652598* ▢ *(lunch) to* ▥ ▣ ▣ ▣ *Closed Mon. Last orders 11.30pm. Tram 7, 8 to Mauritskade.*
A spacious and elegant Oriental restaurant with upturned parasols hung from the ceiling — an exotic effect pioneered in the sister restaurant in Amsterdam (see page 140). The menu features exotic cooking from Thailand, India and China. Some dishes are strewn with fiery spices, while others are subtly flavored with lemon grass. The ideal place for a special dinner.

SAUR

Lange Voorhout 47-53 ☎*(070) 3463344* ▥ ▣ ▣ ▣ *Closed Sat lunch, Sun. Tram 12 to Tournooiveld.*

Saur has built up a loyal following by offering excellent fish dishes in a handsome wood-paneled restaurant. Saur also boasts an oyster bar, which is open from noon to midnight, and a delicatessen offering takeout gourmet food.

SAUVAGE

Schoolstraat 15A ☎*(070) 3647399* ▥ *to* ▥ ▨ ▣ ▣ ▨ *Closed Sun lunch. Last orders 10.30pm. Tram 3 to Grote Kerk.*

Don't let the name put you off. Sauvage is one of the most civilized restaurants in town. It occupies a curious building with bay windows on a quiet lane in the heart of the old town. The interior is tastefully decorated with Oriental chairs and modern paintings. Like its sister restaurant in Amsterdam (see page 143), Sauvage offers a choice of three set menus featuring superbly-prepared seasonal rarities. Parking nearby is impossible, but you can phone in advance to reserve a space.

SEINPOST

Zeekant 60, Scheveningen ☎*(070) 3555250* ▨*(070) 3555093* ▥ *to* ▥ ▨ ▣ ▣ ▨ ◁€ *Closed Sat lunch, Sun. Tram 7, 8 to Haringkade.*

Standing on the windswept dune where Mesdag painted his celebrated Panorama, Seinpost offers the double attraction of a splendid sea view and exquisite fish dishes.

SHIRASAGI

Spui 170 ☎*(070) 3464700* ▥ *(lunch) to* ▥▥ ▨ ▣ ▣ ▨ *Closed Sat lunch, Sun lunch. Last orders 10pm. Tram 1, 8, 9, 10, 12 to Spui.*

A spacious Japanese restaurant next to the Muziektheater, where fastidious chefs work with the freshest and crispest ingredients. You can have your food brought to you by waitresses dressed in traditional flowing gowns, or you can opt to sit at one of the Teppan tables where the chef grills the meat as you watch. The set menus are inexpensive by Japanese standards, particularly if you eat at lunchtime. The *Licht complet,* a light three-course lunch served with tea, is good value. Or you can reserve an entire Teppan table, seating up to eight, with your own personal chef on hand. You each choose what you want to eat and drink from the *"Teppan Séparé"* menu and pay a fixed sum for the entire table. It might be a good idea for businessmen who want to entertain in style, while keeping the bill manageable. For a pre-concert meal, order the *Theatermenu* (6-8pm), which the chefs at the Teppan tables serve at lightning speed.

Cafés

Many cafés in The Hague exude an atmosphere of false glamor or snobbery that few outsiders find attractive. Yet there are a few places where you can drink a Dutch beer amid a friendly crowd of locals. Old fashioned Dutch courtesy is still found at the comfortable café **De Posthoorn** *(Lange Voorhout 39, open 8am-1am, closed Sun, tram 12 to Tournooiveld),* where graying ex-cabinet ministers, artists and locals engage in animated disputes. In summer, sit on the terrace under the chestnut trees.

The **Kurhaus café** in Scheveningen (in the STEIGENBERGER KURHAUS hotel) is a cherished survival from The Hague's grander days. The café occupies a tiny corner of the magnificent frescoed Kurzaal, where stars such as Edith Piaf, Duke Ellington and Marlene Dietrich once performed.

In summer, elderly couples like to sit on the glassed-in terrace of the ·café **Corona** *(Buitenhof 40-42),* and in winter they retreat indoors to the dark wood-paneled interior.

The **Zwarte Ruiter** *(Grote Markt)* is a modern café on two floors with a terrace that catches the late afternoon sun. There are several café terraces on Plein, but the square is too windswept to be truly *gezellig*.

Young students sit squashed alongside stiff elderly couples in the austere interior of the **Wiener Konditorei** *(Korte Poten 24* ☎ *(070) 3600549, tram 3, 7, 8 to Centrum)*. The pastry shop, which has been there since 1934, may not have much Viennese elegance, but its moist *Sachertorte* comes close to perfection. Try the plump *Apfelstrudel* with a frothy capuccino if you fall victim to The Hague blues. When the sun shines, and the wind relents, you can sit outside.

The café of the **Haags Filmhuis** (see NIGHTLIFE AND ENTERTAINMENT) is a quiet spot for a drink in the evening; it is open to non-film-goers. **De Bok** *(Papestraat 36)* is a cluttered 19thC brown café complete with a screeching parrot. It draws a cosmopolitan crowd, especially to its jazz concerts on a Sunday evening.

Today we drove as far as Scheveningen. The road is a shady path, narrow and long, piercing the heart of the wood in a straight line. It is cool and dark there whatever may be the heat of the sun or the haze of the air. The sun leaves you at the entrance and rejoins you at the exit. At the exit is a vast undulating desert, thinly sown with meagre grass and with sand, as on the edge of a great beach. We drove through the village, looked at the casinos, bathing halls, the princely pavilions adorned with the colours and the coat-of-arms of Holland; we climbed the dune, we plodded heavily through it to reach the shore. Now we have in front of us - level, grey, reeking, and foaming - the North Sea. Who has not been there and seen that? We think of Ruysdael, of Van Goyen, of Van de Velde.
(Eugène Fromentin, *The Masters of Past Time,* 1876)

The Hague: nightlife and entertainment

The Hague by night

The Hague is admittedly not one of the world's liveliest cities after dark, but there are usually concerts, movies, or the occasional jazz session to tempt you out of your hotel room. The liveliest quarters after dark are around the **Koninklijke Schouwburg** and along **Denneweg**. If the action in the old town seems too tame, head out to **Scheveningen** where the mood is frequently tropical, or tries to be. Otherwise, take a train to **Delft**, just 15 minutes from Centraal Station, where the brown cafés are packed with likeable students.

BARS AND CAFÉS
Many bars in The Hague are frequented by loutish males in leather jackets with shaggy Bouviers sprawled amid the sawdust. You are best to avoid anywhere that requires you to ring the doorbell. For a civilized drink in the evening, go to **Schlemmer** (see WHERE TO EAT, page 263), or the scruffy and amiable **De Paraplu** (*Bagijnestraat 9*), where musicians sometimes play. For a more formal setting, try the **Kurhaus Bar** in the STEIGENBERGER KURHAUS hotel, or the **Pullman Bar** in the PULLMAN CENTRAL HOTEL (see page 262)

CASINO
The **Kurhaus** in Scheveningen has the only legal casino in town (*Gevers Deynootplein* ☎ *(070) 3512621, open daily 2pm-2am, minimum age 18*). Wear a suit and take along your passport to play roulette, baccara or the one-armed bandits.

CLASSICAL MUSIC AND BALLET
You can watch exciting interpretations of classical and modern ballets at the new **Nederlands Danstheater** (*Spui* ☎ *(070) 3604930*), or listen to the Residentie-Orkest perform classical works in the adjoining **Dr Anton Philipszaal** (*Spui* ☎ *(070) 3609810* ▣ ♿). Tickets for major concerts are inevitably difficult to obtain on short notice. You can make an advance reservation up to one month before a concert.

The **Circustheater** in Scheveningen (*Circusplein 1* ☎ *(070) 3558800*) provides a grand setting for opera and musicals. The **Regentenkamer Theater**, situated in an 17thC almshouse, the **Hofje van Nieuwkoop** (*Warmoezierstraat 44* ☎ *(070) 3888436*), provides an intimate Classical setting for performances of chamber music and songs on Sunday afternoons. Organ recitals occasionally take place in the **St Jacobskerk**, the **Kloosterkerk** and other old churches. Pick up a copy of the monthly *VVV Info* magazine at the tourist office for details of concerts in The Hague.

MOVIES

The Hague has only a few movie theaters left standing, and most have predictable programs of Hollywood murder and mayhem movies. **Metropole** *(Carnegielaan 16)*, **Odeon** *(Herengracht 13)*, **Asta** *(Spui 27)*, **Babylon** *(facing Centraal Station)* and **Cineac** *(Buitenhof 20)* screen the latest US movies. Those serious about artistic European and Japanese films have to go to the **Haags Filmhuis** *(Denneweg 56 ☎ (070) 3656030)*, a three-screen complex that is worth a visit simply for its magnificent Art Nouveau architecture.

PLAYS

The **Koninklijke Schouwburg** *(Korte Voorhout 3 ☎ (070) 3469450)* is home to the Dutch national theater company, Het Nationale Toneel. The company performs contemporary European plays translated into Dutch.

The Hague: shopping

Where to go

The Hague is well served with traditional shops specializing in ornate visiting cards for diplomats, or Havana cigars for ceremonial dinners, but there are few places for youthful fashions or modern fiction. In recent years, however, the city has begun to thaw, and several fashionable Amsterdam boutiques have opened branches in The Hague.

The ultimate in luxurious shopping is mostly found in the neighborhood of the royal palaces. **Noordeinde,** which runs N from Paleis Noordeinde, is a pleasant pedestrianized shopping street rich in Art Nouveau details. It boasts some of the city's most exclusive boutiques, antique stores and art galleries. The parallel **Denneweg**, which runs N from the former palace on Lange Voorhout, contains a lively mixture of antique stores, art galleries, boutiques, wine stores, cafés and restaurants.

Major department stores are located on **Grote Markt**, while chain stores selling records, clothes, books and toys tend to be found along **Lange Poten** and its continuations **Spuistraat** and **Vlamingstraat**.

DEPARTMENT STORES

De Bijenkorf *(Grote Markt* ☎ *(070) 3624991* AE Ⓒ ⓒⓓ VISA *)* is the most exciting and innovative department store in The Hague. It occupies a handsome building designed in 1926 by the Amsterdam School architect P. L. Kramer. Go there for designer clothes, *The International Herald Tribune*, Dutch chocolates, kitchen equipment or perfume. But for a cheap umbrella or a pair of shoelaces, go to **Vroom en Dreesmann**, or **Hema**. Wealthy Hagenaars continue to patronize the exclusive 19thC department store **Bonneterie en Pander** *(Gravenstraat 2* ☎ *(070) 3656844* AE Ⓒ ⓒⓓ VISA *)*. Multinational executives find lambswool pullovers suitable for the golf course, and women can pick out a dress for a formal dinner.

FOOD AND DRINK

The Hague's one famous specialty is the **Haagsche Hopje**, a toffee candy. An entire museum is devoted to this delicacy, which you can buy in local delicatessens. The old elegance of The Hague lingers on at **G. de Graaff** *(Heulstraat 27* ☎ *(070) 3600533),* a wondrous old tobacconist's store with wood-paneled walls and chandeliers. Try to buy something here just for the experience; if not a pipe or a box of cigars, then at least a packet of English tea. If hunger pangs strike, buy

269

dried fruit and nuts to nibble at **De Notenkoning** *(Passage 35)*. **Leonidas** *(Passage 28)* sells the chocolates that Belgians adore.

MARKETS

You can watch North Sea fish being landed and auctioned off at the **Visafslag** in Scheveningen *(Visafslagweg 1, Mon-Sat, 7-10am, tram 11 to Strandweg)*. An open-air market occasionally takes place under the trees on **Lange Voorhout** *(mid-May to Sept, Thurs 9am-9pm; Sun 11am-5pm)*, and on the windy **Plein** *(Oct to mid-May, Thurs 11am-9pm)*. You will find rusting bird cages, *jenever* glasses, old books and prints. Even if you buy nothing, it is pleasant to sit on the terraces, perhaps listening to a mournful tune from an accordion.

SHOES AND LEATHER GOODS

The Amsterdam designer **Fred de la Bretonière** recently opened a shop in The Hague *(Korte Poten 2)* selling his exclusive shoes and handbags. **Cinderella** *(Passage⬛)* sells the wildest shoes in town.

STATIONERY AND ART SUPPLIES

Go to **Akkerman Creatief Centrum** *(Passage 36 ☎(070) 3466831 [AE] ⬛)* for art supplies and card models of famous buildings (including the Grote Kerk).

WOMEN'S CLOTHING

Women in The Hague favor traditionally elegant but conservative clothes. Nonetheless, there are shops that stock the latest lines by international designers. Young women join the crush in **Lange Poten**, while working women buy their clothes on **Noordeinde** and nearby streets. You will find branches of Richfield, Scapa of Scotland, Benetton and Bognor on **Noordeinde**. A branch of **Pauw of Amsterdam** *(Noordeinde 42)* stocks smart and comfortable styles for tall women, and Amsterdam designers **Puck & Hans** now sell their provocative party dresses at Prinsestraat 92. French designer **Daniel Boudon** *(Heulstraat 25)* sells well-styled dresses for pregnancy.

ART GALLERIES

Galleries in The Hague tend to stock mainly traditional styles of paintings and sculpture. **Pulchri Studio** *(Lange Voorhout 15 ☎(070) 3657178)* is a rambling old building belonging to a private club. You can stroll in to look at the exhibitions of paintings, drawings or sculpture by Dutch artists. Tucked away in a corner of the Pulchri, the **Mesdag Taveerne** *(open Tues-Sat, 11am-5pm; Sun 1-5pm)* is a handsome tiled tavern known only to locals, where you can eat a traditional Dutch *uitsmijter,* or coffee and cake. The leafy garden is pleasant in the summer, but be careful not to stray into the members-only rooms.

The **Haagse Kunstkring** *(Denneweg 64 ☎(070) 3647585 ⬛)* stages stimulating exhibitions of local paintings, architecture and photographs. The **Kijkhuis** *(Noordeinde 140 ☎(070) 3644805)* runs video installations by international artists in a bare interior.

The Hague: recreation

The Hague for children

A wonderful playground in the city center helps solve the problem of fretful toddlers. **De Europese Speeltuin** *(Groenmarkt)* is equipped with exciting rope bridges and slides, plus plenty of benches where parents can flop.

Older children should be captivated by the miniature town of **Madurodam**, the dizzying films screened at **Omniversum**, and the hands-on demonstrations at **Museon**.

If all else fails, take the kids by tram to **Scheveningen**. The beach has fine sand for digging, although you might have to hike for a while to escape the crowds. Energetic kids might be cajoled into climbing up the spiral stairs to the **observation deck** on the pier. For windy days on the beach, go to the **Haags Vliegerhuis** *(Molenstraat 46 ☎(070) 3457715)* for colorful kites and frisbees, plus everything you need to build a kite from scratch.

Duinrell amusement park *(Wassenaar ☎(01751) 40260, NZH bus 90 from Den Haag Centraal Station)* has water slides, rowboats, chair lifts, and daredevil shows. The **Tikibad** tropical swimming pool at Duinrell is a blessing to families with children when boredom threatens, or on days of torrential rain.

Sports

BOWLING

Locals go tenpin bowling next to the Kurhaus in Scheveningen, at the 24-lane **Bowling Scheveningen** *(Palace Promenade 990 ☎(070) 3543212, open 10am-late)*.

CYCLING

Bicycles can be rented at **Centraal Station** *(☎(070) 3853235)* or Hollands Spoor Station *(☎(070) 3890830)*. The same conditions apply as for Amsterdam (see page 36). **Rijwielverhuur du Nord** *(Keizerstraat 27, Scheveningen ☎(070) 3554060)* has bicycles and tandems. There are extensive cycle routes through the dunes along the North Sea coast. The best inland route is from The Hague to **Delft** along the River Vliet.

ICE SKATING

The Dutch wait hopefully each year for the canals to freeze hard so that they can skim across the landscape like figures in an Avercamp painting. At other times they can be found doing daring stunts at indoor ice-skating rinks such as **De Uithof** *(Jaap Edenweg 10 ☎(070) 3299066).*

SAILBOARDING

The hardy Dutch go to **Katwijk** on the North Sea for sailboarding and sailing. Contact **Intersail** *(Zuiderstrand, Kijkduin ☎(070) 3684203).*

SWIMMING

The **Golfbad Scheveningen** *(Strandweg 13, Scheveningen ☎(070) 3542100, open Mon-Fri 11am-10.30pm; Sat, Sun 11am-5.30pm)* is a modern swimming pool next to the Kurhaus, with artificial waves, long water shutes, a children's pool, an outdoor pool and a gym.

Environs of The Hague

The windswept North Sea dunes that attracted the Hague School painters in the 19thC are within easy reach of the city. Trams run to the busy resort of **Scheveningen** (see page 257), or you can take a local bus to the quieter resorts of **Kijkduin** or **Wassenaar**.

The Hague is close to several historic Dutch cities. After looking at Vermeer's *View of Delft* in the Mauritshuis, go to **Delft** (see page 278), and walk down Westvest to reach the **Hooikade**, where Vermeer painted the seductive city view in 1660. The peaceful university town of **Leiden** (see page 299) lies to the NE of The Hague, and the cheese town of **Gouda** (see page 289) is to the E.

Excursions

Randstad
towns and villages

Amsterdam, Rotterdam and The Hague are surrounded by Dutch cities rich in history, art and architecture, each with its own distinctive personality. Among the most interesting are the ports of Dordrecht, Enkhuizen and Hoorn, the university towns of Leiden, Utrecht and Delft, the old-fashioned Haarlem and the cheese-making towns of Edam, Gouda and Alkmaar.

Despite such a concentration of cities and towns, which makes the Randstad one of the most densely populated conurbations in the world, it is still possible to discover quiet villages such as Broek in Waterland and Monnickendam, and landscapes that have not changed since the Golden Age.

ALKMAAR

Noord-Holland, 40km (25miles) NW of Amsterdam. Population: 83,900. By train, 30mins from Amsterdam CS i Waagplein 2, 1811 JP ☎(072) 114284.

A compact market town located amid the prosperous polders N of Amsterdam, Alkmaar is particularly cheerful on a Friday, when an animated cheese market *(mid-Apr to mid-Sept 10am-noon)* is enacted in the main square, **Waagplein**, beneath the flamboyant Renaissance Waaggebouw, or weigh house. A delightful mood of festivity infuses the town for the two hours of the market; carillons, barrel organs and street musicians fill the air with music, and the narrow streets around the market are crammed with stalls selling cheeses and crafts. It is worth arriving early in order to avoid the crowds, as the market is a popular tourist attraction.

THE TOWN

The most seductive area of Alkmaar is the SE corner, which from the station is reached by turning right along Stationsweg, left down Geesterweg and, after crossing a canal, right down Geest. This leads to a landscaped park, through which you can walk to reach the **Molen van Piet**, an 18thC windmill built atop a bastion. Cross Ritsevoort and then turn left down Baanstraat and right along Parkstraat, a charming, although quite unnecessary, detour, which eventually brings you back to the outer canal. Continue along **Kennemerpark** — a leafy area of 19thC Art Nouveau houses — to reach the narrow canal Baangracht, the perfect point at which to enter the city. Turn left, then right along Oude Gracht until you come to the impressive **Wildemanshofje**

(#87), an 18thC almshouse. Retrace your steps to cross the canal, then continue into the heart of the town along Groot Nieuwland and Kapelstraat.

A wooden bridge then crosses Verdronkenoord, with the small **fish market** to the left and the sprightly 17thC **Accijnstoren**, where duty was paid on imported beer, to the right. Continue straight ahead down Hekelstraat to another bridge, which offers an exceptional view of the Renaissance facade of the **Waag**, a 14thC Gothic hospice converted to a weigh house in the 16thC. To reach Waagplein, continue down the beguiling canal **Kooltuin**, then turn left along Dijk.

Across the next bridge, at Houttil 1, is the **Nationaal Biermuseum "De Boom"** (☎ *(072) 113801* 🔤 *open Apr-Sept Tues-Sat 10am-4pm and Sun 1-5pm; Oct-Mar Tues-Sun 1-5pm),* attractively located in a former 18thC brewery. The exhibits are rather impenetrable to the non-Dutch speaker, but you might enjoy the attractive *proeflokaal* (tasting house) with its canalside terrace, which offers a choice of more than 80 Dutch beers, including unusual Trappist brews produced by the Schaapskooi brewery in Tilburg, and Boombier, a traditional beer brewed specially for the museum by a local brewery. A further attraction for epicures is the **Kaasmuseum** in the weigh house *(Waagplein* 🔤 *open Apr-Oct Mon-Sat 10am-4pm),* which demonstrates the art of cheese-making.

The **Stedelijk Museum** *(Doelenstraat 3-9* ☎ *(072) 110737* 🔤 *open Tues-Fri 10am-3pm; Sun 1-5pm),* reached from Waagplein along the exceptionally narrow Magdalenenstraat, contains some interesting paintings, including an Altdorfer-like panorama of the siege of Alkmaar in 1573, when the town successfully resisted a vastly superior Spanish army, thereby turning the tide in the Dutch Revolt. The museum also contains collections of tiles, toys and facade stones.

🚬 If you are in the vicinity of the cheese market and want to eat something more than a *broodje kaas,* try the Indonesian restaurant **Deli** *(Mient 8* ☎ *(072) 154082* ▭ *last orders 10pm, closed Sun).*

SHOPPING Clothing stores and department stores are tightly packed in the narrow streets s of the Waagplein, while the quieter streets to the N are favored by antique dealers and craft stores. Alkmaar is the home of the delightful, but expensive, **Oilily** children's clothes *(Waagplein 11* ☎ *(072) 155984).*

BROEK IN WATERLAND
Map 2B4. Noord-Holland, 12km (7 miles) N of Amsterdam. Population 2,670. By NZH bus 110, 111, 114 or 115 from Amsterdam Centraal Station to Dorp; by car, through the IJ-tunnel, then N on E10.

"Broek... is a little village so remarkable for the neatness of its appearance, as probably to be unique in the world," the writer Charles Tennant observed in 1824.

This very pretty village just N of Amsterdam has been a constant source of amusement to travelers because of its obsessive attention to cleanliness, which was essential for the local manufacture of cheese. Although you are unlikely nowadays to come across inhabitants scrubbing clean

277

the trees — as one visitor observed — the town still has a decidedly prim and cared-for look, with its handsome 18thC wooden gable houses and its tidy streets where even the trees are carefully trained on wooden frames so as not to disturb the magisterial symmetry.

The most picturesque area is **Havenrak**, once a bustling harbor. The 16thC church lies to the W of here, and you can savor something of Broek's attentive domesticity by venturing farther W along streets such as Roomeinde and Leeteinde.

De Witte Swaen ♣ *(Dorpstraat 11 ☎(02903) 1525 ☐ open daily noon-9pm)*, named after the white swan on Broek's coat of arms, is a favorite stop for cyclists, its typical N Holland interior decorated with attractive local watercolors. The delicious, sustaining pancakes are worth a detour, and of the 40 sweet and savory varieties on the menu, the *pannekoek Broekse heerlijkheid*, piled with apple, Calvados and cream, is particularly memorable. You can also sample the local specialty, *gerookte IJsselmeer paling* (smoked eel), but it might be best to avoid the Hertog Jan beer if you seriously intend to pedal back to Amsterdam.

DELFT

*Map 1E2. Zuid-Holland, 58km (36 miles) sw of Amsterdam, 15km (9 miles) N of Rotterdam, 13km (8 miles) s of The Hague. Population: 86,700. By train, 55mins from Amsterdam CS, 15mins from Rotterdam CS, 15mins from Den Haag CS; by tram, line 1 from Scheveningen and Den Haag CS **i** Markt 85 2611 GS ☎(015) 126100 ☎(015) 158695.*

"Delft is the most charming town in the world," sighed Hilaire Belloc in 1906, likening it to "a good woman in early middle age, careful of her dress, combed, orderly, not without a sober beauty." Today Delft inevitably conjures up images of inexpensive, mass-produced Delftware — of blue and white porcelain clogs and windmills — but it would be a pity to dismiss the town as merely a tourist trap, for beyond all the kitsch souvenirs, Delft has a rich history and a wealth of architectural interest.

In the early 16thC Delft was a major center of Catholic humanism and the arts, counting among its painters the Master of Delft and the Master of the *Virgo inter Virgines*. The Reformation brought an end to Delft's monastic days, particularly after William of Orange took up residence in the Prinsenhof, turning Delft for a time into the capital city of the rebel Dutch provinces.

In the 17thC, however, Delft flourished again as a center of art and learning, producing distinguished painters such as Johannes Vermeer and Pieter de Hoogh, the pioneering microbiologist Anthonie van Leeuwenhoek and the legal philosopher Hugo Grotius.

A Vermeer enthusiast might visit the MAURITSHUIS in The Hague to look at the *View of Delft* before visiting the town. Vermeer's paintings, such as this one, and the *Little Street in Delft* (in the Amsterdam RIJKSMUSEUM) have done much to promote an idealized image of the town, and Delft today may be something of a disappointment, particularly as most of the houses were shorn of their distinctive step gables in the 18thC. Giant industrial works on the N edge of Delft and a large modern university

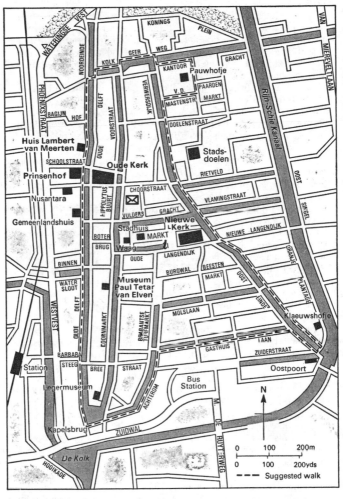

campus to the s now threaten to engulf the town, yet you can still discover many quiet canals where the tranquil, almost monastic, mood of Vermeer's art survives.

EVENTS **A weekly market** is held on Markt every Thursday. **Flowers** are sold along the Hippolytusbuurt quayside on Thursday, and on Brabantse Turfmarkt and Burgwal on Saturday. The **17thC Hemony carillon** in the spire of the Nieuwe Kerk is played on Tuesday, Thursday and Saturday 11am-noon, on Friday 7.30-8.30pm.

THE TOWN

Delft has not changed a great deal since Samuel Pepys described it in 1660 as "a most sweet town with bridges and a river in every street." In the same year, Vermeer painted *The View of Delft,* now in the MAURITS-HUIS in The Hague. The best way to see the town is to follow the canals; those on the W side of town are urbane and prosperous, while those to the E have a more tranquil and forlorn air.

Begin at the rail station and walk through the narrow Barbarasteeg to reach **Oude Delft**, an old canal lined with handsome 17th-19thC houses. Turn left, past the former convent of St Barbara (#59), to reach, eventually, the **Gemeenlandshuis van Delfland** (#167), an exceptionally ornate late Gothic building dating from 1510 and attributed to Anthonis Kelder-mans. Just N of here is the **Prinsenhof**, whose gardens and bricked courtyards retain a medieval flavor. The **Volkenkundig Museum "Nu-santara"** *(St Agathaplein 4* ☎ *(015) 602358* ▨ *open Tues-Sat 10am-5pm; Sun, hols, and Mon June-Aug, 1-5pm)* contains a small, interesting collection of Indonesian artifacts.

Opposite the Prinsenhof is the **Oude Kerk** *(* ▨ 🎫 *open Apr-Oct, Mon-Sat noon-5pm),* looking somewhat sullen with its 14thC leaning tower and unfinished late-Gothic N transept, the work of Anthonis Keldermans and his son. Inside, the tomb of the naval hero Piet Heyn, designed in a solemn Classical style by Pieter de Keyser, is given pride of place in the main choir, while Admiral Maarten Tromp, who died fighting the English in 1653, is commemorated by a lavish Baroque monument designed by Jacob van Campen and Rombout Verhulst. The Oude Kerk also contains a tomb to the scientist Anthonie van Leeuwen-hoek, and the simple, dignified grave of the painter Johannes Vermeer.

From the Oude Kerk, continue down Oude Delft to reach a weather-beaten Gothic portal showing, apparently, St John the Evangelist on the island of Patmos. This leads to the former **Bagijnhof**, now somewhat disappointing except for the narrow **alley** to the right of #118, where the atmosphere of Vermeer's Delft has survived.

Return to Oude Delft and head N, past the attractive **Louis XIV house** (#118), to reach the small canal Kolk. If you are interested in enigmas, continue down Noordeinde to Wateringse Vest and cross the road to the small park to discover, nestling in a dark glade, a **tomb** purported to be that of Louis XVII of France, who apparently lived in Delft under the alias Karl Wilhelm Naundorff until his death in 1845. Retrace your steps down Noordeinde and turn left along Kolk to Geerweg, where the modern buildings on one side contrast with the crumbling 17thC houses opposite. Don't miss the view down **Verwersdijk** to the spire of the Nieuwe Kerk.

Cross the footbridge opposite Kantoorgracht 70 to reach the **Pauw-hofje** *(Paardenmarkt 54),* a pleasant almshouse established in 1707. Around the corner on Van den Mastenstraat is the 16thC **Hofje van Gratie**. Continue E to Verwersdijk and turn left. The first street you pass is **Doelenstraat**, where Rembrandt's gifted pupil Carel Fabritius was living when a gunpowder magazine in an expropriated convent nearby exploded, killing some 200 people including the young artist, and, according to an eyewitness, leaving "nothing but a pool of water."

To reach Markt, turn right off Verwersdijk down **Voldersgracht**, which is the famous *Little Street in Delft* painted by Vermeer, who lived in a house that backed onto this street until bankruptcy forced him to move in 1672. Turn left into the broad market square **Markt**, overlooked by the ornate Renaissance **Stadhuis**, which was built in 1618 by Hendrick de Keyser.

Here is a convenient place to pause, after which you might continue down Oosteinde to reach Delft's only surviving city gate, the 14thC **Oostpoort**, embellished in the 16thC with elegant Burgundian towers. Return along the left-hand side of Oosteinde and turn left along Gasthuis-laan and, later, left down Achterom to reach the Kapelsbrug, where you can still pick out many of the features that appear in Vermeer's *View of Delft,* which he painted from an upstairs window of a house on the far side of the harbor *De Kolk.* Dominating this corner of Delft is the **Armamentarium**, an arsenal established in the early days of the Dutch Republic and now housing the **Legermuseum** (National Army Museum) *(Korte Geer 1* ☎*(015) 150500* 🖾 *open Tues-Sat 10am-5pm; Sun 1-5pm).* Also of interest is the former seat of the Delft Chamber of the Dutch East India Company at **Oude Delft 39**, comprising three former houses grouped around a courtyard.

SIGHTS AND PLACES OF INTEREST

NIEUWE KERK
Markt ☎*(015) 123025* 🖾 ⚅ 🖈 *Open Apr-Oct, daily 9am-5pm; Nov-Mar, daily 10am-noon, 1.30-4pm.*

The exterior of the Nieuwe Kerk is a baffling jumble of jarring styles and periods: the 15thC choir soars above the 14thC transepts, while the tower comprises a late 14thC base, a 15thC High Gothic tier, a 16thC late-Gothic tier and a 19thC spire. However, the interior is surprisingly harmonious, with attention directed toward the choir, where a mysterious golden light is shed on the **tomb of William of Orange**.

Begun 40 years after the death of William, as a symbol to unify the country at a time of religious strife, the tomb is a cold, melancholy design by Hendrick de Keyser, laden with Renaissance obelisks and wailing cherubs. The four corner figures represent the virtues of Liberty (with a hat), Justice, Religion and Fortitude, while behind stands a trumpeting figure of Fame and, at William's feet, his loyal dog.

Numerous other monarchs, most of them called Willem (except for one queen, called Wilhelmina), are buried in the Nieuwe Kerk. The Delft-born jurist **Hugo Grotius**, who laid the foundations of international law and is popularly remembered for his escape from Loevestein Castle in a trunk, is commemorated by a simple Classical monument.

PAUL TÉTAR VAN ELVEN, MUSEUM
Koornmarkt 67 ☎*(015) 124206* 🖾 𝄃 *Open May-Sept Mon-Sat 1-5pm.*

This curious 19thC house, filled with nostalgic memorabilia, belonged to a minor painter who taught at the Delft Polytechnische School and in his spare time assiduously copied the Dutch Masters of the Golden Age. Van Elven's favorite artist was Vermeer of Delft, and he went to the length of fitting leaded glass to his first-floor studio windows to re-create the mellow light that suffuses Vermeer's works. The museum contains an incongruous room in Louis XIV style on the ground floor, which was rescued from a nearby house in the 1970s.

RIJKSMUSEUM HUIS LAMBERT VAN MEERTEN
Oude Delft 199 ☎(015) 602358 ▨ Open Tues-Sat 10am-5pm; Sun, hols (and Mon June-Aug) 1-5pm. Ring bell for entry.

This small museum is famed for its huge collection of tiles, which cover the walls of the house so completely that you might think you had stumbled into a mosque.

The Delft industrialist Lambert van Meerten had this house built in 1891 in an unusual version of Old Dutch Renaissance style, and to make matters worse had genuine 16thC architectural fragments incorporated into the fabric, such as the pillars flanking the entrance and the magnificent Renaissance window on the staircase landing. Van Meerten intended his house to become a museum, but his plans were thwarted by his bankruptcy in 1902, and he committed suicide shortly afterwards.

Some friends tried nevertheless to open the building to the public, although everything movable had already been sold. The architect Jan Schouten came to the rescue, however, presenting to the museum his unique collection of **tiles**. This includes early examples from Mediterranean countries, but its chief interest lies in the extensive range of blue and white Dutch tiles, naively decorated with children, ships, flowers and other cheerful subjects.

Despite these whimsical exhibits, the house is filled with a profound nostalgia for the Dutch Golden Age, especially in the bedroom, where Van Meerten installed leaded glass windows and even a traditional cupboard bed.

STEDELIJK MUSEUM HET PRINSENHOF ★
St Agathaplein 1 ☎(015) 602357. Open Tues-Sat 10am-5pm; Sun, hols (and Mon June-Aug) 1-5pm. The permanent collection is closed for several weeks in Oct or Nov when the annual art and antiques fair is held in the Prinsenhof.

This beautiful 15thC convent with its late Gothic tracery and sagging Burgundian roofs seems to come straight out of an early Netherlandish painting. In spring the museum is especially attractive to visit, with bunches of tulips in every niche and birds singing merrily in the courtyards. However, the main attraction of the Prinsenhof is the gloomy **Moordzaal** (rm 8), where William of Orange was assassinated in 1584 by Balthazar Gerards as he left the dining room (rm 7). The holes in the wall where the bullets struck can still be seen, together with several melodramatic 19thC prints depicting the event.

William took up residence in the Prinsenhof — previously a convent dedicated to St Agatha — in 1572 and conducted many of the crucial battles of the Dutch Revolt from here, including the dramatic **relief of Leiden**. It is popularly believed that the beautiful room at the front of the building known as the **Prinsenkamer** (rm 16), now the museum's restoration workshop, was where William slept and worked.

The museum boasts a fine collection of **paintings** by Delft artists — sadly no Vermeers are among them — which mainly depict the disasters that have befallen the city, such as the conflagration of 1536, the Stadhuis fire of 1618 and the gunpowder magazine explosion of 1654. Also of interest is the capricious view of Delft by D. Vosmaer, and the church interiors by the 17thC Delft School (rm 11-12).

The museum also possesses an interesting collection of 16th-18thC **portraits** of prominent Delft families (rm 7, where William of Orange dined just before his death), a Delftware collection (rm 23), and a trunk (rm 11) that supposedly served Grotius during his famous escape from captivity (although the RIJKSMUSEUM in Amsterdam makes the same claim about a chest in its historical collection).

When visiting the museum, follow this route: rms 3-7, 14-25 (first floor), then 8-13. Don't miss the tiny **gallery for novices** (rm 23), which overlooks the chapel (rm 5).

⌘   Located next to the Prinsenhof and occupying two 17thC houses, the **Museumhotel** *(Oude Delft 189, 2611 HD ☎(015) 140930 ▨(015) 140935*

▢ *47 rms* AE ⊙ ⊙ VISA ▢ ◪ *)* combines tasteful, modern decor with a few well-chosen antiques. If you want to splurge, reserve a room on the canal side for a splendid view of the Oude Kerk. Other hotels in Delft tend to be furnished in Old Dutch style, a classic example of which is **Leeuwenbrug** *(Koornmarkt 16, 2611 EE* ☎ *(015) 147741* Fx *(015) 159759* ▢ *34 rms* AE ⊙ ⊙ VISA ▢ ◪ *),* a friendly hotel with an interior bathed in mellow light.

🍽 **L'Escalier** *(Oude Delft 125* ☎ *(015) 124621* Fx *(015) 158048* ▢ *to* ▢▢ AE ⊙ ⊙ VISA ♥ *closed Sat lunch, Sun, Tues),* located in an 18thC town house on Delft's oldest canal, is consistently praised for its delicate, traditional French cuisine; **Redjeki** *(Choorstraat 50* ☎ *(015) 125022* ▢ AE ⊙ ⊙ VISA *closed Sun lunch)* offers Indonesian cuisine in pleasant surroundings; **Kleyweg's Stadskof-fiehuis** *(Oude Delft 135* ☎ *(015) 124625* ▢ *closed Sun)* is a tasteful coffee house producing excellent pancakes and *broodjes* that draw gasps of admiration; and **Uit de Kunst** *(Oude Delft 140* ▢ *open 10am-7pm)* is a curious café crammed with Art Deco furniture, where you can have a coffee and a *broodje,* or a slice of delicious apple cake.

SHOPPING   The only surviving producer of hand-painted Delftware porcelain is **De Porceleyne Fles** *(Rotterdamseweg 196* ☎ *(015) 560234, shop open Apr-Oct Mon-Sat 9am-5pm and Sun 10am-4pm; Nov-Mar Mon-Fri 9am-5pm and Sat 10am-4pm; bus 60 from rail station).* A small museum linked to the shop boasts several rooms of antique Delftware. You can buy De Porceleyne Fles plates and vases at several shops in town, including **Reynders** *(Grote Markt 45* AE ⊙ VISA *).* For zany modern ceramics by local designers, go to **Terra** *(Nieuwstraat 7* ☎ *(015) 147072* AE ⊙ ⊙ VISA *).*

DORDRECHT
Zuid-Holland. 95km (59 miles) s of Amsterdam, 23km (14 miles) s of Rotterdam, 53km (33 miles) se of The Hague. Population 109,000. By train, 90mins from Amsterdam CS; 30mins from Rotterdam CS; 45mins from Den Haag CS
i Stationsweg 1, 3311 JW ☎ *(078) 132800* Fx *(078) 131783.*
The old town of Dordrecht is attractively situated on an island at the confluence of the Merwede, the Noord and the Kil. The oldest town in Holland, Dordrecht (sometimes known as Dort) dates back to the early 11thC, when Count Dirk III built a castle on the island to control the vital shipping routes. Dordrecht grew into one of the most prosperous cities in the Netherlands, trading in timber and wine.

Situated on an island, the town became an important rebel stronghold during the Dutch revolt against the Spanish, and the representatives of the United Provinces met for the first time in 1572 in the **Statenzaal** (situated in a courtyard, the Hof, formerly part of a friary). The town was later the setting for the Synod of Dort in 1618-19, convened to resolve the religious conflict between the moderate Remonstrants and the extremist Calvinists. The result was a victory for the Calvinists, leading to the imprisonment of Hugo Grotius in Loevestein Castle, and the execution of the elderly Remonstrant statesman Johan van Oldenbarnevelt.

THE TOWN
From the station, walk into town following Stationsweg, Johan de Witt-straat, Bagijnhof and Visstraat. Pause on the Visbrug to look w to the

impressive 19thC **Stadhuis** (town hall). The building spans the canal on the Gothic foundations of an **exchange** built by Flemish merchants in 1383.

Once across the bridge, turn left along Groenmarkt, past the town hall, and continue straight ahead along Grote Kerks Buurt, then follow the canalside Pottenkade to the **Grote Kerk**. Climb the church **tower** for a spectacular view of the Oude Maas.

Upon leaving the church, turn right along the quay Lange Gelderse-kade and cross the bridge (the Engelenburgerbrug) to reach the Nieuwe Haven. The wondrous **Museum Mr Simon van Gijn** overlooks the harbor. Continue past the old warehouses and cross the little drawbridge to reach Kuipershaven. A swaggering 17thC city gate, the **Groothoofds Poort**, stands at the end of this harbor. Festooned with Renaissance decoration, including a plumpish Maid of Holland, the gate once formed the principal entry to Dordrecht. In July and August, a restored 19thC steam tug, the *Pieter Boele,* departs from here on a tour of the local waterways. The boat goes into the eerie Biesbosch (reed forest), a region of islands inundated by the St Elizabeth's Day Flood of 1421, when 72 towns and villages were lost, and more than 100,000 people drowned. The flood — which is depicted in a painting in the RIJKSMUSEUM — turned Dordrecht into an island.

Now walk through the gateway and follow the meandering **Wijnstraat**, an interesting old street of abandoned warehouses and dusty antique stores. Turn left across the Wijnbrug and straight ahead down Nieuwstraat to reach Vest. The **Dordrechts Museum** is just to the left. To reach the **Statenzaal** from here, continue along Vest, then turn left up Steegoversloot. A lane on the left leads into the courtyard **'t Hof**. The Statenzaal *(12 Hof ☎ (078) 134626 open Tues-Sat 1-5pm)* was the room where representatives of the 12 cities backing William of Orange met in 1572 to plan the revolt against the Spanish.

EVENTS   A market takes place on the Grote Markt every Saturday *(8.30am-4pm).*

SIGHTS AND PLACES OF INTEREST

DORDRECHTS MUSEUM
Museumstraat 40 ☎(078) 134100 ☁ Open Tues-Sat 10am-5pm; Sun 1-5pm.
A former lunatic asylum has been modernized to house a modest collection of paintings by Dordrecht artists of the Golden Age, including Albert Cuyp, Nicholas Maes and Ferdinand Bol. A romantic *View of Dordrecht* was painted by the Leiden artist Jan van Goyen from the N bank of the Oude Maas in 1651.

The museum has **Impressionist** works by the Hague and Amsterdam Schools, abstract paintings by **Cobra** artists, and a curious room devoted to the once famous 19thC Dordrecht painter Ary Scheffer.

GROTE KERK
Grote Kerksplein. Open Apr-Oct, Tues-Sat 10.30am-4.30pm; Sun noon-4pm; Nov-Mar Sat only 1-4pm.
The Grote Kerk is beautifully sited at the mouth of the old harbor, and its unfinished 14thC tower, surmounted by four rather bizarre clocks, rises splendidly above the busy Oude Maas. The church was built in 15thC Flemish Gothic style by the Antwerp architect Evert Spoorwater, but the vast Gothic interior is bare compared

to the Catholic churches of Flanders. Carillon concerts are given on Friday 11-noon and Saturday 2-3pm.

MUSEUM MR SIMON VAN GIJN

Nieuwe Haven 29 ☎*(078) 133793 Open Tues-Sat 10am-5pm; Sun 1-5pm. Speelgoedhuis (toy house) open Wed, Sat and Sun.*

A handsome 18thC merchant's house overlooking the harbor contains a collection of decorative art amassed by Simon van Gijn, a local banker, who lived in the house from 1864 to 1922.

The museum reflects the quiet prosperity of Dordrecht, with its 18thC and 19thC interiors, including a spry tiled kitchen, a room furnished with a 16thC Renaissance fireplace rescued from the arquebusiers' guild house, and an evocative study added by Van Gijn in the style of a Vermeer painting.

The museum owns an impressive collection of glass, porcelain, Flemish tapestries, old shop signs, ship models and Dutch paintings. A scale model of Dordrecht in 1544 makes the island city look like a ship sailing downstream. Don't miss the collection of antique toys, including many working models, displayed in the attic and garden house.

◪ The handsome **Grand Café Crimpert Salm** (*Visstraat 3-7* ☎*(078) 145557 open Mon-Sat 9am-1am; Sun noon-1am*) occupies the former fishermen's guild house of 1608. Furnished with antique Belgian wood paneling and brass chandeliers, the spacious interior is particularly attractive on chill winter days. Friendly and cosmopolitan, the café serves good coffee and sophisticated cooking.

EDAM

Map 2A4. Noord-Holland, 22km (14 miles) N of Amsterdam. Population: 24,000. By NZH bus 110, 116 from Amsterdam CS; by car, through IJ-tunnel, then E10 *i Stadhuis, Damplein 1 1135 ZJ* ☎*(02993) 71727.*

The neat, stately town of Edam was a major shipbuilding center in the 15th-16thC, and when the inland seas to the w such as the Beemster and Purmer were drained in the 17thC to create rich pastures, the town adroitly shifted its attention to the cheese trade. The round, red cheese that goes by the name of Edam is one of Holland's best-known exports, although the Dutch themselves much prefer Gouda.

THE TOWN

Edam is a pleasant and interesting town to explore if you have some time. The most dignified canal is the **Schepenmakersdijk** (shipbuilders' dike), with its ornate tea houses and picturesque 18thC offices belonging to the Hoogheemraadschap van de Uitwaterende Sluizen (a body set up in the 16thC to reduce the danger of flooding in this part of Holland).

In contrast, the area N of the main square, **Dam**, is quite modest and in parts even rural, particularly along Nieuw Vaartje, where there is a **farmhouse** with chickens running loose in the yard, as well as a house with a puzzling **decorated beam** (#8). The quay opposite, known as **Groenland**, recalls Edam's former links with the Greenland whaling industry. Farther N is the unexpectedly large **Grote Kerk** (*open Apr-Oct daily 2-4.30pm),* which boasts a handsome late Gothic library on the s side. The **Kaasmarkt** (cheese market), with its 18thC weigh house (*open daily 10am-5pm),* is also worth a glance.

EVENT An open-air market takes place in Edam every Wednesday *(9am-2pm)*.

SIGHTS AND PLACES OF INTEREST

EDAMS MUSEUM
Damplein 8 ▦ ✱ *Open Easter-Oct Mon-Sat 10am-4pm; Sun 2-4pm.*

Occupying a remarkable late Gothic house built about 1550, the most mysterious feature of this museum is a **floating cellar** that rocks gently like a small boat. One local legend has it that this was installed by a retired captain to remind him of his days at sea, although a more plausible explanation is that it was to protect the fabric of the house from changes in the water table.

Equally curious are three large **portraits** of local freaks: the exceptionally fat Jan Claeszoon Clees, the tall Trijntje Cornelisdochter Kever and finally Pieter Dirkszoon Langebaard, who traveled around Holland exhibiting his lengthy beard to raise money for the local orphanage. Another interesting painting shows the Edam shipbuilder Jacob Mathijsz Osterlingh proudly displaying the fleet of some 92 fishing boats and warships constructed in his shipyards. The maze of dark rooms and steep stairs, cupboard beds and other unexpected details make the museum especially appealing to children.

ENKHUIZEN
Noord-Holland, 62km (39 miles) NE of Amsterdam. Population: 15,750. By train, 1hr from Amsterdam Centraal Station; by car, through IJ-tunnel, then A7
i *Stationsplein 1 1601 EN* ☎*(02280) 13164.*

Enkhuizen's flamboyant Renaissance houses and massive warehouses date mainly from the first quarter of the 17thC, when it boasted the largest herring fleet in Holland. The silting of the Zuider Zee in the late 17thC brought its prosperity to an end, and by the 19thC Enkhuizen was one of the famous "dead towns of the Zuider Zee" to which travelers flocked in search of the old-fashioned and picturesque. Nowadays its harbors are crammed with a fascinating variety of sailboats, while the **Zuiderzee Museum** is a major crowd-puller. But you only have to walk a short distance away from the harbor to discover a lingering mood of melancholy decay, especially in the quarter known as the **Boerenhoek**, where an almost rural disorder prevails.

During the summer *(mid-May to mid-Sept)*, passenger boats (which take bicycles) cross the IJsselmeer. One route goes from Enkhuizen to **Urk**, a former island now joined to the mainland by the Noord-Oost polder, and another to **Staveren**, which is linked by rail with attractive Frisian towns such as **Hindeloopen** (famous for its painted furniture), **Workum** (a former port) and **Sneek** (set among picturesque lakes). Another boat service connects Enkhuizen with **Medemblik** to the N.

If the notion of setting sail on a traditional brown-sailed boat catches your fancy, contact **Zeilvaart Enkhuizen** *(Zuiderhavendijk 101 1601 JB* ☎*(02280) 12424* Ⓕ*(02280) 13737)* for information on individual or group excursions in summer lasting one or more days.

THE HARBORS
The best view of Enkhuizen's harbors is from the gusty promontory at the end of **Wierdijk**, the old sea wall. From here, cross the bridge and

turn left along the picturesque street **Bocht**, which bends round to reach a second bridge. Across this bridge is the 16thC tower known as **De Dromedaris**, built to protect the harbor mouth and in the 17thC adorned with a merry **Hemony carillon** *(concerts Sat 4-5pm)*. A second harbor is reached through the gate of the tower. Here, turn right past the fish auction and along the harbor, then right again to reach a third harbor. Cross the bridge and turn right down Dijk, which brings you to the splendid **Snouck van Loosenhuis** (#34-6), built in the 1740s and adorned with an ornate cartouche. Just beyond the bridge, turn left down the quiet canal **Zuiderhavendijk** to reach the town center.

THE TOWN

The distinctive late Gothic spire of the **Zuiderkerk**, with its curious onion-shaped top, indicates the center of the town. The **Stadhuis**, an imposing example of 17thC Classicism, is found just E of here in Bredestraat, while a short distance N is the **Stedelijk Waagmuseum** *(Kaasmarkt 8* ▨ *open Nov-Mar Tues-Sat 10am-noon, 2-5pm; Sun 2-5pm)*, a jaunty 16thC Renaissance weigh house, which contains the magnificent 17thC **wood-paneled chamber** of the Enkhuizen guild of surgeons, and an early-20thC **hospital ward**.

Enkhuizen's main shopping street, **Westerstraat**, runs W from here, passing the exceptionally ornate Renaissance **Weeshuis** (orphanage) dating from 1616 *(Westerstraat 109)*, whose facade stone shows a schoolroom. Nearby is another late Gothic church, the **Westerkerk**, built in 1472-1519, with a curious wooden **belfry** incorporating ships' timbers.

Proudly proclaiming Enkhuizen's prosperity in the 17thC are the former **Mint of Westfriesland** at Westerstraat 125, and the house at **Westerstraat 158**, with the Maid of Enkhuizen adorning the gable top.

Just N of here lies the **Boerenhoek** (farmers' quarter), an intriguing area of Enkhuizen, where the canals have a distinctly unkempt appearance and huge pyramid-roofed farmhouses appear in the streets. To discover this pleasantly bucolic corner, turn right down the canal **Oudegracht**. This leads eventually to the site of the city walls, where a small 17thC watchtower stands guard over a gate through which small boats entered the city. Here, you can take a brisk walk along the ramparts, which offer glimpses of crowded market gardens and (in spring and early summer) bright bulbfields. Turn left and walk to the 17thC city gate known as the **Koepoort**. Just beyond here is an experimental flower garden, the **Summer Garden** *(open mid-July to Aug Mon-Sat 9am-5pm; Sun 1-5pm. Closed if raining)*. Westerstraat then leads back to the center of the city.

SIGHTS AND PLACES OF INTEREST

ZUIDERZEE MUSEUM

Wierdijk 18 ☎*(02280) 18260* ▨ ઙ *only in Buitenmuseum (open-air museum)* ⌐ ▆ ⚲ ◄
Binnenmuseum (indoor museum) open mid-Feb to Dec Mon-Sat 10am-5pm; Sun, hols noon-5pm. Buitenmuseum open mid-Apr to mid-Oct 10am-5pm (last entry 4pm). The Buitenmuseum can only be reached by a special ferry service from Enkhuizen rail station and from the parking lot just E of Enkhuizen on the road to Lelystad. No dogs.

The completion in 1932 of the **Afsluitdijk** (enclosing dike) along the N end of the Zuider Zee was the beginning of the end for the numerous fishing towns on this inland sea. Large-scale land reclamation caused former islands such as **Urk** and **Schokland** to vanish in the polder, while other ports such as **Elburg** and **Harderwijk** were suddenly transformed into inland towns. A mixture of guilt and nostalgia led to the establishment of the Zuiderzee Museum to provide a record of a vanished way of life.

This exceptionally interesting museum consists of two parts: the **Binnenmuseum** (indoor museum), housed in a series of magnificent old warehouses built by the Dutch East India Company, and the **Buitenmuseum** (open-air museum), whose 130 assorted buildings from Zuider Zee towns have been grafted onto Enkhuizen to form a compact unit. It is best to begin by visiting the Buitenmuseum (except in winter, when it is closed). A ferry operates across the picturesque harbor of Enkhuizen to the museum, which is to the NE of the town. Allow three hours to visit the Buitenmuseum and a further hour for the Binnenmuseum, which is located just to the left of the exit from the Buitenmuseum.

BUITENMUSEUM

One of the main charms of the open-air museum is its lifelike disorder, which is achieved by clustering houses into picturesque *buurtjes,* or neighborhoods. Around the perimeter, the *buurtjes* reflect the local styles of small fishing towns such as **Monnickendam** (a port SW of Enkhuizen), **Urk** (a former island with glossy wooden-fronted houses), **Harderwijk** (now landlocked by the Flevoland polder) and **Marken** (with picturesque black wooden houses). The inner area is occupied by more opulent buildings representing market towns such as **Edam** and industrial areas such as the **Zaanstreek**. The town canal interestingly reflects the modest style of a Frisian town on one side and a prosperous North Holland town on the other. Among the attractive buildings overlooking the canal are a 16thC Gothic house from Edam (now a souvenir store) and an imposing green-fronted merchant's house from the Zaan region, with a curious **formal garden** that includes parterres of glass beads originally manufactured in Amsterdam as trading tokens, and a spherical mirror to enlarge the apparent size of the garden.

Many of the modest fishermen's houses have been furnished in 1930s style and their cramped but genteel interiors incorporate delightful period details such as goldfish bowls, trays formally set for afternoon tea and neat rows of clogs by the door. The museum even includes a **church** in which the population of Den Oever (at the SW end of the Afsluitdijk) once worshiped, together with gravestones uprooted from various spots. The museum also has Den Oever's post office, which suggests that there cannot be very much to Den Oever nowadays.

There are also several **shops**, including a baker's *(banketbakkerij)* from Hoorn, where you can buy homemade chocolates, a grocer's *(kruidenier)* from Harderwijk where delicious local sausage is sold and a novelty gift store from Monnickendam. A cheese warehouse from Landsmeer (one of the buildings transported here by boat) serves as one of three museum restaurants, while another boasts a remarkable decorative **tiled interior** from a restaurant in Zandvoort. But perhaps the most attractive place to pause is in the café perched on the dike above the harbor.

Demonstrations are given of traditional activities such as tanning, boat building and house painting, while there are working models of a 19thC **windmill** (which maintains the water-level in the museum) and a steam laundry from near Kampen. Occasional trips are also organized on the reconstructed **Texel fishing boat**, which is moored in the Marken harbor.

There is hardly a corner of the museum that is not beguilingly picturesque, but one of the loveliest areas to explore is hidden behind the souvenir store, and includes an unusual *leugenbank,* literally a liars' bench, where fishermen traditionally gathered to exchange yarns.

BINNENMUSEUM

It is worth visiting the Binnenmuseum simply to enjoy the complex of vast 17thC warehouses set around a courtyard. The main building is the **Peperhuis**, a double step-gabled warehouse built in 1625 and later used by the Dutch East India Company. Mementoes of Enkhuizen's maritime past include the **gable stone** on the Peperhuis, illustrating a herring boat, and another at **Wierdijk 22** showing sailing ships struggling through a stormy sea.

The large **ships' hall** (rm 1) contains a number of **boats** that once sailed on the Zuider Zee and the inland waters of North Holland, ranging from stocky fishing boats to elegant pleasure yachts. The museum also has a collection of **figureheads** and other decorations (rm 2), **ship models** (rm 9) and an interesting display of **methods of fishing and duck hunting** (rm 8).

The low-beamed **attic** (rm 4) contains a collection of **hand-painted furniture and sleighs** from isolated fishing communities such as Marken and Workum. These marvelous examples of folk art are illustrated with mythological or biblical episodes copied from artists' prints. The examples of Classical furniture (rm 7) are very sober by comparison. Another attic (rm 6) is devoted to traditional trades such as boat-building, weaving cloth for sails and cheese-making. There are also several sleighs of the type that feature in the skating scenes of Avercamp.

Finally, the museum contains a series of detailed **furnished rooms** (rms 13-15) illustrating the extraordinary variety of costumes and interiors found around the Zuider Zee. The interiors come from the islands of Terschelling, Urk and Marken, the manufacturing area NW of Amsterdam known as the Zaanstreek, and the former ports of Spakenburg and Volendam.

≡ Probably the most attractive restaurant in Enkhuizen is **Die Drie Haringhe** (Dijk 28 ☎(02280) 18610 ◪ ◪ ◪ ◪ last orders 10pm; closed lunch Sat and Sun, Tues, and Nov-Mar Sun), its name recalling the three herrings on the town's coat of arms. Located in a former Dutch East India Company warehouse overlooking the Oude Haven, it specializes in delicate French cuisine. The restaurant's waterside terrace is a pleasant spot for a drink on sunny days, while its basement bar offers a retreat on days of blustery winds. **De Boei** (Havenweg 5 ☎(02280) 14280 ◻ ◪ ◪ last orders 10pm) is a simple, affordable fish restaurant overlooking Buiten Haven, where the house specialty is all the plaice you can eat. Or head for one of the many fish stores found on the harbors, where you can pick up a *lekkerbekje* (piece of fried fish), *maatjes haring* (cured young herring) or perhaps a huge Dutch gherkin.

GOUDA

Map 1E3. Zuid-Holland, 53km (33 miles) s of Amsterdam, 23 km (14 miles) NE of Rotterdam, 30km (19 miles) SE of The Hague. Population: 65,000. By train, 50mins from Amsterdam CS, 25mins from Rotterdam CS, 20mins from Den Haag CS i Markt 27 2801 JJ ☎(01820) 13666.

The compact market town of Gouda is principally famed for its flat round yellow cheeses, which the Dutch consume in large quantities. Those whose palates are accustomed to vigorous French *fromage* might complain that Gouda is a touch bland, but the Dutch come stoutly to the defense of their beloved national food, and point out that there are five different types of cheese according to age, not to mention exotic varieties with cumin *(komijn)* or cloves *(nagel)*. The youngest Gouda, *jong*, is a creamy soft cheese about four weeks old; *jong-belegen* (eight weeks), *belegen* (four months) and *oud* (ten months) are increasingly hard, while one-year-old *overjarig* is particularly crumbly. A traditional **cheese market** is enacted in the large market square on Thursday *(late July to Aug, 9.30am-noon)*, with much of the action taking place in the **Waag**, designed in 1668 by Pieter Post and decorated with an impressive facade stone by Balthazar Eggers, depicting the weighing of Gouda cheeses.

THE TOWN

Gouda's most striking building is its **Stadhuis** in the middle of Markt, built in 1450 in a soaring Gothic style and adorned with **sculptures** of prominent Burgundian counts and countesses. An ornate Renaissance staircase with unusual caryatids was added in 1603.

From Markt, head down Kerksteeg to reach the **Sint Janskerk**, then walk along the outside of the church to reach a small park. Just beyond here, a short distance to the right down Molenwerf, is a small bridge that offers an almost Venetian view down a canal. Retrace your steps to reach Jeruzalemstraat, where the remains of a **12-sided chapel** dating from about 1500 are visible. Turn right down Spieringstraat, passing on the left the 17thC **orphanage** with its attractive courtyard and on the right the colorful 17thC portal of a former almshouse. Walk through the park at the end of the street and turn right past a windmill to reach a picturesque canal, **Oosthaven**, which you should follow N.

SIGHTS AND PLACES OF INTEREST

DE MORIAAN MUSEUM
Westhaven 29 ☒ *Open Mon-Sat 10am-5pm; Sun noon-5pm.*
The De Moriaan Museum occupies a 17thC tobacconist's and coffee store, which advertises itself to passers-by with a row of tobacco bales and a figure of a North American Indian holding a clay pipe. The labyrinthine interior contains some curious clay pipes, tiles and Art Nouveau ceramics.

STEDELIJK MUSEUM HET CATHARINA GASTHUIS
Achter de Kerk 14 ☒ *Open Mon-Sat 10am-5pm, Sun noon-5pm.*
Located in a hospice dating from the 14thC, this museum is entered from Oosthaven either through the *gasthuis* (hospice) chapel (#10), or through the **Lazaruspoortje**, a picturesque 17thC gateway on Achter de Kerk decorated with sculpture alluding to the building's function as a hospital.

The museum contains several 17th-19thC period rooms, including the delightful *gasthuis* **kitchen** (complete with a turtledove in a cage), a reconstructed **apothecary's store**, the Gouda surgeons' guild room, a schoolroom and a toy collection.

The collection of paintings includes medieval altarpieces from Gouda churches, 17thC civic guard group portraits, 19thC landscapes by the Barbizon and Hague Schools and some interesting modern works.

SINT JANSKERK ★
Achter de Kerk 16. Open Mar-Oct Mon-Sat 9am-5pm; Nov-Feb Mon-Sat 10am-6pm
☎*(01820) 12684.*
Many Dutch churches can be given a miss, but not the Sint Janskerk, with its astonishing Renaissance **stained-glass windows**. Most of these were designed in the 16thC by the brothers Dirck and Wouter Crabeth while Gouda was still a Catholic city, and the scenes are mainly religious and mythological. Works by these brothers include: *King Solomon receiving the Queen of Sheba* (window 5); *Judith and Holofernes* (window 6); *The Last Supper,* donated by Philip II of Spain, who

is shown with his wife Queen Mary Tudor of England (window 7); *Jonah and the Whale,* given by the Guild of Fishermen (window 30); *The Nativity* (window 12); *John the Baptist* (window 14); *The Baptism of Jesus* (window 15); and *Christ Preaching* (window 16).

The stained-glass windows craze continued after Gouda turned Protestant in the late 16thC, the themes then shifting to heroic episodes in Dutch history, such as the dramatic relief of Leiden, given by the city of Delft and designed by the burgomaster of Leiden (window 25). A more tenuous Dutch connection is alluded to in the illustration of the Capture of Damietta by Dutch crusaders in 1219 (window 2), and the cornerstone of the Dutch constitution is illustrated in the symbolic group of figures representing Freedom of Conscience (window 1).

Many of the windows were restored in the late 19thC by Jan Schouten of Delft, who created a number of curious, almost surreal, windows using leftover fragments of glass (windows 1A-C, 20 and 21). Finally, a window depicting Occupation and Liberation was added after World War II (window 28A).

HAARLEM

Map 1B3. Noord-Holland, 23km (14 miles) w of Amsterdam, 79km (49 miles) n of Rotterdam, 59km (37 miles) ne of The Hague. Population: 152,500. By train, 15mins from Amsterdam CS, 50mins from Rotterdam CS, 40mins from Den Haag CS i *Stationsplein 1, 2011 LR* ☎(023) 319059 🖾(023) 340537.

Haarlem has held onto its antique character more than any other town in the Randstad. Although only fifteen minutes by train from the bustle of Amsterdam, the town still seems under the sway of sober 17thC virtues. Haarlem boasts an abundance of odd antique stores filled with the sort of objects that appear in Dutch still-life paintings, and apothecaries where you can buy not only aspirin but a dozen different types of *drop* (liquorice).

Haarlem has the most opulent **19thC rail station** in the Netherlands and, at the **Teylers Museum**, one of the best-preserved 18thC museum interiors in Europe. It is an immensely rewarding town to explore on foot, with its decorative brick-paved streets, rosy Renaissance gables and secluded *hofjes.* But it is perhaps the paintings in the FRANS HALS MUSEUM, and the vast GROTE KERK, that will most impress visitors.

THE TOWN

Perhaps the best approach is from the station (a grand Art Nouveau building built in 1908) down Jansweg, which passes the impressive **Hofje van Staats** *(Jansweg 39),* built in Louis XIV style in 1730, and then crosses the former moat to enter the old city. On the right is the 14thc **Janskerk** *(Jansstraat 38),* where the 15thC painter Geertgen tot Sint Jans lived. A tangle of crooked lanes to the e surrounds the 14thC **Waalsekerk** (formerly the Begijnhof chapel), which retains its charm despite having a number of brothels in its vicinity. Toward the end of Jansstraat, notice the beautiful **portal** of the **St Barbara Gasthuis** *(Jansstraat 54),* with a colorful relief showing the interior of this 17thC hospital.

Turn left at the Grote Kerk and head down Damstraat to the river Spaarne, where you find the rugged 1598 **Waag** (weigh house), attributed to Lieven de Key, the **Teylers Museum** and the picturesque **Grave-**

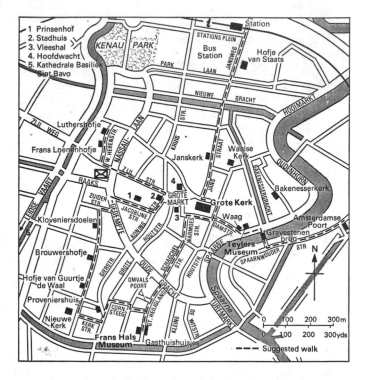

1 Prinsenhof
2. Stadhuis
3. Vleeshal
4. Hoofdwacht
5. Kathedrale Basiliek Sint Bavo

stenenbrug. Cross the bridge and turn left along Spaarnwouderstraat to reach the unexpected **Amsterdamse Poort**, a 15thC city gate. Bakenessergracht is also worth a glance, particularly the exquisite late Gothic spire of the **Bakenesserkerk**. But the best of Haarlem lies S of Grote Markt: head down Warmoesstraat (notice the patterned brick paving) to Schagchelstraat, then across Gedempte Oude Gracht (formerly the town moat) and down the gently curving Groot Heiligland. The **Omvalspoort**, squeezed between Groot Heiligland 22 and 24, is a particularly attractive medieval lane. Facing the **Frans Hals Museum** are the **Gasthuishuisjes**, a harmonious row of 12 identical step gables, built about 1610 for the St Elisabeth's Gasthuis. (Notice the 1612 **facade stone** at Groot Heiligland 47, showing a woman being carried into the hospital on a stretcher, and the inscription: "Bodily sickness is a medicine for the soul.")

Continue w along Ravelingsteeg and Cornelissteeg to reach the spacious **Proveniershuis**, formerly belonging to the civic guard of St George (painted several times by Frans Hals). It was converted to a home for old people in 1707. Continue w along Kerkstraat, at the end of which looms the grim Classical facade of the **Nieuwe Kerk**, erected by Jacob van Campen in 1645-49 alongside a jaunty Renaissance tower designed by Lieven de Key in 1613. Head N along Lange Annastraat, past the compact **Hofje van Guurtje de Waal** with its 1661 portal, and the 1586 **Brouwershofje** with its bright red and white shutters *(both open to the public)*. Farther N, the former **Kloveniersdoelen**, rebuilt by Lieven de Key in 1612, is indicated by the **crossed muskets** above the entrance on Gasthuisstraat *(courtyard open to the public)*. The civic guard of St Adrian, which was the subject of Frans Hals' finest group portrait, met here to exercise and banquet.

Turn right along Zuiderstraat and then continue along Jacobijnestraat, past a former **monastic garden**, which in the 18thC was planted with medicinal herbs. The monastery was once used by William of Orange as his residence (Prinsenhof), and its **cloister** (entered from Grote Markt) now forms part of the Stadhuis (town hall). If energies are flagging by this stage, an ideal place to pause is in one of the many **cafés** on the N side of Grote Markt, after which you should continue W down Zijlstraat to reach Witte Herenstraat, where you find the **Frans Loenenhofje** with its 1625 portal in Dutch Renaissance style, and the **Luthershofje** *(open to the public)*, which contains an open-air pulpit that is attached to the Lutheran Church.

SIGHTS AND PLACES OF INTEREST

FRANS HALS MUSEUM ★
Groot Heiligland 62 ☎*(023) 319180* 📷 💻 🚗 *in De Witstraat. Open Mon-Sat 11am-5pm; Sun, hols 1-5pm.*

The Frans Hals Museum is located in the beautiful **Oudemannenhuis**. Built in 1608 by Lieven de Key, it was once, as its name suggests, a home for old men. The building retains several rooms in 17thC style overlooking exactly the sort of dull formal garden that caused David Hume to grumble in 1748 that: "Nothing can be more disagreeable than the heap of Dirt & Mud & Ditches & Reeds, which they here call a country, except the silly collection of shells and clipt evergreens which they call a garden."

The museum possesses a distinguished collection of Dutch paintings, including eight large **group portraits** by the Haarlem artist Frans Hals (1580-1666), which illustrate the development of his style. The earliest group portrait is the rather stiff *Banquet of the Officers of the Civic Guard of St George* (#123), painted in 1616 when Frans Hals was 36. By 1627, when he painted the *Banquet of the Officers of the Civic Guard of St Adrian* (#125) and again the *Officers of St George* (#124), his style had become more animated. His finest work is undoubtedly the 1633 *Assembly of Officers and Subalterns of the Civic Guard of St George* (#126), which shows the Kloveniersdoelen, where they met, in the background. The last group portrait, showing again the officers of the civic guard of St George, was painted in 1639 in a rather stiff style (#127). It includes a somewhat apprehensive self-portrait behind the two rotund officers at the bottom left.

When in 1641 Frans Hals painted the *Governors of the St Elisabeth Hospital* (#128), he adopted a particularly somber style to depict the black-clothed officials who administered the hospital directly opposite the museum. His last group portraits, showing the governors (#129) and governesses (#130) of the Oudemannenhuis, were painted in 1664 when Frans Hals was himself an old man under their care. The bitterness of these paintings — notice the caustic depiction of a drunkard, with his hat set at a rakish angle — is sadly out of keeping with his cheerful early works.

Another painter to look out for is **Jan van Scorel**, who during a brief period of exile in Haarlem in the late 1520s painted the *Knightly Brotherhood of the Holy Land* (which includes a self-portrait, third from the right).

Haarlem artists of the 16thC included Cornelis Cornelisz. van Haarlem and the remarkable Maerten van Heemskerck, whose eccentric Mannerism is illustrated by the study of St Luke (patron saint of artists) painting the Virgin and Child. Hendrick Cornelisz. Vroom, also from Haarlem, captured the bustling prosperity of the 17thC in his maritime painting of the arrival of the Elector palatine's fleet at Vlissingen in 1616, and in his view of Haarlem from the Noorder Spaarne. Jan van Goyen suggests a more sleepy mood in his 1649 *River Scene,* with a gently crumbling town (probably Leiden) in the background. The views of Haarlem by Gerrit Berckheyde, on the other hand, convey an almost surreal perfection.

GROTE KERK ★
Oude Groenmarkt 23. Open Mon-Sat 10am-4pm. Closed Sun.

Rising magnificently above the city is the Grote Kerk, one of the most popular subjects of Dutch painting. The oldest part is the **late 14thC choir**, built of rough-hewn stone on the site of a 12thC church. Its **nave** dates from the 15thC, while the curious **Renaissance Baptistry** on the s side was added by Lieven de Key in 1600. The **spire** is a delicate late Gothic ornament built in 1520.

Perhaps the most remarkable feature of the church is the cheerful muddle of small **shops** clustered around the walls. At one time there were 37 separate shops, which the church rented out to greengrocers, clog-makers, spectacle-sellers and the like. The church also received an income from the **fish market** *(Vishal),* which was built in 1603 against the N wall of the church.

Another curious feature of the Grote Kerk is its tiny **entrance** on the picturesque s side, from which a narrow corridor leads into the vast and rather bleak church, with its pavement of gray tombstones and its stark whitewashed walls. Most of the Gothic sculpture was destroyed during the Reformation, to be replaced by notice boards inscribed with the names of church officials in fine calligraphy.

The glory of the Grote Kerk is its **organ**, built by Christian Müller in 1738 and lavishly decorated with Baroque sculpture by Jan van Logteren. The organ, with its 4,295 pipes, has been played by Handel, Mozart (aged ten), Liszt and Saint-Saëns *(concerts Tues 8.15-9.15pm, Thurs 3-4pm.)*

GROTE MARKT
Haarlem's breezy main square stands on the site of a medieval tilting yard formerly overlooked by a hunting lodge of the Counts of Holland. The mainly Renaissance **Stadhuis** now encloses the w side with its rather haphazard collection of buildings, including an Italian loggia, a small arcade and a slender late Gothic spire. Perhaps the most harmonious part is the N wing, with its lofty chimneys, designed by Lieven de Key in 1620. Also by De Key is the riotous 1603 **Vleeshal** on the s side of the market square, advertising itself as a meat hall by a display of carved oxen heads. Opposite is the neat Classical **Hoofdwacht** (guardhouse) of 1650, while the E side of the square is enclosed by the soaring **Grote Kerk**. A statue of L. J. Coster, who was, at one time, credited with the invention of printing, stands alongside the church.

KATHEDRALE BASILIEK SINT BAVO
Leidsevaart 146 ☎*(023) 313336* 🖾 *Open Apr-Sept Mon-Sat 10am-noon, 2-4.30pm. Bus 4, 8 from station to Emmastraat.*

The cathedral of St Bavo, one of the largest churches in the Netherlands, was built by Jos. Th. Cuypers in 1895 in a quiet residential area to the sw of the old city.

The picturesque confusion of chapels, turrets and gargoyles at the apsed E end (best seen from Emmastraat) is a fine example of late 19thC eclecticism, mixing Romanesque, Gothic and even Moorish elements. The towers at the w end, added in the 1920s, are sober by comparison, with just a hint of Art Deco at the top.

The remarkable interior contains a wealth of late 19thC and early 20thC art, including a set of Art Nouveau tile tableaux by Jan Toorop in the Kapel H. Aloysius, just to the left of the altar. Notice too the exquisite dome above the crossing, with its almost Moorish delicacy.

TEYLERS MUSEUM ★

Spaarne 16 ☎*(023) 319010* ▇▇ ▇ *Open Tues-Sat 10am-5pm; Sun, hols 1-5pm. Closes 4pm Oct-Feb.*

With its marble floor, Neoclassical pilasters, chaste marble statues, and ornate coat racks, Teylers is more like an aristocratic country house than a museum. It is the oldest public museum in the Netherlands, founded in 1778 by Pieter van Teyler, a wealthy silk merchant stirred by the ideals of the Enlightenment. The overblown Neoclassical facade on the Spaarne waterfront seems calculated to deter the faint-hearted, but it is worth pushing open the heavy door to enter the vast hall. The **Oval Room** is a wonderful Neoclassical interior, and you can pore over the handwritten labels attached to everything from fossils to electricity generators.

Had Teylers been in Amsterdam, it would probably have been altered beyond recognition in the 1970s, as happened to the STEDELIJK MUSEUM and TROPENMUSEUM, but Haarlem is a far less revolutionary town, and the collection has scarcely altered in the two centuries since its foundation. Frozen in the 18thC, the Teylers no longer offers much scientific instruction, and its coterie of admirers appreciate it simply as a curious antiquity. The **picture gallery** is still lit only by daylight, with the result that the museum has to close one hour early in the winter months.

The collection contains a few good works by **Dutch Impressionists** (including Breitner, Josef Israels and Weissenbruch), but rather a preponderance of Victorian sentimentality. Those in search of Dutch painting are better off devoting their time in Haarlem to the FRANS HALS MUSEUM, but the **Print Cabinet** has a superb collection of drawings by Dutch, Flemish and Italian Masters (including Michelangelo), although only a few are on display at any time.

On leaving this rather melancholy museum, one's spirit is immediately lifted by a picturesque **white wooden bridge** across the Buiten Spaarne, overlooked by a pair of merry step gables that belonged to a 17thC brewery, De Oliphant (The Elephant).

▬▆ A beautiful late Gothic arch leads into the former Bank van Lening (lending bank), which has been expertly converted into a restaurant: **Peter Cuyper** *(Kleine Houtstraat 70* ☎ *(023) 320885* ▥ ▣ ◉ ☙ *last orders 11pm; closed Sat lunch, Sun, Mon dinner)* has a pleasant brick-paved inner courtyard where you can enjoy an aperitif if the weather permits. Since you can almost smell the North Sea in Haarlem it is worth sampling a fish dish such as the *filets de sole cuits en croûte*.

▣ Haarlem's most popular cafés are mainly ranked along the N side of Grote Markt. Probably the most famous is the café-restaurant **De Kroon** *(Grote Markt 13, open Mon-Sat 9am-1pm),* occupying a 19thC neo-Renaissance building which fastidiously copies the bustling Mannerism of the **Vleeshal** on the opposite side of the square. The nearby café-restaurant **Carillon** *(Grote Markt 27, open 7.30am-2am)* offers a varied menu in an Old Dutch interior with wood paneling, comfortable armchairs and dim Art Deco cinema lamps.

Farther E is the **Proeflokaal De Uiver** *(Riviervischmarkt 13, open Mon-Sat 10am-2am, Sun 4pm-2am),* a tasting-house located in a former fish store, which boasts a magnificent tile tableau of fishing boats as well as some curious relics of Douglas DC-2 aircraft.

Finally, do not leave Haarlem without glancing at the 1908 Art Nouveau **station restaurant**, which is the pride and joy of the Dutch railway system. Haarlem Station originally boasted no fewer than five waiting rooms earmarked for first-, second- and third-class passengers, plus women and lunatics.

SHOPPING   Haarlem's stubborn resistance to progress has left it with a number of traditional 18th and 19thC shop interiors, which are a pleasure to enter, even if only to buy a tube of toothpaste. Among many old-fashioned tobacconists are **W. H. Voet en Zonen** *(Kruisstraat 39)*, located in an ornate Neoclassical interior, and **Prinsenhof** *(Jacobijnestraat 8)*, which is named after the nearby building where William of Orange stayed in 1580. Haarlem-made **Droste** products, including cocoa sold in cans decorated with a nun, are available at **Haarlemmer Halletjes** *(Kruisstraat 37)*, while traditional Dutch *drop* (liquorice) is, for some obscure health reason, sold by pharmacies *(drogisterijen)* such as **A.J. van der Pigge** *(Gierstraat 3)*.

Antique stores, which Haarlem has in abundance, congregate in Zijlstraat, Kruisstraat and the area s of Grote Markt. Book-lovers should make a point of visiting **H. de Vries** *(Gedempte Oude Gracht 27)*, which is furnished in the style of a 17thC Dutch painting, with brass chandeliers, solid oak furniture and old stone fireplaces. Although this shop is particularly famous for its books on sport, it also offers a good range of art books and English novels.

For chain stores, the main shopping street is **Grote Houtstraat**, which runs s from Grote Markt and passes close to the main department store, **Vroom & Dreesmann** *(Gedempte Oude Gracht)*. **Barteljorisstraat** has a few slightly more unusual fashion stores.

HOORN
Noord-Holland, 43km (27 miles) N of Amsterdam. Population: 56,000. By train, 30mins from Amsterdam Centraal Station; by car, through IJ-tunnel, then A7
i Nieuwstraat 23 ☎(02290) 18342.

Hoorn was one of the foremost Dutch ports in the 17thC. It produced a host of mariners and explorers, including Willem Schouten, who named Cape Horn after his home town, and Jan Pieterszoon Coen, who founded the Dutch colony of Batavia, now the Indonesian capital Jakarta. After the silting of the Zuider Zee in the late 17thC, Hoorn's fortunes rapidly declined and it became in the 19thC one of the famous dead towns of the Zuider Zee. In recent years, however, Hoorn has risen from the grave and it is now a bustling center for excursions on the IJsselmeer.

During the summer months (May to mid-September) gleaming steam trains depart from Hoorn rail station amid clouds of black smoke and head N to the port of **Medemblik** *(☎(02290) 14862, May-Sept)*. Passenger boats connect Medemblik with Enkhuizen rail station, where you can catch an ordinary train back to Hoorn. Contact NS (Dutch Railways) for details of special excursion rates.

Not to be outdone, an enterprising skipper has restored the jaunty **steam tug** *Gabriëlle*, built in Brandenburg in 1903. Excursions *(late June-Aug Wed and Sun afternoon only)* depart from the pier in front of the Hoofdtoren. For information about excursions on traditional wooden sailboats,try contacting **Zeilvaart Hoorn** *(Hoofd 15, 1621 AM Hoorn (☎(02290) 17695* Ⓕ*(02290) 17143)*.

THE HARBORS
From the rail station, follow signs to "Havens" to reach the Westerdijk, which follows the broad sweeping bay known as the Hoornsche Hop.

The dike leads eventually to the plump, round **Hoofdtoren**, built in 1532 to protect the harbor and adorned with a bell tower in 1651. The sculptural group on the harbor wall shows three boys from a seafaring romance set in the 17thC.

Veermanskade has a splendid row of step-gabled merchants' houses dating from the early 17thC when Hoorn's prosperity was at its peak. A pleasant detour can be made along Korenmarkt; then cross the bridge to reach Bierkade, where the warehouse **Dantzig** at #8 dates from the time when Hanseatic ships unloaded beer shipments on this quay.

Returning to the harbor, turn left, then pass two jaunty **Renaissance houses** at Oudedoelenkade 17-19 and 21, with ships carved on the gable stones and names indicating that the merchant on the left traded with the Baltic while his neighbor dealt with the Mediterranean. Cross the wooden bridge on the right at the end of the harbor and continue straight ahead to reach the former Chamber of the Dutch West India Company, sited in a rather isolated spot. From here, you should walk back along the promontory known as **Baatland** to obtain a superb panorama of the harbor front.

After recrossing the bridge, continue straight ahead down Slapershaven to discover the curious three houses known as the **Bossuhuizen**, which are decorated with magnificent **friezes** depicting the Battle of the Zuider Zee in 1573 at which a fleet of Dutch rebels defeated Admiral Bossu's Spanish fleet.

THE TOWN

After completing the harbor route, explore the rest of the town by turning left along Grote Oost, a handsome street of mainly 18thC houses running from the splendid 1578 Oosterpoort to the **Rode Steen**. Side streets such as Schoolstraat provide picturesque distractions, but do not miss the theatrical 17thC **Staten-College** (now the Westfries Museum) or the dignified **Waag** on Rode Steen, the main square of Hoorn.

Kerkstraat runs N from here past the Renaissance facade of the **St Jans Gasthuis**, built as a hospital in 1563. Behind the 19thC **Grote Kerk**, which now contains shops and apartments, are two 17thC gates, one of which gave access to the Admiralty offices, while the other was the entrance to a home for elderly women. Both buildings were established in former convents, abolished during the Reformation.

A picturesque lane leads through a former cloister to Nieuwstraat. The **Statenpoort** at Nieuwstraat 23 was built in Dutch Renaissance style in 1613 as the meeting place for representatives from the seven cities of West Friesland. Nearby, in Muntstraat, is the late 17thC office of the Hoorn Chamber of the Dutch East India Company. Continue N along Korte Achterstraat, passing the protestant Orphanage, where Admiral Bossu was imprisoned after the Battle of the Zuider Zee. Farther N is the 17thC hall of the Guild of St Sebastian. Turn left at the end of this street and you will come across the attractive Munnickenveld, with a small *hofje* founded in 1682. At the end of the canal, turn right on Spoorstraat and left down Baanstraat to reach the **Noorderkerk** *(Klein Noord* ☎ *(02290)*

34650, open Easter-Sept Mon-Sat 11am-5pm, Sun noon-5pm), which contains a detailed scale model of 17thC Hoorn. Kleine Noord takes you back to the rail station.

SIGHTS AND PLACES OF INTEREST

WESTFRIES MUSEUM ★
Rode Steen 1 ☎*(02290) 15597* ▣ *Open Mon-Fri 11am-5pm; Sat, Sun 2-5pm.*

The museum of West Friesland is devoted to the history of the area N of the IJ, bounded to the W by the North Sea and to the E by the IJsselmeer (formerly the Zuider Zee). The museum occupies the splendid 1632 College of the States of West Friesland, a dazzling masterpiece of Dutch Mannerism. The growling lions that hold aloft the coats of arms of the seven cities of West Friesland (Alkmaar, Hoorn, Enkhuizen, Medemblik, Edam, Monnickendam and Purmerend) are a reminder of the former importance of these now-slumbering satellites of Amsterdam. Although the exhibits are labeled only in Dutch, the Westfries Museum is well worth visiting to catch the flavor of the Golden Age.

The chilly **14thC cellars** (rms 1-5) are all that survive of the house on this site occupied by the representative of the Bishop of Utrecht. Among the facade stones salvaged from demolished buildings are two ornate 17thC stones, one showing **Mary Queen of Scots** and her unfortunate husband Darnley, the other, which may once have decorated the house of a Scottish merchant resident in Hoorn, depicting **James I and Anne of Denmark**.

The three floors directly above preserve fine 17thC Mannerist paneled rooms, connected by steep staircases that creak like old galleons. The delegates of the seven cities used to assemble in the magnificent room at the front of the building (rm 7), which is now overwhelmed by huge 17thC Civic Guard group portraits. The attic (rm 12) is also appealing, and offers intriguing glimpses of the open water on one side and the Waag and Grote Kerk on the other.

The final rooms occupy the 18thC Rococo annex and are furnished in various French styles, with pastel colors and delicate moldings that contrast vividly with the bold detail and robust construction of the 17thC rooms.

▬ In an area of Holland in which eating well is sometimes regarded as a deadly sin, **De Oude Rosmolen** *(Duinsteeg 1 (off Nieuwe Noord)* ☎*(02290) 14752* ▣ *(02290) 14938* ▥ ▬ ▣ ▣ ▣ *last orders 9.30pm; closed lunch and Thurs),* a small restaurant located in a characteristic 17thC house, is unique. The friendly owner, Constant Fonk, claims a lifelong dedication to all aspects of the culinary arts, displaying a photograph of himself as a young boy proudly bearing a birthday cake he had baked. The inventive cuisine, carefully selected wines (including some rare white wines from Dutch Limburg) and a groaning cart of homemade gateaux amply demonstrate his commitment. Nor does the experience end with dessert: coffee is served with a delicious selection of *petits fours.*

Located directly opposite Hoorn rail station, **Azië** *(Veemarkt 49* ☎*(02290) 18555* ▣*(02290) 49604* ▢ ▣ ▣ ▣ ▣ *last orders 11pm)* offers exquisite Chinese cuisine, ranging from delicate Cantonese to fiery Szechuan dishes, together with a range of *rijsttafels.* The specialty menu, offering a range of rare Oriental dishes, is particularly good value.

SHOPPING Most shops are located on the pedestrianized **Grote Noord**. **Schoolstraat** contains an interesting cluster of antique stores, including one that specializes in dolls and another that sells Wurlitzers, street organs and circus paraphernalia. Hoorn's most attractive shop is **P. Kaag Antz.** *(Breed 38),* selling tea, coffee and tobacco in a beautiful 19thC building with a gable stone showing a horse-drawn barge.

LEIDEN

Map 1D2. Zuid-Holland, 41km (26 miles) sw of Amsterdam, 34km (21 miles) N of Rotterdam, 19km (12 miles) NE of The Hague. Population: 104,260. By train, 30mins from Amsterdam CS, 30mins from Rotterdam CS, 15mins from Den Haag CS i Stationsplein 210 2312 AR ☎(071) 146846.

Located on a branch of the Rhine, Leiden's cloth and beer industries made it a very prosperous city in the Middle Ages. Besieged in 1573-74 by the Spanish, the city was eventually relieved in October 1574 when William of Orange broke the dikes to flood the surrounding countryside, allowing Admiral Boisot's fleet to sail up to the city walls.

In recognition of Leiden's stoic stand against the Spanish, William granted the town its own university, the first to be established in Holland. As a result, Leiden became a major center of Protestant learning in the 17th-18thC, and its intellectual and religious tolerance attracted refugees, such as the printer Louis Elsevier, from the southern Netherlands. It was here, too, that the Pilgrim Fathers, led by John Robinson, settled in 1609 before they departed for the New World in 1620.

The names of numerous artists are linked with Leiden, including Jan van Goyen, Gabriel Metsu, Jan Steen (who ran a tavern on Lange Brug) and Rembrandt, who was born here in 1606.

Like the untidy study of a forgetful professor, the old city of Leiden now possesses a dishevelled charm, which is best preserved in the narrow streets around the two enormous churches. Despite several heroic attempts at restoration, Leiden seems to be in permanent decline, and even in the 17thC paintings of Jan van Goyen has an air of neglect. Perhaps this is only superficial, however, for in the secluded world of Leiden's *hofjes* there reigns a brisk orderliness, while its museums display everything from stuffed birds to clay pipes with an academic precision.

EVENTS A fruit and vegetable market takes place along the quays of the Nieuwe Rijn on Wednesday and Saturday 9am-5pm.

THE TOWN

Boat tours of Leiden *(mid June to early Sept)* depart from Beestenmarkt, skirting the edge of the old city on the outward journey and returning through the city along the Rhine. However, you have to walk through the town to discover the hidden *hofjes* and picturesque corners and lanes that are the particular charm of Leiden.

From Beestenmarkt, head down Morsstraat to the 17thC Morspoort and turn left to reach the **Rembrandtbrug**, a white wooden drawbridge whose name recalls the fact that Rembrandt was born just s of here in 1606. However, the only building hereabouts that the young Rembrandt might have seen is the **Dutch Renaissance house** built in 1612 on the Stadstimmerwerf, where the municipal carpenters and sculptors worked. The wooden windmill nearby called **De Put** *(open Sat 10am-6pm, Sun 2.30-6pm)* was built recently to show the type of mill owned by Rembrandt's father. **Rowboats** can be rented on the opposite side of the Rembrandtbrug *(☎ (071) 149790)*.

Cross the bridge to head s down Weddesteeg and Rembrandtstraat to **Groenhazengracht**, a picturesque canal of crumbling brick houses. The

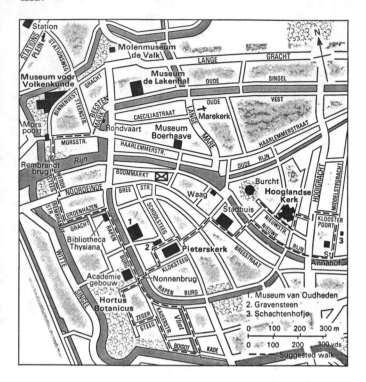

figure of St George adorns a flamboyant **gateway** that once led to the Civic Guard exercise ground. Continue to Rapenburg and turn right past the dignified **Bibliotheca Thysiana**, a pleasing 17thC Classical building designed by Arend van 's-Gravesande, to reach the **Academiegebouw**, a former convent chapel that was given to the university in 1581. Walk down the lane to enter the **Hortus Botanicus**.

From here, follow Zegersteeg and Kaiserstraat to reach the picturesque spot where the river Vliet enters the city. Follow the river N to Rapenburg, then turn left to reach the Nonnenbrug, which you should cross to reach Kloksteeg. A plaque on the 17thC **Jean Pesijnshofje** at Kloksteeg 21 recalls that the Pilgrim Fathers' leader, John Robinson, lived and died in a house that stood here.

Dominating the square is Leiden's oldest church, the **Pieterskerk** *(open 1.30-4pm)*, a gracefully soaring 15thC edifice with a few interesting gravestones (including those of Rembrandt's parents) and guild relics. The Pieterskerk has fallen victim to the distressing Dutch habit of converting old churches into secular cultural centers, and the building is now used for examinations and graduation parties, rather than services. It may seem tasteless to let students drink amid the tombs of the eminent, but

300

the pragmatic Dutch seem unconcerned by the fact. From the Pieterskerk, head w past the **Gravensteen**, a picturesque jumble of buildings of various vintages surrounding a 14thC prison of the Counts of Holland. Former courtrooms and cells now accommodate Leiden university's law faculty. The *Koffiehuis* opposite is a pleasant brown café with dim green lamps hung low above wooden tables.

On the corner of Schoolsteeg is the **Latin School**, which Rembrandt attended from 1614-20. It was built in 1599 by Lieven de Key, as was the splendid 1595 **Stadhuis** on Breestraat, which can be reached along Pieterskerkchoorsteeg. Beyond the Stadhuis, turn left and cross the Nieuwe Rijn by the Koornbrug, then continue right to **Middelstegracht**, a filled-in canal that formed part of an ambitious 17thC extension plan modeled on that of Amsterdam. The grandeur of Amsterdam was never attained, however, and the main delights on this canal are the 16thC **St Annahof**, with its own chapel, and the 17thC **Schachtenhofje** *(both open to the public)*.

Turn left down Kloosterpoort to reach Leiden's second massive church, the **Hooglandsekerk**, with its curious 14thC wooden tower, 15thC choir and squat 16thC nave. You get a striking view of the red pantiled roofs and old church towers of Leiden from the top of the **Burcht**, a curious 12thC fortress built on an artificial hill (turn right along Nieuwstraat and continue through the **Renaissance gateway** decorated with lions).

SIGHTS AND PLACES OF INTEREST

BOERHAAVE, MUSEUM
Lange Sint Agnietenstraat 10 ☎*(071) 214224* ▨ *Open Tues-Sat 10am-5pm; Sun, hols 1-5pm.*

Named after Leiden's distinguished professor of medicine, Herman Boerhaave (1666-1738), the Dutch national science museum reflects the intense intellectual atmosphere in the Netherlands. The museum recently moved to the restored **Ceciliaklooster**, a 15thC monastery later used as a hospital.

Dutch scientific inventions are arranged chronologically in a series of restored rooms, including the old anatomy theater and some wards where Boerhaave once taught medical students alongside the sickbeds. The scientific rarities include three microscopes made by Anthonie van Leeuwenhoek of Delft and a complex 17thC planetarium known as the Leiden Sphere. The museum's collection of some 200 Delftware apothecary jars, pendulum clocks, microscopes and surgical instruments is of great interest to experts, although children may find the displays rather too dry to enjoy.

HORTUS BOTANICUS
Rapenburg 73 ☎*(071) 275188. Open Apr-Sept Mon-Sat 9am-5pm; Sun 10am-5pm. Closed Sat Oct-Mar.*

Tucked away down a lane behind the old university, Leiden's botanical garden is one of the city's secret delights, with its sheltered herb gardens, willows trailing in ponds, and greenhouses full of exotic orchids. The garden is one of the oldest in the world, dating back to 1575. Don't miss the reconstructed Old Dutch garden, the **Clusiustuin** (named after the 17thC Leiden botanist Carolus Clusius, who introduced the tulip to Holland), reached through a gate and across a bridge.

RIJKSMUSEUM VAN OUDHEDEN ★
Rapenburg 28 ☎*(071) 146246* ▨ ♿ *Open Tues-Sat 10am-5pm; Sun, hols noon-5pm.*

Founded in 1818, the national museum of antiquities contains objects from the ancient civilizations of the Mediterranean, together with archeological finds from the Netherlands.

The Egyptian Temple of Taffeh forms a dramatic and somewhat menacing centerpiece to the collection. Built in the district of Nubia in the 1stC AD, the temple shows evidence of alterations made in the 4thC when winged sun-discs and friezes of crowned cobras were added by worshipers of the goddess Ibis. It was later used as a Christian temple and finally as a house, before being dismantled in 1960 during the construction of the Aswan dams. It was then presented to the Netherlands in recognition of Dutch assistance in the rescue of the Nile temples.

The museum's **Ancient Egyptian collection** has always been its chief glory and includes numerous mummies, sarcophagi, tombs and chapels, as well as less gloomy relics such as writing equipment and toys. The three statues from the tomb of Tutankhamun's minister, Maya, are particularly impressive.

The Ancient Roman rooms contain several interesting finds from the Netherlands, such as the remarkable **Simpelveld sarcophagus**, decorated inside with reliefs of a reclining figure surrounded by various pieces of furniture. Other remarkable finds are the **altars** dedicated to the goddess of merchants and seamen, Nehallennia. These were lifted from the sea off the coast of Zeeland in 1970.

An unusual feature is the **Panorama of Archeology**, which presents parallel displays of artifacts from different civilizations from 5000BC to AD500.

RIJKSMUSEUM VOOR VOLKENKUNDE
Steenstraat 1 ☎*(071) 211824* 🔲 ⓖ 🏛 *Open Tues-Sat 10am-5pm; Sun, hols 1-5pm.*
The rather old-fashioned Dutch National Museum of Ethnography is in the throes of modernization. Nevertheless it is worth a visit for its excellent **Japanese lacquer boxes** (the museum was founded by the first Europeans allowed to travel freely in Japan), its **furnished rooms** from Japan, Korea and Nepal, the **South American exhibits** and **Javanese sculpture** — a curious but pleasing blend of Hindu and Buddhist art.

STEDELIJK MOLENMUSEUM DE VALK
Tweede Binnenvestgracht 1 ☎*(071) 254639* 🔲 ✱ ◀€ *Open Tues-Sat 10am-5pm; Sun, hols 1-5pm.*
This imposing 8-floor-high working corn windmill was erected in 1743 on a bastion on the N edge of the city. It now houses an interesting museum of milling, with furnished living quarters on the ground floor, and storage and machinery rooms on the upper floors. The ascent by steep wooden steps is rewarded by a panoramic view of Leiden.

STEDELIJK MUSEUM DE LAKENHAL ★
Oude Singel 32 ☎*(071) 254620* 🔲 ⓖ *Open Tues-Sat 10am-5pm; Sun, hols 1-5pm.*
Leiden's municipal museum is housed in the former cloth hall, an attractive building in sober Dutch Classical style designed by Arend van 's-Gravesande in 1640.

The Lakenhal is best known for the **triptych** by Lucas van Leyden of the *Last Judgment* (rm S17). Painted for the Pieterskerk in 1526, this work shows a hesitant transition from Gothic to Renaissance style. Among the interesting 17thC works (rm S18) is a view of Leiden by Jan van Goyen and several "Vanity" pieces, whose morbid symbolism seems to have appealed to Leiden's collectors.

The **tile collection** (rms L3-4) illustrates the development of designs from the complex Islamic styles favored in the southern Netherlands in the 16thC to the whimsical blue Holland tiles of the 17thC.

The Lakenhal also contains several attractive period rooms, including an **18thC kitchen** (rm L7), the Louis XIV-style **Groene Papezaal** (rm P23) and the mainly Louis XVI-style **Gele Papezaal** (rm P24). Of the 17thC rooms on the first floor, the **Grote Pers** (L8) is the grandest, but the intimate **Staalmeesterskamer** (L10), where the syndics of the cloth guild met, is somehow more attractive. On the opposite side of the main hall is the charming **Bierbrouwerskamer** (L13), which was rescued from the demolished brewers' guild hall, with delightful 18thC paintings showing harvesting of the hops, the malting house, the brewery, transporting the beer, and the malting mill, De Juffer.

The historical collection (L15) contains some interesting maps of Leiden and a series of paintings by Isaac Swanenburg illustrating the cloth trade. The courtyard in front of the building, where the quality of cloth was examined in daylight, contains an intriguing collection of old gable stones, including one curiosity illustrating the five senses.

For overnight stays, the **Golden Tulip Leiden** *(Schipholweg 3, 2316 XB* ☎ *(071) 221121* Fx*(071) 226675* ▥ *51 rms* ▣ AE ◉ ⊙ VISA*)* is a striking glass-fronted hotel facing the rail station, offering pleasant bedrooms and a comfortable lounge stacked with international newspapers. **Nieuw Minerva** *(Boommarkt 23, 2300 EA* ☎ *(071) 126358* ▥ AE ◉ ⊙ VISA*)* is a friendly hotel located in a row of 17thC houses overlooking the Rhine.

Leiden's most respected restaurant, **Oudt Leyden** *(Steenstraat 51* ☎*(071) 133144* ▢ *to* ▥ AE ◉ ⊙ VISA *last orders 10pm; Rôtisserie closed Sun lunch and Mon, pancake house closed Sun lunch)*, is divided into a sophisticated *nouvelle cuisine* **Rôtisserie** and a modestly priced creperie-restaurant, **'t-Pannekoekenhuisje**. The latter offers an excellent-value Tourist Menu, as well as pancakes served on large blue Delft plates.

For Indonesian food try **Surakarta** *(Noordeinde 51* ☎*(071) 123524* ▢ *last orders 10pm; closed Mon)*, which offers delicate Javanese dishes in a brown café ambience. Students tired of traditional *hutspot* (Dutch stew) head for **Camino Real** *(Doelensteeg 8* ☎*(071) 149069* ▢ AE ◉ ⊙ *last orders 10pm)*, a spacious café-restaurant furnished in an eccentric Italian-inspired Post Modern style. Although specializing in Latin American dishes, it also offers traditional *broodjes* (sandwiches), and has the added attraction of a garden.

The most inviting places in which to drink in Leiden are the student cafés clustered around the university. Try **Barrera** *(Rapenburg 56)*, a friendly, somewhat shabby brown café on the town's principal canal, where students pontificate after classes. In the shadow of an old city gate, **Huis de Bijlen** *(Morsstraat 60)* is a popular student café with a spacious terrace for summer days. Local cafés in Leiden are perhaps *too* local for tourists to visit, but you might want to glance into **Harmonie** *(Breestraat 16)*, with its 19thC stained-glass windows showing boisterous drinking scenes, or **De Bonte Koe** *(Hooglandsekerkchoorsteeg 31)*, a local café decorated with giant tile tableaux of grazing cows.

SHOPPING   Department stores and a few interesting shops are found on **Breestraat**, while boutiques and chain stores can be found along the meandering **Haarlemmerstraat**, which was originally a dike along the N bank of the Rhine. Unusual antique stores and specialized antiquarian bookstores abound in the narrow streets around the Pieterskerk, such as the alluring **Diefsteeg** and **Pieterskerkchoorsteeg.**

MARKEN
Map **2**B5. *18km (11 miles)* NE *of Amsterdam. Population: 2,000. By NZH bus 111, hourly from Amsterdam Centraal Station; by car, through the IJ-tunnel, then* N *on E10; by boat, Marken Express, every 45mins from Volendam and Monnickendam Mar-Oct.*

The curious fishing community on the island of Marken in the Zuider Zee was discovered by French travelers in the 19thC, who were amazed at the eccentric locals dressed in bright costumes and living in remarkable black tarred houses on stilts. Soon steamboats were bringing flocks of visitors to the island and Marken became an early casualty of the tourist industry. Marken suffered a further blow to its identity when the enclosure of the Zuider Zee in 1932 destroyed its fishing industry, and, since the construction of a causeway to the mainland in 1957, the community has become a parody of itself.

But Marken is at least not vulgarized, and its tightly packed clusters of houses perched on hillocks *(werven)* are architecturally fascinating. Marken is particularly jolly on Monday, when large quantities of old-fashioned laundry (not a T-shirt or pair of fluorescent socks in sight) are strung along the clotheslines in a manner that is a touch too regimented to ring true.

The busiest areas of Marken are the **Havenbuurt** (harbor quarter) and **Kerkbuurt** (church quarter), and to the E are quieter *werven* such as **Rozenwerf**. A brisk walk along the dike leads to a lonely lighthouse.

Regular boat services are operated by **Marken Express** *(Mar-Oct daily 9am-4.45pm* ☎ *(02995) 1707)* from Marken to Monnickendam or Volendam. An interesting option for those without a car is the NZH C-toer, a combined boat-bus pass that allows one to take a bus from Amsterdam to Monnickendam, boat from Monnickendam to Marken and from Marken to Volendam, then bus back to Amsterdam *(tickets obtainable from NZH kiosk at Centraal Station, opposite Victoria Hotel)*.

SIGHTS AND PLACES OF INTEREST

MARKER MUSEUM
Kerkbuurt 44-47 🖼 ♿ *Open Easter-Oct Mon-Sat 10am-4pm; Sun noon-4pm.*
This tiny house packed with bright furniture gives an idea of the remarkably cramped interiors of fishermen's dwellings on Marken. Slide shows (with commentary in English or German) portray life on the island and explain the significance of the local costumes, which range in color from bright red to black depending on the occasion.

🍴 **De Taanderij** *(Havenbuurt 1* ☎ *(02996) 1364; open Tues-Sun 10am-9pm; Sept-Easter reduced hrs; closed Mon)* is a pleasant café-restaurant overlooking the harbor, with a pottery in the basement.

MONNICKENDAM
Map 2B4. Noord-Holland, 16km (10 miles) N of Amsterdam. Population 9,500. By NZH bus 115 from Amsterdam Centraal Station; by car, through IJ-tunnel, then E10 i *De Zarken 2 (in the Grote Kerk tower) 1140 AA* ☎*(02995) 1998.*
Monnickendam is a small and rather sleepy fishing town with pleasant canals and attractive buildings. The main activity is centered around the harbor, where a few eel smokehouses survive and a ferry departs *(Mar-Oct)* to the former island of Marken *(* ☎ *(02995) 1707 for departure times)*.

EVENTS Saturday is market day in Monnickendam.

🍴 On Monnickendam's harbor front, where the smell of smoked eel wafts around enticingly, the café-restaurant **Nieuw Stuttenburgh** *(Haringburgwal 4*

☎ *(02995) 1869* ▭ *to* ▣ AE ☉ VISA *)* offers an interesting menu of fish and meat dishes, including the inexpensive *Monnickendammer twaalf uurtje* (a lunch platter of three types of smoked fish). The interior is engagingly eccentric, with its mechanical musical instruments, pond, stuffed alligator and canary.

UTRECHT

Map 2D4. 35km (22 miles) s of Amsterdam, 57km (35 miles) NE of Rotterdam, 61km (38 miles) E of The Hague. Population: 230,400. By train, 30mins from Amsterdam CS, 45mins from Rotterdam CS, 50mins from Den Haag CS
i Vredenburg 90 3511 BD ☎06-34034085 Ex(030) 331417. For information on public transportation in Utrecht ☎(030) 363500.

Originating in the 1stC AD as a Roman outpost on the Rhine frontier, Utrecht grew to become a major religious center in the Middle Ages; much of its interest lies in its numerous churches and convents, and in the sculpture and painting that developed during this period. During Holland's Golden Age, Utrecht declined into a quiet backwater, and the hurricane of 1674, which toppled most of its church towers, did nothing to boost morale. The mood of melancholy continued into the 18thC, when the Scottish writer James Boswell, sent to Utrecht by his father to study law, complained: "I groaned with the idea of living all winter in so shocking a place."

The development of the **Hoog Catharijne** shopping and office complex in the 1970s has brought a new, restless energy to the city, although there are still areas such as **Nieuwegracht** where the mood of genteel decline has not totally vanished.

EVENTS　　On Saturday Utrecht is given over to markets, including a genial **food market** on Vredenburg (also on Wednesday), crammed with stalls selling waffles and raw herrings to eat on the spot, or cheese and plants to take home. There's also a Saturday **stamp market** on Vismarkt *(noon-5pm)*, a **flea market** on Willemstraat and around the Jacobikerk *(8am-1pm)*, an **antique market** in **De Ossekop** *(Voorstraat 19)* and a **plant market** on the Janskerkhof. The most spectacular sight, however, is the **flower market**, which spreads along Oude Gracht from Lange Viestraat to the Stadhuisbrug. A peak of excitement is reached at around 5pm when the market-traders hawk gigantic bunches of flowers at irresistible prices.

Utrecht is a music-loving city, and scarcely a day goes by when there is not a classical concert in the modern **Vredenburg Muziekcentrum** *(☎(030) 313144)* or in one of the many churches. There are regular concerts in the **Pieterskerk** *(☎(030) 311485)*, the **Nicolaikerk** *(☎(030) 315734)* and the **Domkerk** *(Sat at 3.30pm ☎(030) 310403)*. August is a quiet month, but in early September the town comes alive with the **Holland Festival Oude Muziek Utrecht** *(for info: Postbus 734, 3500 AS Utrecht ☎(030) 340981)*, which features music from the Middle Ages to the early Romantics. Concerts are also played on the **Dom carillon** every Thursday evening, and the cloisters are kept open for listeners.

The cultural center **'t Hoogt** *(Hoogt 4 ☎(030) 328388)* offers an interesting film program; the **Oude Pothuis** *(Oudegracht 279 ☎(030) 318970)* is a basement jazz café; and **Astaire** *(Voorstraat 102 ☎(030) 319362)* is a café-disco that appeals to the 1960s generation.

The fortnightly *Uit in Utrecht,* available from the VVV, lists music, movies, theater and other events.

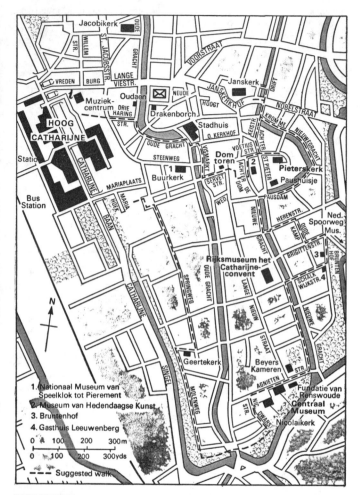

THE TOWN

Like it or not, a visit to Utrecht is bound to begin in the brash Hoog Catharijne complex, which contains the rail station and parking lots, as well as shops and offices. Its only redeeming feature is the **Muziekcentrum**, a sympathetic modern design by Herman Hertzberger (follow signs to Muziekcentrum Vredenburg to avoid the crowds). As you leave the Muziekcentrum, you may be puzzled by some fragments of masonry below the bridge. These are all that remain of an **Italianate fortress** which was built in the 16thC by Charles V to keep the rebellious citizens in check. The strangest relic of all is the **gun emplacement** in the cellar below the tourist office. Several fragments from a demolished Art Nouveau office building, **De Utrecht**, also decorate the tourist office.

On leaving Vredenburg, cross the square of the same name and head down the lane Drie Haringstraat to reach **Oude Gracht**, a sunken canal with deserted quays, winding gracefully through the old city. Several medieval tower houses survive on Oude Gracht, notably **Oudaen** (#99), dating from 1320, and **Drakenborch** (#114), built in 1280. By descending to the lower quay, you can discover numerous lamp-post consoles with modern sculpture illustrating scenes from Utrecht's history.

Head s down Oude Gracht, pausing on the bridges to enjoy the lively scene, completed by the exquisite cathedral tower. After passing the **Stadhuis**, continue down Vismarkt and turn left along Servetstraat, which leads to the cathedral tower. Just before you come to the tower, a gate on the right leads into a quiet garden, **Flora's Hof** *(open Mon-Sat 10am-5pm)*, which formerly belonged to the bishop's palace. A narrow lane leads from here to **Domplein**, the site of the nave of the cathedral, which was brought down by a hurricane. Cross the road and walk through the **Pandhof** (cathedral cloister) *(Domplein* 🖸 *open Sat 11am-5pm, Sun noon-5pm, and Apr-Oct, Mon-Fri 10am-5pm, but to 8.30pm on Tues, Thurs in May only)*, to reach Achter de Dom. Turn left, past the **Museum van Hedendaagse Kunst** *(Achter de Dom 12-14* ☎ *(030) 314185* 🖸 ⬛ *open Tues-Sat 10am-5pm, Sun, hols 1-5pm)*, which exhibits Dutch and international art of the 1970s and '80s, and right down Voetiusstraat to reach the tranquil precinct of the **Pieterskerk**.

On leaving the square, turn right and follow Achter St Pieter to **Keistraat**. The unusual corner house (#8) was built by a 17thC eccentric, Everard Meyster, who won a bet by persuading the people of Amersfoort to drag an enormous **boulder** into the center of the town, where it is still to be seen. The pretzel-shaped doorhandle is a reminder of the famous feast of beer and pretzels that Meyster threw in honor of this achievement, remembered too in the street name **Keistraat** (Boulder Street).

Keistraat leads into the Janskerkhof, which boasts several dignified buildings, especially the neat 17thC Classical house at **Janskerkhof 13**. Yet this former precinct of the Janskerk is now a somewhat frantic area of town, and to get back to more tranquil parts, head back down the canal Drift, then turn left along **Kromme Nieuwegracht**, a quiet canal of 18thC town houses that follows a former loop in the Rhine. This leads to **Pausdam**, a picturesque convergence of quiet streets and canals, which is overlooked by the beautiful late Gothic **Paushuisje**, built in the early 16thC by Adriaen Florisz., who in 1522 became the first (and only) Dutch pope.

Nieuwegracht is a deep 14thC canal with deserted, overgrown quays along the waterside and quiet streets of 18thC houses above. A rusticated 17thC portal at **Nieuwegracht 7** leads into a courtyard containing a fragment of an 11thC Benedictine abbey, which formed one point in a cross of five Romanesque churches planned by the ambitious Bishop Bernold. The Baroque gables at **Nieuwegracht 15-17** are unusually flamboyant for Utrecht, while the house at **Nieuwegracht 37** is a fetching example of miniaturized Classical architecture.

A short detour can be made to the left down Herenstraat, turning right down Oude Kamp and left into Brigittenstraat, to reach a quiet land-scaped **park** overlooked by elegant 19thC villas. Turn right here to reach the **Bruntenhof**, a row of 17thC almshouses built by the city wall. The **Governors' Chamber** (#5) was reached through an ornate Renaissance portal adorned with melancholy symbols of mortality.

Walk along Bruntenhof to the **Gasthuis Leeuwenberg** — a 14thC hospital for plague victims — and turn right along Schalkwijkstraat to get back to Nieuwegracht. Turn left and follow Nieuwegracht to the SE corner of the old city, where a Classical portal (#205) marks a *hofje* founded in 1651 by Maria van Pallaes. The simple almshouses are located around the corner in Agnietenstraat, while a second *hofje* — the late 16thC **Beyerskameren** — is discovered by turning right into Lange Nieuw-straat. From here enjoy also the full effect of the 18thC Rococo facade of the **Fundatie van Renswoude**, an enlightened orphanage for boys, on Agnietenstraat.

Continue along Agnietenstraat past the **Centraal Museum** (see below) and turn left down Nicolaasdwarsstraat to reach a 19thC park romantically laid out on the site of the old city walls. Turn right, walk through the tunnel and cross the road. You can then continue through the park, following the former moat N and passing on the right a series of convivial 19thC working-class streets known locally as **De seven steegjes** (The Seven Alleys). Leave the park when you reach the snug medieval parish church, the **Geertekerk**, turning right, then left along Springweg. At **Springweg 110-30** is a row of 11 almshouses founded in 1583 by Cornelis van Mierop, Dean of the cathedral, while at Springweg 104 is the colorful 16thC gateway of the municipal orphanage.

At the end of Springweg, turn left and cross the square to reach a tiny doorway (#29), which leads into a warren of medieval alleys known as the **Mariahoek**. This eventually brings you to the cloister of the **Maria-kerk**, all that remains of the Romanesque church that completed Bishop Bernold's cross of churches.

CHURCHES

In the Middle Ages, Utrecht was the main religious center of the north-ern Netherlands, and although its skyline no longer bristles with spires, it still boasts numerous interesting churches. Most of these are open during the summer, and enthusiastic guides are on the spot to explain the curiosities.

The cathedral, or **Domkerk** *(Domplein* ☎ *(030) 310403* ▣ *ʎ* ▪ *open May-Sept 10am-5pm, Oct-Apr 11am-4pm; Sun 2-4pm),* begun in 1254, was still unfinished when a hurricane ripped through the town in 1674 and brought the inadequately buttressed nave crashing to the ground.

All that now remains of the Gothic masterpiece is the soaring **choir**, built during 1254-1321 in the style of Cologne Cathedral, and the 15thC **cloisters**, with tympana showing scenes from the life of St Martin (who gave his cloak to a beggar), and a curious traceried window made to look as if it were held together with rope.

Utrecht also has two Romanesque churches, which formed part of a cross of four churches planned in the 11thC by Bishop Bernold. His favourite church was the **Pieterskerk** *(Pieterskerkhof 5 ✗ open Tues-Fri 10am-4.30pm),* built in 1048 of a distinctive grayish tuff, with vivid red sandstone columns in the nave. A peaceful mood is conferred by the arc of houses enclosing the **Pieterskerkhof**, which until the Reformation was a walled precinct which was immune from municipal jurisdiction.

Bishop Bernold's second church, the **Janskerk** *(Janskerkhof ☎ (030) 316440* ◼ *open Mon-Fri 9am-5pm),* was completed about 1250. The design was faulty, however, and the red sandstone columns later had to be enclosed by brick pillars (one of which has been exposed to show the original column). The choir was rebuilt in late Gothic style in the 16thC. After the Reformation, a chapel at the w end was converted into a guard house and adorned with gaudy military emblems.

Utrecht's oldest parish church is the **Buurkerk**, which now houses Utrecht's marvelous museum of mechanical musical instruments. The present building is a good example of a Gothic hall church, although the choir was demolished in the 17thC. The church tower, intended to rival the Domtoren (see page 310), attained only a modest height before funds ran out.

Another parish church, the **Nicolaikerk** *(Nicolaaskerkhof* ◼ *open May-Sept Tues-Sat 10am-5pm, Sun 1-5pm; enter through Centraal Museum),* was built at the s end of the city in the mid-12thC. Romanesque details can still be seen in the **Westwork**, although the interior was rebuilt under Bishop David of Burgundy as a late Gothic hall church. The 12thC **Jacobikerk** *(St Jacobsstraat ☎ (030) 317862* ◼ *open June and Sept Tues-Fri 1-5pm, July, Aug Tues-Fri noon-5pm),* which stands at the N end of the city, was also rebuilt in the 15thC as a hall church. Its spire, recently restored after being brought down by the 17thC hurricane, lends dignity to an otherwise abandoned area of the city. The 19thC **Willibrorduskerk** *(Minrebroederstraat 21* ◼ ✗ *open Mon, Tues, Thurs, Fri 10am-4pm, Wed noon-4pm)* contains an exuberance of neo-Gothic detail in its murals, sculpture, iron-work, wood carvings and stained glass.

SIGHTS AND PLACES OF INTEREST

BOTANISCHE TUIN (Botanical Gardens)
Fort Hoofddijk, Budapestlaan 17 ☎(030) 531826 ◼ *Open Mon-Fri 8.30am-4pm; Sat 10am-4pm, Sun. Closed weekends Oct-Mar.*
A former 19thC fort near the Utrecht university campus has been imaginatively planted with an extensive collection of botanical specimens. The flourishing **rock garden** is reckoned among the best in the world, with rare plants from China, the Himalayas and the Alps. Avoid Fridays, when newly-weds scramble up the rocks to pose for romantic portraits.

CENTRAAL MUSEUM ★
Agnietenstraat ☎(030) 362362 ▣ ◗ *Open Tues-Sat 10am-5pm; Sun, hols 1-5pm. Bus 2 to Agnietenstraat.*
Housed in a 15thC convent, the Centraal Museum in Utrecht is a confusing but captivating hodgepodge of collections brought under one roof, including a cos-

tume museum, a set of period rooms in Gothic, Renaissance, Classical and Louis XIV-XVI styles; a Modern Art collection; a collection of Old Masters; a coin collection; a department of applied art; and a Utrecht historical collection.

Be sure to see the collection of paintings by the 16thC Utrecht artist **Jan van Scorel**, which is displayed on the upper floor of the 16thC **Agnietenklooster** chapel. These include several early 16thC group portraits of members of the Utrecht Jerusalem Brotherhood, carrying palm leaves to signify that they had completed a pilgrimage to Jerusalem. Their faces are rendered with a penetrating Netherlandish Realism, apart from the face of the one woman — referred to simply as Dirck Evert's daughter — whose fair complexion seems too good to be true amid so many warts and wrinkles. Other works such as the *Entry into Jerusalem* show the influence of the Italian Renaissance, which Van Scorel encountered during his time as keeper of the Vatican treasures under Pope Adrian VI.

The museum also has works by Utrecht Masters such as Abraham Bloemaert, whose early paintings are highly Mannerist; Gerard van Honthorst, a follower of Caravaggio; and Jan Both, who fell under the spell of the Italian landscape. The 20thC collection includes several disturbing works by Dutch Magic Realists such as Carel Willink and Pyke Koch.

Not to be missed is the **17thC dollhouse** (in the Classical period room), with its collection of remarkably detailed furniture, porcelain, Old Master paintings and globes.

DOMTOREN ★

Domplein ☎(030) 919540 ▣ ⨍ *compulsory, on the hour up to 4pm. Open Apr-Oct Mon-Fri 10am-5pm; Sat 11am-5pm; Sun, hols noon-5pm; Nov-Mar Sat 11am-5pm; Sun, hols noon-5pm. Bus 2 or 22 to Domplein.*

The ethereal cathedral tower of Utrecht is one of the masterpieces of Burgundian architecture and appears in the background of numerous medieval paintings. Three architects worked on the 112m (364-foot) tower during its construction from 1321-82, the most notable being Jan van den Dom II, who gave the **octagonal lantern** at the top its delicate lace-like tracery. Not everyone was pleased with this Gothic extravaganza, however; the ascetic monk Geert Groot denounced it as a symbol of vanity and pride, and during its construction had recurrent dreams of its collapse.

Yet even the hurricane of 1674 did not shake the Domtoren and it remains today a symbol of Utrecht's religious greatness, despite the unwarranted indignity of having buses pass through its arch.

NATIONAAL MUSEUM VAN SPEELKLOK TOT PIEREMENT ★

Buurkerkhof 10 ☎(030) 312789 ▣ � ⨍ *compulsory, lasting 1 hour, beginning on the hour 10am-4pm* ✸ ▣ *Open Tues-Sat 10am-5pm; Sun, hols 1-5pm. Commentary given in English, French or German on request. Bus 2 to Domplein.*

One of the most enjoyable museums in the Netherlands is the Nationaal Museum Van Speelklok tot Pierement (From Carillon to Barrel Organ), which is located in the 13thC **Buurkerk** (see page 309). The museum illustrates the development of mechanical musical instruments from the 18th-20thC.

What gives the museum its particular appeal is that many of the instruments are played during the guided tour, which is given by highly informed and enthusiastic music students. Among the more unusual inventions are a mechanical rabbit, a musical chair and an extraordinary "Phono-Liszt Viola" from a Berlin café, which conceals three pneumatic violins in its casing. The most striking exhibits, however, are the street and dance-hall organs.

It is worth the ascent to the "promenade" floor to view the architecture and medieval frescoes. There is also a small exhibition on the history of the Buurkerk, including the story of Sister Bertken, who occupied a penitential cell in the choir for some 57 years, until her death in 1514.

NEDERLANDS SPOORWEGMUSEUM

Maliebaan ☎*(030) 306206* 🖼 ✴ � ☕ *Open Tues-Sat 10am-5pm; Sun, hols 1-5pm. Bus 3 to Maliebaan.*

Situated in a handsome 19thC rail station that closed down in 1939, the Netherlands national railway museum is a must for all rail enthusiasts. Three disused platforms are lined with gleaming steam ,rains and wood-paneled coaches, while the station building contains an impressive display of model trains, tin signs, and antiquated furniture. One highlight is the a station master's desk, complete with a mechanical mouse nibbling at a cheese sandwich. Children can work the controls of a marshaling yard or clamber up into a signal box, then gulp down a chocolate milk served in a 1911 Hungarian restaurant car. The most recent addition is the *Spoorbermtuin*, a small garden showing the types of weeds that flourish along Dutch rail embankments.

RIETVELD-SCHRÖDERHUIS

Prins Hendriklaan 50a ☎*(030) 517926* 🖼 ✗ *compulsory. Open Tues-Sun 12.30-5pm. Visits by appointment only; to reserve* ☎*Mon-Fri 11am-5pm. Bus 4 to De Hoogstraat.*

Built in 1923, the Rietveld-Schröderhuis had a profound influence on modern Dutch architecture. Tacked onto the end of a dull row of 19thC houses, the red, blue, yellow and gray house was designed by the local architect Gerrit Rietveld in collaboration with the recently-widowed Truus Schröder. To give the house a modern appearance, the walls, which are in fact made of brick, were concealed under a layer of plaster.

Ingenious design features are demonstrated during the guided tour, including **sliding walls** that convert the upper floor into a single space, and a **cupboard** in the hall built to hold a child's wooden beach cart (the original, designed by Rietveld, is now in the Centraal Museum in Utrecht).

Rietveld and Schröder later lived together in the house, and the architect converted the garage into a studio. The house once stood on the edge of the city, but the idyllic location was destroyed in 1963 by the construction of an elevated section of the N222 freeway a few yards from the house. Rietveld died the following year.

RIJKSMUSEUM HET CATHARIJNECONVENT ★

Nieuwegracht 63 ☎*(030) 313835* 🖼 ⚅ ☕ *Open Tues-Fri 10am-5pm; Sat, Sun, hols 11am-5pm. Bus 2 to Lange Nieuwstraat.*

The history of Christianity in the Netherlands is the theme of this fascinating museum, located in an attractively restored 15thC monastery that once belonged to the Knights of St John. The highlight of the collection is the sculpture and painting from the Burgundian era, including several Renaissance works by Jan van Scorel of Utrecht, whose tomb is also displayed.

The museum is arranged thematically and the medieval works are mainly found on the ground floor of the *kloostergebouw* (convent building), which is reached from the entrance hall through a cellar passage. The Reformation and the theoretical quarrels of the 17thC are also covered in the *kloostergebouw*. Religious developments from the 17th-20thC are dealt with in the *grachtenhuis* (canal house).

🛏 **Des Pays Bas** *(Janskerkhof 10, 3512 BL* ☎*(030) 333321* ℻*(030) 313169* 🔲 ☕ ⛁ AE ✦ 🅾 VISA *bus 3 to Janskerkhof)* is a distinguished traditional Dutch hotel close to the Dom, blessed with an airy Winter Garden. A modern alternative is the **Scandic Crown** *(Westplein 50, 3531 BL* ☎*(030) 925200* ℻*(030) 925199* 🔲 � AE ✦ 🅾 VISA *120 rms* 🍽 ⟨€ *)*, a comfortable hotel hidden behind a dazzling glass front, a 5-minute stroll from the rail station and **Jaarbeurs Congress Center**. The **Malie** *(Maliestraat 2, 3581 SL* ☎*(030) 316424* ℻*(030) ·340661* 🔲 *29 rms* AE ✦ 🅾 VISA *bus 4, 11 to Oude Kerkstraat)* is a small, friendly hotel occupying two handsome 19thC houses in a elegant quarter of the city. With its attractive bedrooms, ubiquitous flowers, and leafy garden, it is the perfect choice for travelers on a budget.

Martin Fagel's **Café de Paris** *(Drieharingstraat 16* ☎*(030) 317503* ▥▯ ▣▣ ▣▣ *closed Sun)* offers traditional French brasserie cooking amid a decor of old iron lamps and bizarre antiques; **Selamat Makan** *(Voorstraat 100* ☎*(030) 368917* ▭ *last orders 11pm; closed Tues, Wed, mid-July to mid-Aug)* is a pleasant Indonesian restaurant offering dishes to please most palates. Try the friendly, fern-filled **Hedendaags Lunchcafé** *(Achter de Dom 12-14, open Tues-Sat 10am-5pm, Sun 1-5pm)* for an *uitsmijter* or *broodje*, or sample Dutch *poffertjes* (tiny pancakes served with butter and a heavy dusting of icing sugar) in the mirror-filled 19thC ambience of **Victor Consael** *(Neude, open daily 10am-8pm)*. Enticing Italian *broodjes* piled high with salami, cheese and peppers are sold in large numbers at the **Broodje Mario** stall on Oude Gracht (near Café Oudaen).

Utrecht's most distinguished café is **Stadskasteel Oudaen** *(Oudegracht 99)*, opened in 1986 in a renovated 14thC tower house. **Graaf Floris** *(Vismarkt 13)* is a handsome café with wood paneling and old lamps, popular with students and professors alike. For a more typical brown café, try the pleasant **Tapperiji De Luifel** *(Neude 36)*, where flowers grace the tables, although sawdust is strewn on the floor. Student cafés, including the picturesque **De Vingerhoed** *(Donkere Gaard 11)*, are concentrated on Donkere Gaard and Wed. **Café Zeezicht** *(Nobelstraat 2)* is a friendly, modern café featuring art exhibitions, live groups and women's events.

SHOPPING   **Hoog Catharijne** is a vast modern shopping center with shops of every description, while **La Vie** on Vredenburg is a more elegant center with fashion stores and an elegant **Bijenkorf** branch. A large pedestrianized shopping area spreads to the s of here. **Lichte Gaard** and **Lijnmarkt** contain some enticing clothes stores in 18thC buildings, while **Oude Gracht** to the s of here is good for interesting boutiques, avant-garde jewelers and art galleries. **De Witte Tandenwinkel** *(Oude Gracht 226)* sells nothing but toothbrushes, while Utrecht's most inviting pâtisserie is **Noteboom** *(Oudekerkhof 9)*, which has a tearoom where you can sample the local specialty *botersprits* (butter shortbread). Concealed in an alley beside the 't Hoogt cultural center is a restored 19thC shop **Erven Betje Boerhave** *(Hoogt 6* ☎*(030) 316628)*, which sells mustard, coffee and tea in traditional packaging, as well as old-fashioned candies such as *drop* (liquorice) and *kerk-pepermuntjes* (church peppermints).

VOLENDAM

Map 2A5. Noord-Holland, 21km (13 miles) N of Amsterdam. Population: 16,890. By NZH bus 110; by car, through IJ-tunnel, then E10 **i** *Haven 39 1130 AA* ☎*(02993) 63747.*

Life in the small fishing town of Volendam has never been quite the same since its discovery in 1873 by an art historian, who described its quaint local costumes in the sort of glowing terms reserved today for remote South Sea island paradises. A few years later artists began to arrive in Volendam to paint romantic scenes of fishermen in baggy black breeches and women in curious peaked hats.

Much of Volendam is now tacky, with English fish-and-chip shops and photographers specializing in group portraits in local costume. However, the SPAANDER HOTEL (see page 313) — where the international community of artists was based — retains an old-fashioned charm. The hotel café in particular should be visited for its remarkable collection of **19thC Romantic paintings** donated by former guests. The café waitresses wear traditional costume.

The warren of streets behind the dike known as the **Doolhof** (maze) is also worth a glance.

For an overnight stay in Volendam, the **Spaander Hotel** *(Haven 15-19* **☎**(02993) 63595 [Fx](02993) 69615 [II] *81 rms* ⊟ AE ⊕ ⊚ VISA ⇎ ⬗*)* has bedrooms tastefully furnished in a modern style, many with views of the IJsselmeer. The old part of the hotel is crammed with mementos of the artists who stayed here in the late 19thC.

ZAANSTAD

Map 2B4. Noord-Holland, 16km (10 miles) N of Amsterdam. Population: 65,390. By train, 10mins from Amsterdam Centraal Station to Zaandam, 15mins to Koog-Zaandijk; by car, through Coentunnel, then A8 **i** *Gedempte Gracht 76, Zaandam* **☎**(075) 162221; *also at the tea house, Zaanse Schans.*

The string of towns (now collectively known as Zaanstad) along the river Zaan was a major center of industrial activity as early as the 17thC. By the 18thC there were some 1,000 windmills in operation, supporting a diversity of industries such as shipbuilding, paper-making, oil-milling and whaling.

The main town of **Zaandam** still reverberates with the excitement of Czar Peter the Great's incognito visit in 1697, which has something of the air of an old Russian fairy-tale. Posing as the sailor Peter Mikhailov, the Czar came to Zaandam to study local shipbuilding methods and lodged for a few days in the humble dwelling of Gerrit Kist, a smith who had worked in the Czar's service in St Petersburg.

Located in a baffling maze of streets near Zaandam harbor, the **Czaar Peterhuisje** ★ *(Krimp 23* ⬛ **✗** *open Tues-Fri 10am-1pm, 2-5pm, Sat, Sun 1-5pm)* — now with a decided tilt and enclosed by a protective structure — has become a shrine to which emperors (including Napoleon), politicians, poets and writers have paid homage. The concierge, a Russian emigré, communicates an extraordinary store of knowledge, and enthusiastically points out numerous mementos ranging from the box bed in which the Czar slept to a final demand for unpaid property tax sent to Czar Alexander III, who was at one time the owner of the house.

On leaving the house, turn right, then left along Hogendijk to reach the **harbor** and, slightly farther on, a **statue of Peter the Great** working on a ship.

To obtain an idea of how the Zaan area once looked, visit the **Zaanse Schans** (on the river Zaan at Zaandijk, a short walk from Koog-Zaandijk rail station), where a number of typical 17th-18thC houses and windmills have been reconstructed. Some are open to the public *(*⬛ *open Apr-Oct daily, Nov-Mar Sat and Sun only)* and include a 19thC grocer's store, a museum of clocks, a furnished interior, a clog-maker and an antique store.

If all this seems somewhat artificial, cross the river to the town of Zaandijk and visit the fascinating **Zaanlandse Oudheidkamer** *(Lage-*

dijk 80 ☎ *(075) 83628* ▨ *Ƙ compulsory; open Tues-Fri 10am-noon, 2-4pm, Sun 2-4pm; closed Sat, Mon; ring bell for entry)*, a local history museum located in the early 18thC home of a Mennonite merchant. The 18thC rooms, toys, kitchen utensils and paintings of the Zaan are all of interest, but the best feature of the house is undoubtedly the room at the front overlooking the river. Since the river Zaan was once the main thoroughfare of the region, most of the houses face the river, and a boat excursion from the Zaanse Schans is therefore the best way to appreciate their eccentric green wooden gables.

❧ **De Saense Schans** *(Lagedijk 32-34, Zaandijk* ☎ *(075) 211911* ▥ ➡ ⊒ ☐ ▱ ❦ ◄€ *)* is a comfortable modern hotel enjoying a panoramic view across the river to the windmills and green gables of the Zaanse Schans.

⊨ **De Hoop op d'Swarte Walvis** *(Kalverringdijk 15, Zaanse Schans* ☎ *(075) 165540* Fx *(075) 162476* ▥ *to* ▥ ➡ AE ☉ ☐ VISA *last orders 10pm; closed Sun)* — the name means "In the Hope of a Black Whale" — is one of Holland's most idyllic restaurants, occupying a cluster of 18thC wooden buildings that includes the former orphanage from the village of Westzaan and a store for whaling gear. The restaurant, tastefully decorated with seafaring memorabilia, enjoys a splendid view of the river Zaan, and the French-style cuisine is excellent.

Words and phrases

An introduction to Dutch

"Here, though destitute of what may be properly called a language of their own," wrote Oliver Goldsmith in 1759, "all the languages are understood, cultivated, and spoken." While it is certainly true that the Dutch are conscientious linguists (speaking good English, German and French), it is wrong to see Dutch merely as a corruption of German. Moreover, even as a casual visitor, it is rewarding to master the basic pronunciation and learn a few essential words.

In common with German, Dutch fuses words together into unwieldy compounds, but unlike German it has streamlined its case system and manages quite well with only two genders: *de* for masculine and feminine words and *het* for neuter. A curious habit of the Dutch is to reduce everything to diminutives by the addition of the suffix — *je* (e.g., *broodje,* a sandwich; *pilsje,* a harmless little beer).

VOWELS

Dutch vowel sounds are particularly baffling to foreigners, and some sounds have no equivalent in English. There is also a distinction between short and long vowel sounds. Words are divided into syllables, each syllable beginning with a consonant; e.g., Haar/lem, Ap/pel. If a syllable ends in a vowel, this will be a long vowel even if it is only a single vowel; e.g., E/dam. Double vowels will always be long.

a	(when short)	as the u in cut; e.g Damrak
a	(when long) or aa	as the a in are; e.g. Haarlem
e	(when short)	as the e in bet; e.g. Delft
e	(when long) or ee	as the a in baby; e.g. Steen, Edam
i	(short)	as the i in sit; e.g. Prinsengracht
ie	(long)	as the ie in pier; e.g. bier
o	(when short)	as the o in dot; e.g. bos
o	(when long) or oo	as the o in no; e.g. Volendam, telefoon
u	(when short)	as the e in the (unstressed); e.g. brug
u	(when long) or uu	as the u in tune; e.g. Utrecht, buurt

eu	as the e in the (unstressed); e.g. Beurs
ui	a treacherous diphthong, close to the ou in out, but ending with a slight i as in item; e.g. zuid
ij or ei	another tongue twister, close to the i in light; e.g. Rijksmuseum, IJsselmeer, Leidseplein (but when ij unstressed at end of word, as the e in the (unstressed); e.g. Stedelijk
ou	as the ou in loud; e.g. oud
oe	as the ou in soup; e.g. soep
ieuw	similar to the ew in few; nieuw

CONSONANTS

w	as the v in vole; e.g. Waterland
j	as the y in yawn; e.g. Jordaan
th	as the t in tea; e.g thee
ch or g	as the ch in loch; e.g. Schiphol, Gouda
b and d	soften to p and t sounds at the end of words
n	when unstressed, becomes silent at the end of a word; e.g. Leiden

REFERENCE WORDS

Monday	*maandag*	April	*april*
Tuesday	*dinsdag*	May	*mei*
Wednesday	*woensdag*	June	*juni*
Thursday	*donderdag*	July	*juli*
Friday	*vrijdag*	August	*augustus*
Saturday	*zaterdag*	September	*september*
Sunday	*zondag*	October	*oktober*
January	*januari*	November	*november*
February	*februari*	December	*december*
March	*maart*		

1	een	11	elf	21	eenentwintig
2	twee	12	twaalf	22	tweeëntwintig
3	drie	13	dertien	30	dertig
4	vier	14	veertien	40	viertig
5	vijf	15	vijftien	50	vijftig
6	zes	16	zestien	60	zestig
7	zeven	17	zeventien	70	zeventig
8	acht	18	achttien	80	tachtig
9	negen	19	negentien	90	negentig
10	tien	20	twintig	100	honderd

First	*eerste*	quarter-past....	*kwart over....*
Second	*tweede*	half-past one	*half twee* (i.e.,
Third	*derde*	half of two)	
Fourth	*vierde*	quarter to....	*kwart*
....o'clock	*....uur*	*voor....*	

316

Mr   *mijnheer*
Mrs   *mevrouw*
Miss   *mejuffrouw*

Ladies   *dames*
Gents   *heren*

BASIC VOCABULARY

Yes   *ja*
No   *nee*
Please   *alstublieft* (formal),
alsjeblieft (informal)
Thank you   *dank u wel* (formal),
dank je (informal)
Thanks   *bedankt*
You're welcome   *geen
dank/graag gedaan*
Sorry   *sorry*
Excuse me   *neem me niet kwalijk*
(formal)
Good   *goed*
Bad   *slecht*
Well   *goed*
Badly   *slecht*
And   *en*
But   *maar*
Very   *zeer*
All   *alle*
Open   *open*
Closed   *gesloten*
Hello   *hallo*
Good morning   *goede morgen*
Good afternoon   *goede middag*
Good evening   *goede avond*

goodbye   *dag/tot ziens*
Left   *links*
Right   *rechts*
Straight ahead   *rechtdoor*
Day   *dag*
Month   *maand*
Year   *jaar*
Here   *hier*
There   *daar*
Big   *groot*
Small   *klein*
Hot   *warm*
Cold   *koud*
Toilet   *toilet/WC*
I speak English   *ik spreek Engels*
Do you speak English?   *spreekt u
Engels?*
I don't know   *ik weet het niet*
I am English/American   *ik kom
uit Engeland/Amerika*
Do you have?   *heeft u?*
Where is?   *waar is?*
How much does it cost?   *hoeveel
kost het?*
What time is it?   *hoe laat is het?*
Is there a...?   *is er een...?*

SIGNS DECODER

Stadhuis   *town hall*
Gracht/kanaal/singel   *canal*
Brug   *bridge*
Straat   *street*
Laan   *avenue*
Steeg   *alley*
Poort   *gate*
Perron/spoor   *platform*
Station   *station*
Ingang   *entrance*
Uitgang   *exit*
Trap   *staircase*

Verdieping   *floor/story*
Wisselkantoor   *foreign exchange*
Loket   *ticket office*
Nooduitgang   *emergency exit*
Noodtrap   *emergency stairs*
Geen toegang/toegang verboden
no entry
Niet roken   *no smoking*
Kassa   *cashier*
Trekken   *pull*
Duwen   *push*
Rondvaart   *boat tour*

ROAD SIGNS

Doorgaand verkeer   *through
traffic*
Omleiding   *detour*

Centrum   *center*
Uit   *exit*
Parkeerplaats   *parking lot*

317

Parkeergarage *multistory parking garage*
Rijverkeer gestremd *no through road*
Uitrit vrijhouden *keep exit clear*
Niet parkeren *no parking*
Pas op/let op *danger*
Snelheid *speed*
Langzaam rijden *go slow*
Fietspad *cycle lane*

Voetganger *pedestrian*
Zachte berm *hard shoulder*
Vrachtwagen *truck*
Bromfiets *moped*
Motor *motorcycle*
m.u.v. *with the exception of*
Oversteken *crossover*
(Loodvrije) benzine *(lead-free) gasoline*

SHOPS

Winkel *shop*
Apotheek *pharmacy, chemist*
Bakker *baker*
Slager *butcher*
Groenteboer *greengrocer*

Boekhandel *bookstore*
Viswinkel *fish store*
Reisbureau *travel agent*
Postkantoor *post office*
Warenhuis *department store*

FOOD AND DRINK

Breakfast *ontbijt*
Lunch *lunch*
Dinner *diner*
Glass *glas*
Bottle *fles*
Beer/lager *bier/pils*
Draft beer *bier van het vat*
Carbonated water *mineraalwater*
Fruit juice *sap*
Orange juice *sinaasappelsap*
Apple juice *appelsap*
Tomato juice *tomatensap*
Milk *melk*
Buttermilk *karnemelk*
Red wine *rode wijn*

White wine *witte wijn*
Dry *droog*
Sweet *zoet*
Salt *zout*
Pepper *peper*
Mustard *mosterd*
Oil *olie*
Vinegar *azijn*
Bread *brood*
Butter *boter*
Cheese *kaas*
Coffee *koffie*
Tea *thee*
Chocolate *chocolade*
Sugar *suiker*
Steak *biefstuk*

MENU DECODER

Aalbessen *red currants*
Aardappels *potatoes*
Aardbeien *strawberries*
Amandelen *almonds*
Ananas *pineapple*
Andijvie *endive*
Anijs *aniseed*
Appel *apple*
Asperges *asparagus*
Bami *egg noodles*
Banaan *banana*
Basilicum *basil*
Biefstuk *steak*

Bieslook *chives*
Bloemkool *cauliflower*
Borst *breast*
Bosbessen *bilberries*
Broodje *roll*
Champignons *mushrooms*
Citroen *lemon*
Dagschotel *dish of the day*
Deeg *dough*
Doperwten *peas*
Dragon *tarragon*
Eend *duck*
Ei *egg*

Erwtensoep *pea soup*
Fazant *pheasant*
Flensjes *small pancakes*
Forel *trout*
Frambozen *raspberries*
Fricandeau *cold, cooked lean pork or veal*
Gambas *king prawns*
Gans *goose*
Garnalen *shrimps*
Gebak *cake*
Gebakken *fried*
Gebraden *baked*
Gekookt *boiled*
Gember *ginger*
Gepocheerd *poached*
Gerookt *smoked*
Gestoofd *stewed*
Gestoomd *steamed*
Gevogelte *poultry*
Gevuld *stuffed*
Groenten *vegetables*
Haas *hare*
Ham *ham*
Haring *herring*
Hazepeper *jugged hare*
Heilbot *halibut*
Hoofdgerecht *main dish*
IJs *ice cream*
Inktvis *squid*
Kabeljauw *cod*
Kalfsoesters *medallions of veal*
Kalfsvlees *veal*
Kalkoen *turkey*
Kaneel *cinnamon*
Karbonade *chop/cutlet*
Kerrie *curry*
Kervel *chervil*
Ketjap *soy sauce*
Kikkerbilletjes *frogs legs*
Kip *chicken*
Knoflook *garlic*
Komkommer *cucumber*
Konijn *rabbit*
Kool *cabbage*
Kotelet *chop/cutlet*
Kreeft *lobster*
Kroepoek *prawn cracker*
Kruidnagel *clove*
Kwartel *quail*
Lamsbout *leg of lamb*
Lamsvlees *lamb*
Lever *liver*
Linzen *lentils*

Loempia *spring roll*
Maatje *small, cured herring*
Mais *sweet corn*
Makreel *mackerel*
Marjolein *marjoram*
Meloen *melon*
Mosselen *mussels*
Munt *mint*
Nagerecht *dessert*
Nasi *fried rice*
Nieren *kidneys*
Oester *oyster*
Ossehaas *fillet of beef*
Ossestaart *oxtail*
Paling *eel*
Pannekoek *pancake*
Paprika *(green or red) pepper*
Parelhoen *guinea fowl*
Passievrucht *passion fruit*
Pasteitje *vol-au-vent*
Peer *pear*
Perzik *peach*
Peterselie *parsley*
Peulen *mange-tout peas*
Pinda *peanut*
Poffertjes *tiny pancakes drenched in sugar and butter*
Pommes frites/patat *French fries*
Poon *gurnard*
Prei *leek*
Rauw *raw*
Rijst *rice*
Rode kool *red cabbage*
Rog *skate*
Rosbief *roast beef*
Rozemarijn *rosemary*
Rundvlees *beef*
Salie *sage*
Sambal *very hot crushed chilies*
Saté *meat on a skewer*
Saucijzebroodje *sausage roll*
Saus *sauce*
Schelvis *haddock*
Schol *plaice*
Sla *lettuce/salad*
Slagroom *whipped cream*
Slakken *snails*
Sneetje *slice*
Snijbonen *runner beans*
Soep *soup*
Speculaas *ginger-and-spice biscuit*
Spek *bacon*
Spekkoek *layered spice cake*

319

Sperciebonen *green beans*
Spinazie *spinach*
Stokbrood *French bread*
Tarbot *turbot*
Taugé *bean sprouts*
Tong *sole*
Tonijn *tuna fish*
Ui *onion*
Uitsmijter *fried eggs on bread with ham or cheese*
Varkenshaas *fillet of pork*
Varkensvlees *pork*
Venkel *fennel*

Vers *fresh*
Vis *fish*
Vlees *meat*
Voorgerecht *hors d'oeuvre*
Wafel *waffle*
Waterkers *watercress*
Wild *game*
Witlof *chicory*
Wortels *carrots*
Zalm *salmon*
Zalmforel *salmon trout*
Zeeduivel *anglerfish, monkfish*
Zoetzuur *sweet and sour*
Zwezerik *sweetbreads*

Index

Page numbers in **bold** type indicate the main entry. *Italic* page numbers refer to illustrations and maps.

The letters **ij**, when they appear together in Dutch (e.g., IJsselmeer, Bijbels Museum), sound as **y** and have been filed alphabetically as such (e.g., as if they were Ysselmeer, Bybels Museum).

INDEX OF PLACES

321

GENERAL INDEX

List of Amsterdam street names

All streets mentioned in this book that fall within the area covered by our maps of Amsterdam are listed below. Map numbers are printed in **bold** type. Some smaller streets are not named on the maps, but the map reference given below will help you locate the correct area. For information on how to master Amsterdam's distinctive network of canals and streets, see WHERE TO GO, page 64.

Albert Cuypstraat,
6I4-H6
Amstel, **6**F5-7J6
Amstelstraat, **10**F5-6
Amstelveenseweg,
3E2-F2
Amstelveld, **6**G5
Anjeliersdwarsstraat, 2ᵉ·,
9C3
Antoniesbreestraat, St,
11D6-E6

Baerlestraat, Van, **5**I2-3
Barberenstraat, St, **10**E5
Barndesteeg, **11**D5-6
Begijnhof, **10**E4
Berenstraat, **9**E3
Beulingsloot, **10**E4
Beulingstraat, **10**E4
Beursplein, **10**D5
Binnen Bantammerstraat,
11D6
Binnenkant, **11**D5-6
Blauwburgwal, **10**C4
Bloemdwarsstraat, 1ᵉ·,
9C2-D3
Bloemgracht, **9**D2-
C3
Breestraat, Van, **5**H1-2
Brouwersgracht,
9A3-**10**B5
Brouwersstraat, J. W.,
5H2-I2
Buiksloterweg, **11**A6

Buiten Bantammerstraat,
11D6-7
Buiten Oranjestraat,
10A4

Ceintuurbaan, 6J4-7I7
Churchilllaan, **3**E3
Clercqstraat, De, **3**D2-3
Coenenstraat, J. M.,
5J2-I3
Concertgebouwplein,
5H2
Constantijn
Huygensstraat, 1ᵉ·,
5F1-H2

Dam, **10**D4
Damrak, **10**D5-C5
Damstraat, **10**D5
Drie Koningenstraat,
10D4

Egelantiersdwarsstraat,
1ᵉ·, **9**C3
Egelantiersdwarsstraat,
2ᵉ·, **9**C3
Egelantiersgracht, **9**C2-3
Egelantiersstraat, **9**C2-3
Elandsgracht, **9**E2-3
Elandsstraat, **9**E2-D3
Enge Kapelsteeg, **10**E4
Enge Lombardsteeg,
10D5-E5
Entrepôtdok, **8**E8-F9

Ferdinand Bolstraat,
6H4-J4
Frederiksplein, **7**G6

Gasthuismolensteeg,
10D4
Gedempte
Begijnensloot, **10**E4
's Gravenhekje, **11**D7
Gravenstraat, **10**D4 5
Grimburgwal, **10**E5
Groenburgwal, **10**E5-6

Haarlemmerhouttuinen,
10A4-B5
Haarlemmerstraat,
10B4-5
Harmoniehof, **5**J3
Hartenstraat, **9**D3-**10**D4
Hazenstraat, **9**D2-E3
Heiligeweg, **10**E4
Heisteeg, **10**E4
Helststraat, van der, 2ᵉ·,
6I5-J5
Herengracht, **6** and **10**
Herenmarkt, **10**B4
Herenstraat, **10**C4
Hirschgebouw, **5**F3
Hobbemakade, **5**J3-G3
Hobbemastraat, **5**G3-H3
Hooftstraat, P. C.,
5H1-G3
Hoogte Kadijk, **8**E9-
F10

337

CONVERSION FORMULAE

To convert	Multiply by
Inches to Centimeters	2.540
Centimeters to Inches	0.39370
Feet to Meters	0.3048
Meters to feet	3.2808
Yards to Meters	0.9144
Meters to Yards	1.09361
Miles to Kilometers	1.60934
Kilometers to Miles	0.621371
Sq Meters to Sq Feet	10.7638
Sq Feet to Sq Meters	0.092903
Sq Yards to Sq Meters	0.83612
Sq Meters to Sq Yards	1.19599
Sq Miles to Sq Kilometers	2.5899
Sq Kilometers to Sq Miles	0.386103
Acres to Hectares	0.40468
Hectares to Acres	2.47105
Gallons to Liters	4.545
Liters to Gallons	0.22
Ounces to Grams	28.3495
Grams to Ounces	0.03528
Pounds to Grams	453.592
Grams to Pounds	0.00220
Pounds to Kilograms	0.4536
Kilograms to Pounds	2.2046
Tons (UK) to Kilograms	1016.05
Kilograms to Tons (UK)	0.0009842
Tons (US) to Kilograms	746.483
Kilograms to Tons (US)	0.0013396

Quick conversions

Kilometers to Miles	Divide by 8, multiply by 5
Miles to Kilometers	Divide by 5, multiply by 8
1 meter =	Approximately 3 feet 3 inches
2 centimeters =	Approximately 1 inch
1 pound (weight) =	475 grams (nearly $\frac{1}{2}$ kilogram)
Celsius to Fahrenheit	Divide by 5, multiply by 9, add 32
Fahrenheit to Celsius	Subtract 32, divide by 9, multiply by 5

Clothing sizes chart

LADIES
Suits and dresses

Australia	8	10	12	14	16	18
France	34	36	38	40	42	44
Germany	32	34	36	38	40	42
Italy	38	40	42	44	46	
Japan	7	9	11	13		
UK	6	8	10	12	14	16	18
USA	4	6	8	10	12	14	16

Shoes

USA	6	$6\frac{1}{2}$	7	$7\frac{1}{2}$	8	$8\frac{1}{2}$
UK	$4\frac{1}{2}$	5	$5\frac{1}{2}$	6	$6\frac{1}{2}$	7
Europe	38	38	39	39	40	41

MEN
Shirts

USA, UK	14	$14\frac{1}{2}$	15	$15\frac{1}{2}$	16	$16\frac{1}{2}$	17
Europe, Japan Australia	36	37	38	39.5	41	42	43

Sweaters/T-shirts

Australia, USA, Germany	S	M	L	XL
UK	34	36-38	40	42-44
Italy	44	46-48	50	52
France	1	2-3	4	5
Japan		S-M	L	XL

Suits/Coats

UK, USA	36	38	40	42	44
Australia, Italy, France, Germany	46	48	50	52	54
Japan	S	M	L	XL	

Shoes

UK	7	$7\frac{1}{2}$	$8\frac{1}{2}$	$9\frac{1}{2}$	$10\frac{1}{2}$	11
USA	8	$8\frac{1}{2}$	$9\frac{1}{2}$	$10\frac{1}{2}$	$11\frac{1}{2}$	12
Europe	41	42	43	44	45	46

CHILDREN
Clothing

UK

Height (ins)	43	48	55	60	62	
Age	4-5	6-7	9-10	11	12	13

USA

Age	4	6	8	10	12	14

Europe

Height (cms)	125	135	150	155	160	165
Age	7	9	12	13	14	15

AMSTERDAM tram & metro system

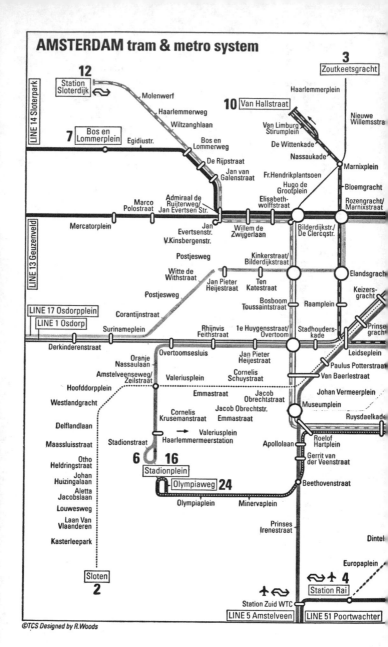

12 Station Sloterdijk

3 Zoutkeetsgracht

LINE 14 Sloterpark

Molenwerf

Haarlemmerweg

Wiltzanghlaan

Haarlemmerplein

10 Van Hallstraat

Nieuwe Willemsstra

7 Bos en Lommerplein

Egidiustr.

Bos en Lommerweg

Van Limburg Stirumplein

De Wittenkade

Nassaukade

De Rijpstraat

Jan van Galenstraat

Fr.Hendrikplantsoen

Marnixplein

Hugo de Grootplein

Bloemgracht

Admiraal de Ruijterweg/ Jan Evertsen Str.

Marco Polostraat

Elisabeth-wolffstraat

Rozengracht/ Marnixstraat

LINE 13 Geuzenveld

Mercatorplein

Jan Evertsenstr. V.Kinsbergenstr.

Willem de Zwijgerlaan

Bilderdijkstr./ De Clercqstr.

Postjesweg

Witte de Withstraat

Kinkerstraat/ Bilderdijkstraat

Jan Pieter Heijestraat

Ten Katestraat

Elandsgrach

Keizers-gracht

Postjesweg

Bosboom Toussaintstraat

LINE 17 Osdorpplein
LINE 1 Osdorp

Corantijnstraat

Raamplein

Prinse gracht

Surinameplein

Rhijnvis Feithstraat

1e Huygensstraat/ Overtoom

Stadhouders-kade

Derkinderenstraat

Overtoomsesluis

Jan Pieter Heijestraat

Leidseplein

Oranje Nassaulaan

Amstelveenseweg/ Zeilstraat

Valeriusplein

Cornelis Schuystraat

Paulus Potterstraa

Van Baerlestraat

Hoofddorpplein

Emmastraat

Jacob Obrechtstraat

Johan Vermeerplein

Westlandgracht

Cornelis Krusemanstraat

Jacob Obrechtstr. Emmastraat

Museumplein

Delflandlaan

Ruysdaelkade

Valeriusplein

Maassluisstraat

Stadionstraat

Haarlemmermeerstation

Apollolaan

Roelof Hartplein

Otho Heldringstraat

6 **16**

Gerrit van der Veenstraat

Johan Huizingalaan

Stadionplein

Aletta Jacobslaan

Olympiaweg **24**

Beethovenstraat

Louwesweg

Olympiaplein

Minervaplein

Laan Van Vlaanderen

Prinses Irenestraat

Dintel

Kasterleepark

Europaplein

Sloten **2**

4 Station Rai

Station Zuid WTC

LINE 5 Amstelveen   **LINE 51 Poortwachter**

©TCS Designed by R.Woods

342

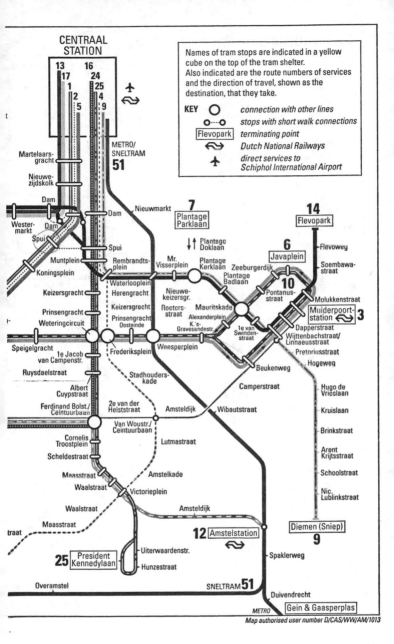

CENTRAAL
STATION

13   16
17   24
1   25
2   4
5   9

✈
⇌

METRO/
SNELTRAM
51

Names of tram stops are indicated in a yellow
cube on the top of the tram shelter.
Also indicated are the route numbers of services
and the direction of travel, shown as the
destination, that they take.

KEY   O   connection with other lines
       o⋯o   stops with short walk connections
       Flevopark   terminating point
       ⇌   Dutch National Railways
       ✈   direct services to
              Schiphol International Airport

Martelaars-
gracht

Nieuwe-
zijdskolk

Dam

Dam   Nieuwmarkt

Wester-
markt   Dam

Spui

Muntplein   Spui

Koningsplein   Rembrandts-
                plein

Keizersgracht   Waterlooplein
                Herengracht

Prinsengracht   Keizersgracht

Weteringcircuit Prinsengracht
                Oosteinde

Speigelgracht
                1e Jacob
Ruysdaelstraat van Campenstr. Frederiksplein

                Stadhouders-
Albert   kade
Cuypstraat
                2e van der
Ferdinand Bolst./ Helststraat   Amsteldijk   Wibautstraat
Ceintuurbaan
                Van Woustr./
                Ceintuurbaan

Cornelis   Lutmastraat
Troostplein

Scheldestraat

Maasstraat   Amstelkade

Waalstraat   Victorieplein

Waalstraat   Amsteldijk

Maasstraat

traat

25 President   Uiterwaardenstr.   **12** Amstelstation
     Kennedylaan   ⇌

                Hunzestraat   Spaklerweg

Overamstel   SNELTRAM **51**   Duivendrecht

                                METRO   Gein & Gaasperplas

7
Plantage
Parklaan

↑↓ Plantage
   Doklaan

Mr.   Plantage   **6**
Visserplein   Kerklaan   Javaplein

               Plantage
Nieuwe-   Badlaan   Zeeburgerdijk
keizersgr.
               Mauritskade   **10**
Roeters-   Pontanus-
straat   straat
               Alexanderplein
               K.'s-
               Gravensandestr.   1e van
                                 Swinden-
Weesperplein   straat

                                 Beukenweg

               Camperstraat

14
Flevopark

Flevoweg

Soembawa-
straat

Molukkenstraat

Muiderpoort-
station ⇌ **3**

Dapperstraat
Wijttenbachstraat/
Linnaeusstraat

Pretoriusstraat

Hogeweg

Hugo de
Vrieslaan

Kruislaan

Brinkstraat

Arent
Krijtsstraat

Schoolstraat

Nic.
Lublinkstraat

Diemen (Sniep)

9

Map authorised user number D/CAS/WW/AM/1013

343

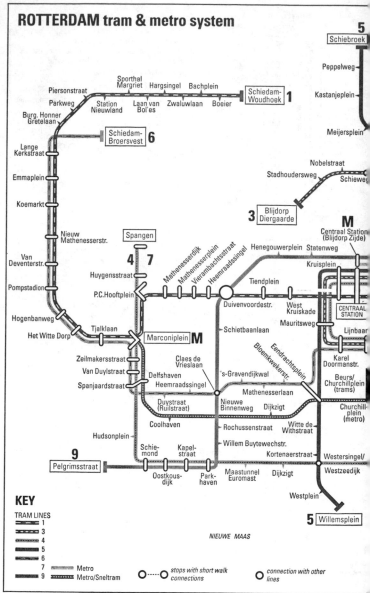

ROTTERDAM tram & metro system

KEY

TRAM LINES
- 1
- 3
- 4
- 5
- 6
- 7
- 9

Metro

Metro/Sneltram

○-----○ stops with short walk connections

○ connection with other lines

NIEUWE MAAS

©TCS Designed by R.Woods

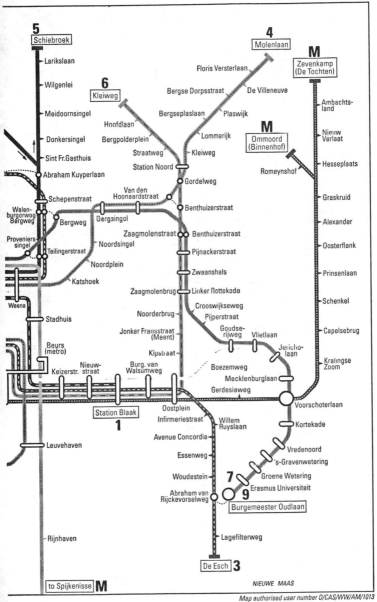

5 Schiebroek

- Larikslaan
- Wilgenlei
- Meidoornsingel
- Donkersingel
- Sint Fr.Gasthuis
- Abraham Kuyperlaan
- Schepenstraat

Walen-
burgerwog
Bergweg
- Bergweg
Proveniers-
singel
- Teilingerstraat

Weena
- Stadhuis

Beurs
(metro)
Nieuw-
Keizerstr. straat

Burg. van
Walsumweg

Station Blaak
1

- Leuvehaven

- Rijnhaven

to Spijkenisse **M**

6 Kleiweg

Hoofdlaan
Bergpolderplein
Straatweg
Station Noord

Van den
Hoonaardstraat
Dergsingol

Zaagmolenstraat
Noordsingel
Noordplein
Katshoek

Zaagmolenbrug
Noorderbrug
Jonker Fransstraat
(Meent)
Kipstraat

Oostplein
Infirmeriestraat
Avenue Concordia
Essenweg
Woudestein
Abraham van
Rijckevorselweg

De Esch **3**

4 Molenlaan

Floris Versterlaan
Bergse Dorpsstraat
De Villeneuve
Bergseplaslaan
Plaswijk
Lommerijk
Kleiweg
- Gordelweg
- Benthuizerstraat
- Benthuizerstraat
- Pijnackerstraat
- Zwaanshals
Linker Rottekade
Crooswijkseweg
Pijperstraat
Goudse-
rijweg
Vlietlaan
Jericho-
laan
Boezemweg
Mecklenburglaan
Gerdesiaweg
Voorschoterlaan
Kortekade
Willem
Ruyslaan
Vredenoord
's-Gravenwetering
Groene Wetering
7
Erasmus Universiteit
9
Burgemeester Oudlaan

Lagefilterweg

M Zevenkamp
(De Tochten)

Ambachts-
land
Nieuw
Verlaat
Hesseplaats
Graskruid
Alexander
Oosterflank
Prinsenlaan
Schenkel
Capelsebrug
Kralingse
Zoom

M Ommoord
(Binnenhof)
Romeynshof

NIEUWE MAAS

What the papers said:

- "The expertly edited American Express series has the knack of pin-pointing precisely the details you need to know, and doing it concisely and intelligently." (*The Washington Post*)

- "*(Venice)* ... the best guide book I have ever used." (*The Standard* — London)

- "Amid the welter of guides to individual countries, American Express stands out...." (*Time*)

- "Possibly the best ... guides on the market, they come close to the oft-claimed 'all you need to know' comprehensiveness, with much original experience, research and opinions." (*Sunday Telegraph* — London)

- "The most useful general guide was *American Express New York* by Herbert Bailey Livesey. It also has the best street and subway maps." (*Daily Telegraph* — London)

- "...in the flood of travel guides, the *American Express* guides come closest to the needs of traveling managers with little time." (*Die Zeit* — Germany)

What the experts said:

- "We only used one guide book, Sheila Hale's *Amex Venice*, for which she and the editors deserve a Nobel Prize." (Eric Newby, London)

- "Congratulations to you and your staff for putting out the best guide book of *any* size (*Barcelona & Madrid*). I'm recommending it to everyone." (Barnaby Conrad, Santa Barbara, California)

- "If you're only buying one guide book, we recommend American Express...." (*Which?* — Britain's leading consumer magazine)

What readers from all over the world have said:

- "The book *(Hong Kong, Singapore & Bangkok)* was written in such a personal way that I feel as if you were actually writing this book for me." (L.Z., Orange, Conn., USA)

- "Your book *(Florence and Tuscany)* proved a wonderful companion for us in the past fortnight. It went with us everywhere...." (E.H., Kingston-on-Thames, Surrey, England)

- "I feel as if you have been a silent friend shadowing my time in Tuscany." (T.G., Washington, DC, USA)

- "We followed your book *(Los Angeles & San Francisco)* to the letter. It proved to be wonderful, indispensable, a joy...." (C.C., London, England)

- "We could never have had the wonderful time that we did without your guide to *Paris*. The compactness was very convenient, your maps were all we needed, but it was your restaurant guide that truly made our stay special.... We have learned first-hand: *American Express — don't leave home without it*." (A. R., Virginia Beach, Va., USA)

- "Much of our enjoyment came from the way your book *(Venice)* sent us off scurrying around the interesting streets and off to the right places at the right times". (Lord H., London, England)

- "It *(Paris)* was my constant companion and totally dependable...." (V. N., Johannesburg, South Africa)

- "I could go on and on about how useful the book *(Amsterdam)* was — the trouble was that it was almost getting to be a case of not venturing out without it...." (J.C.W., Manchester, England)

- "We have heartily recommended these books to all our friends who have plans to travel abroad." (A.S. and J.C., New York, USA)

- "Despite many previous visits to Italy, I wish I had had your guide *(Florence and Tuscany)* ages ago. I love the author's crisp, literate writing and her devotion to her subject." (M. B-K., Denver, Colorado, USA)

- "We never made a restaurant reservation without checking your book *(Venice)*. The recommendations were excellent, and the historical and artistic text got us through the sights beautifully." (L.S., Boston, Ma., USA)

- "We became almost a club as we found people sitting at tables all around, consulting their little blue books!" (F.C., Glasgow, Scotland)

- "This guide *(Paris)* we warmly recommend to all the many international visitors we work with." (M.L., Paris, France)

- "It's not often I would write such a letter, but it's one of the best guide books we have ever used *(Rome)* — we can't fault it!" (S.H., Berkhamsted, Herts, England)

American Express Travel Guides

spanning the globe....

EUROPE
Amsterdam, Rotterdam
  & The Hague
Athens and the
  Classical Sites ‡
Barcelona & Madrid ‡
Berlin ‡
Brussels #
Dublin and Cork #
Florence and Tuscany
London #
Moscow & St Petersburg *
Paris #
Prague *
Provence and the
  Côte d'Azur *
Rome
Venice ‡
Vienna & Budapest

NORTH AMERICA
Boston and New
  England *
Los Angeles & San
  Diego #
Mexico ‡
New York #
San Francisco and
  the Wine Regions
Toronto, Montréal and
  Québec City ‡
Washington, DC

THE PACIFIC
Cities of Australia
Hong Kong & Taiwan
Singapore &
  Bangkok ‡
Tokyo #

*   Paperbacks in preparation   #   Paperbacks appearing January 1993
‡   Hardback pocket guides (in paperback 1993)

Clarity and quality of information, combined with outstanding maps — the ultimate in travelers' guides

Airport Departure Tax?
5.50 for train ticket